Metacognitive Interpersonal Therapy for Personality Disorders

Patients with personality disorders need targeted treatments which are able to deal with the specific aspects of the core pathology and to tackle the challenges they present to the treatment clinicians. Such patients, however, are often difficult to engage, are prone to ruptures in the therapeutic alliance and have difficulty adhering to a manualised treatment.

Giancarlo Dimaggio, Antonella Montano, Raffaele Popolo and Giampaolo Salvatore aim to change this, and have developed a practical and systematic manual for the clinician using metacognitive interpersonal therapy (MIT) and including detailed procedures for dealing with a range of personality disorders. The book is divided into two parts, Pathology, and Treatment, and provides precise instructions on how to move from the basic steps of forming an alliance, drafting a therapy contract and promoting self-reflections to the more advanced steps of promoting change and helping the patient move toward health and adaptation.

With clinical examples, summaries of therapies and excerpts of session transcripts, *Metacognitive Interpersonal Therapy for Personality Disorders* will be welcomed by psychotherapists, clinical psychologists and other mental health professionals involved in the treatment of personality disorders.

Giancarlo Dimaggio is a co-founding member of the Center for Metacognitive Interpersonal Therapy. He is the author of four books and numerous articles.

Antonella Montano is a founding member and director of the psychotherapy school at A. T. Beck Institute for Cognitive Behavior Therapy. He is a teacher and supervisor of the Associazione Italiana Analisi e Modificazione del Comportamento (AIAMC), a certified trainer/consultant/speaker/supervisor of the Academy of Cognitive Therapy (ACT), a member of the International Association for Cognitive Psychotherapy (IACP) and a member of the International Society for Sexual Medicine (ISSM).

T03939G9

Raffaele Popolo is a co-founding member of the Center for Metacognitive Interpersonal Therapy, a trainer at the Società Italiana di Terapia Comportamentale e Cognitiva (SITCC) and a trainer of the psychotherapy school 'Studi Cognitivi'. He has written papers on psychopathology and the treatment of personality disorders and psychosis.

Giampaolo Salvatore is a co-founding member of the Center for Metacognitive Interpersonal Therapy, a trainer at A. T. Beck Institute for Cognitive Behavior Therapy. He has written papers about the psychotherapeutic process and the pathology and treatment of schizophrenia and personality disorders, and in particular of persons with paranoid features.

Metacognitive Interpersonal Therapy for Personality Disorders

A treatment manual

Giancarlo Dimaggio, Antonella Montano, Raffaele Popolo and Giampaolo Salvatore

LONDON AND NEW YORK

First published 2015
by Routledge
27 Church Road, Hove, East Sussex, BN3 2FA

and by Routledge
711 Third Avenue, New York, NY 10017

Routledge is an imprint of the Taylor & Francis Group, an informa business

British Library Cataloguing in Publication Data
A catalogue record for this book is available from the British Library

Library of Congress Cataloging-in-Publication Data
Dimaggio, Giancarlo, author.
[Terapia metacognitiva interpersonale per i disturbi di personalit?. English]
Metacognitive interpersonal therapy for personality disorders : a treatment manual / Giancarlo Dimaggio, Antonella Montano, Raffaele Popolo, and Giampaolo Salvatore.
pages cm
1. Personality disorders–Treatment. 2. Metacognition. I. Montano, Antonella, author. II. Popolo, Raffaele, author. III. Salvatore, Giampaolo, author. IV. Title.
RC455.4.B5D5613 2015
616.85'81–dc23
2014033799

ISBN: 978-1-138-02415-1 (hbk)
ISBN: 978-1-138-02418-2 (pbk)
ISBN: 978-1-315-74412-4 (ebk)

Typeset in Times
by Deer Park Productions

Contents

Abbreviations

ABC	antecedent, belief, consequence
ACT	acceptance and commitment therapy
APA	American Psychiatric Association
A-PST	Advanced Picture Sequencing Task
ATT	attentional training
BDI	Beck Depression Inventory
BLERT	Bell-Lysaker Emotional Recognition Task
BVAQ	Bermond-Vorst Alexithymia Questionnaire
CAS	cognitive attentional syndrome
CBT	cognitive behavioural therapy
CBT-E	enhanced transdiagnostic CBT for eating disorders
CCRT	core conflictual relational theme
DBT	dialectical-behaviour therapy
DERS	Difficulties in Emotion Regulation Scale
EIS	Emotional Inhibition Scale
ERP	exposure and response prevention
ERQ	Emotion Regulation Questionnaire
IIP	Inventory of Interpersonal Problems
MAI	Metacognition Assessment Interview
MAS-R	Metacognition Assessment Scale – Revised
MBSR	mindfulness-based stress reduction
MCMI	Millon Clinical Multiaxial Inventory
MCT	metacognitive therapy
MIT	metacognitive interpersonal therapy
MOSST	Metacognitive Oriented Social Skills Training
MSCEIT	Mayer-Salovey-Caruso Emotional Intelligence Test
PD	personality disorder
PDNOS	personality disorder not otherwise specified
SCL	Symptom Checklist
STAI	State-Trait Anxiety Inventory

TAS	Toronto Alexithymia Scale
ToM	theory of mind
TR	thought recording
TZPD	Therapeutic Zone of Proximal Development
YSQ	Young Schema Questionnaire

Introduction

Time was ripe. Psychotherapies for personality disorders (PDs) have undergone a major leap during the last twenty years. We know better their self-sustaining mechanisms, that they respond to treatment (unlike the pessimism of some decades ago) and that drop-out can be kept to a reasonably low amount. But it is a patchy evolution. The majority of progress was made with borderline PD, for which many treatments of proven effectiveness exist and are currently under refinement and further empirical testing. For all the other PDs, except avoidant and narcissistic, the literature is scanty and fragmented. The clinician wanting to treat dependent, paranoid, obsessive-compulsive PD or depressive, passive-aggressive and schizoid traits, has to dig hard to find a well full of water. The bias towards borderline PD is unjustified, as the other PDs are overall much more prevalent and can be just as severe as the former.

There is another problem. Many patients do not present with pure disorder. Co-occurrence among PDs or of a PD with traits of other disorders is the rule more than the exception. Knowing how to treat a patient with narcissism is one matter. A totally different matter is treating a patient with narcissism and obsessive-compulsive, paranoid and passive-aggressive traits. Leaving specific orientations aside, we thought a guide for the clinician treating these conditions was lacking. For this reason, this volume deals with the PDs listed above, taking into account their occurrence. Borderline PD is not discussed here. It was about filling a gap.

We chose to describe common procedures across different PDs, without devoting specific chapters to the various disorders. We designed precise sequences of interventions that can be applied to any kind of personality features the patient presents with. Leaving the diagnosis aside, we think the best way to understand a PD in a way that makes treatment planning easier is a carefully devised case formulation. Needless to say, diagnosing a specific PD is relevant for treatment planning and the model of pathology described in our previous manual are still valid (Dimaggio, Semerari, Carcione et al., 2007).

Our focus here has been on showing how to make an extremely careful case formulation. The aim is for both clinician and patient to have a map of the patient's mental functioning. This allows for optimisation of therapy work, moving step-by-step towards healing personality problems and alleviating symptoms.

Thanks to the case formulation, the therapist and patient come to understand that the patient's suffering is fuelled by a functioning that early in treatment can be described as follows: '*You are driven by the wish to be appreciated. In order to fulfil it you show others your deeds and long for a positive judgement, but then you expect the other will criticise you and invalidate you. When you imagine yourself being criticised, you feel an uncanny tension you can't name and we understand that it predates anxiety symptoms, though we still don't know the process unfolding within you that leads to this outcome. Then if you are actually criticised, your reactions swing between shame at the idea the other is right and anger at the idea the judgement is unfair and you did deserve the appreciation you longed for. Finally, after having received a negative reaction, you tend to either shut yourself in or protest in vain. Over time, you isolate more and more because you took for sure that negative judgement would systematically arrive, so avoiding receiving it is the only way you know to prevent pain. You lost sight of your qualities and the possibility others will note them and appreciate them, though in some moments of less tension you still catch a glimpse of them.*'

This functioning portrays a combination of avoidant, narcissistic, dependent and obsessive-compulsive features. The clinician can choose to describe the patient either by listing the PD features or adopting the formulation we have just drawn. The categorical language helps make the connection to what is known, but drives understanding apart. Shared formulation of functioning instead fosters the patient's awareness that she accepted these negative images of herself as the truth, instead of just an internalised image, one that has been formed over the lifetime that does not necessarily reflect reality. This paves the ground on which to build the therapy parts aimed at making the patient aware another life exists, one where he can express the self-aspects filled with a sense of worth and motivation. Therapy work is about bringing these aspects of personality to light and letting them become generators of adaptive actions. In a way, this volume is for clinicians who first learned the pathology of a specific PD and then decided to forget it, seeing the patient in her uniqueness.

About uniqueness: writing a treatment manual means supplying generalised, standardised and reproducible procedures. It means asking the therapist, to a certain extent, to make their actions uniform. The challenge we faced in the formulation of our model was to formalise how to treat each case as unique, to teach the therapist how to listen to the text of the discourse, distilling its structure and making it visible to the patient. Awareness of the structures of personality revealed by the understanding of the text can then lead the patient and therapist towards the path of health and creativity. Procedures are common; the case formulation is unique.

Our attention to the therapy relationship should do justice to our attempt. In MIT, we consider the therapist as a person with a story, reactivity, personal goals, vulnerabilities and weaknesses, weaving with the patient an ever changing web. Ever changing does not mean that it cannot be analysed and used as a template for understanding other stories. We leave it to the reader to judge whether our attempt to be both unique and reproducible was a success or failure. Our bet is that the procedures we outlined here do not lead therapists to act mechanically, but make them able to be swift and nimble in identifying difficulties and overcoming them with a mixture of intuition and a well-coded action repertoire.

Manuals are written to be tested empirically. One of the reasons behind writing this volume was to provide the clinician with a reliable guide that is easy to apply and makes therapy action reproducible. The ultimate goal was testing the effectiveness of Metacognitive Interpersonal Therapy (MIT), and it was the moment to try. To date, MIT has been judged as credible for the treatment of PD (Karterud, 2012; Warren, 2012) and has shown preliminary effectiveness in some selected single cases (Dimaggio, Carcione, Salvatore et al., 2010, 2011; Dimaggio and Attinà, 2012; Dimaggio, Attinà, Popolo et al., 2012; Dimaggio, Salvatore, Fiore et al., 2012). A small benchmark study is currently underway by the Centre for Metacognitive Interpersonal Therapy in Rome. In order to disseminate the model and pave the way for outcome studies, there are training courses and supervisions of expert therapists underway in Italy, Norway, Denmark and Portugal, and it will likely spread to the USA as well.

As a last remark, treating PD requires a vast array of skills: flexibility, empathy, ability to formulate the case with sensitivity and precision, tolerance of frustrations, the capacity not to overreact, the ability to work through one's own vulnerabilities in order to avoid the escalation of problems in the therapy relationship, changing strategies as therapy evolves, and the expression of warmth, attention and presence. These qualities are needed in order to treat these patients. Given that working with these patients is already difficult enough, we wanted to spare the therapist the fatigue of difficult reading. We have tried to adopt simple, non-jargon language, describing with details any operations in order to take out the sense of esoteric magic that only the faithful understand. This is to allow the clinician to say: 'Is it as simple as this? So I can do it too!' Every reader who has been caught by surprise by such a thought will give us a glimpse of joy.

Chapter 1

Personality disorder psychopathology

Form and contents of subjective experience

Once the important aspects of personality pathology have been defined it is possible to develop reliable tools for conceptualising the case in a ready-to-use way and then for accurate treatment planning. Personality disorders (PDs) are complex pathologies, contributed to by various aspects, whether temperamental, learnt or developmental, and dysfunctions in relationships and in the capacity to understand mental states. They include difficulties in undertaking independent actions, regulating affects and consciously managing subjective suffering.

The areas delineating PD psychopathology and which are focused on by metacognitive interpersonal therapy (MIT) are the following:

- impoverished narratives/intellectualising narrative style;
- limited or fluctuating sense of *agency*;
- pathogenic interpersonal schemas;
- dysfunctional interpersonal cycles;
- recurring mental states;
- metacognitive dysfunctions;
- maladaptive forms of coping and cognitive biases;
- problems regulating affects.

Given that in this book we are proposing a treatment model that can be applied consistently to all the PDs treated, we are not going to systematically describe how each area is altered in each single disorder. The reason for this choice is that, on the one hand, there are numerous dysfunctions and elements of subjective experience appearing transversally in the various disorders and, on the other, the co-occurrence among the various PDs and the presence of dysfunctional personality disordered traits of one in another PD render the pathology boundaries fuzzy. As regards mental states, the forms of subjective experience reoccur in the various PDs and there is no mental state that is pathognomonic of one disorder. Certainly disdainful grandiosity characterises narcissism but also surfaces in avoidant PD as a result of positive reinforcements of self-esteem. Diffidence towards others seen as humiliating, mocking and threatening is the most evident feature of paranoid PD but avoidant PD displays it in the same way and many vulnerable narcissists experience this same state. Harsh criticism, driven by morally perfectionist standards, is characteristic of obsessive-compulsive PD and is also found in passive-aggressive, depressive and narcissistic PD and, directed mainly towards the self, in avoidant PD.

The same applies to metacognitive dysfunctions. No single dysfunction in the system for comprehending mental states is specific to one PD and many have been found to varying degrees in several disorders. There is a lack of convincing research evidence to show that each PD has its own characteristic metacognitive malfunctioning profile (Carcione, Semerari, Nicolò et al., 2011; Dimaggio, Semerari, Carcione et al., 2007; Dimaggio, Carcione, Conti et al., 2009; Semerari, Dimaggio, Nicolò et al., 2005).

The rationale for our description of psychopathology is, therefore, to provide clinicians with an insight into the alterations in cognitive/affective processes, interpersonal and metacognitive functioning and what patients typically think and feel, to give them the ability to construct patient-specific case formulations. We shall, however, point out what aspects are most closely linked to specific disorders. The reader will therefore be able to recognise that shame, avoidance of relationships in which one feels judged and difficulties in naming one's own emotions are elements that frequently point to avoidant PD. Shifts between icy and contemptuous rage and emptiness, the idea that others are hampering the pursuit of one's goals and a proneness to get paralysed when the other does not provide admiration, together with a tendency towards an intellectualising narrative style, probably point to narcissism.

In this chapter we will concentrate on the pathologies of both the narrative structure and the contents of experience, while in the next chapter we will describe metacognitive dysfunctions, reasoning biases, maladaptive coping, and difficulties in regulating affects and behaviour.

Impoverished narratives/intellectualising narrative style

We define impoverished narratives as a difficulty in recalling rich and detailed autobiographical memories describing the cognitive, emotional and somatic aspects of subjective experience, as well as a true and proper lack of conscious personal memories establishing one's identity and guiding one's actions. Patients with personality disorders or dysfunctional traits such as narcissistic, avoidant, obsessive-compulsive, paranoid, dependent and passive-aggressive, depressive and schizoid experience difficulty using episodes from their own autobiographies to explain their suffering and psychological problems to others (Dimaggio, Salvatore, Popolo et al., 2012; Spinhoven, Bamelis, Molendijk et al., 2009).

They often motivate their requests for psychotherapy in only vague terms or ascribe their problem to external causes, based on generic theories about human functioning. They offer abstract reasons and intellectualisations about others hampering their goals or undermining their possibilities of living a successful life

(Dimaggio, Salvatore, Fiore et al., 2012). A clinician may see a static and scarcely outlined self-portrait. The narrative style is of the intellectualising type and the use of autobiographical memory to make meaning of events is marginal.

Giulia is a typical example of intellectualising narrative style. She suffers from generalised anxiety disorder and hypochondria, and has difficulties in her relationship with her partner. She is 33 years old, has a five-year-old son and works as the press officer for a political party. She suffers from passive-aggressive PD and below threshold obsessive-compulsive PD, and complies overall with 16 SCID-II criteria. We shall describe her history in more detail in the chapters about treatment. In her third session she talked about how she had reacted to an anonymous telephone call, whom she recognised was the partner of her lover. Because of the abstract way in which she narrated, it was not possible, however, for the therapist to grasp her inner world:

> *Patient*: On my side there's been a fall in my feelings for him because I've had so many experiences like that regarding relationships. It's been a journey made up of little things. Perhaps not even the subject of a total, spoken, evident, explicit becoming aware and then, how can I say, a gesture counts and reveals everything, doesn't it? What we hadn't said to each other too … in this case this calling me on Sunday of his, he'd become desperate because he was alone, he'd been abandoned, hadn't he? This searching for me, but not as a specific striving towards me, but as a stage in his desperation. This made me give him a wide berth because I however much it's a little human to stretch out to another person to react to the suffering that they give you, however one should try a bit, how can I say?[1] … And then he's a bit insistent in this, let's say, that is he's a very delicate person, isn't he? Then one feels a bit overbearing too saying one hundred times 'No, I don't want to any more', doesn't one? … Last night I was trying to find an explanation for these things and he was. He could hear from the tone that it was a fight, an argument I mean. It was as if he was, let's say, not up to conflict, that's it!

As one can see, Giulia has a strong tendency to resort to generalisations and consequently provides very little information about her own inner world. Faced with comments like '*It's been a journey made up of little things. Perhaps not even the subject of a total, spoken, evident, explicit becoming aware and then, how can I say, a gesture counts and reveals everything, doesn't it?*' can lead the therapist to feel disoriented. What does Giulia feel? What does she think? How did others affect her feelings or thoughts? Giulia describes other's behaviours as '*but as a stage in his desperation*', which does not allow the clinician to form an idea of his own. What does a person '*not up to conflict*' think and feel? Moreover, Giulia often uses the third person (e.g. '*one feels a bit overbearing too*'), which forces the therapist to ask himself to whom she is referring.

To understand the patient, the clinician requires circumstantiated and contextual descriptions of suffering and the factors making it arise and persist, which is what we refer to as narrative episodes regarding interpersonal relationships. A good narrative episode is characterised by the following. It is communicating a specific autobiographical memory that took place within precise spatial (*where*) and time (*when*) boundaries. The actors on stage need to be identified (*who*) and there should be dialogue between the actors. Lastly, the topic covered (*what*) and the reason for which the story is being related (*why*) should be communicated (Neimeyer, 2000).

Narratives by patients suffering from PD often do not comply with these requirements. The stage where the action takes place is typically undefined and the time boundaries are often vague. The others are described in a generic fashion – 'people', 'colleagues', 'men', 'women', 'relatives' – and behaviours are explained on the basis of stereotypes or generalisations.

For example, when asking a narcissistic patient with paranoid traits reasons for his difficulties with relationships he may restrict himself to generic statements like: '*I have to keep women at a distance because they try to trap me and restrict my freedom.*' A patient with avoidant PD and dependent traits declares: '*If I lose my girlfriend, no woman will want me anymore because I'm useless.*' Statements like these provide very little information about what is actually eliciting thoughts and emotions that cause suffering, and they leave clinicians without the necessary data to understand the patient's functioning.

An example of impoverished narrative comes from Riccardo, a 30-year-old biologist with a severe avoidant personality disorder, with passive-aggressive and schizoid traits and covert narcissism features. He attempted suicide by cutting his veins in a park the year before starting therapy. A few months after starting treatment he began an affair with a woman but he denied he was romantically involved and it was not possible to pick up any verbal indicators of a real interest in this person. When his therapist tried to ask him why he had started the relationship, Riccardo was unable to provide clear reasons, except for sexual ones. He resorted, rather, to abstract explanations to convince himself and the therapist that there was no relation whatsoever by stating, '*We're different in every respect. Our families have different backgrounds and her friends are all far left, while I'm right of centre.*' Riccardo expatiated in his theorisations. He was affectively flattened and described himself as '*one able to surf between situations. I've got my way of navigating with a certain stylishness so as to manage any possible problems, which then in fact do not necessarily crop up.*' The therapist as a result had trouble grasping how Riccardo felt and why he acted in a certain way. Requests for autobiographical details led only to a minimal enrichment of an action scenario. Riccardo's ability to access autobiographical memory was seriously hampered.

To make a joint case-formulation with the patient, the clinician needs details of the latter's subjective experience in order to determine what impacted his behaviours during stressful interpersonal circumstances. In MIT, therapists do not look for abstract causes to ascribe to events but instead look at the ways in which patients, in specific situations of their episodes and interaction with others, think and feel and how thinking and feeling are at the root of their suffering and how it influences behaviour that hampers their well-being and stability of their relationships.

One reason for persisting in the search for specific autobiographical episodes is that these facilitate access to emotions (Gonçalves, Mendes, Cruz et al., 2012). People somewhat unconsciously evaluate significant and important events on the basis of their goals and these evaluations elicit emotions which then assume control of all behavioural systems. Emotions are the force driving actions. Emotionally driven behaviour is, therefore, at the top of the list of things a therapist should investigate. Abstract theories, on the other hand, provide little or no knowledge of the processes associated with emotions.

The narratives of the PD patients described here are lacking emotions and the patients have difficulty identifying both positive and negative emotions. This is a core aspect of the metacognitive dysfunction we will be discussing in Chapter 2. PD patients also underrate emotions, have difficulty labelling emotions, repress emotions and do not use them as a guide to social action, replacing them with general theories about the functioning of the human mind.

A good autobiographical memory, therefore, will include information from which one can deduce the *wish* pushing the person to act, what he did or thought to achieve it or what the conditions were as a result of which he thought it would be achieved, how the others responded and how the patient reacted to the others' response. Typically in the impoverished narratives of patients suffering from PD, one or many of these elements are difficult to pinpoint.

PD patients display varying degrees of impoverished narratives but there are important individual differences. Some manage to describe recurring scenes but have trouble focusing on a specific episode. Others, on the other hand, are almost totally unable to transform the reasons for their problem into a narrative.

It is possible for autobiographical memories to have been simply not *stored* in long-term memory so that the subject has a scanty personal memory base (Liotti, 2004). When confronted with a request to recall the memories providing the foundations to their identity, patients can feel frustrated because they have to look for something that is missing. It is useful to remember that in these patients, autobiographical memory continues to be unutilised and, as such, it becomes atrophied. The non-activation of the brain areas underlying the fixing, recalling and use of personal narrative episodes leaves them, in a certain sense, hypotonic. Impoverished narratives do not only concern development history, but it represents a dysfunction that continuously self-perpetuates, which authorises a clinician to retrain patients in narrating themselves, as we shall see in Chapter 6.

Less typical of these patients are disorganised narratives, which are more characteristic of borderline and histrionic personality disorders (Adler, Chin, Kolisetty et al., 2012). These patients display a fragmented discourse, have problems prioritising the topics of a narrative, talk chaotically and open many parentheses that they do not close, and jump from one subject to another without grasping any easily understandable links. Clinicians therefore have difficulty deciding what topic to concentrate on.

Limited or fluctuating sense of agency

The sense of *agency* refers to the subjective awareness of being inhabited by wishes, intentions and goals and of the ability to initiate, carry out and control actions aimed at achieving them. It is a question of the conscious awareness of being the origin of one's own actions. PD patients can act and carry out choices in their social lives without being aware of generating these choices from within. Lack of agency in PDs involves: (1) lack of internal sources generating behaviour; (2) difficulty recognising internal sources when present; (3) inability to programme plans arising from wishes that are self-generated, and behave accordingly and sustain them over time (Adler, Clum, Kolisetty et al., 2012; Dimaggio, Vanheule, Lysaker et al., 2009). Reality-testing is not affected and patients do not feel controlled by alien forces.

In the fields of cognitive science, neurological disorders and psychosis, lack of agency refers to a severe shortfall in the ability to see physical movements and thoughts as self-generated. Patients with neurological deficits or a diagnosis of schizophrenia may find it difficult to perceive that their own free will moved an arm (which is seen, instead, as being moved from outside) or that a thought has arisen in their own mind and has not been inserted by another entity (Frith, 1992; Lafargue, Franck and Sirigu, 2006).

We are not referring here to breaks in these basic, often unconscious forms of *agency* but, instead, to a lack of conscious awareness of acting in the personal and social domains while being driven by goals over which we have ownership. In the absence of an awareness of intentionally generating an action, PD patients do not realise they have control to alter these actions. Patients with obsessive-compulsive PD might say, '*I do this because it's the right way*'; a patient with dependent PD might say, '*I don't work because, if I did, my mother would feel abandoned and hurt.*' When confronted with the idea that the problem is not the feared reaction from the mother but instead feeling guilty or at risk of being abandoned, the patient does not see she has the power to choose. She stays convinced that there is no alternative. Other declarations indicating the problem might be stated as '*I don't know what to do*', '*I have no idea*', '*Others would be put out*' and '*It's the only way I know.*'

A lack of agency can be partly connected to cognitive biases, such as a constant referring to a sense of duty as an action guide (Ellis, 1962) but cannot be reduced to these. Should a patient with obsessive-compulsive PD perceive that she refers excessively to moral standards for acting and grasp that this causes suffering, she will continue to have difficulty finding alternative inner sources to depend upon for actions. In other words, once the cognitive bias hampering intentional actions has been overcome, a patient is bereft of an internal guide that she feels is hers and is capable of activating.

The reduction of the sense of agency therefore causes problems in the regulating of choices, in particular two types. The first is the tendency to act with reference to others' goals and intentions. Lacking an inner guide coupled with the need to act, decide and choose leads patients to submit, please, and depend on others and, therefore, lose a foundation to their identity (Dimaggio, Semerari, A., Carcione et al., 2007). The second, a consequence of the first, is that through the lack of an inner guide, there is a strong perception of external pressure. The others are likely to be seen as tyrannical, constricting and ready to impose their own will. This combination of limited agency and perception of the others as pushy and dominating leads to the opposing behaviour. This is seen frequently in passive-aggressive PD, patients with *covert* narcissism and sometimes in patients with avoidant PD as well. When patients with limited agency do not regulate their behaviour based on the will of others, do not model themselves after others or rebel and oppose others' will, they become paralysed.

Giovanni was 35 years old and suffered from obsessive-compulsive and paranoid PD and generalised anxiety. He spoke about going camping with a friend. The friend had some modern, high-tech and efficient equipment that made the patient envious. Once his therapist helped him to overcome his sense of inferiority and envy, the patient felt dismayed and paralysed. He now sensed that there was nothing in theory to stop him from being able to get the equipment but he had no idea of how to do it. He felt empty, broken apart, confused, ineffective and paralysed. The paralysis had somatic correlates in the form of muscle weakness and difficulty in moving his limbs.

The basis of building a stable sense of *agency* begins with secure attachment. A child needs to feel secure in the relationship with their caregiver before proceeding to explore the surrounding world (Bowlby, 1988). A child's exploratory system involves a desire to have new experiences as well as a fear of the unknown. The activation of the exploratory system remains but at the same time the fear activates attachment. If a child has an attachment figure that is present and validating and encourages his independence, he will continue to explore and over time will develop agency and personal efficacy. Should the attachment figure instead be absent or invalidating, the child's fears will persist and will lead him to quickly give up exploring. Repeated experiences of this type prevent us from discovering the destiny of our desires and ideas while we are planning and pursuing them. We would not even feel the satisfaction deriving from these desires when we manage to accomplish them. As a result, we would not keep memories of our bodies and minds at the times when we are initiating, carrying out and completing a project. Subsequently, we would not learn to monitor how our plans are modified with the various unforeseen events that we overcome. As we mature, a lack of these experiences leaves us bereft of structures providing a link between the start of an action and its completion. The result is likely to be a feeling of emptiness, confusion, paralysis and the feeling that one is being controlled from outside.

We can find traces of what led to the lack of agency in Tiziano, a 37-year-old patient suffering from avoidant PD with sub-threshold obsessive-compulsive and paranoid PD and a total of 20 SCID-II criteria complied with obsessive-compulsive disorder and social phobia. At six years old the patient asked his mother if he could enroll in soccer classes while she was engaged in crocheting. His mother did not look up from her work but belittled his request: *'What do want to be doing with soccer?! Didn't you want to do piano? It's less dangerous and much nicer!'* When Tiziano recalls this autobiographical memory in session, he remembers wanting at that moment to enroll for the soccer lessons but now he doubts the authenticity of what he felt. We should like to stress that the story contained the origin of a desire which was not supported by his mother.

Adults' agency experiences probably come from episodes in their development in which caretakers acknowledged the child's independent desires and intentions and appreciated their desires, while paying attention to the child. Among the foundation of adult *agency* is the capacity of parent figures to accompany the destiny of the child's desires in a respectful manner, providing suggestions without superimposing themselves on what the child is doing (Tomasello, Carpenter, Call et al., 2005).

The low level of *agency* in PDs (Dimaggio, 2011; Dimaggio, Vanheule, Lysaker et al., 2009) can lead to a loss of identity, given that acting without an awareness of voluntarily affecting events deprives a person of the idea that he has stable nuclei driving him, being capable of mirroring himself, and being able to say: *'That's how I am. I'm driven by these tendencies and desires.'* Patients with dependent PD, for example, may see themselves without the power to make decisions and view their actions as being controlled by partners whom they consider to be charismatic leaders. They certainly can see that the idea and the drive to please their partner is from within their own minds but they are not capable of seeing that the impulse has an internal source and does not derive from threatening, mysterious, and abstract rules. When their therapist tries to help them see that their actions are dictated by their own wishes, they become paralysed, confused or frightened. They are unable to find any reliable guide in their minds (Dimaggio, Semerari, Carcione et al., 2007).

In a similar example, patients with obsessive-compulsive PD are driven by moral rules outside of their own minds and by inflexible and perfectionist ethical and performance standards (Millon and Davis, 1996) and, consequently, do not know they have the power to decide (Dimaggio, Carcione, Salvatore et al., 2011).

Patients with narcissism display a particular agency anomaly. They are, in a certain sense, 'hyperagentic' (Ronningstam, 2009) in the competitive system but experience a lack of agency if driven by other motivational systems. No sooner are they outside the competitive context, that is when facing needs such as cultivating friendships, enjoying life or persisting in a goal while overcoming difficulties and frustrations, they try but quickly enter states where they reactively accuse the other, become paralysed, relive primordial experiences of inadequacy and then surrender. Narcissists may have had neglectful parents as children, who did not help them focus on their inner drives and passions, and lend support and trust so they can achieve their goals. Narcissists lack the experience of being lovingly accompanied in the journey from a wish to its accomplishment.[2]

Riccardo had a serious lack of agency. In his romantic relationships he never said he was attracted to a woman, except for a sexual desire, which he felt sporadically. Only when a woman displayed a lasting interest towards him did he go out with her but without ever declaring he felt involved. He described himself as being driven externally and often forced to be in a relationship. In the professional field the problem was even more marked. Once he got his degree he did not display any vocation and passively remained in the laboratory where he had done his training, but without showing interest in anything. His therapist asked him if he had wishes, plans or ambitions professionally but nothing emerged. Riccardo stated that everything had the same value and he did not do anything to find a stable or gratifying job. Passivity was displayed with a sense of emptiness, boredom, lack of motivation and confusion about his identity. Only when he lost opportunities did Riccardo discover that there were some action tendencies in him. When his partner, whom he declared he did not love, left him, he attempted suicide with a medication overdose. For several years after the incident he said he was in love with her. When he started a relationship with another girl, he again experienced a sense of apathy, passivity and lack of enthusiasm and claimed he was in the relationship just because she wanted it and he did not want to disappoint her.

Pathogenic interpersonal schemas

Human beings' actions on the social stage are driven by goals, wishes and beliefs about the conditions under which it will be possible to achieve these wishes. Based on temperament and repeated relational experiences, adults form stable belief structures about how others will respond to their wishes and about what reactions they themselves will have to others' responses, and put together plans for achieving the wishes (Caspar and Ecker, 2008; Kramer, Rosciano, Pavlovic et al., 2011). The cognitive-affective-somatic structures that persons construct both consciously and automatically to make sense of social relationships are termed *interpersonal schemas* and clinicians can infer them from patients' conversation and non-verbal behaviour.

These schemas are formed from primary motivations, selected during evolution (Gilbert, 1989; Lichtenberg, 1989; Panksepp, 1998). A typical example is attachment (Bowlby, 1988), which is the need for love, protection, stability, attention and acceptance (which contribute to the forming of stable bonds with parents and with one's group). Another example is the need for autonomy and independence in order to explore the environment. Every individual activates behaviour driven by these so-called *interpersonal motivational systems* (Liotti, 2004; Lichtenberg, 1989) or social mentalities (Gilbert, 1989, 2005), otherwise known as systems of innate rules that organise behaviour to satisfy goals (motivations) aimed at survival and adaptation to the social niche.

The main interpersonal motivational systems active in human beings are:

- attachment;
- agonism/social rank/competition for access to limited resources;

- caregiving;
- belonging to a group;
- mating/forming stable sexual bonds;
- cooperation to achieve goals;
- autonomy/agency/exploration.

More sophisticated human motivational systems are: *acting spontaneously and playing symbolically, acquiring a sense of competence and mastery, constructing a sense of stable identity* to help one find one's way as contexts change, and maintaining a good level of *self-esteem*. In adulthood, a good self-image depends to a great extent on a person's perception that the wishes underlying the various motivational spheres can be potentially satisfied. One can esteem oneself because one feels loved, feels effective when taking care of children, is a skilled seducer or reaches success, power and money.

Behaviour driven by motivational systems needs to be validated and supported by caregivers as early as infancy. Based on the child's innate predispositions, a caregiver responds to requests in line with the activated motivational systems, and performs regular and recurrent actions. The child progressively memorises these recurring features and formulates abstractions which are then internalised and transformed into relational schemas.

Should, for example, a child have a parent that repeatedly presents as unavailable to listen to and satisfy the child's emotional needs, then the child will learn that if she wants attention and expresses this explicitly, the parent will once again be unavailable.

These predictions about the behaviour of a caregiver could lead the child to defensively withdraw and distance herself from others to protect against being misunderstood and rejected. In adulthood this may lead her to feel unloveable, in which she may not be fully aware. The predictions about others' behaviour will, over time, form into an interpersonal schema that the individual will use to interpret events and guide her in social relationships.

A schema leads one to automatically and dysfunctionally attend to information that confirms the schema, while ignoring or underrating any information that might disprove it. For example, an individual with the schema '*I am unloveable*' will look in his environment for clues as to whether others love him or not. In a social interaction context, he will pay attention to the slightest signs of rejection in others' behaviour.

The schema is based on a *wish* and a *core belief*, which is defined as the self-image underlying the wish. A typical core belief in PD is 'I am not loveable.' Judith Beck (2011) describes how the prevailing self-image, the core belief, leads to systematic information-processing biases (see Figure 1.1).

In Figure 1.1 the core belief '*I am not loveable*' corresponds to the self-image underlying the attachment motivation. Under the pressure of this motivation and driven a priori by this conviction, a subject is hyper-attentive to any signs of a possible rejection ('*I felt like he was being distant*') or acceptance ('*She gave me a present*').

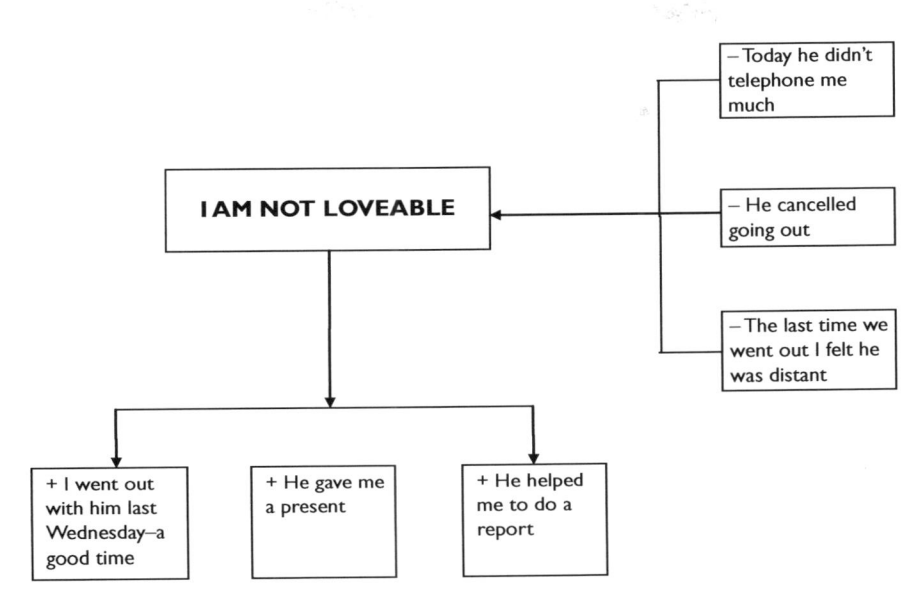

Figure 1.1 The *core belief* and biases in the processing of information.

An environmental cause-response schema carries out numerous functions:

1   It selects incoming information: we pay attention to what is important with regard to our active wish – if I am looking for food, I will take note of restaurant signs and not those of clothing stores.
2   It interprets events in line with forecasts: if I fear that the other will judge me, I will be hypersensitive to signs of judgement and my reading of facial expressions will probably be biased in this sense.
3   It leads an individual to forecast/anticipate what will happen: if my schema foresees that the other will reject me when I seek attention, I will then tend to foresee that this is likely to happen when I seek attention.
4   It affects, to a certain extent, others' intentions and leads them to behave in accordance with my schema.

Temperament plays a role in the creation of schemas. Temperament is defined as innate character inclinations, such as pessimism, optimism, openness to exploration and so on. Attachment style is important but not fundamental in our model. Attachment styles are not necessarily stable over the lifespan, meaning an insecure attachment in infancy can become secure in adulthood due to corrective experiences.

The history of a person's other motivational systems is another likely factor leading to the formation of maladaptive schemas in adults. For example, how someone learned to modulate a quest for status in the social rank motive may be helpful in understanding a schema. An individual's temperament becomes integrated with what occurs in his life and subsequently produces personal responses. The consequent emotions then shape inner and interpersonal experiences and generate meanings. Schemas are malleable and continuously evolving, and a schema formed in the early years of life can become modified more or less radically as a result of subsequent life events. Interpersonal schemas have their origin in the success or failure experienced by patients when carrying out actions driven by their motivational systems. Pathology can arise in the presence of a secure attachment if other motivational systems have not found an environment favorable for their fulfilment. An adolescent living in a rural context, in which he is loved and cared for, moves to a high school in a big city. Here he does not get included in the larger social group, and his peers consider him an outcast, poke fun at him for his manners and accent, and do not invite him to parties. The girls avoid him and consider him to be a loser. He lacks the conversational ease typical of his peers and is unable to rectify his initial exclusion. At this point he feels socially rejected and experiences a profound existential dissatisfaction because his belonging-to-the-group motivational system is not satisfied by his environment. His self-esteem can collapse and this will provide a fertile terrain for psychopathology, even if attachment was secure.

In clinical practice carried out according to MIT, one should not pay attention exclusively to the earliest years of a patient's life, as cases can be conceptualised by focusing on relatively recent events. Recent events can nevertheless have contributed to the crystallisation of a pathogenic schema.

Pathogenic interpersonal schema structure

We repeat that interpersonal schemas are an intra-psychical procedural structure, a subjective representation of the destiny that will be met by our wishes in the course of our relations with others. They are a structure that has become consolidated over time and are derived from innumerable learning experiences, from the earliest to the most recent, regarding relations between peers and colleagues, and are of a romantic nature, which then become generalised. A schema is a 'generalised memory' about how one's wishes have been received in the past and about how much they were satisfied. At the same time, it is an internalised expectation, a cognitive-affective outline with a prediction (e.g. 'Things will go like that'), which drives actions (e.g. 'Given that things will go like that, I'll try to do this').

The organisation of a schema starts with the activation of a wish driven by self-images tending to anticipate whether this wish will be satisfied or not. The wish activates plans or procedures aimed at satisfying the wish. These plans and procedures are of the 'if … then …' type and typically elicit a *response from the Other*. This response generates a *response from the Self* (in reaction to the Other's response) of an emotional, behavioural and cognitive type. We shall describe the structure of interpersonal schemas (Figure 1.2) in greater detail in Chapter 3.

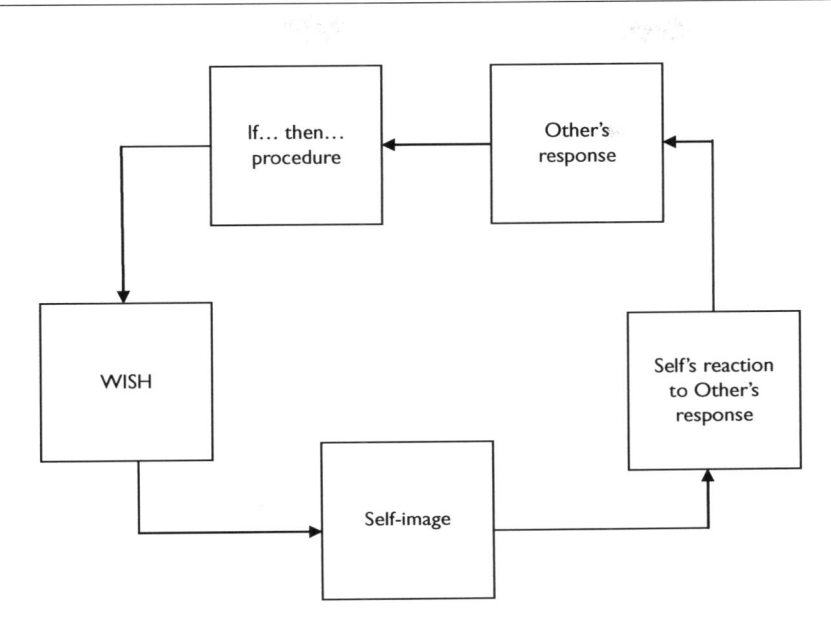

Figure 1.2 Interpersonal schema structure.

In PD, schemas are easily activated and often generate intense and dysregulated emotions that are difficult to modulate (i.e. anger or distress) because patients are unable to question whether the assumptions underlying the schema are true or false. Interpersonal schemas are not, therefore, accurate readings of what is actually occurring in relationships, but instead generate rigid and dysfunctional interpretations that prevent alternative views. For example, if an individual expects the Other not to respond to his wish to be cared for, he may approach the latter with anxiety, maintain a defensive and closed stance and talk with a strained and tense voice. His behaviour betrays a mixture of distress and resentful anger deriving from an unconscious fear of being abandoned.

This way of interrelating will induce responses from the Other that are likely to be schema-confirming (Safran and Muran, 2000). The Other will react towards the subject's hostility and defensiveness either by acting aggressive or by distancing himself from the subject. At this point the Other's distance or hostility will confirm the self-representation: 'I do not deserve to be loved and cared for'. In PD patients the most common self-representations underlying the achievement of wishes are linked to the following basic beliefs: *unloveable, inadequate, defective, undeserving, of limited value, powerless, paralysed, guilty, incompetent, untrusting, betrayed* and *omnipotent* (Beck, 2011). The typical representations of the Other include the following beliefs: *threatening, rejecting, abusing, hypercritical, controlling, inept, incapable, deceiving, deserving punishment, ideal* (Beck, 2011).

Several interpersonal schemas can grow out of the same wish; for example, in addition to the wish '*I want to be loved*' and representation of the Other as rejecting, critical and disdainful, there can be a healthy and adaptive underlying representation of the Self such as '*I deserve to be loved.*' In this case, the Other's rejecting and critical response will be seen as unjust, violent and aggressive and the Self's reaction to the Other's response will not be a depressive closing up, but instead anger at the non-satisfying of an equitable need (see Figure 1.3).

Patients will display their pathogenic self-representation to their clinicians similar to the example mentioned above of non-loveability. If, however, a patient had only this self-representation, she would be unlikely to ask for therapy because she would not imagine that there was a welcoming other able to offer her assistance. She would instead expect rejection right from the start and her depression would continue.

A clinician, therefore, has to presume that there is, at least minimally, a more functional self-representation, of being loveable and deserving attention that may have been acquired and constructed via a secondary caregiver such as the other parent, a grandparent, an elder brother or sister. This would explain the angry response in the face of a rejecting other (e.g. '*If I deserve to be loved and you*

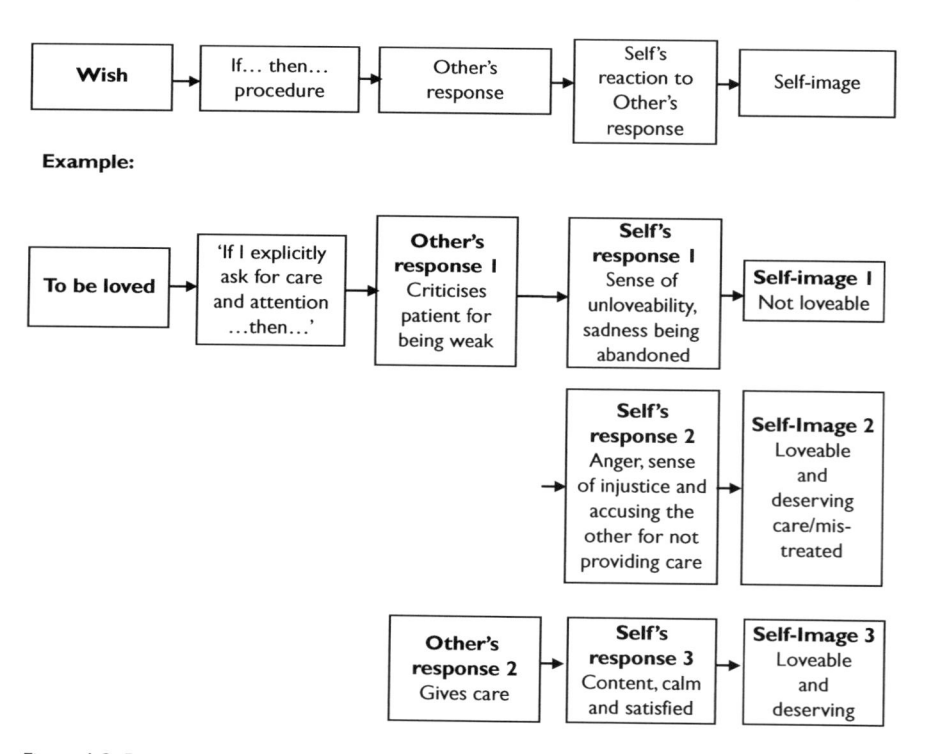

Figure 1.3 Pathogenic interpersonal schema structure.

don't love me, you're at fault'). The dysfunctional self-representation contained in the pathogenic schema is, therefore, the cause underlying the suffering or social dysfunction for which a patient starts therapy, while the functional self-representation underlies a parent's hope of finding a relational partner, starting with the therapist (Weiss, 1993). Table 1.1 displays some of the schemas most frequently found in the PDs discussed here.

Interpersonal cycles

On the basis of an individual's interpersonal schema and how his wishes match others' wishes, perspectives, intentions and projects, some *interpersonal cycles* can become activated in current relationships (Safran and Muran, 2000).

We would stress that the interpersonal schema and interpersonal cycle concepts are distinct: the first is an intra-psychical structure that organises experience and behaviour while the second is an inter-subjective process. Put concisely, a schema occurs within a person while a cycle occurs between persons. Over the course of a person's life, there are reciprocal exchanges between these two elements: inner structures shape inter-subjective processes and repeated inter-subjective processes become internalised and stable structures which modify a person's schema repertoire (Hermans and Dimaggio, 2004).

An interpersonal cycle starts when an individual, driven by his schema, acts and witnesses the response of the other who, in turn, reacts. The other's reactions evoke thoughts and emotions in the individual, confirming his pathogenic schema, which strengthens the force driving dysfunctional behaviours. At this point, the exit from the problematic communicational cycle is blocked. The interpersonal cycle is thus a sequence of inter-subjective events, a mutual inducing of actions, behaviours and affects that sustains the relational dysfunction, to which the participants end up contributing both automatically and unconsciously.

Let us think of a patient with obsessive-compulsive PD who typically tends to take on too many commitments and finds it difficult to delegate or ask for help. The patient is unaware of the fact that there is no help when he needs it because he did not ask for it. This leads him to view the other as inattentive, selfish and uninterested. Given that the other does not receive any requests for help, he keeps his distance. The other feels his help to be useless or his interventions inadequate and the target of criticism. At certain moments, however, the patient, overloaded with work and irritable as a result of fatigue, bursts with anger at the sight of the other not supporting him and protests about the lack of help that has been offered. At this point, the other feels unjustly criticised and reacts angrily to these accusations or becomes less inclined to provide help. This interaction has confirmed the patient's idea that when he needs help, he is left alone and criticised. The awareness of one's own contribution to causing the problem is, generally, lacking or minimal. Of course, attitudes and personality traits in the other play a prominent role in the activation of these cycles as well.

Table 1.1 Typical interpersonal schemas

Wish	Other's response	Self's response	Self-image	Type of personality disorder
CARE	Distant Disinterested Rejects care	Sad Depressed Lonely	Not loveable	PERVASIVE
	Rejecting Critical	Shame Undeservingness	Imperfect Not loveable	AVOIDANT DEPENDENT OBSSESSIVE-COMPULSIVE
	Intruding Tyrannical Aggressive	Closing up, switching off/shutting down Fright, withdrawal Trying to please to placate the aggressor	Vulnerable	DEPENDENT AVOIDANT OBSSESSIVE-COMPULSIVE
APPRECIATION	Critical Disdainful	Humiliation Failure Defeat Depression	Unworthiness	NARCISSISTIC OBSSESSIVE-COMPULSIVE AVOIDANT DEPENDENT DEPRESSIVE
	Critical Dissatisfied	Perfectionistic Standards	Conditionally acceptable Subordinated	NARCISSISTIC OBSSESSIVE-COMPULSIVE PARANOID
	Critical Disdainful	Anger Injustice undergone Protest Opposition	Deserves recognition Capable but misunderstood Harmed	PERVASIVE
	Accepts Judges positively	Temporary relief Effective Continues to fear judgement	Morally deserving Acceptable but only thanks to the other's positive judgement	OBSSESSIVE-COMPULSIVE DEPENDENT

Need	Other's response	Self's reaction	Self's view	Disorder
AUTONOMY[a]	Hampers Controls Underrates Suffers Blames	Paralysis Anxiety Dependence Guilt	Inadequate Weak Incapable Powerless Guilty Harmful	DEPENDENT AVOIDANT PASSIVE-AGGRESSIVE COVERT NARCISISSISM DEPRESSIVE
Autonomy	Hampers Controls Underrates	Anger Sense of oppression Flight from the relationship	Capable but not supported by the environment	NARCISSIST DEPENDENT AVOIDANT PASSIVE-AGGRESSIVE PARANOID
Appreciation[b]	Admires	Exaltation High self-esteem	Grandiose	NARCISSIST
Security	Threatening Humiliating	Fear Flight Diffidence Reactive Anger	Vulnerable	PARANOID PASSIVE-AGGRESSIVE AVOIDANT COVERT NARCISSISM
Group inclusion[c]	Different Incomprehensible Inaccessible	Alienation Isolation	Different Inferior Lonely	AVOIDANT DEPENDENT (IF SOCIALLY ISOLATED)

[a] This is a description of Other's responses and Self's reactions which are different from each other and put in chart form for brevity. In the face of the patient's wish for independence, the other hampers in various ways: by explicitly underrating and triggering paralysis or displaying suffering at the idea that the patient is neglecting him and causing sadness and guilt.

[b] The schema linked to the need for appreciation in which the other judges positively is not pathogenic in its structure, but because the patient does not manage to free himself from the need for approval, then the opposite schema in which the other underrates, surfaces. It is, therefore, a compulsive coping schema.

[c] The schema linked to the need for inclusion in the group that is found in dependent disorder is only for patients depending on a few reference figures (e.g. parents or partner) and unable to connect with others.

During the description of the treatment, we will make clear how we tackle schemas and interpersonal cycles in various different ways in MIT. The first goal of MIT is to help patients understand they are driven by internal structures, specifically interpersonal schemas that determine their behaviour. We would instead advise against prematurely attributing the patients' issues from stemming from within. Such an awareness is likely to be seen as criticising, blaming or mocking, in which the patient may respond defensively, '*So you think I'm the cause of my suffering?*' Patients' awareness that they themselves create the conditions for maintaining their problems should be promoted only during advanced stages of treatment, when they have already built knowledge of their schemas and more adaptive forms of functioning begin to surface.

Right from the first contact with a patient, the interpersonal cycle is a fundamental tool for understanding what happens in the therapeutic relationship and, especially, for helping a therapist to avoid contributing to pathological intersubjective processes (see Chapter 5). Therapists should be aware that they contribute to building the relationship and can have an active role in rendering it either beneficial or dysfunctional. We shall look at several typical interpersonal cycles in Chapter 5 on the therapeutic relationship.

There are not enough longitudinal studies clarifying the origins of dysfunctional interpersonal schemas. Certainly, various factors occur in their development and subsequent perpetuation. MIT agrees with the idea that every individual is born with a set of innate dispositions which constitute his temperament (Cloninger, 1994). For example, someone may possess a tendency to pessimism or optimism and to emotional instability or stability. Temperament can help determine the type of sensitivity and attitudes with which humans tackle events in their lives and condition others' responses. The outcome of childhood attachment processes (Bowlby, 1988), the satisfying of primary needs via the activation of motivational systems (Gilbert, 2005; Lichtenberg, 1989) and the learning of recurrences and regularities in the interaction between individual characteristics and life experiences (Young, Klosko and Weishaar, 2003) then get embedded into temperament.

Recurring states of mind

States of mind are forms of subjective experience characterised by a stable and recurring group of elements such as thoughts, beliefs, emotions, feelings, physical sensations, intentions and wishes that together manifest themselves in the flow of consciousness (Horowitz, 1987; Semerari, Carcione, Dimaggio et al., 2003a).

Some states of mind such as distress and fear are subjectively laden with suffering and patients try to avoid them. Others are *coping* states and are aimed at managing distress or avoiding negative experiences; they are dysfunctional not so much for the negative quality of the experience but because they are pursued compulsively in order to consciously or semi-automatically avoid the feared negative states. *Egosyntonic* states, which an individual seeks for their own worth and not in order to shun negative experiences, are also fundamental. These are states featuring ideas that an individual deems not needing to be discussed and considers values and questions of principle or identity-definition. During development, an egosyntonic state may have had a coping valence but, when observed clinically, the patient is not aware of this function and in his subjective experience does not consider it. The same action may be experienced as coping or as a value. A man with dependent traits may compulsively seduce women because he is terrified by loneliness (*coping*), whereas one with narcissistic traits does it because he finds it fun, gives him pleasure and considers it a natural part of male identity (*egosyntonic*).

Every patient oscillates between these states (Dimaggio, Semerari, Carcione et al., 2007). Persons with avoidant PD may suffer because of a negative opinion received and feel ashamed (*distressing and feared state*); they then seek for pleasurable activities they perform alone in order to soothe the pain of the feared criticism and the detachment from others (*coping state*). A paranoid patient may fear aggression and feel trodden on, humiliated and scorned (*feared state*), switch to a defensive counter-attack laden with anger and fantasies about revenge (*coping state*) and angrily claim respect from others because he considers it a primary and unquestionable human value (*egosyntonic state with a moral valence*).

There are, lastly, *wished for states*, which are not disorder-specific but correspond to forms of experience that are healthy, beneficial and context-sensitive, such as the ability to relax, feeling the pleasure of belonging, the enjoyment of social play or a sense of activity and independence when pursuing one's inclinations or effectively mastering one's abilities, or persisting in an activity while overcoming tiredness and frustration.

Patients often experience states of mind that are not specific to PD but characterise the suffering linked to symptom disorders. There are, therefore, multiform states of anxiety or depression, from fantasies about catastrophes found in panic attacks to depressive despair and the fear of getting ill found in hypochondria.

Another aspect of subjective suffering not specific to PD but often found in them, is the tendency for consciousness to disgregate under stress, in other words, dissociation proneness (Farina and Liotti, 2013). These are not in themselves states with typical contents. What is at stake is, rather, a succession of many and various themes, sensations, mental images and emotions appearing as in a fog. In these states subjects are afraid of going crazy and breaking up; they are confused and dazed and have trouble putting together projects, while their sense of identity wobbles (Van der Hart, Nijenhuis and Steele, 2006). Sometimes their sensation is of a true and proper mental vacuum, with characteristics, however, different from the sense of emptiness and boredom found in states of affective lifelessness. In the latter the prevailing sensations are coldness, lack of drive and detachment. Dissociation instead is an experience of dizziness, confusion, loss of control, fragmentation and an inability to master one's own mind. Another difference is that some patients may seek states of emptiness and coldness to silence their distressing experiences, while states of emptiness with a dissociative valence frighten them. The impending absence of sense, loss of goals and fragmentation associated with dissociation can be terrifying.

In PD, patients' states of mind are recurrent and vacillate between one another, interspersed at times by states of well-being in which the patient reacts appropriately to contexts. It can be said intuitively that the more a person is capable of experiencing healthy states or responding congruously to what happens, the less pervasive their PD is.

In many PDs there are groups of states that alternate in a rigid manner and in line with foreseeable transition rules. There is no state typical of a disorder, but it is the alternating among themselves of several states with rigid transition rules that assists in diagnosing a specific personality prototype (Dimaggio, Carcione, Petrilli et al., 2005; Dimaggio, Semerari, Carcione et al., 2007). For example, in narcissistic PD a patient vacillates between emptiness, grandiose fantasies, angry states where they believe others are blocking their path to glory, and depressive or distressing states where they feel defeated or excluded. An analysis of three narcissistic patients' session transcripts showed that the states of mind were consistent with what was hypothesised, in particular a state of anger emerged at the idea that others were hampering, harming, hurting and cheating them and excluding them from the group. Fragile and needy self-aspects were not expressed by the women, which is congruent with the idea that these patients will not place their trust in others and prefer self-soothing instead (Dimaggio, Nicolò, Fiore et al., 2008).

The schema-focused therapy approach (Young, Klosko and Weishaar, 2003) has explored so-called *schema modes* in PD, a concept in part similar to that of state of mind and inspired by Horowitz's work (1987). A schema mode is an emotional, cognitive and behavioural state active at a particular moment in an individual (Lobbestael, van Vreeswijk and Arntz, 2007; Young, Klosko, and Weishaar, 2003). Schema modes were initially divided into four categories: innate child, maladaptive coping, maladaptive parent and healthy adult. The child modes included the *vulnerable child, angry child, impulsive/undisciplined child* and *contented child*. The maladaptive coping mode included the *detached protector, compliant surrender* and *overcompensator*, and the maladaptive parent mode included the *demanding or critical parent* and *punitive parent*. Seven new modes were then added (Lobbestael, van Vreeswijk and Arntz, 2008; Bamelis, Renner, Heidkamp et al., 2011) characterising more fully Cluster C PDs (paranoid, histrionic and narcissistic): *isolated child, abandoned/abused child, dependent child, avoidant protector, attention and approval seeker, perfectionist overcontroller* and *suspicious overcontroller*.

Schema therapy has, therefore, hypothesised associations between particular modes and specific PDs. Some of these associations have recently been confirmed (Arntz, Klokman, Sieswerda, 2005; Bamelis, Renner, Heidkamp et al., 2011; Lobbestael, Arntz and Sieswerda, 2005). Overall, paranoid PD is characterised by the *angry child* and *suspicious overcontroller* modes, while the expected *abandoned/abused child, angry child* and *avoidant protector* modes were found to be absent. Narcissistic PD was found to be correlated with the *attention and approval seeker* and *impulsive child* modes, associations that had not been theorised previously and which could: (1) lead to a conceptualisation of narcissism as a response to an extreme need for attention, and (2) provide grounds for the hypothesis that narcissism depends on there not being adequate limits imposed on a child during infancy. The other correlations expected with the *detached protector* mode were confirmed.

The main modes hypothesised in the Cluster C disorders were confirmed: *avoidant protector*, *detached protector* and *compliant surrenderer* in avoidant PD, *dependent child* and *compliant surrenderer* in dependent PD and *perfectionist overcontroller* in obsessive-compulsive PD.

Several unlikely associations emerged between certain personality disorders and schema modes, including dependent and avoidant PD and the *abandoned/ abused child* mode and between avoidant PD and the *suspicious overcontroller* mode. The first is consistent with the hypothesis in the literature that there is a history of deprivation/emotional abuse in avoidant patients' infancy; the other can be explained by their fear of critical judgements and humiliation, which renders them wary and suspicious. Although research in schema therapy supports the idea that there are specific experience patterns for some PDs, there is still a great need for empirical research. In particular, research should focus on discourse analysis rather than responses to predetermined questionnaires. The description of mental states in MIT has been based principally on clinical experience.

No single state of mind is pathological in itself. Pathology is determined by the pervasiveness of a set of states, the level of subjective distress accompanying the states, the lack of states linked to well-being and adaptation, and their tendency to become activated under minimal cues in the face of disparate stimuli.

For example, defence against relational danger (i.e. physical vulnerability, humiliation, submission) and a tendency to an anticipatory counterattack is not specific to paranoia. The automatism dictated by the need for security and protection from danger puts humans in a hyper-vigilant state aimed at finding any danger and preparing a reaction in accordance with rectilinear attack-flight formats. The title of Dostoevsky's novel, *Humiliated and Insulted*, and wanting to make good of one's losses or seeking revenge describes human beings, not paranoid PD.

Persons suffering from paranoid, avoidant and narcissistic disorders remain indefinitely in such states and, if they manage to get out of them, do this in an equally problematic way. A person with paranoia, therefore, sticks to an angry counterattack (*fight*) or isolates himself (*flight*) to avoid the hovering threat; a narcissist withdraws disdainfully into her ivory tower; an avoidant sufferer breaks down with shame at his social ineptitude and in the end feels he is the cause of the humiliation he has received. Relatively well-adapted persons will, instead, remain in these states for a shorter time, due to accepting reassurance from a partner or a diversion of their attention, for example by a friend's telephone call inviting them out shopping. In PD, states of mind are less flexible and less the result of responses consistent with the context.

Table 1.2 The states of mind typical of PDs

Type of state	State of mind	Personality disorder
Distressing or feared states	Abandonment, non-loveability, unworthiness	PERVASIVE
	Group exclusion, outsiderness, alienation	AVOIDANT, NARCISSISTIC
	Vulnerability, weakness, perception of relational danger	PARANOID, AVOIDANT NARCISSISTIC, PASSIVE-AGGRESSIVE
	Unworthiness, fear of negative judgement, shame	PERVASIVE
	Moral guilt, survivor's guilt	OBSESSIVE-COMPULSIVE, DEPENDENT, NARCISSISTIC, DEPRESSIVE
	Constriction, forced submission	AVOIDANT, DEPENDENT, PASSIVE-AGGRESSIVE, PARANOID, NARCISSISTIC
Coping states	Self-protective anger, opposition to an oppressor, rebellion against constriction	PARANOID, NARCISSISTIC, PASSIVE-AGGRESSIVE AVOIDANT
	Mistrustfulness	PARANOID, COVERT NARCISSISM, AVOIDANT
	Devitalised emptiness	NARCISSISTIC, DEPENDENT, AVOIDANT
	Avoidance, protective isolation	AVOIDANT, PARANOID, NARCISSISTIC
	Compliance, sought-for submission	DEPENDENT, AVOIDANT
	Workaholism, perfectionism, overload	OBSESSIVE-COMPULSIVE, NARCISSISTIC, DEPENDENT, DEPRESSIVE
	Idealisation of other, ideal protector	DEPENDENT
	Stupefaction	ASPECIFIC
Egosynthonic states	Grandiosity	NARCISSISTIC, PARANOID, AVOIDANT (TRANSITORY)
	Moral superiority, critical judgement, disdain	OBSESSIVE-COMPULSIVE, NARCISSISTIC, PASSIVE-AGGRESSIVE, DEPRESSIVE, PARANOID
	Seeking and maintaining of status, territoriality, consolidation of power	PARANOID, NARCISSISTIC
	Pleasure-seeking, hedonism	NARCISSISTIC

The states typical of PDs are summarised in Table 1.2 with a cross-reference to which disorders are most typically linked to them among those of interest here (avoidant, narcissistic, dependent, obsessive-compulsive, paranoid, passive-aggressive, depressive and schizoid traits).

We would recall that the first group refers to those *distressing* or *feared* states that a patient tries to avoid; the second group is made of *coping* states, usually aimed at managing distress or avoiding feeling it. The third group refers to *egosyntonic* states, which a patient actively seeks and which generally have the characteristic of being considered moral values that define the patient's identity.

Feared or distressing states

Abandonment/non-lovability

This is probably one of the most important states and is found in all PDs. It describes a feeling that one is alone and not loved, while others are distant, lost and unreachable, and that in the face of one's need for support, love and warmth, one will remain alone. The self-image at these moments is that this abandonment is deserved because one is unworthy, inadequate and deserving of rejection. Patients feel weak, fragile and depressed at the idea that the abandonment will be endless. If there is hope of attention and support, it is dominated by anxiety at the idea that the hope will be unmet. This state can lead to various coping states, depending on the dominant personality traits. For example, it can generate compliance and submission to please the other or switch to the competitive/social rank system culminating in perfectionism (e.g. '*If they find out who I really am, they'll reject me, but If I'm perfect, up to the challenge and irreproachable, perhaps I'll be accepted*').

Alienation/group exclusion/outsiderness

This state features a sensation of being different from the others, inferior and that social inclusion is way beyond one's reach. Sometimes patients have a sense of being different because they are better than others, but the dominant idea is to be alien and doomed to rejection and being ostracised. Patients often feel it impossible to connect with others or see themselves as similar and capable of sharing common topics, values or emotions. Others are seen as distant, critical and *normal* but incomprehensible. There is not, therefore, a perception of group inclusion. Patients often describe this state with metaphors like: 'I see the others as if through glass' or 'There's a wall separating me from the others' or 'I'm a fish out of water'. In this state a person is prone to thinking that others reject and criticise and are united with each other in mocking him, and such ideas lead to shifting between the *fear of judgment/shame, vulnerability/weakness/perception of relational danger* or *mistrustfulness* states.

Vulnerability/weakness/perception of relational danger

This consists of a subjective experience of weakness, both physical and character fragility. It includes the sense of incapacity to defend one's territory, one's private space and the group to which one belongs from the others' overbearing and domineering influence (Salvatore, Lysaker, Procacci et al., 2012). The sensation that boundaries are being violated is immediately perceived as threatening. Characteristic emotions are anxiety and ineffectiveness in handling aggression. Sometimes there is the fear of a true and proper physical attack. The belief is that one is inferior and risks being subjugated. This is a state with a strong somatic side, characterised by a sense of weakness or physical inadequacy; for example, one feels one's virility or femininity to be threatened. Others, on the contrary, are felt to be strong, dominating, powerful and influential. The idea is that there will soon be a contest, a confrontation in which others, ill-intentioned and superior, will end up achieving their goal of squashing, dominating and excluding. Sometimes the state includes a feeling of loneliness, the idea that there are no reliable allies with whom to tackle a hostile world. This state is likely to shift into states involving *protective isolation* or *self-protective anger/mistrustfulness*. Moreover, the experiencing of vulnerability, especially in patients with Paranoid PD, can lead to a searching for a position with a high social rank, with the idea that the power resulting from it will allow them to subjugate others and thus control the danger. This strategy can lead to the status maintenance/power consolidation state.

Unworthiness/fear of judgement/shame

Based on the idea that one is unworthy, the core theme is that others will notice our defects and criticise and mock, and because of this exclude or reject us. The dominant emotions are shame and embarrassment. Self-esteem is low and the sense of self-efficacy minimal. The dominant action tendency is to avoid others looking at us, distance oneself from relationships and, thus, isolate oneself. Patients long for appreciation to the point of displaying a false self-image. One can wear a mask or lie with the aim of presenting a more socially acceptable self-image. Alternatively, one can opt for submission to get accepted in the group again. The bodily state is one of intense activation, widespread alarm and tension, often accompanied by evident expressive correlates, like blushing or avoiding eye contact. In this state patients are likely to feel transparent.

Moral guilt and survivor's guilt

The individual feels guilty because he broke a rule, did not perform a duty or harmed others through incompetence or carelessness, or unjustly enjoyed greater good fortune than the others (Basile, Mancini, Macaluso et al., 2011). The action tendencies include making amends or renouncing one's good fortune. Self-esteem can easily collapse and self-blaming is pervasive, often in a ruminative form; the subject accurately evaluates their own behaviour and asks themselves whether it is a sign of evil intentions or moral weakness on their part or if they will harm others. They readily criticise their own spontaneous inclinations or their seeking pleasure or relaxation because they consider them immoral or harmful to others.

Constriction/injustice suffered/forced submission

The core of this state is represented by feeling constrained by the other's will. A patient believes she is unable to control her own choices because expressing her own point of view could lead the other to punish, subjugate or abandon her. As a result, she falls in with the other's goals but does it disgruntledly and feels she is suffering an injustice and does not have the power to rebel. She broods silently on her anger. She thinks she deserves a different, better treatment, but only the other's stamp of approval would allow her to achieve her wishes and this does not happen. In her brooding over rebellion, she fantasises about resisting her tendency to fall in and imagines little, hidden rebellions but does not see herself being able to openly defy the will of the other, seen as oppressive, tyrannical and powerful. Sometimes a patient is afraid of his own aggressiveness and fears that, if he asserted himself, he would do it laden with a destructive anger for others and for himself. Patients shift from this state to isolation and protective avoidance, so as to create for themselves an area of freedom far from the other's influence. Sometimes, instead, they pass to a state of *self-protective anger/rebellion against the tyrant*, an anger that can spiral out of control.

Coping states

Mistrustfulness

This state features hyper-vigilance and watchfulness when faced with the idea that others could threaten, deceive, humiliate, betray or cause harm to the patient. The social safeness and threat-detection system (Gilbert, 1989) is hyperactive. Attention is focused on others' minds with a rapid attribution of ill-intentioned contents, often with very sophisticated psychological cause-effect chains explaining why the other should want to harm them. These chains are sometimes plausible but always impossible to criticise. The subject can be an individual or an entire group that a patient imagines in a coalition against herself. This is not a psychotic state and reality testing is still intact. The dominant emotions are anxiety and irritation. The body is vigorous, vigilant and ready to react should the threat prove to be real. This vigilance is linked to a sense of good self-efficacy and a person feels capable of reacting and hard to deceive. This is a state linked to positive metacognitions such as 'It is a good idea to be on watch because I can protect myself better from dangers' (see coping strategies of the ruminative type). The dominant theme, as in the vulnerability state, is the defence of one's territory, physical integrity and protection of self-esteem when faced with potentially deceiving, predatory or humiliating others. If the danger feared is considered true and impending, a patient, often with paranoid or narcissistic aspects, shifts from this state to one of self-protective anger or rebellion towards an oppressor. If the battle is seen as risky, it leads to a shift into protective isolation, typical of paranoia or avoidant PD.

Self-protective anger/opposition to an oppressor/rebellion against constriction

This state is activated when a patient sees threats to his self-esteem, social rank, image, physical and territorial integrity, independence, or access to resources.

It represents a reaction to the vulnerability state, in situations in which the patient feels a sense of mounting power and strength when faced with others who humiliate, attack, prey, subjugate or hamper. This state follows the activation of the danger warning system during the mistrustfulness state, when the danger is by now seen as certain and the oppressor acting. The patient has stopped oscillating between feelings of fear and irritation at the least perception of impending failure, humiliation and submission.

By now the harm has been suffered and the injustice carried out. Wounded pride accompanied by anger is typical of this state, and similarly accusing and underrating others by considering them undeserving, morally inferior, deceiving or incapable. The aggressiveness can be fantasised about or enacted. Behaviour is directed not so much towards achieving one's wishes but rather towards preventing the other from continuing to cause harm, threaten and hamper. This state can prelude an entry into states of disdainful distance from relationships, like paranoid isolation or narcissists' seeking of an ivory tower. In some cases, patients feel a sense of belonging to a group with which they jointly confront the enemy.

The anger in this state, even if unexpressed, silently insinuates itself in a patient's behaviour so that he begins to do things like not showing up to work, avoiding friends or progressively shunning romantic ties due to feeling offended. This is a state frequently found in paranoid, narcissistic and passive-aggressive PD and in certain cases of obsessive-compulsive PD. It is also found in a silent form in avoidant PD.

Patients can shift from this state to states involving anger directed at the self; they think they are suffering injustices because they are weak and dependent on others. For example, patients with avoidant or dependent PD or with passive-aggressive aspects feel constrained to give up propounding their own point of view for fear that others will abandon them and they consider themselves inept for this reason.

Devitalised emptiness

Patients feel lifeless, emotionally flat, apathetic and cold. Their lives take on a metallic tone and they feel estranged and disconnected. There is a sort of affective anaesthesia: not only are pain, weakness, fragility, depression and distress distant echoes, but all sensations arrive deadened. Others are distant not because they exclude, but because patients do not have the drive to look for them. In part, it is an anaesthesia they desire because it ensures there is no pain, but it is unpleasant at the same time. In fact, everything seems, at intervals, unreal. Body is distant and inanimate, except in brief episodes of intense, often erotic or chemically induced stimulation generated by compulsively repeated activities (for example, electronic games or pornography). This state is at times accompanied by a sort of artificial sense of safety and unattackability. Some narcissistic patients can also fantasise about success and omnipotence, but in a cold form, without the triumphal echo filling the grandiose state. If this state persists, it too becomes unpleasant, and a hardly self-confessed desire for relationships surfaces among the iciness and boredom.

This is a state typical of narcissistic PD, frequent in avoidant PD and linked to schizoid traits. Paranoid patients can experience it as a consequence of prolonged relational isolation. Patients with passive-aggressive traits can enter it as a result of not pursuing goals other than opposing an oppressor.

Avoidance/protective isolation

This state is activated when a patient sees others as critical, threatening, aggressive and hostile, no longer doubts the others' evil intentions and is sure danger is imminent. The patient feels he does not have the strength to fight anymore. He subsequently feels the need to physically and mentally isolate himself with the aim of putting an end to his relational suffering. He feels afraid and ashamed for avoiding relationships, but also experiences security and diminished anxiety. Arousal is high at the time the patient enters the state but falls when the patient sees it is possible to avoid the feared situation. Patients suffering from different disorders seek isolation in particular ways (Dimaggio, Semerari, Carcione et al., 2007): a person with paranoid PD isolates herself in an armored bunker, a person with narcissistic PD closes himself in an ivory tower (Dimaggio, 2012; Modell, 1984) and an avoidant sufferer isolates himself in a hidden lair. Sometimes this state leads to another, pleasure-seeking state, where patients seek solitary gratification.

Compliance/sought-for submission

This state becomes activated when the idea of contradicting the other is too frightening because the other is stronger and could attack or abandon the patient. Thus the patient feels at fault and gives up pursuing her own goals. She complies almost automatically with the other's plans and as a result momentarily obtains a sense of calmness, relief and security. Signs of submission are evident: the patient wants to make it clear to the other that she will not threaten or disobey him and will be loyal. In this state a patient can arrive at a sincere conviction that she is in agreement with the other, almost to the extent of losing any memory of her own point of view.

Workaholism/perfectionism/overload

In this state patients focus on the target they want to reach and set high performance standards for themselves. They carefully monitor the gap between expected and actual performance, with the constant idea that this gap will persist and they need to make a bigger effort to correct their mistakes. The difference between expected standards and recorded performance is so intolerable that the patients do not heed any signs of tiredness or fatigue. In the perfectionist state, ideal performance is sought either via a single goal or several of them (Dimaggio, Semerari, Carcione et al., 2007). Everything has to be done correctly and this is likely to be linked to a sense of overdoing things, accompanied by the idea that it is not possible to give up anything. The fear of making mistakes is strong, doubts about making the wrong choice are oppressive, and the idea that one is not up to expectations are pervasive, as is the expectation that others will harshly and disdainfully criticise and, often, abandon them (Frost, Marten, Lahart et al., 1990; Hewitt and Flett, 1991). Guilt, shame and anxiety anticipating the failure to achieve the perfectionist standard are typical emotions. Self-efficacy is very low but at certain moments in which patients feel they are mastering some of the goals, it can be high. Patients can shift from this state to states involving paralysis in decision-making and depressive impotence.

Idealisation of the other/ideal protector

In this state the other is seen as strong, full of qualities, able to ensure protection, guidance and comfort. This is an image accompanied by a sense of comfort, security, self-efficacy and warmth. The idea is that the other is always available and able to solve problems and ensure protection, security and well-being. Sometimes the state acquires both dream-like nuances and elements from reality. Sometimes elements from reality are ignored, as if problems and dangers were unimportant when the other is around, who is seen as perfect and ready to succour. Patients search for an ideal other to soothe their feelings of solitude, incapability and vulnerability, or simply because having an ideal protector at their side is considered a normal condition for self-achievement. The other's nearness, be it physical or mental, is seen as indispensable. If the other is far away or unavailable, patients imagine themselves to be fragile and incapable, with life losing its meaning. When they are in this state, they see this risk as marginal; as long as the other is here they just experience a mixture of low anxiety (e.g. *'let's hope he will not disappear'*) and relief for the danger avoided (e.g. *'he's here with me after all'*).

Stupefaction

When feeling distress or uncontrollable emotions and thoughts in this state, a patient intentionally seeks to lower his state of wakefulness, or stupefy himself. This is achieved through overworking (different from perfectionist overworking as the goal is not performance but to avoid thinking), physical exercise or substance abuse. He feels a sort of pleasant dulling, a temporary relief from psychic pain and ruminations.

Egosyntonic states

Grandiosity

A patient feels superior, self-sufficient and admired, is convinced he rules the world and considers himself different from the persons around him, whereas he belongs to a fantasised elite often distant in space and time. A characteristic emotion is disdain, followed by a sense of strength and self-efficacy and sometimes temporary euphoria. His experiences are characterised by coldness and detachment; nothing touches him as if he is wrapped in a mantle of omnipotence. The grandiosity can turn into true and proper exaltation with an accelerating thought flow but does not last as long as in a hypo-maniacal or maniacal state. This state can be tinged by a sense of revenge, as if their due recognition has not arrived and can be displayed to those who previously did not believe in one. The attitude towards others is often condescending, like that of a benevolent feudal landowner towards his subjects, whom he considers inferiors. The grandiose state is likely to extinguish when faced with frustrations such as one's worth not being acknowledged or a perception that others are abandoning, rejecting or criticising the self, and this leads to a shift into states involving shame and fear of judgement, exclusion/alienation, self-protective anger (in which others are blamed for failures) or protective isolation. These are processes typical of narcissism but temporarily found in avoidant PD as well when a subject has social success. In obsessive-compulsive and paranoid PD, the moral superiority can induce a move to the grandiose state when a person feels special and omnipotent because he is better than the others.

Moral superiority/critical judgement/disdain

This consists of a sense of being just, upright and faultless. Patients exalt themselves to being bearers of ethical and moral values they feel to be absolute, universal and indispensable. The expectation is that the same values are automatically shared by others. Compared to others, patients feel on a higher level with the right to judge. The sense of duty drives ideation and, if thoughts and emotions surface that are inconsistent with the value pursued, they get warded off with a sense of strength and mastery (e.g. '*I'm able to control my impulses*'). Memories of upright behaviour, respectful of the rules and self-defined as altruistic, come to the surface. In this state, patients carefully screen other's intentions and behaviour and are prone to judging them as being immoral or self-centred and, as a result, reprove, accuse and disdain them. Other's failings are interpreted as being caused by ill will or lack of values. This is a state accompanied by energy and a sense of efficacy.

Seeking and maintaining of status/territoriality/consolidation of power

Core features in this state are the extent of the power over and domination of others. This state and the grandiose state strongly overlap, because even if power generates a gratification of self-esteem and is intrinsically pleasant, it is actually functional to dominating and controlling others. In other words, in the grandiose state patients seek domination only if it is useful for supporting the grandiosity, while in this state there is a seeking of grandiosity in order to dominate. The grandiose state is most typical of narcissism and a pure narcissist wants to subjugate in order to win; the current state is most frequent in paranoid PD and a pure paranoid wants to win in order to subjugate and feel the strength and control deriving from status.

What is actively sought via the subjugation of the other is a mixture of revenge and of reacquiring control over the danger. With an avoidant patient occupying a position of power, the other, usually represented as judging and critical towards the self, is finally 'made to feel' inadequate. Patients exalt in reducing someone, who previously humiliated them, to silence. A paranoid patient who has achieved power feels safe and strong when he sees that others belonging to the group fear him and are obliged to respect or obey him.

As in the grandiose state, patients are disdainful and arrogant. The affects are euphoria, sense of strength and self-efficacy. Diffidence and anger can tinge this state. But in this case, even if angry inside, persons can avoid letting their emotions show, and act with cold calculation. Lastly, it should be said that any winning of a position of elevated social power does not usually alter the idea of being vulnerable vis-à-vis stronger and more dangerous others. This leads the state to self-perpetuate itself and the actions aimed at obtaining status or domination of others to increase.

Pleasure-seeking/hedonism

Seeking pleasure is a universal and unavoidable human principle, but for some patients it is a state pursued blindly and compulsively. A subject thinks almost exclusively about how to enjoy himself and get pleasure and other projects and ideas are put on the back burner. He is likely to see others as either instrumental to his enjoyment or an obstacle to it. Gratification can be of the sexual type or in the form of games and is both pursued in relationships with others and artificially induced, for example through substance abuse. With some patients the pleasure-seeking is solitary and arises after the pleasure of social life has been seen to be unachievable. A patient, closed up in his isolation, dedicates himself to gratifying activities, from pornography, to music, to surfing the Internet, watching films and television series, or playing videogames. Sometimes this state has explicit coping valences. When it has intentionally consolatory functions after receiving frustrations, we classify it among ego-syntonic states because pleasure is sought in this moment as an end in itself, accompanied by cynicism, determination and disinterest about the consequences for others of one's actions.

The rules guiding between-states shifts

With each patient not only is it necessary to define which states of mind she experiences recurrently but also the internal and interpersonal factors causing the shifts from one state to another. Personality pathology is constituted not only of problematic states but also of the fact that patients shift rigidly between dysfunctional states as a result of minimal triggers of which they are often unaware (Dimaggio, Carcione, Petrilli et al., 2005; Dimaggio, Semerari, Carcione et al., 2007). Some triggers are endogenous. For example, if a patient suffers from mood fluctuations on a temperamental basis, with a tendency towards depression, at these times it is more likely that she will start to go through a series of negative states. In other cases, and more commonly in the case of PD, the triggers are of an interpersonal nature or are in any case represented by outside stimuli from the environment. We are going to illustrate these maintenance mechanisms using narcissistic and obsessive-compulsive PD as examples.

A patient with narcissism wishes to be appreciated for his special qualities and, in particular, supported in his goals. If this happens, he is able to remain in the grandiose state or temporarily pass through good functioning states in which he feels satisfied, efficacious, active and productive. These positive states do not, however, last long. Exiting from such a state can be provoked by minimal environmental events. The subject thinks he has achieved something exceptional but others do not appreciate him, acknowledge his merit or, worse still, hamper or exclude him. Initially the narcissistic patient shifts into the self-protective anger state and begins thinking that others are inept, disdains them and labels them incompetent, lazy and inadequate. In this state he is temporarily combative and is likely to induce hostile responses in others that confirm his idea that he is being blocked, ostracised and excluded, instead of admired and supported as he profoundly wishes. At this point the easiest way out of his frustration is protective isolation or entering the devitalised emptiness state. In the latter he can cling to a special or superior self-image and fantasise that whenever others stop hampering him, then his enormous skills, intelligence and abilities will be acknowledged. This is a lifeless image, which does not produce a true and proper sense of grandiosity. Affective lifelessness and relational isolation are automatisms protecting one from the suffering generated by images of rejection, negative opinions from others' lack of support and, in the end, abandonment. If relational frustrations and lack of support of one's special value persist, as when a partner fails to provide the necessary and expected attention and admiration, the length of the devitalised emptiness increases. This leads to an entry into states involving depression and intense anxiety, often laden with symptoms.

For example, a patient realises that the dreams of his youth have not come true, or else that the people around him have obtained greater gratification and personal and professional success. Isolated and deadened, he is likely to become a prey to intense depression and feel that life has no meaning. He may experience anxiety attacks, dissociative states or fear for his health. Exiting from the depression is difficult and requires time; generally it is possible by resorting to the grandiose self-image, with the idea that, given particular conditions, one's special value could again be acknowledged. Thinking that there is someone admiring them is a fundamental trigger that reactivates the patient and makes it possible for him to return to the grandiose state, although it reactivates the disorder maintenance circuit.

Obsessive-compulsive PD patients are driven by schemas where they need approval and believe others are critical, or need attention and view others as distant, judging and punitive if they break the rules. As they feel rejected, they attempt to be accepted by seeking perfectionism and aiming for moral exceptionableness. In such situations, they set unachievable standards for themselves, overload themselves with commitments and tasks, have great difficulty delegating and do not ask for help. When they do not receive help (because they did not ask for it), patients see the other as inattentive and immorally lacking in the will to help. As the other hears no requests for help and indeed finds himself before a person with compulsive self-sufficiency, the other prefers to keep his distance as he feels that his help would be useless, inadequate and subject to criticism. However, in some situations patients are overloaded with work and become irritable, which leads them to angrily explode when they see the other not supporting them. At this point, the other is likely to feel unjustly criticised and reacts to the accusations in ways that diminish his inclination to provide help. Patients feel abandoned and criticised again but shift easily into states in which they feel guilty for the harm caused and egotistic for asking for help. This starts up their self-accusations again and reinforces their perfectionist standards. Exiting from overworking is impossible due to views of self-criticism and guilt, while entering states involving pleasure and relaxation is censured. One factor that reduces the possibility of exiting the cycle is the difficulty in accessing internal states: an obsessive-compulsive PD patient can scarcely recognise fatigue and tiredness and this, added to her moral self-criticism, prevents her from realising when she exceeds her limits. In fact, if she had functioning monitoring and the capacity to modulate effort, she might relax in order to work better later. An obsessive-compulsive PD patient, therefore, is unable to exit the self-perpetuation cycle among states of mind.

Notes

1 We did not edit Giulia's dialogue to illustrate how her communication becomes very abstract and incomprehensible.
2 We would recall that a phenomenon similar to lack of agency has been described in borderline personality disorder and termed 'alien self' (see Allen, Fonagy and Bateman, 2008). As the result of an ineffective parental style and a disorganised attachment relationship in which the caregiver fails in the precious task of mirroring and modulating affective states, the child is considered to develop a core/nucleus of thoughts, emotions and sensations seen as part of the self, but not as belonging to the self, a sort of alien self in fact, composed of the internalised other. In adulthood individuals with borderline disorder are considered to continue to act under the guidance of this alien self and to go along with its will as they feel they have no other choice except to comply with its requests, even if sometimes it is possible to see from verbal and non-verbal signals that what is expressed is not their true will. Sometimes they themselves have a limited awareness that the goals they are fixing are not those they would try to achieve if they were not driven by their alien controller. If they become more aware of their own needs, they nevertheless feel powerless because the alien self is operating.

Chapter 2

Personality disorder psychopathology

Functions

To usefully conceptualise clinical cases and plan treatment, we need to pinpoint the problematical experiences and the supporting interpersonal schemas. In addition, it is also important to identify dysfunctions in understanding, as well as affect and behaviour regulation processes. In this chapter we will discuss *metacognitive dysfunctions*, *maladaptive forms of coping*, *cognitive biases* and *disorders of affect regulation*.

Metacognitive dysfunctions

According to MIT (Carcione, Dimaggio, Conti et al., 2010; Dimaggio, Procacci, Nicolò et al., 2007; Dimaggio and Lysaker, 2010; Semerari, Carcione, Dimaggio et al., 2003b) metacognition is the human ability to understand one's own and others' mental states, as well as the ability for reflection and mastery.

We engage in *metacognitive activity* by identifying and understanding how we feel and what drives us to act, and by forming an integrated view of ourselves despite the various mental states continuously alternating in our minds. We identify the contents of experience on the basis of perceptual and linguistic cues as well as chains of inferences. For example, we can identify our emotional state by focusing on our bodily sensations: a stomach ache could indicate that we are worried about the outcome of an exam. We also use metacognitive skills when trying to understand how others are feeling and the intentions that are likely to be guiding their behaviour. For example, we can guess others' emotions by observing their facial expressions, postures and prosodies. Lastly, metacognition includes the ability to use an understanding of mental states to manipulate and master them. For instance, mastery may be evidenced by manipulating conditions in which we calm down, concentrate, relax or enjoy ourselves. A knowledge of mental states is beneficial for the maintenance of relationships as well because it helps us foresee probable occurrences when we interact with others, solve any relational conflicts that may transpire and achieve mutual relational goals.

Metacognition greatly coincides with various functions analysed in the research of the *theory of mind* (TOM) (Baron-Cohen, Leslie and Frith, 1985), *social cognition* (Brüne, Abdel-Hamid, Lehmkämper et al., 2007), lack of emotional awareness or *alexithymia* (Taylor, Bagby and Parker, 1997; Vanheule, Verhaege and Desmet, 2011), *mentalisation* (Allen, Fonagy and Bateman, 2008; Fonagy, Gergely, Jurist et al., 2002) and *affect consciousness* (Monsen and Monsen, 1999; Solbakken, Hansen, Havik et al., 2012). Although metacognition and the various constructs listed above are similar in many ways, there are notable differences present.

The most significant difference between metacognition and ToM and social cognition is the context in which these functions are observed. ToM and social cognition describe how persons in experimental settings ascribe punctiform mental states in response to structured stimuli. For example, a person observing a comic strip is able to identify that the actions of the characters (typical theory of mind task) are driven by an intention to hide their mental states in an attempt to deceive the other, or can deduce what emotion the characters are feeling by observing their facial expressions. However, metacognition as conceived in MIT describes the ability to use mental states to ascribe meaning to personally significant events, and to employ this knowledge in the course of real and emotionally warm interactions. Surprisingly, many individuals evidence mentalistic reasoning skills in a laboratory setting, but then do not apply these skills in daily life or implement them in a timely manner. Lastly, ToM and social cognition describe punctiform mental state attributions, such as identifying which emotion a person is experiencing by examining her facial expression in a video. In other words, metacognition is the ability to summarise various aspects of mental knowledge into a general picture which we can use to give meaning to our actions (Lysaker, Gumley, Leudtke et al., 2013) and to reply to questions such as: *'What impact does that face have on me? Now that I feel discouraged, how am I going to react? What can I do to deal with my fear of being abandoned?'*

Unlike laboratory-based ToM, metacognition includes the tendency to recall various mental states when thinking about past interactions, and the reconstruction of the events by reflecting on the memory of what we and the others thought and felt, and the motivations which drove the behaviours that were present. When an individual with limited metacognitive skills thinks about a person he has interacted with, he recalls the latter's behaviour and gestures, but not his emotions or intentions. Metacognition is also distinct from ToM in that it includes both the ability to regulate subjective experience (calming down, exiting from symptoms and so on) and the ability to solve relational problems (Carcione, Semerari, Nicolò et al., 2011). In this case it overlaps with the concept of emotional regulation, because metacognition is a form of emotional regulation that is based on the knowledge of mental states.

Mentalisation differs from metacognition due to the former being considered active in an attachment context (Fonagy, Gergely, Jurist et al., 2002) compared to metacognition, which is considered to be active in the context of all motivational systems (e.g. rank, sexuality or belonging to a group) (Dimaggio, Semerari, Carcione et al., 2007; Liotti and Gilbert, 2011). In addition, mentalisation has been perceived as an overall skill, whereas metacognition is composed of variables that operate semi-independently (Semerari, Carcione, Dimaggio et al., 2007; Semerari, Cucchi, Dimaggio et al., 2012).

An individual's metacognitive skills can fluctuate as the quality of relationships vary. For example, metacognition related to the diagnosis of schizophrenia tends to be more stable as the disorder becomes chronic (Hamm, Renard, Fogley et al., 2012), even as it continues to respond to psychotherapeutic treatment (Lysaker, Buck and Ringer, 2007), whereas metacognition related to PD greatly depends on the emotional context and the quality of relationships (Fonagy, Gergely, Jurist et al., 2002).

With a well-modulated emotional atmosphere and a cooperative relationship context aimed at pursuing common goals, a patient can read her own mind more easily, and the other's mind consequently unfolds before her in a more copious and expressive manner. Perceiving others as similar to us (Dimaggio, Lysaker, Carcione et al., 2008; Mitchell, Macrae and Banaji, 2006) or belonging to the same group as us (Ames, 2004), or knowing their history (Ciaramelli, Bernardi and Moscovitch, 2013) leads us to ascribe more thoughts, emotions and intentions to them, and to reason in a less stereotypical manner. Conversely, if the perception of relational danger is activated, in which we expect the other to attack, abuse or dominate us, or to become a dangerous alien belonging to a hostile social group, it compresses our minds and leads us to believe that the other's mind is inhabited by hostile or malicious intentions (Liotti and Gilbert, 2011; Lysaker, Gumley, Brüne et al., 2011). In toxic relationships individuals tend formulate sophisticated hypotheses about what inhabits others' minds, but out of preference they do so based on negative expectations. For example, if we are in need of attention but alarmed at the idea that the other may take advantage of us when he sees we are weak, we will likely formulate complex arguments about how he can use our weak points to harm us. However, if we deduce that the sullen look on the other's face is a sign of tiredness and worry rather than of evil intentions, the negative expectations previously identified will not even cross our minds. The idea that metacognition or mentalisation (Bateman and Fonagy, 2004) is context-dependent and consequently tied to an affective and motivational state is at the core of MIT (Dimaggio, Semerari, Carcione et al., 2007) and guides our work in the therapeutic relationship (see Chapter 5). The primary goal of an intervention is to create the relational conditions in session that make it possible for a patient's metacognitive skills to operate fully, while avoiding the toxic contents suffocating mentalistic skills.

As a reminder, metacognition refers to the combination of skills which enable humans to:

1   *identify mental states and ascribe them to themselves and others*;
2   *think, reflect and reason about* their own mental states (*self-reflectivity*) and think, reflect and reason about other's mental states (*understanding others' minds*);
3   *use the knowledge and reflections of their own and others' mental states to make decisions, solve problems or psychological and interpersonal conflicts, and master subjective suffering (mastery)*.

(Carcione, Dimaggio, Conti et al., 2010)

Table 2.1 Metacognitive skills

Identifying mental states and ascribing them to self and others		Using metacognitive knowledge to identify and solve problems, and master subjective suffering
Self-reflectivity	Understanding other's minds	Mastery
Monitoring	Monitoring	
Cognitive identification	Cognitive identification	
Emotional identification	Emotional identification	
Thinking, reflecting and reasoning about own and other's mental states		1st level strategies
		2nd level strategies
Relating variables	Relating variables	3rd level strategies
Differentiation	Decentring	
Integration		

Dividing metacognition into distinct skills meets both diagnostic and treatment planning needs, with the latter targeting skills that are the most defective. Let us review them (see Table 2.1).

Basic requirements

The most basic metacognitive skill is an individual's ability to be aware that she has thoughts and emotions that originate in her own mind and are not inserted from outside, even if the environment influences what she experiences and feels. It therefore includes the ability to distinguish one's mind from others' and grasp that others' behaviour is inspired by intentions and motivations. This awareness represents a basic requirement for self-reflectivity and is lacking in conditions like schizophrenia (Lysaker, Gumley, Leudtke et al., 2013).

Identifying mental states and ascribing them to self (self-reflectivity) and others (understanding others' minds)

The metacognitive skill outlined previously consists of identifying mental states and ascribing them to the self and others. The subject of *self-reflectivity* is one's own mental states, whereas *understanding others' minds* focuses on others'. It includes the ability to ascribe cognitions ('I believe that …'), intentions ('I wish to …'; 'he's decided to …') and emotions ('I feel cheerful'; 'I feel angry'; 'He looks sad'). This skill also includes identifying and monitoring one's own cognitive functions such as memory, attention and learning: 'I realise I can remember that poem well', 'Under pressure I'm not as good at concentrating'.

Thinking, reflecting and reasoning about one's own mental states (self-reflectivity), and thinking, reflecting and reasoning about other's mental states (understanding others' minds)

When an individual has identified her thoughts and emotions she can reflect and reason about them. More specifically, she can make inferences about the link between behaviour and intentions, cognitions and emotions, and about how choices and behaviour are driven by psychological reasoning and how interpreting social stimuli influences mental states.

Self-reflectivity is composed of the *monitoring, differentiation and integration* of functions. *Monitoring* primarily encompasses the ability to identify one's own thoughts (*cognitive identification*) and emotions (*emotional identification*). Problems with metacognitive monitoring make it difficult for a patient to:

- (at increasing levels of appropriateness and complexity) define and describe thoughts, beliefs, images and memories. A patient tackling a difficult problem might say: 'I don't know what's happening to me; I'm confused';
- perceive bodily responses as aspects of an emotion, and describe them by using rich and expressive terminology.

Problems with emotional monitoring may lead a patient to use statements such as: 'I'm tense', 'I feel uneasy', 'I'm nervous', 'I'm bothered', or to talk endlessly about facts, theories, abstractions and series of behaviours; the affective engine generating the action is undefined or poorly defined. Put simply, 'I'm tense in public' is a sign of a lack of monitoring, which is confirmed if the therapist asks what it means and the patient replies, 'I don't know. I'm nervous. It makes me feel uneasy.' With good monitoring, however, the patient would be able to reply, 'I feel embarrassed, I tend to blush like a tomato and I feel like I want to sink into the ground.'

One fundamental difficulty for patients diagnosed with a PD is to find causal psychological links between different representations, i.e. to grasp the *relationship between variables*. Many patients can describe how they think and feel to a certain degree, but have difficulty perceiving what links a thought to an emotion, or how a certain behaviour can be generated by an affect and not an automatism. Additionally, they lack the ability to connect symptoms and somatic sensations with cognitive, affective and relational antecedents.

For example, a patient with avoidant PD may tell about leaving a party or distancing themselves from work colleagues or a partner without an explanation. Only with careful work, and sometimes after several sessions, is it possible to understand that the patient felt criticised and reacted by fluctuating between shame and resentment, both of which led him to distance himself.

Somatisation symptoms frequently develop due to this dysfunction. For example, a narcissist patient may describe receiving a sign that he is being abandoned by his partner, which he reacts to by asserting that he does not feel anything. During the subsequent session he tells about suffering from tachycardia and consequently fearing a heart attack. The feelings of abandonment triggers a somatic response – palpitations – which the patient does not recognise; the somatic signal with its unrecognised origin is then interpreted catastrophically. Vice versa, with good relating of variables the patient would be able to identify that the feeling of a tight chest was a somatic manifestation of his displeasure and fear related to being abandoned. Difficulty in relating variables makes it difficult to work with standard CBT tools, such as ABC: a patient is unable to make the psychological cause-effect links because he cannot detect a maladaptive belief, recognise an emotion, or understand that an emotion is driving an action or a thought activating an affect. Here, instead, are some examples of well-functioning relating variables: *'When I think of my mother far away, I feel guilty and rush to telephone her'*, *'When I'm in front of my teacher and he looks at me a bit frowningly, I imagine he's thinking I haven't studied enough and I begin to stutter'*, *'My husband's aggressiveness worries me; when he calls me on my cellphone, I go straight back home to stop him from getting edgy.'*

As well as the monitoring functions, self-reflectivity includes the ability to take a critical distance from one's convictions and grasp that one's wishes have a limited impact on reality, a skill termed *differentiation*. The differentiation concept is similar to other cognitive therapy constructs, such as *defusion* (Hayes, Strosahl and Wilson, 2011), critical distance or cognitive insight, which is the degree of certainty in a conviction (Beck, Baruch, Balter et al., 2004). Differentiation is activated when a person perceives the representational nature of thoughts, distinguishes between internal and external reality, and adopts a perspective from which he sees his ideas as hypotheses and not certainties. It is, therefore, the ability to look at oneself from an outside perspective, and understand that things can appear differently from this more independent viewpoint. A fundamental element of differentiation is the ability to understand that our evaluations of others' behaviour sometimes depend on our stable tendencies (interpersonal schemas) to interpret behaviour, rather than on what they really think and feel.

A patient who has difficulty differentiating falls into spirals such as: *'I'm a disaster. The exams is going to go awfully. I'm hopeless'*, even when faced with positive evidence. At the slightest inkling of inattentiveness from a partner, a patient diagnosed with dependent PD may think: *'I'm worthless. I don't deserve to be loved. The colleague he's going out with this evening is certainly prettier and more intelligent than me, and they'll become lovers. I've got to stop him from going out, otherwise he'll be unfaithful to me. But, on the other hand, what's the point? Sooner or later he's going to find someone better than me.'* When faced with her therapist's suggestion that this is an idea and not a truth, a patient who does not have the skill to *differentiate* will be unable to doubt her idea and will consequently reject alternative explanations.

Another aspect of the inability to differentiate is confusion between dreams, fantasies, hypotheses and beliefs, difficulty understanding whether one is awake or dreaming, and an absence of a clear idea of the space-time coordinates within which action takes place: '*I dreamt about being inside a coffin. I was shouting with all my might but nobody came. When I woke up, I thought I was about to die. I'm still frightened. Something horrible is happening to me*'. Lacking the ability to differentiate also entails not being aware that thoughts, wishes, dreams or forecasts of the future are unable to influence events or modify reality: '*If I'm thinking of yelling at my daughter, it means I'm a potential murderer*', '*I dreamt of kissing a man and so I'm going to turn gay*', '*I had a thought that my partner was going to have an accident and so I must stop him from leaving*'.

Self-reflectivity includes *integration*, which is the ability to keep a unified view of oneself, notwithstanding different, even contradictory, mental states alternating in consciousness, or the variability of our behaviour in different contexts. Integrating also means being aware of how we have evolved, and having the ability to describe who we are today compared to the past. For example, the skill of integrating would allow an individual to describe how she has changed during therapy, or after life events with a profound personal meaning, such as a transfer, success or failure at work, or a death or birth.

Patients with PDs generally have difficulty integrating. They are unable, for example, to describe how a mental state has changed over time, and what events, thoughts, emotions, memories or actions generated the shift from one state to another: '*When I was young I was a braggart. Nowadays I see myself as a bundle of fears. I don't know what happened that changed me.*' An inability to integrate makes patients lose their sense of identity, or when faced with contradictory behaviour makes their self-image wobble: '*I told my daughter off. Does that mean I don't love her? That I'm a bad father?*' At the same time, when faced with changes in the direction of a relationship with a significant other, a subject not integrating loses her memory of the other aspects of the relationship that are not in play at that moment: if on one occasion her partner does not provide attention, he gets described as untrustworthy and selfish, whereas only a day before is described as reliable and loving.

Thinking and reflecting about others' mental states is termed *understanding others' minds*. Understanding others' minds includes TOM (Baron-Cohen, Leslie and Frith, 1985), which is the ability to ascribe intentions, motivations and wishes to others, and to deduce the mental contents of behaviour and language. It also includes the ability to ascribe emotions on the basis of actions, discourse and non-verbal behaviour, in particular facial expressions, especially in the eyes area, posture and tone of voice: '*That look doesn't convince me; he's hiding something.*' *Relating of variables* entails the ability to identify the link between others' cognitive-affective processes and their actions.

Persons not perceiving the other's thoughts often do not mention the contents of the other's mind, and tend to provide descriptions of the other's behaviour which makes it impossible to understand the personality of the person being described. In the same way, poor emotional monitoring leads patients to describe others without heeding their affects; they are aware that the other experiences emotions, but they find it difficult to identify which. They might say: '*He has a tense tone of voice, but I can't grasp what he's feeling*', '*He has a strange expression on his face, and isn't talking or opening up.*' A patient may ascribe emotions to others on the basis of verbal and non-verbal signals, but does so in a distorted manner with a bias toward a specific affect and in situations where it ought to be easy to correctly identify the emotions present. For example, in the presence of a tense tone of voice, he might think that the other is undoubtedly angry and exclude the possibility that he might, for example, be worried, distracted by other thoughts or feel embarrassed due to an awkward situation.

Relating variables, in the case of understanding others' minds, consists of the ability to plausibly pinpoint the cause-effect links leading others to act: '*He was expecting the girl to say "yes". When she rejected his advances, his world fell apart. He thought he'd done something wrong and then convinced himself that he wouldn't get another chance like this, and that's why he got depressed.*' Without an ability to establish links similar to these, a patient is unable to comprehend complex mentalistic actions such as irony. To comprehend irony it is necessary to parse out the real communicational intention hidden behind the textual content of a statement. For example, if we fear being abandoned and a friend makes fun of us ironically by saying, '*Have no doubt; he's sure to chuck you!*', we need to be able to deduce that the friend is not truly thinking, what he said, but has used a communicational strategy to make us laugh and help to minimise our fears. Patients diagnosed with PDs often have difficulty making these inferences or doing so with the necessary speed to make interaction fluid. Problems with this function lead patients to misunderstand what is driving others to act, or leads patients to provide stereotyped motivations for others' behaviours: '*She's jealous because that's the way she is; she's a woman*' or '*He's distracted because he's a man, and men are rigid and not interested in the nuances of the soul.*'

Decentring is the ability to put oneself in others' shoes and to formulate likely inferences about their mental states without taking account of one's own perspective, ways of evaluating and interpreting events, and involvement in the relationship. Patients with PDs often do not have the ability to decentre themselves, and consequently have difficulty realising that others have cognitive and affective processes different from those that they would have in the same circumstances: '*If I'd been in his shoes, I'd have been very ashamed. I can't see why he doesn't feel ashamed*', '*I'd have rushed to lend help to my friend during his difficult time even if he attacked me. He's selfish so he backed off.*'

Individuals not thinking in a decentred manner have difficulty understanding that they are not always present or at least prominent in the other's mind. For example, one may think: '*He didn't greet me, he's angry with me*', when the most likely hypothesis is that the other has simply not seen them, or '*They're splitting their sides with laughter at that table; I'm sure they are laughing at me because of my dress*', when it is more probable that it is a group of friends who are merry and rather noisy but without any interest in the patient.

Using metacognitive knowledge to make decisions, solve problems and master subjective suffering (mastery)

Unlike self-reflectivity and understanding others' minds, which are operations involving metacognitive knowledge, *mastery* is more precisely a *metacognitive control process*. It, therefore, joins mentalistic knowledge with an ability to plan (Carcione, Dimaggio, Conti et al., 2010; Carcione, Semerari, Nicolò et al., 2011). It consists of an intentional and fully aware use of psychological knowledge to decide, formulate strategies for tackling subjective suffering, solve interpersonal conflicts, find ways to achieve one's wishes in the relational world, help others and cooperate on the basis of a knowledge of one's perspective and others' ideas, preferences and types of reaction. The fundamental prerequisite for practising *mastery* is being capable of representing problematic mental states or conflictual relational situations to oneself in terms of psychological problems to solve, and adopting an active attitude towards solving them. The strategies used by an individual to solve these problematical situations can be grouped into three levels of increasing complexity. Below we list the main *mastery* strategies and summarise the dysfunctions that occur.

First-level mastery strategies are the simplest in that they require, for the most part, the activating of behaviours without a significant reflective effort. First-level strategies include:

- Direct action aimed at the body, where an individual tries to affect his problematic state by modifying the general state of his organism through the consumption of medicines, alcohol or narcotics, or by participating in physical activity. Problems that can arise include the uncontrolled use of medicines and narcotics, and compulsive sexual activity to soothe anxiety, or dieting and excessive physical exercise to relieve tension or regulate self-esteem.
- Avoidance: an individual averts the conditions in which a problematic state arises by actively and consciously avoiding the feared situation.
- Searching for interpersonal coordination: an individual turns to others to get help and support. Problems that may occur include a difficulty in asking others for help, an inability to recognise that others would be willing to help if one asked for it, and a tendency not to trust oneself and consequently ask others for help when the slightest difficulty is perceived without considering if the other is willing or able to provide assistance.

These first-level strategies are considered metacognitive when a subject deliberately and voluntarily behaves in a certain manner in order to manage his problematic mental state. Let us take the example of a young man who has had an argument with his girlfriend. If the young man attempts to ameliorate his sadness and disappointment by becoming excessively drunk, avoiding places he might see his girlfriend, or asks the first friend available to go for a walk with him, he is using first-level strategies. To use them one does not need to be particularly reflective of his mental states; it is enough to be aware, even if only based on past experience, that a certain behaviour is capable of modifying them positively.

Second-level mastery strategies require a greater reflective effort and are aimed at obtaining an independent regulation of one's mental layout. Second-level strategies include:

- Voluntarily self-imposing or inhibiting a certain behaviour. Patients with PDs have difficulty concentrating, abstaining from actions they can perceive as harmful or carrying out beneficial actions. A patient in a stressful mental state may forget that physical activity helps him reduce his stress level and therefore stays closed up at home unproductively brooding.
- Actively modifying one's attention towards and concentration on an intra-psychical or interpersonal problem. For example, a patient worrying about being abandoned is unable to engage in activities that require effort because he does not bear in mind that if he did so, the emotional salience of the problem would decrease.

Patients need to identify their thoughts and emotions, and have a clear idea of the contents from which they want to divert their minds to be able to use these strategies. They also need to be capable of self-exhorting or self-imposing certain behaviours. Second-level strategies do not require the contemplation of a sophisticated mentalistic knowledge of the other; they are restricted to using a general theory of the functioning of others' minds, which is sometimes stereotyped but nevertheless possesses a certain degree of efficacy. What is lacking is a careful and individualised analysis of what the persons with whom one interacts feel and experience. If we go back to the young man who had an argument with his girlfriend, if he lacked second-level strategies he might say, '*I've been tempted several times to reach out to her and I've done it. She attacked me, and she was angry and hostile.*' If the patient had recalled past situations he would have remembered that his girlfriend never shows signs of understanding when she is irritable, and would have avoided telephoning her and, as a result, suffering and rejection.

Third-level mastery strategies require a strong reflective effort and include:

- The use of a detailed and critical knowledge of one's own problematical mental state and ordinary functioning in the handling of psychic suffering and the solving of problems. A patient with dysfunctions in this area is incapable of thinking, '*I have a tendency to become irritable and I fly off the handle easily when I'm disappointed or hurt. It would be better if I don't call her because I wouldn't be able to accept her explanations.*' In addition, a patient with PD is often incapable of saying, '*I feel she doesn't love me enough and neglects me, but the problem is that it's me that's too demanding and I'm never satisfied with what others give me.*'
- The use of an adequate knowledge of others' minds in the solving of interpersonal problems. A patient in the midst of an argument with her partner who is

jealous is incapable of thinking, '*Marco is impulsive and very jealous, and he doesn't realise he exaggerates and finds reasons everywhere to be jealous. I need to wait for him to get over it so that I can speak to him calmly and explain what happened.*' On the contrary, she will tend to deal with her partner's jealousy by uselessly trying to calm him, being submissive in order to avoid abandonment and attacking him for his unfair accusations, amid forgetting that none of these strategies have ever worked with her partner in the past.

- Mature acceptance of the limitations of one's ability to influence change in oneself and others, and affect events. If we continue with the example of the jealous partner, the patient might find relief if she thought, '*Marco has a big insecurity problem. His jealousy originates in this and he's just not able to control it. Unfortunately, however much I behave in an exemplary manner and try to get him to understand how much I love him, I can't stay shut up at home! However, if I don't waver when faced with his accusations, his jealousy doesn't harm me. If I then manage not to get angry, he doesn't feel attacked, and after a bit he calms down.*' The inability to accept one's own limitations includes a difficulty in understanding that if one is shy, there is no point being self-critical about not being, for example, a brilliant orator, but one can instead feel proud about many other professional qualities.

- The ability to make predictions about the effect our actions will have on us and others. A good use of mentalistic *mastery* might be: '*If I telephoned her now, she'd be sure to think that I'm in the wrong and have something for which I need to ask forgiveness. She would then become increasingly more defensive and I'd consequently become irritated, which would lead the discussion to degenerate.*' Poor third-level mentalistic *mastery* leads a patient to impulsive action: '*She replied to me jokingly when I asked her if she loved me. I haven't spoken to her for three days; that'll be a lesson to her.*' This patient does not, on the one hand, use differentiation (questioning the truth of his own assumptions) and, on the other, forgets that his closed behaviour will likely have a negative impact.

A command of mastery is particularly important. More specifically, most of the problems experienced by patients diagnosed with PDs is due to a lack of mastery because many are incapable of using mentalistic knowledge pragmatically for coping and problem-solving purposes. It is, in fact, defective to varying degrees in all individuals diagnosed with PDs (Carcione, Semerari, Nicolò et al., 2011).

Metacognition: empirical state

The primary objective of metacognition research has been to test four main hypotheses: (1) that metacognition has the structure hypothesised and described above; (2) that the more serious patients diagnosed with PD have a more widespread metacognitive malfunctioning; (3) that the various PDs have different dysfunctional metacognitive profiles; (4) that metacognition improves throughout successful therapy treatments and is a valuable predictor of treatment outcome. Much of metacognitive research is completed using tools designed specifically to test the above mentioned hypotheses, such as the Metacognition Assessment Scale Scale – Revised (MAS-R) (Carcione, Dimaggio, Conti et al., 2010; Semerari, Carcione, Dimaggio et al., 2003b) and the Metacognition Assessment Interview (MAI) (Semerari, Cucchi, Dimaggio et al., 2012),

Research on a non-clinical sample using the MAI suggests that the structure of metacognition seems to be composed of two distinct factors: the understanding of one's own mental states and the ability to understand others' mental states (Semerari, Cucchi, Dimaggio et al., 2012). Conversely, other preliminary analyses on clinical samples confirm a four-factor structure: monitoring, differentiation, integration and the understanding of others/decentring (Pellecchia et al., 2014).

Moreover, research on the non-clinical sample found that the ability to differentiate, that is to adopt a critical distance from one's convictions, has a greater correlation with understanding other's minds compared to understanding one's own (Semerari et al., 2012; Pellecchia et al., submitted). This result is likely due to the fact that we often adopt a detached perspective and in a certain sense reference the viewpoint of others when we question our own ideas. Adopting a critical distance, therefore, seems to be a starting point to adopting the other's point of view.

Overall, the idea emerging from this initial research is compatible with *neuroimaging* studies (Mitchell, Macrae and Banaji, 2006; Saxe, Moran, Scholz et al., 2006) demonstrating how reflecting on oneself or others involves distinct neural mechanisms. In addition, the research reinforces the initial idea (Semerari, Carcione, Dimaggio et al., 2003b) that it is possible to dismantle metacognition into basic functions. The primary clinical implication, which is similar to the treatment manualisation in the present book, is that it is beneficial to concentrate clinical attention on the most impaired metacognitive domain, without, however, expecting that any success will extend to other domains. In other words, if an individual has difficulty both in describing inner states (*monitoring*) and in *differentiating*, any work on monitoring will not automatically improve differentiation, and it will be necessary to give that domain special attention as well. Let us recall that research on the structure of metacognition in various clinical populations suggests that mastery has a certain degree of independence (Lysaker, Erickson, Ringer et al., 2011), which supports the idea that mentalistic understanding does not automatically translate into a functional coping.

The second hypothesis – the more serious the overall personality pathology, the more extensive the metacognitive dysfunction – has also been supported by findings in metacognitive research. For example, patients fulfilling a greater number of criteria for the various PDS and consequently having greater dysfunctional personality traits, often have the poorest metacognitive abilities (Semerari, Colle, Pellecchia et al., 2014).

Another hypothesis generated in the initial stages of metacognitive research (Semerari, Carcione, Dimaggio et al., 2003b) was that each PD had a different dysfunctional metacognitive profile. Evidence so far shows that the metacognitive differences among the various PDs do not appear to be as clear-cut as originally hypothesised. A characteristic of each psychological disorder is to a varying degree a difficulty in acquiring a critical distance from one's convictions, adopting a decentred point of view of others' minds and using psychological knowledge to master interpersonal problems and subjective suffering (Carcione, Semerari, Nicolò et al., 2011; Dimaggio, Carcione, Conti et al., 2009). If we consider an even broader range of research, studies examining constructs akin to metacognition (alexithymia, affect awareness or mentalisation), a number of associations between specific PDS and precise metacognitive profiles emerge. Perhaps the most convincing result is that patients with *avoidant PD* have difficulty identifying and describing their own affects, integrating them into their self-representation and mastering them (Dimaggio, Procacci, Nicolò et al., 2007; Nicolò, Semerari, Lysaker et al., 2011; Gullestad, Johansen, Høglend et al., 2013). This difficulty does not, moreover, seem to depend on a depressive state, unlike dependent PD, in which moments of depression reduce the ability to successfully explore the range of emotions (Nicolò, Semerari, Lysaker et al., 2012). Among patients with PDs and substance abuse suffering from alexithymia, poor *mastery* indicated a high probability of having prominent Cluster C traits (Lysaker, Olesek, Buck et al., 2014).

Earlier research hypothesised that individuals diagnosed with *narcissistic PD* have difficulty understanding their own mind and others' (Dimaggio, Semerari, Falcone et al., 2002), and this idea was then supported (Given-Wilson, McIlwain and Warburton, 2011). Not only do patients with narcissistic PD have a tendency to describe their experiences in a hyper-generalised, abstract and intellectualised manner, they also have difficulty precisely investigating their own affective states. In particular, even if they experience an emotion, they often lack an understanding of the interpersonal *trigger*. In regard to the ABC sequence (*antecedent, belief, consequence*, situation, thought, and emotional and behavioural consequence), individuals diagnosed with narcissistic PD are often able to describe B well and C fairly well, but are unable to identify A. In a non-clinical population, the use of MAI has shown that narcissism is correlated with a difficulty in describing one's own mental state, which supports the idea that such patients often have problems describing their own inner world more so than understanding others' (Semerari, Cucchi, Dimaggio et al., in preparation).

In regard to empathy, which can be conceptualised as metacognition plus a tendency to react by caring about the other, it has emerged that narcissism features an ability to understand others' thoughts but emotional resonance is more impaired. Individuals with narcissistic tendencies often perceive themselves as being empathetic, but studies using fMRI of brain areas supporting empathy suggest they are not (Ritter, Dziobek, Preißler et al., 2011). Narcissism and a limited capacity for empathy are also associated with poor awareness of one's emotions (Fan, Wonneberger, Enzi et al., 2011). Although there has been an adequate amount of studies examining avoidant and narcissistic PD, the primary focus of research has been on borderline PD (not discussed in this book) and consequently there is a substantial need for the investigation of other disorders using a wide variety of methods.

Lastly, the idea that metacognition improves with effective treatment has also seemed to be confirmed: using the MAS-R to analyse session transcripts, it appears that impaired metacognitive skills have a tendency to improve over the course of a successful therapy treatment (Carcione, Semerari, Nicolò et al., 2011; Dimaggio, Procacci, Nicolò et al., 2007; Dimaggio, Carcione, Conti et al., 2009). In regard to metacognition as a predictor of treatment *outcome*, preliminary research on patients with borderline PD suggests that a patient's overall level of metacognition is linked to psychopathological severity at the onset of treatment, and that poor decentration skills predicted a worse outcome after three months. Due to the small sample size of this study (Maillard, Kramer and Dimaggio, 2013), the correlation between metacognition and clinical improvement is so far little more than anecdotal. There is an MIT effectiveness trial underway at the Center for Metacognitive Interpersonal Therapy to test the hypothesis that metacognition improves in successful psychotherapies.

Maladaptive coping forms and dysfunctional reasoning

PD patients use dysfunctional forms of coping and affect regulation to tackle feared consequences while pursuing goals in relationships. Coping and affect regulation are flanked by maladaptive cognitive styles, in the form of *cognitive biases*. Some coping styles tend to forestall the other's feared response. The avoidance of exposing oneself to a feared opinion expected from a contemptuous and rejecting other is a typical example. Other styles tend to protect against the distress that surfaces after the feared response has actually been received. An example of this protective mechanism is a patient reacting in a perfectionistic manner when he feels rejected for something he has done. Another example is a patient with obsessive-compulsive PD, who wishes to be accepted, expounds his ideas, sees himself as criticised and consequently feels unloveable and undeserving. He then reacts by adopting a perfectionist coping style, and therefore may shift his belief: '*If she sees I'm perfect, she'll accept me and perhaps admire me.*'

In patients diagnosed with PDs, coping is directed primarily toward:

- managing the distress generated by social interaction, for example by avoiding a feared situation;
- protecting oneself from stressors by avoiding the emotional distress associated with them, stopping them from arising or soothing them as quickly as possible;
- acting as if the *stressor* does not exist at all, so as not to have to react to it at either an emotional or a behavioural level.

In this chapter we are not going to systematically discuss dysfunctional *coping* or reasoning and affect regulation strategies in patients with PDs, but we will instead list a few of the most pervasive and problematic coping styles.

Avoidance

Avoiding is an attempt to prevent the emergence of distressing states that one foresees as being activated by contact with others. It can take the form of behaviour, such as social withdrawal or excessive independence: patients actively try not to get involved in relationships, especially intimate ones, or isolate themselves and use their time for solitary activities such as reading, spending time on the computer or watching television. To avoid relational distress they may compulsively seek out environmental stimulation for excitement or enjoyment in the form of compulsive shopping, sex, gambling or excessive physical activity. They may also attempt to self-regulate their emotions by affecting their bodies through substance abuse, hyper-alimentation, compulsive masturbation, etc. An avoidant coping style may include cognitive as well as behavioural avoidance (Borkovec, Alcaine and Behar, 2004): this involves acting so as not to think of or recall situations that could possibly activate negative relational images, even to the extent of using psychological escape such as dissociation or excessive fantasising.

Apart from the fact that some of these strategies are in themselves a cause of problems –alcohol abuse for example – they are generally ineffective at reducing distress in the long term due to the failure of the strategies to impact a patient's perceptions of real threats and their ability to tackle them. Avoidance also prevents having new experiences and automatically leads an individual to act as if the feared scenario is true. Moreover, for many stressors, the longer the avoidance and the more insurmountable the problem appears, the greater the paradoxical increase in intrusive thoughts relating to the stressors. This in turn worsens one's negative mood and anxiety. Avoidant-type coping responses are quite common in avoidant, dependent and obsessive-compulsive PD but can occur in all of the disorders analysed here.

Hyper-compensation

Hyper-compensating (Young, Klosko and Weishaar, 2003) means attempting to elevate to extreme levels those self-aspects and behaviours that are the opposite of those that one fears generate problems. A child that gets neglected can learn to capture others' attention by behaving in a charming, provocative or theatrical way. For example, a child who felt profound shame or impotence while growing up may manage to be successful in the workplace as an adult by developing an aggressive and dominating style that helps him reach the top, or a victim of bullying or abuse may become a bully in an attempt to hide his fear behind a tough facade. Narcissism is perhaps the prototype of the hyper-compensatory coping style. Sufferers often tell about being raised by parents who ignored their basic emotional needs leading them to have felt lonely, useless and inadequate. Resorting to the grandiose self-image makes it possible to temporarily overcome such negative sentiments.

Worrying/rumination

Worrying is a particular strategy for coping with threats which takes the form of persevering thought (Wells, 2008) and consists of both negative and positive metacognitive beliefs about the *worry* itself. This style of coping is considered a fundamental psychopathogenic factor in the majority of disorders in the anxious cluster. We will quickly recall that there are two types of worry. Type I worries are composed of chains of thoughts and mental images emotionally connoted in a negative sense, which a subject sees as being relatively uncontrollable (Borkovec, Robinson, Pruzinsky et al., 1983). These chains regard external events or physical symptoms. Type II worries are composed of positive evaluations about the need or opportuneness of brooding over questions ('*worrying will help me to tackle the problem better*'), and of negative thoughts and evaluations about the uncontrollability or physical, psychological and social harmfulness of the worrying itself ('*worrying this much will make me go crazy*').

The coexistence of positive and negative beliefs about a worry leads to uncertain attempts to eliminate it by resorting to dysfunctional mental regulation strategies. For example, a patient may try to suppress his thinking, which prevents discovering that the worry will not have catastrophic outcomes, or he may seek reassurance which prevents learning that the worry can be self-limited. Tendency to worry is a typical characteristic of paranoid PD, which actively searches for memories of wrongs suffered and recalls others' evil intentions.[1] The metacognitive evaluation associated with this is that worrying is useful because it makes it possible to hone defensive strategies and make plans about revenge, thus increasing one's sense of safety. In reality, worry heightens the activation of anger and stops one from letting go of negative paranoid-type thoughts.

In obsessive-compulsive PD worry is centred on searching for any mistakes made with the aim of achieving a perfect and impeccable performance, and thus avoiding harming others or being subjected to criticism. In this disorder the metacognitive belief that brooding is useful leads to enduring states of *workaholism* and an inability to relax or focus on pleasant experiences.

In avoidant PD worry tends to focus on the idea that others are threatening and is aimed at forestalling harm by acting in ways that are considered to be more adaptive, although this behaviour is often criticised as being strict and rejecting of the other. In this case worry focuses its attention on negative images, which persist in consciousness with associated negative emotions.

Perfectionism

Perfectionist coping is aimed at protecting self-esteem and assuring the possibility of being loved and accepted. It is found in numerous PDS (Ayearst, Flett and Hewitt, 2012) and is a reaction to a pathogenic interpersonal schema in which the other reacts to a wish to be loved and cared for by rejecting and criticising. It is typical of PDS such as narcissistic or obsessive-compulsive, but it can also be found in avoidant patients (who are usually overwhelmed by it) or in patients with depressive personality traits. For example, a patient may set high standards for himself to achieve goals in various fields such as professional performance and physical attractiveness, and he may consequently resort to plastic surgery in an attempt to regulate negative states (Fitzpatrick, Sherry, Hartling et al., 2011). Pursuing such high standards protects an individual from anticipated criticism, and in the case of a narcissistic structure, helps him to feel vital. Nevertheless, the slightest inquiry related to the attempts of achieving perfection leads to a collapse in self-esteem and the emergence of self-accusations that reactivate the perfectionism in a vicious circle that feeds itself. In fact, a successful perfectionist strategy leading the other to guarantee approval paradoxically confirms the fact that one is not loveable for what one is, but only if one acts and behaves in a perfect manner. Perfectionism has a very high cost, and its pursuit often leads to a constant fear of committing mistakes that would undermine the perfection and to doubts as to whether one's actions will lead to the desired consequence (Frost, Marten, Lahart et al., 1990).

Although patients with PDS can have a predominant coping style, the majority use several forms. For example, in an attempt to obtain others' approval or avoid others' disapproval, an avoidant patient may behave submissively towards those she perceives as superior, and behave in a dominant and arrogant manner – hyper-compensating – towards those she perceives as inferior. The relationship among PD interpersonal schemas and coping styles is not univocal; three people driven by the same wish to be approved, underpinned by an *inferior/inadequate* self-image, can react differently to criticism from the other. For example, one may develop an arrogant coping style to conceal his feelings of inferiority; the second may give up and consequently reinforce his beliefs of being a failure and inferior; the third may avoid people or situations, likely the most attractive and successful ones, which will likely trigger his sense of inferiority.

In certain disorders, such as avoidant or dependent, patients have a preference for disengaging from feared situations and avoiding thinking about activities that would expose them to criticism or rejection by the other. An automatism in dependent PD is thinking that if one pays too much attention to one's own wishes, one will find oneself forced, sooner or later, to tackle the feared consequences, such as the other's criticism, anger or abandonment. Feeling frightened, a patient diagnosed with dependent PD may suppress any thoughts that might support independent action and avoid behaviour consistent with these thoughts.

Dysfunctional reasoning and cognitive biases

The patients with PDs described here automatically use multiple dysfunctional reasoning strategies, which is often typical of symptom disorders such as depression and anxiety as well. Due to a limited amount of space, we are only going to describe two of these maladaptive strategies: *self-enhancement*, typical of narcissism, and *better-safe-than-sorry*, a pervasive mechanism involving anticipatory protection from danger, which are relational in PDs.

Better-safe-than-sorry strategies (Gilbert, 1989) consist of overestimating future damage, which leads one not assume risks, even limited ones, when satisfying a wish. This heuristic underestimates the cost of not achieving desirable goals which are potentially safe. This strategy is frequently used in many disorders and supports both the avoidance of judgment – '*Why expose myself if I risk being criticised? Better not to take the exam*' – and the inhibiting of independent exploration – '*Why do it on my own if I risk contradicting my partner, who then might leave me?*'

Self-enhancement is a true and proper cognitive bias and consists of the tendency to overestimate one's personal value. More specifically, self-enhancement may present as a patient perceiving his performance to be worth more than it objectively is or the belief that he is better than others in a social comparison. This dysfunctional strategy is often a bias typical of narcissistic disorder.

Dysregulation and over-regulation of affects

Much research has focused on examining the difficulty that patients with PDs have in regulating emotion (Van Dijke, 2012; Iverson, Follette, Pistorello et al., 2012, Glenn and Klonsky 2009; Gratz, Rosenthal, Tull et al., 2006). Most of this research has concentrated on the difficulty in regulating affective states in patients with borderline PD and identified a particular dysfunctional pattern featuring an inability to regulate *arousal*, difficulty in diverting attention from emotional stimuli, distortions in information processing, inability to control impulses and a tendency to 'freeze' or dissociate emotions in conditions of acute stress (Linehan, Bohus and Lynch, 2007). In reality, difficulties in regulating affective states seem to be a common characteristic of PD patients in general. The most intuitive hypothesis suggests that patients with borderline or histrionic disorder, and in general those with symptoms categorised in Cluster B, have dysregulation problems, whereas the patients who are the subject of this book have a tendency to over-regulate, that is undervalue, neglect, repress, ignore or inhibit emotional experience.

However, this may not always be the case. The patients described here have both a tendency to over-regulate emotions and, when they experience them, to lose control and dysregulate themselves. Both strategies are dysfunctional. Research finds that an optimal regulation strategy is the reappraisal of the emotional triggers, which is more useful than suppressing the emotions (John and Gross, 2004). Instead, the patients we have discussed have a tendency to become irritated, embarrassed or ashamed when they identify themselves as being upset. The more negative feelings they have toward their emotions, the more difficult it is for them to use their cognitive resources to reflect on the emotions and engage in modulating them. Patients with avoidant and depressive personality traits, for example, tend to not accept the experiencing of negative emotions.

The tendency to inhibit the verbal expression of emotions, likely for fear of being judged, correlates with avoidant and obsessive-compulsive personality traits, and shame related to socially displaying one's affects is correlated with dependent traits. And finally, attempting to regulate emotions independently, without involving others, seems typical of avoidant personality traits (Popolo, Lysaker, Salvatore et al., in press). Overall, these patients (avoidant, obsessive-compulsive and dependent) tend to suppress and hide their emotions, especially those feelings related to negative experiences. The tendency to inhibit affects in these PDS is linked to anxiety and depression.

In general, emotional suppression strategies are linked to an increase in negative sensations experienced and a worsening of symptoms (Wenzlaff and Wegner, 2000). An acceptance of emotions and a trust in the idea that one can share negative emotions with others are therefore necessary for the promotion of a functional regulation of emotions. As briefly mentioned before, emotional dysregulation is found in varying degrees among the PDS discussed in this book: avoidant, dependent, narcissistic, passive-aggressive and paranoid patients and those with depressive personality traits. When an emotion that is primarily kept at bay surfaces in consciousness, it often escapes control in the above-mentioned individuals (Dimaggio, Salvatore, Montano et al., 2012). Such patients are no longer able to divert their attention from the emotion and often continue to brood and lack confidence in the possibility of retaking control once the affect has become intense, and thus become further overwhelmed.

Note

1 In session a patient with paranoid PD asked the therapist to read a transcript of a telephone call in which she had overheard her husband accusing her of being inadequate in front of her son. She described that she believed the telephone call had harmed her son, though reported that the call occurred 16 years earlier! The therapist politely refused to read the transcript and asked the patient why she had this desire. The patient began to understand that there was no need to read it and came to the realisation that every time she reread it she felt worse.

Chapter 3

Assessment and case formulation in metacognitive interpersonal therapy

The present chapter provides a detailed description of MIT assessment and specifically covers:

- the goals and duration of assessment;
- what to look for (i.e. the components of a schema);
- how to identify these components (i.e. exploration of narrative episodes);
- obstacles of the assessment process (i.e. metacognitive dysfunctions);
- restitution: a delicate moment in the therapeutic relationship.

Goals and duration of assessment

The purpose of assessment in MIT is to construct a case formulation to plan treatment. It is necessary to: (1) identify a patient's set of pathogenic interpersonal schemas; (2) outline the metacognitive difficulties hampering treatment and adapt therapy to a patient's mentalistic abilities; and (3) formulate a diagnosis consistent with DSM criteria.

Identifying a patient's interpersonal schemas is the core of MIT assessment and is carried out in three steps: (1) recalling a recent narrative episode; (2) use of associative memory to collect other narrative episodes linked to and consistent with the first; (3) conceptualisation of prevailing interpersonal schemas and shared formulation with the patient using non-technical language. At the same time, it is important that a therapist formulate a DSM diagnosis which considers both symptoms and personality disorders. A therapist should then reflect upon the unique characteristics of the patient and decide whether to describe her psychological disorder using a categorical diagnosis or provide a description using non-technical language to help her to focus on her dysfunctions without the use of medical labels. A therapist should provide the patient with a diagnostic label if the need for a shared formulation prevails, such as if the patient requests it: *'Doctor, what am I suffering from?'* A description of the patient's dysfunction, rather than a label, is preferential if it is suspected that the patient may feel judged or demoralised. The choice about communicating the diagnosis and how to do so is, therefore, case-specific.

In any case, a therapist formulates a categorical diagnosis serving the purpose of rapidly forecasting what route of treatment may be the most beneficial and what obstacles may arise. The therapist should then join the patient in an assessment of psychopathological functioning and reconstruct the latter's primary interpersonal schemas. In all cases the main aim of diagnosis restitution in MIT is co-constructing the therapeutic project in an atmosphere of trust and hope. As in a figure-ground relationship, the words used by a therapist should highlight possible solutions to the problem and the strengths and resources possessed by the patient rather than the problem itself. To put it simply, the therapist should communicate to the patient that the available solutions are more important than the problem.

Therapists often realise the difficulty in collecting information related to a patient's interpersonal schemas during the early appraisal of metacognitive dysfunctions. For example, the patient may have trouble comprehending which interpersonal events elicit specific emotions and, without this information, it is impossible to reconstruct a schema. If he is aware of any present metacognitive problems, a therapist can formulate an initial therapeutic plan aimed at discovering the patient's mental world rather than changing personality dysfunctions. It is important to note that the MIT therapist administers symptom-centred techniques consistent with the patient's metacognitive capacities (see Chapter 10). For example, behavioural techniques are preferred with patients lacking the basic skills to understand and describe their mental states.

At the completion of the assessment a therapist should be capable of:

- understanding whether the patient has metacognitive difficulties and formulate interventions aimed at improving them;
- identifying present symptoms or PD;
- comprehending and helping the patient comprehend the main interpersonal schemas underlying the latter's relational and psychological difficulties.

According to MIT, the same PD can be sustained by interpersonal schemas that differ from patient to patient. For example, in a patient with dependent PD various pathogenic schemas can surface, such as:

- Self wishing to obtain recognition of its independence, but perceiving itself as ineffective and inept;
- Other perceived as undervaluing and not acknowledging Self's independence;
- Self continuously trying to satisfy Other's requests by adapting to the latter's expectations and giving up the pursuit of its own goals to the point of feeling a sense of constriction.

In another case dependent PD can be supported by a schema consisting of:

- Self seeking appreciation to improve its self-esteem, but perceiving itself as faulty and not up to standard;

- Other critical and demanding of a better performance;
- Self tending to pay more attention to its faults, correct these faults and adopt perfectionistic criteria for deciding whether its performance will ensure it the appreciation it desires.

In both cases, the main DSM-5 categorical diagnosis (APA, 2013) is dependent PD, but the associated interpersonal schemas and mental states (sense of constriction and irritation in the first case and anxiety in the second) are different. The second case can also be conceptualised as including obsessive-compulsive PD as co-occurring due to the Self seeking approval in the eyes of another, and setting perfectionist and unachievable performance standards. In general, clinical reality and research (Bamelis, Renner, Heidkamp et al., 2011) suggest that there is not a precise overlapping between PDS and schemas, not only because two patients with the same diagnosis can have quite different interpersonal schemas, but also because it is infrequent to find a pure PD not displaying at least dysfunctional traits typical of other PDS.

Assessment in MIT is not limited to a psychiatric diagnosis, schemas and metacognition. In fact, it also appraises the most prominent symptoms, even if the emphasis is primarily on cognitive-affective disorder maintenance processes such as the classical ABCS of Rational Emotive Behavior Therapy (Ellis, 1962). For more information on *emotional regulation processes* and *coping strategies* see Chapter 2.

A patient's resources and strengths should also be evaluated, with an emphasis on promoting protective factors and action driven by the patient's own inclinations and wishes. It is important to note in advance that a key element of MIT for the PDS described in this chapter is the pursuit of a social life that is richly filled with exchanges with others, and based on the pursuit of qualities and talents aligned with a patient's own vocation and resources. For this reason, an analysis of resources, forces and unexpressed wishes is fundamental at the start of therapy. Lastly, the possible need for drug treatment should also be evaluated. The duration of the assessment varies. Nevertheless, in the absence of severe metacognitive dysfunctions it is possible after two or three sessions to reconstruct the patient's dominant interpersonal schema or schemas and most frequently used forms of coping with stressors or emotional regulation styles. If metacognition is defective the assessment may require longer, such as up to about eight sessions. If a therapist is still unable to understand the patient's dominant interpersonal schemas, the opinion of a more experienced therapist or supervisor is likely required.

Metacognitive dysfunctions are one of the aspects to be evaluated at the *assessment* stage and are, at the same time, the target of the start of treatment. Helping a patient to achieve progress in basic self-reflectivity is necessary for a formulation of interpersonal schemas. Elements of general self-reflectivity include understanding one's own thoughts and emotions and an initial intuition related to the mutual links among emotions, thoughts and behaviour. The formulation of the first dominant interpersonal schema represents the completion of *assessment* and the achievement of the first therapeutic goal.

What to look for: the components of an interpersonal schema

In this chapter we place emphasis on the essential components of interpersonal schemas and describe the procedures for gathering information about the schemas and conducting the interview in Chapters 4 and 6. To conceptualise the interpersonal schema or schemas underlying the personality disorder displayed by a patient, it is useful to follow Luborsky and Crits-Christoph (1990) and break any schema identified into its essential components, which are: (1) wish; (2) relational procedures of the 'if ... then ...' type; (3) Other's response; (4) Self's response to Other's response.

The term *wish* refers to a series of universally shared human motivations which a person can explicitly or implicitly express while narrating his interpersonal experiences. Based on the main theories of human motivation in the clinical sphere (Gilbert, 1989; Lichtenberg, 1989), some of the wishes that PD patients most frequently see as being chronically frustrated are outlined below:

1 Self-assertion and independent exploration of the environment; being motivated toward autonomous and inwardly-driven action.
2 Depending on protective and supportive figures in situations of suffering and need.
3 Safety and protective reactions to danger (fight/flight/freeze).
4 Having and maintaining an adequate level of self-esteem acknowledged by others.
5 Being loved and understood.
6 Having success and improving one's position in the social hierarchy.
7 Helping others seen as weak, in need or in difficulty.
8 Belonging to groups and feeling part of the community.
9 Having a satisfying sensual, sexual and love life, and forming stable affective ties during adulthood
10 Accessing limited resources.
11 Cooperating to achieve common goals.
12 Resentfully withdrawing from harmful stimuli.

To understand a patient's wish on the basis of her narrative episodes, the patient needs to describe a real or imagined interpersonal interaction. Given that a schema gets reconstructed from recurring themes, in many cases it is necessary to gather several specific autobiographical memories.

A wish can be expressed independently and explicitly by a patient in his narratives with expressions like: '*I wish*', '*I want*' or '*I'd like*'. When this does not happen it is the therapist's duty to reconstruct it using a detailed analysis of the patient's narrative episodes and, in particular, pinpointing the basic motivations underlying the emotions experienced by the patient. Patients often begin narratives with a symptom. For example, the patient may complain about being depressed and lonely and speak with a low tone of voice. When asked to broaden her field of observation and to recall a specific relational episode in which she felt 'depressed and lonely' it might emerge that the patient experienced this unease because she felt rejected. Her therapist should then help her realise that her initial wish was to receive attention, be accepted and feel deserving of love, and that her depression followed due to her perception that this goal would be permanently missed.

Let us reference a patient who is just beginning psychotherapy, is depressed and self-critical, underrates himself because he feels incapable of doing anything and consequently feels like he is in a rut. After gathering a narrative episode, it emerges that two months earlier he was left by his girlfriend. With this information one can trace his interpersonal schema, in which the *wish* is represented by his desire to be loved. The procedure he follows in an attempt to obtain closeness is of the 'hide your emotions to avoid being unpleasant' type. However, the Other's response was one of rejection and interruption of the relationship. The Self's consequent reaction to the Other's response was to underrate itself and become depressed, which confirmed the underlying representation of the Self as unloveable, not listened to and without value. The presenting symptom state, therefore, often corresponds to the Self's reaction to the Other's response (Crits-Cristoph, Connolly Gibbons, Crits-Christoph et al., 2006), which is the depressive state as a reaction to the romantic rejection. However, before an intervention involving this symptomatic state, it is necessary to trace the true problem underlying the psychopathology, which is the anticipation that the Other will reject him due to the Self-image as being unloveable.

Once he has identified the wish (in this case receiving attention and being accepted), a therapist can gather additional details regarding the relational episode and try to identify:

- the 'if … then …' procedure, which is the cognitive and behavioural method usually used by a patient in an attempt to satisfy her wish (for example, avoiding displaying exaggerated or overly intense emotions because this feeds the expectation that the other will reject or criticise her);
- the way in which a patient foresees that the other will react (for example, by criticising or rejecting) and the reactions she notices from the other in response to her requests;
- a patient's prototypical reactions to the other's expected or real response (for example, shame generated by the other's criticism and closing-up aimed at warding off any further exposure to judgement).

A therapist should also focus on a patient's *tendency* or *action readiness* (Frijda, 1986), by asking the patient how she felt at a precise moment in her narrative episode or what she would have done if she had not had certain ties. Such action tendencies are a powerful wish identification marker and clarify the approach/ avoidance conflict. For example, a patient suppressing his emotions might say he felt an impulse to proclaim his distress but did not do so because he was sure that he would be punished or turned away by the other.

Another element of the formulation of an interpersonal schema is the *Self-representation*, also known as the *self-image* or core belief about the self, underlying the pursuit of the wish. Put simply, a patient may think, 'I can wish to be successful but I think that I am incapable.' The incapable core self-image leads one to arrive at negative expectations about the chances of achieving the wished state. Including the self-image in the overt formulation of the interpersonal schema is fundamental because among its goals therapy is aimed at helping patients to identify their schematic representations of self and others and understand that they are ideas rather than truths.

Only after this operation, which means differentiating or taking a critical distance from their own schemas, can therapy attempt to promote a change toward more benevolent and adaptive representations of self and others. For example, as well as isolating themselves and getting depressed, patients seeking attention and expecting a rejecting other cultivate a self-representation which is unloveable and therefore deserving of rejection. They will consequently tend to avoid presenting their qualities to others in order to avoid critical judgement, but this reduces their chances of being appreciated and increasing social contacts with persons who can be sources of reward. When they begin to understand that they perceive themselves as unloveable and that this belief is not necessarily true, they can start to feel more able to share qualities of themselves with others with greater hope.

Let us now look at the same elements of the assessment applied to a hypothetical patient suffering from paranoia. After gathering a narrative episode a therapist might extract the following structure:

> Self desires to be protected and looked after (*wish*), but perceives itself as vulnerable, easily submissive and physically fragile (self-image). For this reason its approach to the other is cautious and diffident (if-then procedure). The other is seen as being unforeseeably dominant and ridiculing of Self when the self displays its need for protection and care (Other's response), and Self's reaction is to hyper-compensate by becoming angry (Self's response to Other's response). In this case the anger protects against Other's attacks and helps a person to enter a mental state based on strength, which temporarily removes the perception of a vulnerable Self from consciousness.

We underscore that the same wish is supported by both forecasts linked to the pathogenic schema, which is based on a negative self-image (unloveable or vulnerable), and forecasts driven by the idea that the wished state will be achieved and, for example, the Other will supply attention and validation, or will not ridicule or dominate. In the second case Self will feel gratified, liked and capable, which confirms an underlying loveable self-image. According to Weiss (1993), patients come to therapy with an active pathogenic schema but are, at the same time, driven by an adaptive plan in which there is a clear hope that their unsatisfied wish will be achieved (Caspar and Ecker, 2008; Kramer, Berthoud, Keller et al., 2014). A major part of therapy consists of trying to help patients begin to believe that there is hope and for the patients to act so as to render the achievement of the wish, which is supported by positive self-representations, closer in both reality and their anticipatory constructions. Usually, however, healthy self-representations, such as *capable* and *deserving attention*, get overwhelmed by negative ones. In an assessment it is essential to identify the pathogenic schema and, at the same time, get the adaptive schema, which includes the healthy and vital self-parts, to surface. A good formulation will define a patient's interpersonal schema on the basis of his search for positive states.

This is a very important concept in MIT. More specifically, it is the form taken by the restitution of a schema so a patient can either stress that there is a pathology requiring dismantling or a healthy situation to aim for. MIT always tries to opt for the second. In the first case we might tell a patient with avoidant disorder: '*You fear being judged by others because you're not up to it, and consequently you suffer from shame and tend to close in on yourself to avoid the feared judgement coming true. Therapy can help us to see that this idea is not necessarily true.*'

In the second case we might tell the same patient: '*You harbour within you the hope of being accepted and appreciated, but this is easily eclipsed by the idea that others will criticise you. At this point you feel ashamed and close in on yourself to avoid the distress of being judged. And yet a part of you still hopes that approval and acceptance will turn up and therapy can help you to throw light on this self-aspect by attempting to discover what has led you to believe that you're worthless.*'

Patients generally respond well to this type of formulation and this leads to a context in which it is possible to tackle maladaptive interpersonal schemas while building a self-vision that is more positive and encouraging for the patient.

How to search: exploration of narrative episodes

In MIT patients are not asked for details of their life stories in their earliest sessions, but are assisted in gradually identifying current unpleasant sensations and emotions first, and then linking and associating them with significant past events. One should begin by asking a patient to describe an example of a recent life experience. If she, for example, states that she became angry with someone, the questions should be focused on *where* the episode took place, *when* it took place, *who* was present, the *contents* of the dialogue and the *action and reaction sequences*. When useful, one should ask for very precise details regarding the scene such as, '*In what room were you? Had you only just arrived home?*' etc.

Immediately after this it becomes important 'to put oneself in the patient's shoes' and pay attention to what he felt and experienced in the context of the episode he is telling about. For this to be successful, questions need to be precise and aimed at understanding the schema through focusing on the feelings and emotions experienced and on the dynamic triggering them. Following the guidelines of the more strict cognitive aspect, a therapist should never ask patients *why* they reacted in a certain way but *what* they thought at that precise moment that drove them to act in a particular way. They should be careful to avoid being arbitrary in their interpretation of the event and stay focused on the cognition prevailing at the moment of the event.

Let us reference an example of the elicitation of a narrative episode with a patient declaring: '*At work my bosses always treat me poorly.*'

The therapist can begin by saying, '*Can you describe an episode, that occurred recently or in the past – it's your choice – where you can show me what your boss does when he treats you badly? What happened? What did your boss say to you at that moment? Where were you?*' The therapist can then pull for greater detail by asking, '*What did you do at that point? How did you feel? What did you think at that moment? Did you think about reacting differently? Did you have any physical sensations that you can recall? Let me imagine that scene. Help me to experience it with you by taking me as close as possible to it.*'

Alternatively, the therapist might ask a patient who states, '*I don't trust my husband. I believe he's being unfaithful to me. It's an absolutely unbearable relationship,*' to describe the exact moment she started to suspect her husband was being unfaithful. He should ask the patient to place the sensation precisely in space and time and possibly to describe, with as many details as possible, *what* was happening at that moment or immediately before. If details are requested in this manner the relational narrative episodes that emerge will likely have a significant emotional importance.

As mentioned previously, to understand a patient's prevailing interpersonal schema it is necessary to start with an analysis of various narrative scenarios and not become satisfied with a single story (Dimaggio, Salvatore, Fiore et al., 2012; Dimaggio, Popolo, Carcione et al., in press). Once a first episode has been collected the therapist can tell the patient who felt he was ill-treated by his boss: '*Very good. One way or another you expect your work to be recognised. However, your boss had a disdainful attitude toward you, criticised you while you were conversing, and gave you the impression that he appreciated another colleague's work more than yours. At that point you did not feel appreciated, and consequently felt resentful and angry, which makes me think that you believe your work deserves recognition. In addition to the story about how your boss treated you, I'd like you to recall another episode where you wished to be appreciated and acknowledged but got the same sensation about not being appreciated, or felt angry or resentful, or felt you were being treated unfairly.*' This linking of episodes helps a patient alter his perspective and shift his attention to another narrative scenario, potentially one of more importance because it regards a significant other. The technique used to ask for associated memories is described in greater detail in Chapter 6.

A danger to be avoided when interpreting narrative episodes is the act of patients uncritically accepting their clinician's considerations without truly understanding them. In an attempt to avoid this danger a therapist should continually ask for feedback on the restitution of the set of schemas that are identified and reconstructed (Dimaggio, Carcione, Salvatore et al., 2010; Safran and Muran, 2000; see Chapter 5 on the therapeutic relationship).

Even if it is not predetermined, the number of episodes explored can indicatively vary between two or three and five or seven. The episodes should be selected by the therapist on the basis of the intensity and richness of the emotions experienced, with particular attention placed on the negative emotions.

A trained MIT therapist is capable of internally reconstructing the essential elements of a patient's schema immediately after the first narrative episode is recalled if the episode is carefully selected. A less trained clinician may find his ability to understand the essential elements of a schema becoming progressively more refined as he acquires familiarity and experience in the practice and understanding of MIT.

Obstacles to assessment: metacognitive dysfunctions

A therapist can arrive at an inductive reconstruction of a schema, that is extract it from the narrative elements in the episodes related from time to time by patients, only if the latter do not contain serious metacognitive dysfunctions that hamper or prevent a patient's reading of their experience in emotional terms. As we described in Chapter 2, metacognitive difficulties prevent patients from describing their experiences in a way that helps their therapist comprehend their inner worlds. To achieve a good assessment one needs to intervene with a reinforcement of basic self-reflectivity and a focus on patients' awareness of their emotions and thoughts and the relationships between them.

In the most extreme cases, patients' metacognitive dysfunctions can be so pronounced that they prevent them from reconstructing narrative episodes and relating them to their therapist. In these cases clinicians should not give up on reconstructing a set of schemas. However, during approximately the first two months of therapy they should carry out an operation to improve patients' metacognitive skills. In order to evaluate and promote their ability to relate their experiences in a narrative form, the therapist should make explicit the relationship between the patient's metacognitive problems and his consequent difficulty in accessing the information necessary for reconstructing the causes of his suffering, and for identifying his interpersonal schema or set of interpersonal schemas. In less serious cases patients may simply not be up to performing a reconstruction in 'antecedent, belief, consequence' (ABC) terms because they cannot manage to identify the emotions they feel or separate the automatic thoughts occurring in their minds during particular situations.

Patients with constrained traits may display a difficulty in self-reflectivity, which prevents them from thinking about their profound motivations, which hampers a therapist in his comprehension of the wish and other salient schema aspects. In some cases patients may relate a narrative episode rich only in facts and without any emotional connotation. A patient's facial expression while recalling an episode in session can constitute a significant and reliable marker of the emotion experienced by him in that particular situation, notwithstanding what he expresses in words. Let us imagine a patient describing feeling guilty toward his girlfriend due to their sex life, and his therapist noticing that the patient turns up his nose as if disgusted while reflecting on the episode. At this point the therapist can ask the patient whether the expression he can see on his face really corresponds to disgust and whether, by chance, the patient is aware of feeling a sort of repulsion for the experience he has recalled. In the concrete instance in which this intervention was performed, the patient promptly nodded and added that he realised for the first time that in some respects he found sex with his partner 'disgusting'.

A patient's facial expression is important not only when in contrast with his words, but also when it changes abruptly in session, especially when a serene expression gets replaced by a disturbed one. It is very important to point out any change in expression as soon as possible because this helps the patient to more precisely identify the emotional state linked to the thought. When patients are very constrained and inhibited it can be useful to ask them: *'How do you feel when I ask you these questions and you answer me? Do you feel I'm being intrusive or critical? Do you feel understood or not understood?'* If a patient reports negative experiences, the therapist can ask: *'In what way have I contributed to making you feel like that? It's important that you help me to understand how you feel and what I've done to prompt you to feel like this because it allows me to correct my mistakes.'*

Tests

Assessment in MIT includes an appraisal via tests which allows the clinician and the patient to rapidly identify symptoms and dysfunctional processes that may not appear in the earliest session but are nevertheless useful for treatment planning. In the appendix there is a concise description of the tests most frequently used in MIT but the choice of tests largely depends on the unit where a patient is being treated.

In any setting the set of tests that should be used include:

- at least one tool, perhaps an interview, for appraising the possible personality disorder;
- tools for appraising general and specific symptoms such as anxiety, depression, obsessions, dissociation or eating disorders;
- tools for appraising interpersonal dysfunctions;
- tools for appraising the various aspects of metacognition. It is preferable for the assessments to include an analysis of the metacognition elicited through interviews or looked for in transcripts of the earliest sessions. Self-reports for awareness of emotions and also the complex theory of mind/social cognition or emotional intelligence tasks are recommended. It is advisable, on the other hand, not to appraise metacognition exclusively via self-reports;
- tools for appraising emotional regulation and impulse control processes.

Restitution: a delicate moment for the therapeutic relationship

The assessment stage formally ends with the sharing of the test results, but only if the patient inquires about them. The clinician may share an illustration of the patient's dysfunctional schema with regard to the recurring symptoms reported by the patient and the latter's dysfunctional metacognitive profile. Whether one opts for a description of functioning in process terms or gives a name to the pathology from which a patient suffers, restitution is followed by an agreed upon plan for a therapeutic goal hierarchy placed in order of importance. One of the fundamental aims of restitution is to get a patient to understand the strict relationship existing between his schema or schemas and symptoms. He needs to understand not only why he has such symptoms, but also why they have appeared (*predisposing factors*), why precisely at that stage in his life (*precipitating factors*) and why they still continue (*perpetuating factors*). Restitution can be presented as follows: '*You wish this. To achieve it, you tend to do this. The Other responds like this and you react to the other's response like this.*'

With some patients it is possible to summarise by stating: '*On the basis of what you've told me, I think you're coming to therapy because you feel you're not doing enough and wish to be appreciated by others, but instead picture them as being judging and disdaining. This, on the one hand, makes you angry, but on the other it makes you suffer ... I have the feeling that therapy could represent the path by which this destiny does not come to pass. It can be seen in your narratives that you've been learning these dynamics over the course of your life and that they are rooted in your history and your mind. However, in reality, others can give a different response and you can have a different self-worth of yourself. Do you consider that this could be a goal of your therapy?*' Assessment can be completed with a formulation letter or a diagram of functioning. Examples will be described in detail in Chapter 9.

With certain patients who have better metacognitive skills, the formulation letters, verbal summaries or diagrams can be dealt with more quickly than with others. It is important, moreover, as part of the conceptualisation, for the coping mechanisms activated by patients vis-à-vis their discomfort to also be identified. Both constructive and maladaptive strategies which reinforce and perpetuate their disorders should also be identified. A typical example of dysfunctional coping is avoidance (see Chapter 2). In assessment we would stress that patients tend to close up and avoid any confrontations in the hope of protecting themselves from the distress of rejection or abandonment. At the assessment stage the therapist should note how much a patient feels that such a behaviour is necessary and determine that one of the patient's therapy goals will be to stop using this coping strategy. It is important that the therapist highlight that although the coping strategy is partly protecting him from psychical distress, it is also contributing to his suffering. However, patients should clearly comprehend that their therapist will not exert any pressure to make them give up protection mechanisms due to them being necessary at this point in therapy.

But what occurs if patients do not agree on the reconstruction of their schemas created by their therapist? Even if there is a clear basis for the reconstruction, it is possible that the therapist realises that a patient does not agree with what is stated and consequently views the patient more negatively. This shift in perception often occurs due to the patient including the therapist in her schema so that the latter ends up embodying and adopting the Other's position and makes the patient feel underrated, judged, despised and so on. In this case the problem is not metacognitive but relational, and the therapist needs to immediately switch his attention to the therapeutic relationship. He should not, therefore, try to convince the patient that his hypothesis is well grounded because this would create a session dominated by a competitive atmosphere and mutual defiance. Rather, the therapist should investigate those aspects about which the patient does not agree while being careful to catch the non-verbal signals of any emotional change by the latter. In other words, a problematic and dominant schema emerges during the earliest sessions. The therapist may have correctly identified one (for example, the patient not feeling capable) but in the context of the therapeutic relationship another appears (the patient not feeling accepted) and the latter becomes the main focus in subsequent sessions and further material for the shared formulation of functioning.

After identifying and agreeing upon the patient's schema, a therapist needs to make a constant effort through internal discipline procedures (we are going to describe these operations in detail in Chapter 5 on the therapeutic relationship) not to embody the character of the Other in the schema. For example, if the latter believes that the Other is invalidating the therapist should be careful to keep any countertransferal signals under control in an effort not to become invalidating. For this purpose, it is important at the beginning of therapy for a therapist to get patients to express any kind of negative feelings they have towards him. They should be encouraged to do so at any point in a session, and it should be explained that this is precious and useful material that helps to avoid damaging the relationship. The patient needs to be reassured that all the feelings he experiences, even those he would prefer to not manifest, can be rendered explicit and shared because they could lead to a conflict which would likely damage the alliance and thus lead to a premature termination of treatment.

The therapist is responsible for a precise understanding of what a particular question may mean for a patient at any given moment. For this purpose he should ask himself: '*How does the patient see a question of an exploratory nature? Does he perceive it as being intrusive? Does it provoke unbearable anxiety or distress? Is my interpretation seen as being critical? Could the attitude I adopt be considered as a rejection or lack of respect?*' It is particularly important, for example, to avoid using one's diagnostic knowledge to stigmatise or label patients. Even at the assessment stage it is important always to keep the therapeutic relationship under control and to intervene quickly in an attempt to salvage minor ruptures through relational and technical strategies. This will help patients arrive at an agreement about other therapeutic tasks and allow patients to protect the work of caring for themselves that they have decided to undertake.

Diagnosis formulation can be performed within a competitive relationship in which the therapist, more or less consciously, adopts a dominant position, especially if he formulates the diagnosis in a categorical form. The therapist may state: '*You suffer from avoidant personality disorder.*' Moreover, communicating a categorical diagnosis in accordance with the DSM-5 (APA, 2013) can reassure patients that their problem is well-known and has a name, and consequently help them overcome their fear of the unknown and of being taken over by uncontrollable forces. Discovering the typical aspects of their disorder helps them to more easily understand their functioning and recall significant events that are consistent with the profile diagnosed. As we mentioned above, the risk in communicating a diagnosis to a patient is the social stigma, and consequently the evaluation of how to perform the restitution is always case-specific.

Chapter 4

Step-by-step formalised procedures

MIT, as we will systematically describe in the part of this book devoted to pathology and assessment, adopts detailed and formalised step-by-step procedures. In this book, we carefully describe all components and provide rules and a rationale to guide the clinician's transitions from one step to the next (Dimaggio, Carcione, Salvatore et al., 2011; Dimaggio, Attinà, Popolo et al., 2012; Dimaggio, Salvatore, Fiore et al., 2012). In this chapter, we synthetically show the sequence of interventions; we also highlight the progress markers, signalling whether it is possible and advisable to pass to more complex interventions after the simpler ones have been successfully accomplished. As treatment progresses towards more advanced stages, interventions will in fact call for more complex metacognitive acts on the patients' side. Once patients have built a clear understanding of their functioning, the clinician will need to renegotiate the therapy contract in order for the patients to be willing and motivated to engage themselves in activities in-between sessions in order to build new modalities of meaning-making and relating.

We broadly divide MIT into two sections. The first section is *shared formulation of functioning* (see Figure 4.1 below) and is aimed at improving patients' self-reflecting skills. It consists of forming, side by side with the patient, an agreed upon and detailed map of his or her own mental functioning.

This map guides the path towards the second section, which is *change promoting* (see Figure 4.2 below), where actions are aimed at reducing suffering, building new self-narratives, accessing healthier subjective experiences and enacting more adaptive behaviours in order to build personality parts which will guide more effective social action.

MIT procedures

Shared formulation of functioning (Figure 4.1) includes the whole set of operations aimed at understanding the states of mind of the patients, their reasoning processes and eventually their underlying maladaptive interpersonal schemas.

Therapists can start by promoting the more basic level of metacognitive self-reflection, such as awareness of feelings and the recognition of agency, that is the awareness to be the cause and source of one's own actions and subjective experiences.

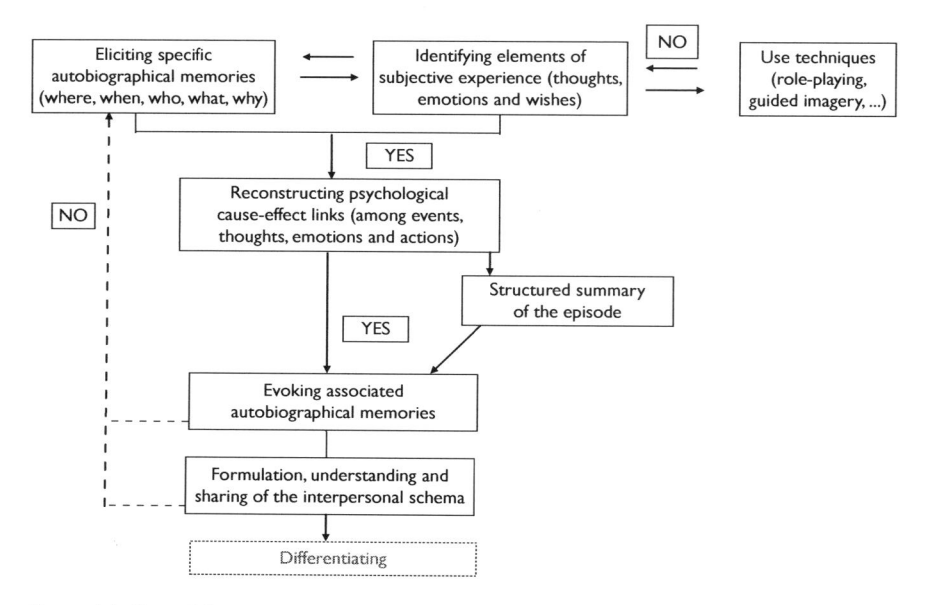

Figure 4.1 Shared formulation of functioning.

Once patients have achieved these levels, it is possible to move towards more complex operations, such as forming plausible hypotheses about psychological cause-effect links between interpersonal events and elements of subjective — experiences – in metacognitive terms: *relating variables* (see Chapter 2). For example, if the patient is aware she is angry, the therapist will assist her thinking: '*I've felt hurt because my boss refused to raise my salary and when I am angry I tend to shut off*.' An even more developed self-awareness is acquired when the patient thinks: '*I understand that when I expect the other will appreciate me and instead I receive a rejection or a criticism, I tend to become angry and to resentfully withdraw*.'

This part of treatment reaches a peak when the patient acquires the ability to differentiate, or to observe his or her own inner world and understand that interpersonal events may be seen from a different angle than the one foreseen by own maladaptive schemas. The ability to differentiate is therefore both the conclusion of the first treatment section and the first step of *change promoting*, a kind of turning point bringing treatment into a different stage. The ability to differentiate allows the patient to think: '*My tendency to shut off when I don't feel appreciated depends only in part from what others do. I am hypersensitive to signals of rejection or criticism and sometimes I see these signals when there are none. Maybe this is rooted in my personal history*.'

We briefly list the procedures of the *shared formulation of functioning* section which we will describe in detail in Chapter 6.

1   (a) *Evoking specific autobiographical memories.* This is about helping the patient recall a series of clear and detailed personal memories, also called *narrative* episodes, that occurred in specific moments in time and in a specific location (*when* and *where*).

   (b) *Identifying elements of subjective experience.* This is understanding what emotions, thoughts and somatic sensations the patient experienced during the narrative episodes. In case the patient is unable to relate specific memories, the clinicians' task is inferring mental states on the basis of more general verbalisations and most of all from in-session non-verbal behaviour.

2   *Reconstructions of psychological cause-effect links.* Once a patient has recollected narrative episodes and has jointly reflected with the therapist on the basic elements of subjective experience, or after reflecting on what is happening in the therapy relationship, the clinician helps the patient to reconstruct and understand the links between events, thoughts, emotions and behaviour, especially with regard to interpersonal interactions. One further goal is to ask for the typical other's actions and intentions, or life events that tend to trigger problematic states of mind (see Chapter 6).

3   *Structured summary of the events.* This is an operation the therapist carries out both in session while listening to the patients and reasoning about their verbalisations and in-between sessions. In this second phase, the therapist reflects about the material evoked during the session and tries to frame his own understanding of the patient according to the interpersonal schema structure (see Chapters 1 and 3). This means understanding the patient's wish, the self-image underlying that wish, the other-image and how the patient reacts to the others' response. During this phase the goal is not a schema-formulation (Chapters 1 and 3), because by definition multiple episodes are needed in order to speak of a schema. The goal is instead to reconstruct the sequence which starts from the wish, passes through the response and of the others, and ends with the reaction of the self once the patient foresees or notices his or her goal will be unmet (see Chapter 6). Once the therapist believes the summary is correct the therapist discusses it with the patient and collects his or her feedback.

4   *Evoking associated autobiographical memories.* Once the structure of the related narrative episodes has been jointly formulated, the therapist asks the patient to evoke a series of autobiographical memories the patient himself feels are similar to the one just told. The goal is to recollect multiple episodes which will then allow for an understanding of how recurrences exist in the relational life of the patient.

5   *Schema reconstruction.* When patients have recalled a series of episodes they feel are psychologically similar, the goal becomes the shared reconstruction of the maladaptive interpersonal schemas underlying the episodes.

For example, the patient may discover that after each time she feels weak or vulnerable, she expects the other will withhold care, reject her or harshly judge her. She may then understand that her tendencies to withdraw and the subsequent sense of isolation are the outcome of the protective avoidance from the feared criticism; she understands how this fear of criticism is generalised to many relationships with relevant others. Operations 1 to 5 are described in Chapter 6.

We consider the shared formulation of functioning section to be completed, and therefore the patients are ready to change, once the schema is felt as egodystonic or a source of suffering and problems that the patient wants to change. If the interpersonal schema is of this kind it will be easier to agree upon how to act in order to bring about change.

A second kind of schematic representation is instead egodystonic only in regard to the self-image and the other's response; the response of the self to the response of the other (which includes the *coping* procedures) is instead egosyntonic. To clarify, the patient may seek safety, while imagining himself as vulnerable and expecting others to threaten or humiliate him. When the patient suffers in feeling vulnerable and threatened, it is egodystonic. When he reacts with anticipatory aggression to minor cues of threat and is convinced this reaction is appropriate and justified, this is the egosyntonic part of the schema. Examples of this kind are: '*My partner does not pay attention to my job and is an obstacle to pursuing my goals. She is weak and always asks for help, which makes me lose time. I criticise her for her weakness and I am forced to yell at her and explain that she should not ask me for help because she ought to know her needs are much less important than my job.*' Another example is: '*I am in danger, people may cheat on me. As a reaction I threaten them when I feel they are about to lie to me and I am never caught off guard.*'

With schemas of such a kind, the differentiation operation the therapist performs in the beginning will be more limited than with the pure egodystonic schemas, as we will detail in Chapter 7. The operation will not be aimed at promoting differentiation from the schema in full, but only from the egodystonic part. The clinician does not work to show the patient that his or her anticipation of others attacking or cheating is ungrounded, nor does the clinician say that the coping response is maladaptive. The therapist will instead try to let the patient achieve critical distance from the egodystonic part of the schema: '*May we talk about you being less vulnerable than you believe?*' Also the therapist tries to foster agency over own state of mind: '*You have a power to master suffering generated from the perception the other is humiliating you; shall we try and use it?*'

Lastly, some interpersonal schemas may be based on goals which are pursued as a compulsion because they are a source of pleasure, such as grandiosity or ideal love. These schemas are fully egosyntonic: '*I like to seduce, it's fun and I love feeling the power to attract women, it makes feel like a god*'; '*I don't want to work, it's my right to pursue my ambitions and I won't surrender to society*

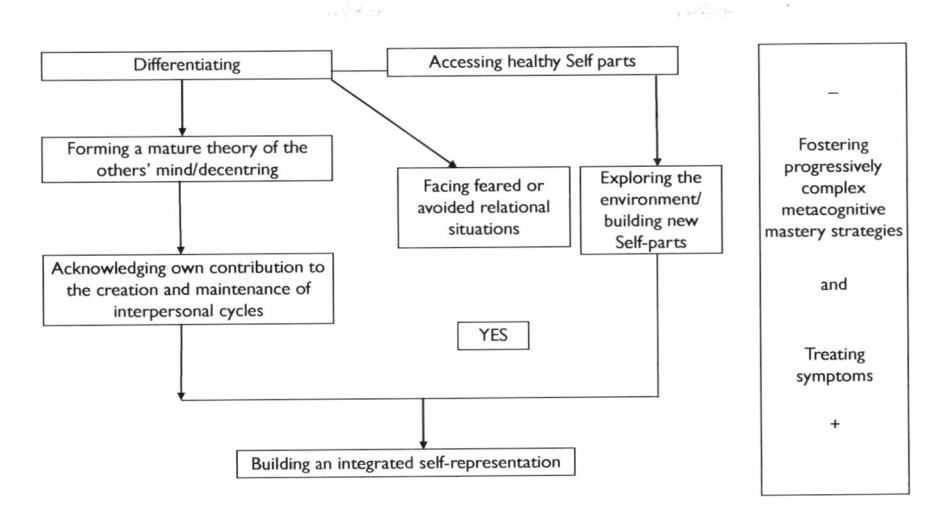

Figure 4.2 Change promoting.

norms and stupid conformism.' In these instances, we suggest the therapist does not prematurely attack the schemas, no matter how dysfunctional they may be. Confronting the patient too early with ideas that these schemas are problematic bears a high risk of eliciting negative reactions that can be counterproductive at best and threaten the therapeutic alliance. Of note, schemas with a relevant chance of generating negative reactions in the therapist are frequent in patients with narcissistic, paranoid and passive-aggressive features.

The second MIT section is *change promoting* (see Figure 4.2) and includes the procedures aimed at assuming a different perspective on interpersonal events, understanding that one's own inner world does not necessarily mirror external reality, and building new modalities of thought and action moving toward wellness, adaption and personal fulfilment.

We briefly list here the procedures of this section which we discuss in detail in the second part of the manual (Chapters 7, 8, 9, 10).

6 *Differentiating.* Differentiating consists of helping the patient understand that his or her ideas about what happens in relationships with others are not necessarily true and things may look different when viewed from a different slant. This way it is possible to start thinking that beliefs about being rejected, mistreated, weak, unworthy, threatened and so on may just be beliefs and not a matter of fact. In particular, the patient may discover that in other moments she feels stronger and safer, with a sense of personal worth and higher self-esteem, therefore predicting more positive responses from the others (Chapters 5 and 7).

7 *Accessing the healthy self parts.* During this step, the therapist helps the patient access in-session positive state of mind and well-functioning parts of the self (Chapters 5 and 7).

8 *Exploration/forming new self-narratives.* Once the patient and therapist have identified and validated the healthy, positive and functioning aspects of the self in the session, the goal is to promote the ability to dwell in these positive states and live them in everyday life. In other words, it is a matter of activating the exploratory system and experimenting with new behaviours in order to enrich the repertoire of relational procedures and meaning-making attributions. In order to do this, the therapist asks the patient to explore new forms of relating and to engage in experiments that once seemed impossible, unreasonable or out of reach. In the next session, reflection is focused on the subjective impact of new actions and whether the patient was able to yield positive experiences. Once the patient has identified personally meaningful wishes and goals, a sense of agency and self-efficacy, it leads to a sensation that he or she possesses power over his or her own life and is no longer a prey of external forces (Chapter 8).

9 *Promote a mature understanding of the mind of the other/decentre.* This operation aims at making the patient aware that others have ideas, preferences, goals and emotions different to ours and we are not necessarily the centre of the others' thoughts. Basically, it is about forming a more and more nuanced and rich awareness of what others think and feel and strive for, and using this knowledge to live a social life with less conflict and more opportunities for personal realisation and overcoming frustrations (Chapter 9).

10 *Acknowledging own contribution to the perpetuation of interpersonal cycles.* This is an intervention for advanced therapy phases and it can only be attempted after the patient has achieved some degree of differentiation, has accessed the healthy self and has started to experiment with new ways of relating in social life. The goal is to help patients understand how their behaviours and attitudes can play a role in the creation and maintenance of the very same relational difficulties that make them suffer. This can help them stop maladaptive behaviours and find more effective ways of relating with others in order to obtain more satisfying reactions (see Chapter 9).

11 *Forming an integrated self-representation.* This aspect of the therapy concerns how to help patients form an integrated view of themselves, make sense of contradictions and lapses, and feel as a coherent whole instead of feeling made up of disconnected pieces. Therapists work in order to foster awareness of the triggers which make the patients think, feel and behave differently as relational contexts change while maintaining a sense of identity and unity at the same time. In parallel, the clinician helps the patients to integrate the new self-parts which arose in therapy, parts that in the past they were unaware of, or that they refused to ascribe to themselves, into their own identity. It is also important to make patients aware of the change obtained thanks to the psychotherapy work and of how the new perspectives they are endorsing and the consequent behaviours led

them to more positive outcomes that are in striking contrast to old dysfunctional patterns. This helps the patients achieve a sense of selfhood and ownership of the parts that have emerged during therapy and foster further trust in the therapy work (Chapter 9).

12 *Fostering metacognitive mastery and treating symptoms.* If patients have poor access to states of mind, the therapist tries to promote mastery strategies for relational problems, and to use techniques for treating symptoms, based mostly on the awareness that a symptom exists because there is a problem for which it is necessary to do something. These forms of strategies are mostly behavioural in nature and in any case minimally mentalistic, such as behavioural activation or helping to divert attention from anxiety-arousing stimuli. During successful therapies then, patients' metacognition improves and they gain a more nuanced understanding of their own mental functioning, together with a more mature theory of the other's mind. Thanks to such a mentalised understanding of symptoms and relational problems, it is possible to deploy a series of strategies to regulate emotions arising from problematic relationships. In parallel, a more nuanced metacognitive awareness is a source for a more flexible, creative and adaptive social behaviour, helping the patient solve relational problems more easily (Chapter 10).

General rules for moving along the procedures

A first basic rule guiding our procedures is that it is not mandatory to start from the first step but from the state of the patient in session. For example, if the patient spontaneously tells clear and detailed autobiographical narratives, the clinician can start with identifying the elements of subjective experience nested within the episodes. If the patient is able to describe their own emotions, the step is to search for triggers and behaviours they activate and so on. In short, therapists' actions should start from an assessment of the metacognitive skills the patient possesses in a specific session and evolve according to the patient's improvement or adapt to a moment of deterioration. One key MIT concept is the one of Therapeutic Zone of Proximal Development (TZPD) (Leiman and Stiles, 2001). The concept stems from the zone of proximal development (Vygotsky, 1978) and means that any therapist's actions must be consistent with the patient's ability to understand mental states and give them meaning. An intervention is likely to be effective if it is around the upper margin of the TZPD, that is it helps the patient reach the level of metacognitive ability immediately more complex to the one that they would display spontaneously. Interventions below the TZPD are likely ineffective because they are not enough to help the patient train and develop their mentalistic skills; interventions far above the upper margin do not work because the patient is unable to give meaning to the therapist's observations when it is overly complex in descriptions of mental states (Ribeiro, Ribeiro, Gonçalves et al., 2013). Put simply, if the patient is unaware of emotions, this is the ability to promote. In the case of emotional unawareness, it is pointless to try and promote critical distance from maladaptive interpersonal schemas – schemas the patient is not aware they possess – and such interventions would easily be rejected by the patient or even have a negative effect.

MIT procedures described here do not imply a *phase model* of psychotherapy, though for the sake of clarity, they have been described as a sequence. In clinical practice, it is necessary to continuously move back and forth between the two sections, *shared formulation of functioning* and *change promoting*, and repeatedly work over the same problems as they rise again until they are solved. It is therefore an iterative model of therapy action. For example, the patient may pass from an abstract and generalised tale about his motivation to reach a higher social status, to telling detailed episodes and then to understanding the underlying maladaptive interpersonal schemas; the goal is to act in order to change that pattern. In parallel, the patient may start bringing up inchoate material about a fear of being abandoned. At this point, the therapist intertwines the work on the social rank motive, which is in the *change promoting* part, with the one about attachment/fear of abandonment which requires starting again from the early steps of the *shared formulation of functioning* part.

During therapy, a problem which seemed to be already solved may reappear. In that case, the therapist will solicit recent narrative episodes which will help in understanding the current functioning, and to walk again through the needed part of the procedures for as long as necessary. Usually, in the course of PD therapy, even when problems reappear, they are described from a more complex metacognitive stance. At the beginning of the therapy, the patient needs to pass from intellectualisation to specific memories. Later on, when the problem surfaces again, the patient will easily tell clearer narratives that are richer in emotional language on her own accord, so the therapist can start directly promoting the connections between events, thoughts, emotions and behaviours in interpersonal relationships.

We remember that MIT does not follow a sequence with fixed starting and ending points. Every session starts from the metacognitive level the patient displays or has just reached in the former session, but if a new self-aspect with different problems come to the fore, or the same problem is spoken in less complex metacognitive language, the therapist steps back to early stages of *shared formulation of functioning* until a new narrative scenario has been built in which to seek states of mind. In the very same session, the therapist can promote operations aimed at a case-formulation in regard to a new emerging area; then, a few minutes later, he can go back to problems the patient understands better and enact change-promoting strategies in order to solve the issues which have already been clearly formulated in mentalising terms (Dimaggio, Salvatore, Nicolò et al., 2010; Dimaggio, Salvatore, Fiore et al., 2012).

Another basic rule is that every time the therapist tries to climb with the patient the steps of the procedures, he must validate the patient's experience and make the patient feel understood, safe, accepted and supported. Therapists can skip the overt validation step as soon as non-verbal markers such as facial expression, prosody and attitude toward the therapist make it clear the patient feels at ease, open and ready to continue exploring any issue in a safe, cooperative or playful atmosphere. As soon as the patient displays any negative reaction, MIT asks the therapist to reassess if her observations or formulations were correct. As an alternative, she will steer attention to the quality of the therapy relationship with the aim of detecting and repairing the alliance rupture (Safran and Muran, 2000; Chapter 5, this volume).

Markers of therapeutic change

How does a therapist know when it is time to move from one step to the next? *Key progress markers* will indicate when a step has been successfully accomplished and that it is time to foster more complex aspects of self-reflection or drive towards change.

Therapeutic markers consist of:

- metacognition;
- quality and intensity of affective reactions, that is the patient's ability to become aware of affects, experiment with them with more intensity than before and modulate;
- quality of the therapy relationship, for example a reduction in confrontation or withdrawal (Safran and Muran, 2000);
- access to more autobiographic memories (Weiss, 1993);
- symptom change.

Interventions are considered effective only if it brings an improvement or at least non-deterioration in some of these factors, and allows for the passage to intervention requiring more complex reflexive skills. Also effective are interventions which promote an increase of intensity of negative affects – such as appropriate sadness for a loss – without activating defensive reactions or emotional dysregulation. It is important to continuously assess how much improvement or impairment is caused by psychotherapy or by external elements. An intervention may be correct but ineffective in the short-term because life events cause a momentary increase in symptoms. Usually short-term reactions are very important because they allow for monitoring through careful observation how the patient's discourse evolves and the quality of the therapy relationship, as evident from non-verbal markers, if an intervention has been accepted and effective or not.

Chapter 5

Therapeutic relationship

In MIT, the therapy relationship consists of the whole interpersonal processes that goes through patient and therapist, both in the context of the 'real relationship' happening in the here and now – including feelings of mutual sympathy, sense of commonality, sharing interests and so on – and in the context of transference and countertransference relationships (Hill and Knox, 2009) where patient and therapist experience relational models and experiences that are not directly related to the here and now but mostly from their respective life histories.

Working on the therapy relationship is one MIT cornerstone and it goes along with every operation aimed at personality change and symptom reduction (Dimaggio, Semerari, Carcione et al., 2007; Dimaggio, Carcione, Salvatore et al., 2010; Semerari, 2010). The therapist works intensively to build a good therapy relationship, repair alliance ruptures and foster a cooperative atmosphere reflecting upon mental states and ensuring patients' metacognitive capacities function at their best possible level (see Chapter 2).

Unfortunately, many patients with the PDs described in this volume tend to build the therapist according to a constricted and dysfunctional set of maladaptive interpersonal schemas. They ask for help, but often anticipate the therapist will be intrusive, spiteful, domineering, incompetent or untrustworthy. They are persons who struggle to build up and maintain relationships based on trust and cooperation, and tend instead to shut down defensively or attack first in order to prevent the predicted aggression they are so intensely afraid of. These patients fear being left alone and react either by clinging to the therapist or by withdrawing to avoid the pain of loss.

One of the main obstacles in treating PDs includes difficulties in forming and sustaining a good therapeutic relationship and the need to constantly repair any rupture. Promoting change in persons who are afraid to open up their soul, are unaware of their emotions and rarely disclose, and who often tend to construct the therapy in ways consistent with their maladaptive schemas presents as hard work that requires shrewdness and a constant focus on the therapy relationship. Moreover, many patients have such a negative self-image that the more therapists come close to the self-aspects they consider unacceptable, the more they are afraid of negative reactions such as harsh criticism and therefore they withdraw from the relationship or attack the therapist to protect themselves from menaces of subjugation, abandonment and rejection.

Relational problems are fuelled by metacognitive dysfunctions. If the patient experiences difficulty in describing how they think and feel, the therapist will hardly understand and empathise. As a result, the therapist will easily feel bewildered, bored, detached or edgy. Lack of access to patients' experience makes it difficult to get along and ally with them: if goals are unclear what is there to agree upon?

Difficulties in understanding others' minds prevent the patients from listening in a fruitful way to the therapist's words. The therapist in turn may sense they are facing a resistant patient and become frustrated or nervous or lose motivation.

Overall, maladaptive interpersonal schemas and metacognitive dysfunctions make it difficult to obtain the needed information to form a shared treatment plan and enact it in a playful, trustful, cooperative and vital atmosphere. This is why in any therapy moment it is of the uttermost importance that the therapist takes care of the therapeutic relationship. Against any marker of relational problems, the therapist will stop working on symptoms and personality structures and steer attention to better understand the kinds of problems that have been created in the therapy relationship. The therapist will work through these issues, and only after they are solved will he will turn back to working on symptoms and personality.

The therapist constantly asks herself: *'How can I create conditions that will allow the patient to better explore his inner experience?'*, *'How can I regulate the in-session atmosphere in order to pave the way for solving problems?'*; *'How can I disentangle myself smoothly and readily from this problematic relational dynamics that may damage the therapy?'*

Markers of problematic relationship

These main rupture markers indicate that the attention needs to shift to the therapy relationship:

- deterioration in the quality of the therapy relationship itself, with a boost in defensive reactions such as withdrawing, confronting or criticising the therapist (Safran and Muran, 2000);
- lack of improvement or deterioration of metacognition;
- increase in negative emotions associated with difficulties of emotional regulation. On the contrary, a well-regulated increase in experiencing negative affects is a sign of better contact with inner experience. For example, the patient is able to experience previously warded-off feelings of sadness and cry;
- lack of access to new autobiographical memories;
- lack of symptom improvement or symptom relapse;
- lack of states of mind shifts in reaction to therapist interventions, for example the patient acknowledges the therapist is right but non-verbal markers do not change.

If therapists' interventions are followed by the above warning signs, it is possible a relational problem exists that needs to be addressed early on. Ignoring the problem and failing to address it swiftly bears the risk of damaging the therapy, risking drop-out and having no chance to repair the relationship.

Functions of the therapy relationship

A good therapy relationship is not just a 'prerequisite' for a successful treatment, it also has specific and relevant functions for the therapy process. We use the therapy relationship as:

- *a source of information*: we draw information about the patients reflecting by the way she relates to us and we relate to her;
- *an instrument*: through the regulation of the therapy relationship, we help the patients overcome difficulties in understanding their states of mind, form a richer and mature theory of the other's mind, and create the condition for making change possible between sessions;
- *a therapy target*: patients found themselves experiencing the relationship with the therapist in a way similar to recalled painful stories. A relationship with their therapist that is less problematic than past ones allows the patient to discover that there are opportunities for developing healthier and safer relationships. Such a discovery can pave the ground to the formation of new representations of *self with others*, cleansed of the toxic influence of maladaptive interpersonal schemas;
- *a prevention of hiatrogenic damage*: the relationship with the therapist may serve as the first healthy relationship the patient has encountered, which challenges his previously held evidence that relating with others will lead to frustration, pain and failure. Avoiding the crystallising of the problematic relational patterns, which are activated over and over again during therapy, helps to prevent damage coming from the therapy itself.

It is clear from our description that this is a complex work, but in MIT therapists do not impose on themselves the unattainable standard to resist reacting negatively to the patients under any conditions. They instead work with a sustained awareness that patients may evoke negative emotions, they would be hurt where personal vulnerabilities arise and therefore they would easily contribute to the maintenance of negative interpersonal cycles. Therapists take for granted that they will never be fully sensitive, attuned and empathic! Failure to create a sense of sharing and understanding, validation and support are impossible to be avoided, and we train therapists to identify any problems surfacing in the therapy relationship early. They then try to do anything they can, at a human and professional level, to prevent the problems from growing from a snowball to an avalanche. This involves softening any conflict, disagreement or lack of attunement, and creating an opportunity for mutual knowledge.

Therapists continuously pay attention to, ask for and listen to patients' feedback, both explicit and non-verbal (Safran and Muran, 2000). If they discover they made an intervention from a non-empathic stance and patients' markers are negative, the therapist may ask what did not work well and what he or she did to make the patient feel misunderstood or invalidated.

Thanks to the dialogue they establish and the feedback the patient provides, the therapist can accustom the initial observation and correct it until the patient again feels understood and accepted. Once the disrupted empathy has been restored and the therapy alliance is again firm, it is possible to turn back and work cooperatively to reach agreed upon therapy goals (Aspland, Llewelyn, Hardy et al., 2008).

Working through the relationship: general principles

MIT works through the relationship first and foremost according to general principles of change known to be effective independently of the treatment model (Norcross, 2002). Synthetically, therapists try to:

- validate patients' subjective experience, highlighting what they consider she thinks and feels as something they understand and accept; they recognise it has a universal human value and is to a certain extent adaptive;
- using conversational strategies to create the optimal relational atmosphere allows the patient to feel a sense of sharing and attunement. Therapists will adopt a positive, welcoming, non-judgemental stance and will always try and put themselves in the patients' shoes. Moreover, they will pay the greatest attention to prevent and repair alliance ruptures. Acknowledging, as we noted earlier, they may have an active role in creating toxic relational patterns, therapists constantly ask themselves if that is happening (Mitchell, 1988). We do not assume that the patient must be charged for the problem, and once the therapist has recognised his role in the problem, he tries to regulate his own reactions (Safran and Muran, 2000), bearing in mind the goal to steer behaviour dictated by his own maladaptive emotions from tension to cooperation and joint reflection;
- considering any information coming from the therapy relationship, be it verbal or non-verbal signals, as opportunities to understand patients' functioning in everyday life. This is a precious way to foster patients' awareness of their own cognitive-affective processes;
- focus the conversation on the therapy relationship itself, therefore *metacommunicating*, that is talking openly about what is happening in session, what kind of feelings are passing through and how the patient and therapist are representing each other (Safran and Muran, 2000; Tufekcioglu and Muran, in press). Metacommunication is a complex operation, including both aspects of repairing the relationship and of honing assessment about patients' inner functioning. It is a conscious effort the participants make in order to come

out from the direct involvement in the interaction, at least for a moment, and openly reflect about what feelings and what kind of intentions they ascribe to each other; the goal is to explain any misunderstanding, restore cooperation and discuss the processes that led to a dysfunction in communication.

Aware as we are that any metacommunication about the therapy relationship bears the risk of deteriorating alliance ruptures (Safran and Muran, 2000), we try to minimise this risk, not using metacommunications by default but in specific moments or when other safer interventions have failed. Expert therapists can more frequently use metacommunications, together with *self-disclosure* (Farber, 2006), for example revealing specific episodes of their own lives, as long as they have acquired the skill to swiftly face and master any unforeseen reaction to what is happening after they have talked about personal issues.

Talking about the therapy relationship is useless if the therapist misidentified problematic relational patterns of both the patients' and her own. A relational intervention can fail even if a therapist, while attempting to repair an alliance rupture, does not consider how developed the patient's abilities are to recognise their inner states. Asking a patient who is struggling to describe his emotions to reflect about the complexities of an interpersonal relationship is counterproductive or useless at best. Explaining to a patient unaware he is angry – in spite of clear non-verbal markers – that he is angry because he appraised the therapist's comment as unproductive and it reminded him of his mother's ineptness is just a waste of time (Bateman and Fonagy, 2004).

The therapy relationship is to be regulated early and constantly during all the therapy. In order to do this, the therapist observes the patients, focusing on communicative signals coming from discourse analysis and non-verbal behaviour. If, for example, a patient talks about feeling threatened and in session shows a wary or sombre look, not making eye contact and having a tense voice, the therapist can guess with good reasons that the patient does not only fear aggression by others, but imagines the therapist as frightful. Before facing patients' difficulties, the first operation is expressing attention, respect, acceptance and empathy for the thoughts and feelings the patient is experiencing in front of the therapist: '*I can understand you are cautious about disclosing your experience, you do not really know me as a person so I imagine it must be difficult revealing parts of yourself when you are not sure I will treat them with due respect and attention*' (Dimaggio, Semerari, Carcione et al., 2007; Dimaggio, Carcione, Salvatore et al., 2010; Semerari, 2010).

In order to regulate the therapy relationship, it is useful for the therapist to steer attention towards herself, looking inside and seeking for any emotions, thoughts and sensations the patient is eliciting: anxiety, anguish, feeling judged, anger, worry, happiness, impotence, low self-efficacy and so on (Dimaggio, Carcione, Salvatore et al., 2010; Semerari, 2010).

Every time the therapist finds herself thinking things like '*the patient is unpleasant, reticent, ambivalent*' or '*I like him a lot*', she must first reflect on the

> Monica was 44 years old, held a clerical job and suffered from not otherwise speci-fied PD with paranoid and obsessive-compulsive traits and post-traumatic stress disorder due to her recent loss of her mother. She had already lost her father when she was 18 and had a brother she described as a trickster and a bully, often harassing and tricking her mother for years. When she needed help, she felt she was being cheated by incompetent and untrustworthy others. In the first session she started by saying that she did not trust psychologists – almost charlatans according to her – and that she was there because others had in some way imposed it on her. For a major part of the session, she looked out of the window. The therapist noticed her defensive withdrawal, which in this case was clear and manifest in her behaviour, and pointed it out early on: '*I sense that you are grieving and suffering a lot and need to tackle the loss of your mum, but I can also see you're afraid I might say some garbage and that the therapy could turn out pointless or, worse still, constrictive. I sense that there is, inside you, a desire to leave. It's something I respect and understand and which I'd like to discuss together with you.*' The patient felt reassured by this intervention and her face relaxed. The therapy continued and only after several months did Monica again, at a moment when distressing memories regarding another loss, that of her father, were surfacing, express the intention of interrupting it. During the session, both parties identified this intention as a defensive strategy for protection from distress and the therapy continued in a cooperative manner and with success.

fact that these are not objective reactions but subjective ways to react to that specific person. Then she can remember her subjective therapist's responses are still informative about the inner reality of the patient, but only to a certain extent. One therapist may perceive the patient as a hateful braggart but another may find him nicely exhibitionist. A patient may evoke feelings of threat and menace in one clinician, while another may note his vulnerable side and appraise him as needing care and not dangerous at all.

On the other hand, there is evidence that many therapists would react in the same way to a specific personality disorder presentation, or with just minimal differences. The hypothesis that there are specific interpersonal cycles for the different PDs (Bender, 2005; Dimaggio, Semerari, Carcione et al., 2007; Tufekcgioclu and Muran, in press) has actually received empirical support (Betan, Heim, Conklin et al., 2005; Colli, Tanzilli, Dimaggio et al., 2014). If a patient demands not to have to pay the fees because he is unhappy about a thera-pist's work, everyone would feel either anger or performance anxiety! When faced with a suicidal patient who is planning out the details of his own death, reacting with anguish would be normal. If instead, for example, the patient does not comply with homework or does not part from an apparently dysfunctional partner, the therapist's irritation cannot be ascribed solely to the patients' dysfunctional patterns. It is to be considered a sign that either the therapist is getting involved in a typical PD interpersonal cycle, and also that the therapist is reacting according to his own subjective schemas unrelated to the patient.

The more severe a patient's personality pathology is, the more the therapist's reactions are constrained and the easier the activating or sustaining of pathological interpersonal cycles (Colli, Tanzilli, Dimaggio et al., 2014; Clarkin, Yeomans and Kernberg, 1999). For example, when a patient with paranoid PD communicates his anger, mistrust and resented accusations, therapists typically experience fear or anger when they consider criticism unfair and undeserved (Dimaggio, Semerari, Carcione et al., 2007; Salvatore, Nicolò and Dimaggio, 2005). A therapist's fear or anger further triggers the concerns that initially activated the patient's protective behaviour and the patient may think, *'If he is scared he has something to hide'* or *'He is aggressive and wants to dominate me.'* This usually increases the therapist's negative reactions and the cycle continues. We hasten to repeat that no matter how typical a cycle is for a particular PD pathology, a therapist's response should not be considered automatic. Instead, a therapist's reaction is always filtered by her personal history and tendencies to react to unique interpersonal triggers, especially when her own vulnerabilities are evoked.

Knowledge about interpersonal cycles typical of PDs is useful because it is a heuristic which helps the therapist who is imbued in the negative emotions often elicited by patients to swiftly think, *'I am facing a person with a paranoid personality so there is no way I can hope to stay in the relationship relaxed, calm and neutral. But on the other hand, what I am experiencing is well-known, there is nothing strange in my reaction and I can allow myself to feel these feelings. I also have the tools to move on and change the climate of the session.'* Nevertheless, just understanding that a PD-specific negative cycle is not enough to break the repetitive sequence. The therapist must implement appropriate technical interventions, which are consistent with a correct case formulation. If he is not able to do this it is necessary that he explore his inner world. It is often the case that the difficulty in delivering interventions correctly is due to the activation of emotional arousal linked to problematic personal memories the therapist is unaware of in the moment. Receiving supervision allows a therapist to become aware that he is not just reacting to the patient, but to internal characters that are shadows of his history, and he becomes able to differentiate himself. A therapist may think, *'I realise I am being reminded of my harsh father telling me that everything I do is wrong.'* This realisation allows him to relax and retrieve the clear mindedness to leave his negative reactions aside. This will enable him to make a correct case formulation and deliver interventions that are able to support the patient's wish underlying the negative schema instead of falling victim to the interpersonal schemas of the patient.

Expert therapists, or even training therapists in moments of good emotional regulation, can quickly and easily use their knowledge about typical interpersonal cycles making patients' personal impact less intense, and therefore do not need to dwell on the investigation of countertransference before finding a solution to the problem. Of note, exploring one's own inner world is not a never-ending and exhausting work of self-analysis on the therapist's side. Usually it is sufficient to be aware of one's own feelings, have the ability to distance one's self from them to select sufficient interventions based on the case formulation to be less driven by one's own interfering internal feelings. Only when negative emotions are interfering with therapy progress and relational problems are sustained is it necessary for deeper exploration in order to assess whether the therapist is prey to problematic reactions he is not mastering swiftly enough.

Overall, therapists working with patients with PDs require an open mind and a readiness to reflect upon their own reactions. When supervising, MIT therapists strongly encourage trainees to freely explore, in a non-judgemental atmosphere, their negative reactions and disclose them to the supervisor until they are resolved at a level that allows them to freely interact with patients without toxic interference. A big issue in PD treatment is the ability to master these negative reactions. A well-functioning therapist does not censor her reactions, no matter how dysfunctional they may be, but she observes and reflects upon them, and works through them until she finds a perspective from which these reactions promote an enriching therapy rather than hamper the therapeutic process. In the early years of training it is especially difficult to achieve this mastery alone, and individual supervision and group discussion of cases are often needed to train a consistent and skilled MIT therapist for PDs.

Dolores, a 45-year-old Portuguese patient, suffered from serious avoidant and depressive disorder, with schizoid traits. She came to sessions with various layers of jumpers, a coat and a hat, and told of chronically feeling cold, tired and weak. She did not work and only left her home for medical appointments, which she wanted in order to solve the physical problems she complained of. She was affectively detached, flat, confused and paralysed. She managed to get by thanks to help from her relatives and various social services, which sent assistants to help her cook, given that she felt physically incapable of doing so independently.

Dolores described a history of sexual abuse by a stepfather beginning when she was 14 years old and continuing until she was in her thirties. Her mother never believed she was abused, and her stepfather threatened he would beat her if she told anyone. The therapist's reaction to this story was one of uncertainty and doubt, and she had the unpleasant sensation of not being able to believe the patient's words. The therapist was disoriented and did not know how to act. In group reflection work it became clear that her reactions consisting of backing off did not mean that the patient was really lying. The patient displayed a dissociation between the content of her thoughts and affects by speaking about the sexual violence with a neutral and detached tone, almost as if it did not concern her. She seemed lacking in trust in the therapist and at the same time fatuous. An emotional tone so inconsistent with the contents of her story could not induce anything but mistrust and incredulity in others. On the other hand, how could a woman, who had had two attachment figures, her stepfather who abused her and her mother who did not believe her, manage, except by attempting to detach herself emotionally.

A person who has learned that her own point of view and the emotions she feels are not important to significant others, or that even expressing herself is risky, likely can only communicate with a therapist in a flat manner, lacking in affect. Dolores' style did not induce a tendency in the therapist to offer treatment in a consistent and loving manner, but rather withdrawal and irritation at her evasive attitude. However, these effects were not the intention of the patient who, instead, sought attention but feared being ignored and maltreated.

Faced with stories like Dolores' a therapist can react critically and think, '*This patient is reticent, she's not cooperating, she's evasive and not motivated toward treatment, and perhaps she's lying.*' This reaction, if carried forward, would be inconsistent with the interpersonal schemas the patient activates in therapy. A therapist should, therefore, internally modulate her reactions and adopt a position consistent with the problem. Her supervisor helped Dolores' therapist to become aware of her reaction and to understand that the patient was reawakening in her distressing memories of her failure to provide care to her own relatives. Once these emotions had been modulated, her supervisor reformulated the case and helped the therapist to achieve the following internal position, '*I can understand that the patient is frightened by the idea of opening herself up. She's afraid that the figures she entrusts herself to will abuse her again and so she automatically keeps an emotional distance. Furthermore, it is likely that she hasn't developed a language for a proper communication of her affects.*' With this representation of the patient, based on an accurate evaluation of her interpersonal schemas and an ability to take a critical distance from her own countertransference reactions, the therapist was able to change her perspective and shift toward a benevolent attitude.

Typical interpersonal cycles

The faster the therapist recognises the presence of a negative cycle, the sooner she starts to disengage. In Chapter 1 we listed some of the typical interpersonal schemas that are treated in individuals with PDs. Interpersonal cycles stem from these schemas, though schemas are not the only factor contributing to their activation. Metacognitive dysfunctions, for example difficulties in describing feelings, also play a role. If the patient lacks the ability to monitor his own emotions (is alexithymic) and consequently does not convey emotions during therapy, the therapist will find it more difficult to be involved, curious, motivated to understand or resonate empathically.

A first group that will be discussed falls into the category of *attachment/ interpersonal dependence*. Patients in this category are best described as needing care and the therapist often embodies the complementary roles of *omnipotent caregiver*, *rejecting* and *judgemental*. The patient expects the therapist will take care of her in full, and the therapist can feel highly effective, capable of helping and occasionally the only person able to give the patient the love, attention and protection she never received in the past. As soon as the patient does not respond, the therapist may feel ineffective or criticise the patient for a lack of results due to being lazy or not willing to comply with the therapy tasks. Alternatively, the therapist may disengage or be disappointed by a patient, in whom he formerly invested a significant amount. He may also think of her as being immature, demanding and dependent, consequently consider her request for help exaggerated and feel exhausted and exploited. These cycles are easily activated with patients suffering from dependent, avoidant or depressive PD. Role-reversal of the therapist feeling abandoned may also occur due to feeling rejected or neglected when the patient does not show up to an appointment, forgets to pay, does not comply with assignments or lacks positive responses in spite of the therapist's enthusiasm and energy.

A second group of cycles occurs in the presence of *antagonism* and *social rank*. For example, the patient wishes for appreciation and recognition of personal worthiness, and at the same time the therapist may criticise the patient who is self-blaming for some mistakes or faux pas he claims he did and consider the patient's self-reproach as realist. The therapist should help the patient take a critical distance from these self-accusations, which should be considered as part of the patient's maladaptive schema, and she should give suggestions related to how to behave appropriately in hopes of role modelling or teaching social skills. This identified cycle is typical of patients with avoidant, dependent or obsessive-compulsive PDs. The result is that the underlying negative self-image of the patient is reinforced and self-criticism increases with the patient providing more and more example of pitfalls and errors.

Another typical condition is the therapist admiring the patient in an atmosphere of reciprocal idealisation (Kohut, 1971). For example, the therapist may succeed in validation and avoid noting appropriately problematic areas driven by the fear of hurting the patient. The therapist can be reluctant to abandon the reciprocal idealisation because he is flattered and pleased by the patient's admiration. This is a typical cycle of narcissistic PD.

Again, role-reversals occur easily in these cycles too. For example, with minimal signs of therapy being implemented, the patient may become critical toward the therapist, which likely will lead the therapist to feel targeted and guilty about the lack of therapeutic progress. He may react by seeking approval, justifying himself, and starting to do anything in an attempt to prompt change without rationale. During this cycle feelings of professional and personal inadequacy and low self-efficacy loom over the therapist, and the patient may be explicitly critical of the therapist and blame him for the lack of expected progress. These criticisms fuel the therapist's tendencies to self-derogation, and the therapist either creates excuses for why the therapy did not work or become disorganised tries to implement many techniques without a vision of what the correct thing to do is. A sense of hyperactivation and anxiety is a typical marker for this cycle occurring on the therapist's side, and the reflective stance is lost and case formulation neglected. Such a cycle typically happens with narcissistic, paranoid, passive-aggressive and obsessive-compulsive PDs. In short, both the patient and the therapist, facing lack of recognition of their own worth, become defensive, critical and edgy, or complain about struggling for an approval that never comes.

In the area of the threat-detection system, and of *fight or flight* reactions, both the therapist and the patient can have a desire to feel safe, and see each other as a menace, intrusive, controlling or domineering. In anticipation of impending danger, both may shut down, be overly cautious and suspicious, or counterattack in turn by grinding their teeth so to speak, in order to prevent aggression. Both fight and flight elicit in the other complementary roles, for example if one flights the other easily thinks he has something to hide and becomes angry. If instead one is angry the other either is scared or aggressive in turn. Fight or flight cycles are typical of paranoia, but frequent in patients with narcissistic and passive-aggressive PDs, particularly if rank and control are at stake.

Another cycle is the one of *reciprocal distance and lack of interest*. The patients, often with avoidant, dependent or obsessive-compulsive PDs, fail to raise the curiosity and attention of the therapist who easily becomes bored and uninvolved, and does not understand the patient because her emotions are neither present in the story nor in facial expressions, and as a consequence loses the motivation to listen. The patient often senses the therapist's disengagement, and her self-image of being unloveable or unworthy is reinforced, which leads to the maintenance of the cycle.

Other cycles happen in the area of *autonomy and agency*, in the context of the activation of the *exploratory system* (Panksepp, 1998). When the patient acts autonomously – and often wisely, we have to admit – from what has been decided during sessions, the therapist can feel defied and react by becoming controlling, intrusive and domineering, and generally hamper autonomy. The therapist can also perceive the patient as not respecting social roles and therefore challenging his or her authority, and consequently feel belittled, invalidated or forced to accept the patient's decisions. This reaction evidences a powerful activation of the social rank motive, and the patient may react by thinking, '*I am the therapist, it's me making the right decision for the sake of your health.*' So the therapist shelters behind this position of dominance and subjugates the patient. These schemas are easily activated with patients suffering from narcissistic, avoidant, passive-aggressive, obsessive-compulsive or paranoid PDs. At times, when patients with dependent PD improve they tend to become autonomous and therapists can feel like they are losing control or worry about patients not being able to follow their own course of action. Again, a problematic response by the therapist is attempting to regain control. Another reaction to be modulated is becoming like an anxious parent in front of a teenage son trying to pursue his own path in life by doing things that look dangerous but can also not be avoided in the growth process.

We can never emphasise enough that the therapist must not focus on how realistic she thinks her fears are related to the patient harming herself if she acts independently, unless of course there are serious markers of problematic behaviour such as reckless driving or impulsive and unsafe sex. If the therapist enacts his worries he will simply reinforce a maladaptive schema such as: '*If I struggle for autonomy my anxiety will paralyse me, and I'll harm him by causing him anxiety.*' As a consequence, inner modulation of the therapist's worry is needed and must not be displayed. Only when both patient and therapist are well aware of the schemas of impaired autonomy, and some differentiation over them has been acquired can the therapist note some behaviours are dysfunctional or risky, for example over-exercising in order to cope with distress, as in the following example.

Arturo was a 36-year-old programmer. He suffered from a serious paranoid personality disorder with narcissistic traits and major depression. In the initial sessions he told about how he performed extreme physical exercise to calm himself. His therapist was, realistically, worried that Arturo could hurt himself because he was straining his body too much, especially because he reported having frequent muscle problems in the past. Her supervisor helped the therapist by, on the one hand, pointing out that physical over-exercise was a form of dysfunctional coping and was therefore to be tackled later, only after understanding its adaptive value and comprehending what mental state it was aimed at soothing. In the case formulation it became clear that the over-training served to overcome moments of weakness and obliteration tied to the idea that others at work were creating problems for and humiliating him. At this point the therapy goal should, reasonably, have become the underlying state of obliteration and vulnerability, tied to his pathogenic schema involving a wish for independence and approval when faced with problematic work situations.

The therapist grasped the sense of the intervention but was unable to carry it out due to feeling that it was not possible to leave the patient to himself while he was engaging in risky behaviour. Her supervisor helped the therapist to focus on personal memories in which her relatives were described as suffering profoundly, and the therapist felt it was her duty to do whatever possible to treat and save them. Thanks to this awareness, the therapist comprehended that she was repeating a pattern where she took on the role of omnipotent caregiver, where the other did not have agency over his own treatment project, and she relaxed. In the following sessions she deftly managed not to block Arturo's over-exercise and to help him to understand its coping value. After a few sessions Arturo negotiated a reduction in the hours spent training.

Progressively going deeper in therapy relationship work

MIT works through the therapy relationship according to growing degrees of relational engagement. We start from interventions focused on symptoms or personality-related issues and if they work the relationship is not a matter of discourse, but if instead interventions are unproductive the focus shifts toward the therapeutic relationship.

Therapy work on the therapeutic relationship starts even before the first assessment session, sometimes during first phone calls or email exchanges when a patient is seeking a visit. The therapist often begins to reflect on his impact on the patient's internal world early on.

Giulia, the patient with predominant passive-aggressive features described in Chapter 1, had missed her first appointment three times. The therapist became annoyed because he felt harmed by this behaviour. When she missed a fourth appointment, Giulia sent a text message to the therapist stating, '*Can I have one more chance?*' Faced with such a request, the therapist agreed to see her, but warned her that from that moment on she would have to pay for every session she booked and then missed. In fact, in order to be able to modulate one's reaction it is important to remember the terms of the therapeutic contract, which is negotiated between responsible adults. In this case, as we shall show later, what is important is that the therapist modulates his reactions, such as his irritation at the idea of having suffered harm. It is correct to refer to the contract for direction, but a therapist should also ask himself what led the patient, who on the telephone seemed motivated to start therapy, to miss her initial appointments. A therapist should tell himself, '*It is likely that there is a valid reason I don't know about.*' This reflective attitude and a willingness to modulate one's negative reactions create the conditions for being more open and inquisitive about what leads the patient to attend sessions. At this point the therapist avoided letting his irritation drive his actions, which probably would have prevented the therapy from even starting. The patient agreed and attended the next appointment she booked and underwent the tests that were foreseen.

However, Giulia did not come to the second session. She then asked for the date of the third one to be changed and the therapist agreed to this. She arrived very late and started by asking if she could miss one session per month as she had problems getting to the clinic. When faced with such behaviour, the therapist started to experience feelings of abandonment. He found that he again felt critical and irritated vis-à-vis the patient's evasiveness and flightiness. The therapist realised he was doing this, but was able to realise that the patient's behaviour was not attributable to hostility or indifference towards the therapy, but to a stable manner of hers of being in the world, conditioned by a very powerful obsessive and anxious ideation. Giulia lived in a state of alarm regarding her loved ones' health and considered herself the only person capable of effectively looking after them. The missing of sessions was, in fact, due to her five-year-old son's health problems and to a close friend having to go into hospital. Due to always being ready to help others, she did not attribute any value to taking care of herself. By acknowledging that his reactions could be traced to experiences of his own and were not totally caused by the patient, the therapist was able not to show himself as being critical and to react with a welcoming formulation. The therapist stated, '*I can feel that you are a generous and affectionate person, with a big need to look after others, which leads you to become over-alarmed and to want to give a lot. This, however, saps your energy, makes you live in a constant state of alarm and stops you from taking care of yourself. But I feel, instead, that there's another part of you that wants to soothe this anxiety and take care of yourself.*' In this way the therapist identified the patient's wish to be cared for, which was being systematically suppressed when the patient saw another as being vulnerable. On this basis the formulation became, '*You have two wishes, both of them very good and positive, but one suppresses the other and this stops you from coming to therapy. Do you agree that this mechanism is what we should be reflecting on?*'

Parameters guiding interventions in the therapeutic relationship are related to how much the therapist has understood patients' functioning and has correctly assessed their metacognitive abilities. If the therapist has not yet acquired a clear awareness of the interpersonal schemas colonising patients' inner lives and of the interpersonal cycles activated in session, he must work to focus more on his clinical intuition and try and limit his interventions during problematic moments by regulating his own problematic internal state. The goal is to make the patient feel accepted and to avoid any potential relational problems turning from a snowball into an avalanche.

When the therapist is better aware of the structures underlying the relational strain, more explicit work on the therapy relationship is possible, one that must be customised to the patient's metacognitive skills in session. If the patient possess limited abilities to make sense of what is happening in a session, the therapist should focus primarily on a non-verbal regulation of the therapy relationship and be as explicit as possible in explaining the reasons guiding his interventions. This therapeutic process helps the therapist have an open mind and requires less inferences, which would likely produce biased readings. If the patient has reached more complex levels of metacognition, the clinician can formulate more nuanced ideas. For example, he can overtly reason about the interpersonal pattern active in session, and invite the patient into a process in which both can reason about how to exit from a conflict or misunderstanding. The therapist should ask the patient for any feedback about his intervention or invite the patient to talk freely about the problem.

In addition to the understanding of functioning and of assessing the level of metacognitive abilities possessed by the patient, the therapist should adopt another parameter in order to gauge the interventions on the relationship, which is her own clinical experience and self-awareness. Expert therapists can use more precocious and intense self-disclosures. When self-disclosing, the therapist relates her own personal experiences and memories that she feels are similar to the ones told by the patient, fostering a sense of sharing and attunement. It is important that when the therapist decides to self-disclose and metacommunicate about the therapy relationship, she makes quick guesses about how the patient would react to her disclosures or to the attempt to engage the patient in a joint reflection about the relationship. Moreover, she has to be able to adjust the tone and topic of the conversation, no matter how accurate early forecasts were, on the basis of the patient's feedback.

Less expert therapists, or those with less mastery of their inner world and personal reactions, might have difficulties modulating their feelings in front of negative or unexpected feedback, for example sourness or judging. In this case it is better that they are more cautious in self-disclosing or readily ask for supervision when facing unexpected and challenging feedback.

We now describe how the therapist works in order to:

- validate;
- prevent and repair alliance ruptures;
- create an optimal relational atmosphere, reach a sense of sharing and be empathic;

- metacommunicate;
- use the therapy relationship as a source of information about the patient.

This classification is more for didactic reasons as the boundaries among these relational interventions are often rather blurred. For example, when modulating one's own problematic reaction the therapist both prevents the entrance into a negative cycle and therefore avoids harming the patient, and heals the relationship by fostering an optimal atmosphere for joint reflection on mental states and contributes to creating new and more adaptive patterns of interpersonal relationships.

Chronologically, the interventions listed above are continuously intertwined and there is no ideal sequence. Nevertheless, the order in which we describe them in the following sections is based on a hierarchy of priorities.

Validating

Patients with PD have prejudice against their emotions and subjective experiences in general. They are often self-critics, afraid of what they feel and tend to underrate or reject it. They also have problems trusting the therapist's proposals of more benevolent ideas of themselves, and adopt a stance of self-inquisition (Popolo, Lysaker, Salvatore et al., in press). These reasons are why it is necessary for the therapist to attempt to validate any emerging experience, starting from an explanation of the bio-psychological role of emotions in adaptation to the environment (Linehan, 1993) and in the construction of meaning (Greenberg, 2002).

Presented with a patient with avoidant PD who is critical of his own shame and a patient with dependent PD who is self-invalidating of her own fragility, the therapist may emphasise that to be ashamed or feel vulnerable, and to need approval and support from others, are universal aspects that are common to every human (Safran and Muran, 2000; Semerari, 2010). Sometimes such basic interventions of validation are sufficient to tone down the ferocity of their self-criticism.

In other instances, in spite of the attempts to accept, validate or understand them, patients persist in self-invalidation and self-derogation. This can depend on how they construct the therapist according to their maladaptive interpersonal schemas. The patient is prone to guess the therapist is just pretending to accept her or does it because of his professional role, but secretly dislikes her. If this is the case, therapist's self-disclosure and metacommunication about the therapy process are necessary, as we will describe later on.

Validation continues throughout the entire duration of therapy. Each time patients raise new themes, become aware of previously unnoticed self-aspects or try to adopt new behaviours in order to enlarge their relational repertoire (see Chapter 8), the therapist should start with validation. Validation has a cognitive component, '*I understand your point of view*', and an emotional component, '*You are feeling this emotion, and it's normal that it happens under these conditions*' (Semerari, 2010).

Lucia was 47 years old, worked as a graphic designer and suffered from avoidant and depressive PD, with 21 SCID-II criteria overall and major depression. She had marked perfectionist traits and high performance standards, was afraid of making mistakes and criticised herself severely. She had difficulty accepting and regulating her emotions and found it difficult to express them socially. She experienced overwhelming sensations of guilt and self-accusation because every time she experienced pleasant feelings while doing something she felt was her own, she was convinced that this meant she wanted to leave her partner, who suffered from bipolar disorder, suicidal ideas and pathological gambling – although the latter was not so severe as to put the family at risk financially. At such moments she started to morally judge herself as a poor partner, became distressed at the idea of him being left alone and abandoned, and fell into a depressive state. At the same time, the idea of giving up everything pleasant that she was doing for herself made her feel angry at her partner, whom she saw as crippling and tyrannical when he asked her for small sums of money. During her initial therapy session her therapist intervened repeatedly by validating the patient and acknowledging how normal and understandable it was to feel powerless, despairing and distressed.

However, the patient's stories also contained positive feelings in many situations not involving her partner, for example a healthy and nutritious breakfast, the pleasure of doing physical exercise, how she liked opening up the office and planning her work in the morning or listening to the radio in the car. Her therapist, therefore, started to systematically stress that when Lucia felt good it did not necessarily represent a wish to leave her partner: '*You have many areas of well-being within you. They are not a sign that you want to leave your partner, instead they just show that you have the ability to feel good. I can see that you accuse yourself and are afraid of abandoning him, but that's not how it is. We can work together on your being able to allow yourself an expansion of these positive experiences, and at the same time find a way of living with the feelings of distress and powerlessness you experience toward your partner when you see him going out, probably to go gambling.*'

Already starting with her second session, the patient, in the face of these interventions, started to vacillate between a persistence of her distress and powerlessness, and feelings of guilt and anger, as well as positive moments where she discovered that there was room for well-being and relaxation. She realised that the therapist's accepting way of seeing things was difficult to adopt, but grasped that this depended on the intensity and pervasiveness of the feelings from which she suffered.

As one can note from this excerpt of Lucia's therapy, validation does not mean reinforcing a patient's negative beliefs. More specifically, the therapist shows that he understands everything as human and with a meaning that can be shared, but with calm steadiness takes up a position against the patient's tendencies to succumb under these ideas.

Prevent and repair alliance ruptures

Preventing and repairing ruptures in the therapeutic alliance is an ongoing process of the therapist trying, from the first contact with the patient to the last session, to avoid contributing to relational strains. The clinician focuses on the awareness of her own reactions and their early inner regulation even if she has not yet identified any clear reasons that elicited them (Dimaggio, Carcione, Salvatore et al., 2010). The simple gut feeling to take action in a problematic way is a sufficient warning sign to invite the therapist to self-regulate. When she has a clearer idea of the patient's maladaptive interpersonal patterns, and of her own personal tendencies to react in specific ways in the face of some cues, she can avoid entering the negative interpersonal cycle or readily find a way out. The awareness of her personal contribution to the negative interaction is of utmost importance here. In sum, the early phase of interpersonal regulation is a therapist's *intuition* that she is about to react in ways that would make problems grow. In a later phase, the therapist can note that she is embodying the role of the problematic Other in the patient's schemas. This essentially is work aimed at *preventing damage* that may come from the therapy relationship.

Transference is active very early on in therapy and even minor cues can lead the patient to mistrust the therapist and leave the patient feeling criticised, ashamed and so on. It is unlikely the therapist can correctly assess the problem in the heat of the moment, though she still needs to understand swiftly what led to the patient's fight or flight. Therefore the therapist needs to perform an intuitive guess as to what the problem at stake is, and thanks to this intuition she can enter a state of *inner readiness to disembed* from the problematic cycle. For example, when facing a patient's displays of closing up or shame, the clinician will readily use an extremely gentle, non-judgemental and non-pathologising language in order to avoid the patient underrating herself and thinking, '*My therapist thinks I am sick too.*' If the therapist instead feels the need to walk on eggshells and vacillates between anger and fear since the first phone contact, this is likely a sign that the patient presents with prominent paranoid features. In this instance the therapist has to take care to avoid withdrawing or counterattacking, even if she does not yet have any awareness of the specific maladaptive schema of the patient. These early operations are made easier if the therapist is aware of what the most typical interpersonal cycles are of PD (Colli, Tanzilli, Dimaggio et al., 2014; Clarkin, Yeomans and Kernberg, 1999; Dimaggio, Semerari, Carcione et al., 2007). In parallel, it is helpful to be able to rapidly adopt a self-observing stance and reach a bird's-eye view on one's own internal world in order to know the impact a problematic patient is likely to have on our personal vulnerabilities.

Training is important in developing these skills, including supervision aimed at identifying typical inner states of the therapist when facing difficult patients (Safran and Muran, 2000). For example, if the therapist knows that when he feels criticised, constrained or abandoned he tends to react with anger and a need for recognition. He may think: '*I am feeling criticised by the patient. I know this is typical of me. This person is affected by narcissistic PD and is consequently prone to scorn others. If I dwell on my need for approval I will end-up depending on the patient's judgement, which will likely be negative, and I will end up feeling frustrated or try to prove my worth. In any case I will contribute to the maintenance of interpersonal processes typical of narcissism. Also I have to bear in mind that the patient is now purposefully enacting this behaviour as it is an automatism so I can't blame him for that. If he was free to choose how to relate with others he wouldn't be here asking for psychotherapy. Putting my need for approval aside is possible and useful, and so I can try and change the state of our relationship by acting differently.'*

When the case formulation is well done, interventions aimed at preventing and repairing alliance ruptures are more effective because they are consistent with the patient's maladaptive schemas which are now clear. The therapist assesses if the patient is portraying him in a schema-consistent way and then tries to gauge his reactions in order to both avoid reinforcing the patient's negative expectations and disconfirming them.

Fulvio, 44 years old and self-employed, suffered from avoidant PD with dependent and depressive traits, compiled with 16 SCID-II criteria overall and presented with social phobia. His dominant theme was a critical perfectionism. He wanted to be accepted and supported in his goals, but saw the other as criticising, hampering and rejecting of him and thus adopted perfectionist strategies to avoid negative opinions. The therapist suggested exposure exercises to overcome his social phobia which stemmed from his worry and embarrassment related to sweating in public. Fulvio's reaction was worry, anxiety and a sense of constriction, and he stated, '*I know it's the right thing to do, however, I don't feel up to it.*'

Although aware of the need for the exposure exercises, the therapist could see that the patient felt constrained and deprived of freedom of choice, and linked these elements to a narrative episode referenced by Fulvio a few days before. He shared that when he was younger he missed his tennis lesson to go out with a girl, and once he got home he was harshly rebuked by his parents. His mother commented, '*You're wasting your time going out with a silly floozy who says the first thing that comes into her mind.*' Fulvio reacted aggressively by throwing water at his mother because he felt she was tyrannical, constrictive and dominant.

The therapist then saw a potential link between the narrative episode and a dynamic of the therapeutic relationship (his suggesting exposure aimed at treating Fulvio's phobic symptom), and hypothesised that in each case there was a specific interpersonal schema in action. In this schema the wish to be independent gets frustrated by a tyrannical and dominant Other, to whom the Self reacts initially with anxiety at the idea of being subjugated and later with anger when it feels that the constriction is unjust.

The therapist hypothesised that if he persisted in suggesting the exposure he would reinforce this pathogenic schema. He therefore addressed the patient as follows: '*I feel that at this moment it's more important for me to not ask you to do this exercise because it's as if you needed to know that you can assert your will freely with me.*' Fulvio relaxed and said that he felt the therapist was respectful. They then agreed that Fulvio would try exposure, which was something he wanted to do, when he felt surer and less anxious, and a rupture in the relationship was prevented. In Chapter 6 we shall see that the therapist continued to explore the episode in session to foster further awareness in the patient and his underlying pathogenic schema.

As evident from the excerpt, the intervention started form the idea that the patient's maladaptive schema was active in the transference (Luborsky and Crits-Christoph, 1990), but the patient was not fully responsible for the relational problem. In that moment the therapist was not guided by negative countertransference but instead was working by using technical instruments well suited for social phobia. Nevertheless, he noted that he was being constructed into the constrictive other in the maladaptive schema, but he stepped back because he realised that persistently promoting the overcoming of social avoidance would have triggered a dysfunctional interpersonal cycle.

The strategies to prevent early alliance ruptures are the very same interventions used to repair ruptures once they have happened. This will be evidenced when we describe the process of metacommunication.

Creating an optimal relational atmosphere: sharing, self-disclosure, empathy and accessing positive states

Patients suffering from PD with inhibited traits rarely feel attuned with others, which often creates an unpleasant atmosphere in session. Moreover, patients with PD often enter the session in negative states and spend most of the session feeling shame, depression, guilt, self-derogation and so on (see Chapter 1 for a list of mental states). Notwithstanding therapists' efforts, patients are often not able to shift to more positive states of mind during the session. But, if patients return home in the same state they came to session, their memories of the interactions with the therapist will be affect-congruent. For example, if they are angry they will be prone to remember hostility. Interestingly, memories of the positive aspect of the relationship will be remembered less and with minor intensity. If this is the case, the gains of the session will not stay, and at the same time the therapist will be constructed more easily in a schema-consistent way. Therefore it is necessary that the therapist promotes a positive atmosphere, for example by focusing the conversation on topics of shared interest which can be a good avenue for accessing positive emotions.

Promoting a sense of sharing

With patients who have difficulty opening up to others and providing detailed narratives, the therapist should seek to identify areas of common interest, such as movies, books, sports and so on, and then try to focus the conversation on those. Of course, if such shared areas exist this is helpful because it allows the therapist to be more involved and invested in the conversation. With this strategy the patient will feel comfortable talking about things she likes and knows well (Dimaggio, Semerari, Carcione et al., 2007; Semerari, 2010) and appraise the therapist as a peer as he is displaying a sincere involvement in the theme of the discussion. Of note, evidence shows that humans tend to perform mental operations that improve the quality of the relationship (Ciaramelli, Bernardi and Moscovitch, 2013).

They also ascribe more mental states, use less stereotypes in order to explain the other's behaviour and do not perceive them as an enemy or a threat if they perceive the other as being similar (Ames, 2004). Overall, these interventions aimed at promoting a sense of sharing improve the understanding of the mind of the other (the therapist's in particular) and make access to self-states easier as they are more relaxed and feel accepted and not-judged.

Talking about shared themes needs to be sustained until psychologically relevant contents surface. From this moment the conversation can be focused on those. Again, it is important that the therapist is authentic when displaying interest in a theme and not just playing along. On the other hand if interests are not shared the therapist can try and learn something about the patient's favourite areas without pretending that she is personally involved in the matter. This is still good for the relationship as the patient understands the therapist is motivated in getting to know him.

During the conversation on shared interest the therapist must have a two-sided position. More specifically, the therapist should simply be involved in the conversation as if she were talking with a friend, while still maintaining a therapeutic stance by reflecting on what is happening during the dialogue and determining how it is relevant to the relationship. This information can be used by the therapist during the processes of reformulation and metacommunication about the therapy relationship (Bromberg, 1998). For example, the therapist can say, '*We were involved in the discussion about the movie we both saw last week. I noticed that you felt relaxed and happy, which is an experience you do not usually feel. Also, you felt like truly sharing something, while at the beginning of the session you said you often feel alone. It seems that during this conversation you had the experience you struggle for, which means it is something within your reach.*'

In short, while talking about themes he likes with a therapist displaying sincere involvement, the patient accesses healthy and functioning aspects of the self, and therefore feels effective, valid, worthy and vital. These self-experiences will be the pillar for the operations aimed at enriching the self (see Chapter 8).

Therapist's self-disclosure

A particularly useful aspect of the relationship is the therapist's self-disclosure. Disclosure can take a variety of different forms. The first type of disclosure is openly describing the reasons underlying an intervention. This disclosure is adopted by default in cognitive therapies, and it is one of the cornerstones of collaborative empiricism. A second kind is disclosing self-aspects aimed at promoting a sense of sharing, similarity and connection. The goal of this disclosure is not just repairing alliance ruptures, but creating an atmosphere that allows the patient to access self-experiences that she usually does not accept by having a sense of being with a peer of the same rank and status and consequently not feeling inferior or judged.

In order to reach this goal, the therapist can talk about his own interests, as noted before, and share episodes from his own life when he felt driven by wishes, emotions and thoughts similar to the patient's. It is of the utmost importance to select well-modulated personal memories that the therapist is not currently struggling with or suffering from in the present. To put it simply, if the patient is suffering from a broken heart and the therapist is facing the very same problem, the therapist should not choose to self-disclose.

Self-disclosure must not focus on providing suggestions for solutions to the problem (i.e. how the therapist suffered from the same problem but then found a way to move on). That would easily evoke a sense of inferiority in the patient. Instead, the therapist must show how she actually experienced similar feelings and lived in similar conditions, and so can see the world from the same angle. We will later describe a third kind of self-disclosure, which consists of a therapist sharing her experience of the therapy relationship. This type of intervention is aimed at understanding and solving in-session relational problems through metacommunication.

There is always a chance that the patient's appraisal of the therapist's disclosure is different from what the therapist expected due to it being inherently unpredictable. For example, the patient may note aspects of the disclosure that the therapist was unaware of and consequently not feel a sense of sharing. Another possibility is that the patient inverts the attachment and takes care of the therapist, which detracts from the need to be understood or feel guilty for creating troubles. Most often the patient can idealise the therapist and feel she is deeply human while he is a failure, no matter the therapist's effort to describe her vulnerabilities with a sense of being at the same level and both immersed in the difficulties of human life. We repeat that in MIT a key aspect of self-disclosure is avoidance of triggering the social rank motive. If this motive is active the patient may react with shame: '*She was able to overcome a problem that I'm stuck in*', or with anger, '*So you did great. So what? How is this helpful to me?*' In order to avoid such problems, self-disclosure must be carefully made distinct from *modelling*, with the latter aimed at problem-solving. It is important to note that modelling can be used but only when the patient is accepting himself, and the risk that the therapist's solution yield self-derogation or passive imitation are minimal. A signal that suggests modelling is appropriate may be the patient stating, '*I understand the reasons for my suffering and that I could not do anything different then. But what can I do now? What would you do if you were in my shoes?*' In this scenario, the patient has already become aware of his own maladaptive schemas and has acquired some degree of differentiation which allowed him to ask for advice without questioning his own personal worth. In such advanced conditions the therapist can describe her own past experience in order to share her personal solution, without pretending that it is universal or the wisest thing to do. The therapist must not think of herself as an example of virtue, but as a unique human subject who found her own personal way to deal with the difficulties of life in the very same way the patient is doing. The therapist must stress that the ultimate goal of self-disclosure is inviting the patient to explore different avenues and find a solution that fits with his personality.

The overarching question is not to self-disclose or not, but whether the therapist's skill is sufficient enough to track the consequences of the disclosure and then adjust the intervention according to the patient's reactions (Safran and Muran, 2000). For example, a self-disclosure may trigger further self-criticism so that the patient states: '*You suffered but it is clear you were able to move on. I'm too stupid, and so I'm stuck in my failures.*' In such cases the therapist must swiftly ask the patient how the self-disclosure increased his self-derogation and then insist that the goal was not to show the patient how she overcame the problem, but to communicate that she has been in similar dark waters and that she can understand how the patient feels. The patient's self-criticism should then become the new focus of the session.

Overall, operations of validation, self-disclosure and the capacity to formulate any intervention starting from a focus on the patient's wish, are part of the fundamental therapy skill of empathy (Kohut, 1971), which is the capacity to see the world with the eyes of the others, resonate with them, and make people feel understood and accepted.

Promoting access to positive elements in the therapy conversation

MIT shares a similar assumption of positive emotions psychology (Frederickson, 2001) and emotion focused therapy (Greenberg, 2002). This assumption indicates that it is important not only to promote change in the direction that goes from cognition to emotion, but also from emotion to cognition so that affect-dependent cognition changes. It is well-known that affects influence ideas in an emotion-coherent way. For example, depressed people will think depressive thoughts, angry people will look for evidence to support their anger and happy people with see the world through a rosy lens (Bower, 1981; Forgas, 2002; Johnson-Laird, Mancini and Gangemi, 2006). Helping the patient access positive states interrupts the vicious affective-cognitive chains and promotes access to more benevolent views of the self and others. This perception helps the patient search for more adaptive coping strategies and foster the belief of having resources and strengths at the patient's disposal.

The first way to evoke positive emotions is the one just mentioned, that is talking about themes of shared interest. Another modality is based on the therapist's awareness of and readiness to identify any shift in the state of mind of the patient. The majority of patients with PD, with the exception of the most severe and socially isolated, hold positive memories but are unable to retrieve them. Steering the conversation toward the details of the narrative episodes will allow the patient to recall moments of well-being, activity, energy, positive self-esteem, curiosity, humour, lightheartedness, social play and self-efficacy. Once such a shift happens the clinician should immediately notice it and bring the positive state to the patient's awareness. The key idea of this intervention is for the therapist to attempt to keep the patient's mind dwelling on the positive state for as long as possible.

Thanks to the strategies of sharing and accessing positive states, the quality of the therapy relationship is more likely to remain intact and any occurring problems are overcome more easily. The patient will build and then retrieve a set of good memories of time spent together and acknowledge that this relation, if not overly positive, is at least better than everyday relationships that are filled with conflicts.

Metacommunication

In MIT the therapist cultivates the art of talking about the therapy relationship with the patient, reasoning together about what happens and, in short, metacommunicating (Safran and Muran, 2000). Metacommunication starts as early as session one or two, and is the default mode of MIT therapists. As soon as the therapist notices signs of maladaptive interpersonal schemas active in the transference, or just senses a minimally problematic relational atmosphere, he invites the patient to freely talk about what is happening. In a typical intervention the therapist may say: '*It is important that you feel comfortable to talk about anything you feel is not working in our meetings. If you think I am not understanding or that I am disrespectful or neglecting please tell me. It will help me better understand what I am doing wrong and correct my actions, and it will allow us to talk about any problems more easily.*' This encourages the patient to have a freedom of expression, and emotions and cognitions such as shame, fear of criticism, fear of hurting the therapist by expressing dissatisfaction, hostility or complaining to be reduced to the minimum.

If the therapist has identified the maladaptive schema from the patient's narratives and foresees that the schema will likely colonise the therapy relationship (i.e. identifying that the patient is feeling fear or rejected due to talking in a low voice and avoiding making eye contact) the therapist can say: '*You are driven by the idea that if you seek appreciation others will criticise you. It is possible that during our sessions you feel criticised by me, both if I actually criticise you even if not on purpose, or if I did not but you still perceive me as doing so. If that happens, please tell me, because if that is the case I am not helping you in that moment. If instead you verbalise the problem, I may reason and understand that I may have been being critical, and then correct my action and learn from my mishap. I can also explain my intentions so that we can understand that I did not mean to harm you, and hopefully you will feel less hurt and feel accepted again.*' These interventions are particularly helpful in reducing the toxicity of schemas in the areas of, for example, mistrust, criticism, hopelessness or rejection. These ideas are less poisonous if they become an object of discourse instead of a force driving from underneath.

Another aspect of metacommunication is inviting the patient to explore the therapist's mind. Many patients with PD have developmental histories in which talking about the mind of caregivers was risky. Relatives who were harsh, distant, depressed, violent, abusing or easily hurt and offended by any comment have taught the patient that reflecting on the other's mind is dangerous. During the therapy, therefore, the patient faces a mind that he has to depend on, but that generates anguish. The process of exploring minds ranges to the impossible as those are eerie and uncanny places. Therapists in MIT often invite the patient to formulate

Giulia sent her therapist an e-mail alluding to something not being right in their relationship. As we shall see, the patient had followed the therapist's suggestion that she speak openly about how she felt about the relationship with him: '*I wanted to tell you something about our therapy. Do you remember when you asked me to declare any doubts or perplexities? My doubt is this. In fact, not a doubt but more an unease. The patient–doctor relationship is – how can I say this? – a bit asymmetric. With the patient telling sharing things that sometimes he doesn't even say to himself, and the doctor's muteness about his personal things, it's a naturally an unavoidable schema. But for me it creates (irrationally, of course) a subtle sense of non-reciprocity.*'

Towards the end of the next session the therapist went back to the question:

T: Listen, Giulia, before saying goodbye … I wanted to go back to that e-mail because it's very important to me that you pointed out that our talks are unbalanced, in the sense that we talk only about Giulia. I've thought a lot about this and I'm very glad you told me that and … but what's your impression about this disparity?

P: In my opinion, it's a topic that has a lot to do with the fact that I'm following a course of treatment with a person, let's say …

T: … who takes care of you.

P: Exactly! I can't do anything for you. Here and now you're fine.

T: [*laughs*]

P: Everything OK?

T: [*laughs*] Everything is fantastic! It is precisely this asymmetry in the sense that it's me who has to take care of you.

P: Yes! For me it's a problem!

T: [*laughs*]

P: I don't know. If, by chance, one day you didn't feel well, tell me.

T: [*ironically*] Today I have to say I'm a bit tired. I'm suffering a bit because I didn't sleep well.

P: [*Giulia's expression changes and relaxes, and her face lights up*] That's better! This would make me feel much more at ease!

T: [*laughs*] Yes, that's right.

P: [*laughs*] Can I give you a few words of advice?

T: In this exchange of ours there's something I was expecting … that is, that occupying the position of someone who accepts care from others, with another person taking care of Giulia … is a role in life that you've always found uncomfortable to play, isn't it? Here it's as if you felt the impulse to …

P: Yes, it's precisely as if I didn't have an interlocutor [*meaning a person to take care of*] who for me is the only one possible

T: You know what's the best thing about this? It was enough for us to talk just jokingly about the possibility of you providing me with care and your expression changed! You're smiling, you're relaxed, you have more colour in your cheeks … it's a miracle!

The therapist continued by explaining that, in general, psychotherapy is a physiologically asymmetric relationship, with the therapist more likely to take care of the patient than the reverse. However, the therapist said that as they increasingly got to know each other it would be easier for him to be open and tell her something about himself so that the relationship would become more equal. He then continued by pointing out that, thanks to the fact that Giulia had freely expressed her problem about not being able to provide care to the therapist and having to reveal intimate parts of herself to the therapist in order to receive care, their relationship had taken on an amusing and relaxed tone. Giulia responded with an increased ability to identify her schema, as well as motivation to work on it:

P: I repeat, in reality after writing you I thought about it too. It's better for me to have to get used to something that's alien to me, I mean allowing someone, a doctor, to devote himself to me.
T: [laughs] But slowly, slowly!
P: Yes, it's difficult!
T: I reckon it's probably the biggest difficulty you will have on this journey. However, it's great that you've pinpointed it immediately and were able to talk about it openly.
P: I realise that this therapy is putting me on a particular track … the good thing is that I thought psychotherapy would be a weird experience. I imagined it could become a sort of brooding, but I've realised it's not at all like that. Things get solved without me using my head. So there's some existential, vital channel that gets opened up … it's bringing me serenity.

The therapist concluded this sequence by revealing to Giulia that he had received psychotherapy and therefore knew the difficulty of finding oneself in that position and displaying one's vulnerabilities. The therapist shared this experience in an attempt to validate the work she was doing to be more open and overcome her embarrassment. Later in the therapy it appeared that Giulia was driven by memories where the caregiver figure abandoned her (her father) or criticised her, and did not respect her independence (her mother), which made it risky to put herself in the position of being cared for.

ideas about what he is experiencing, especially during moment of alliance ruptures. The therapist may state, '*What do you believe I am thinking right now? I'll do my best to help you understand what is actually passing through my mind.*' *If the patient fears abandonment the therapist can say, 'You thought I wanted to dump you. I don't understand why I should, but please help me guess what I may have thought that would lead me to desire to interrupt the therapy together.*'

Another action the therapist continuously performs, sometimes more than once in the same session, is to ask for feedback after an intervention. This way the therapist can constantly monitor the impact of her observations and can utilise optimal moments to identify, discuss and try to solve relational problems.

Metacommunication makes alliance ruptures weaker. It also helps to create a safe environment in which both schema-dependent patterns and schema-discrepant thoughts and feelings surface. Actually, after an effective metacommunication, the patient often relaxes and changes expression and emotional tone. The therapist can readily remark, '*In this moment we once again created a good atmosphere. This means you have the capacity to feel comfortable in a relationship filled with mutual understanding.*' This helps the patient discover previously unnoticed relational capacities.

Metacommunication is key to repairing relational ruptures, as well as finding a way out of pathological interpersonal cycles. The therapist first reads the typical markers of alliance ruptures, such as *withdrawal* – the patients disengages herself from the therapist – and *confrontation* – the patient is critical and negative about the therapist. At that point the therapist opens her mind about what is happening in session and invites the patient in a joint reflection about the process. The therapist places herself as an active part of the process and does not put the burden of responsibility fully on the patient's shoulders. She notes that a problem is present by stating, '*It is like we were competing with each other*' or '*Today is more difficult to understand each other. Is there something different that I can do?*' A next step is another kind of self-disclosure, that is a tactful description of thoughts and feelings directed toward the patient in the here and now.

If the therapist chooses to implement this intervention it is necessary that he carefully weigh the risk of making the patient feel blamed, criticised or like they are the sole cause of the problem. Self-disclosing about feelings and thoughts related to the patient is a thorny and sensitive operation requiring the patient to feel both involved in the cycle and free from the relational dynamics. The therapist must first regulate her own emotions so that what the patient experiences is not the problematic emotion, but the *description* of that emotion. Also relevant is what the therapist decides to reveal. We suggest that the therapist carefully evaluate her inner states until she is able to access primary negative emotions and not those pertaining to the coping processes. In particular we advise therapists not to disclose anger, even in mild forms such as irritation. The antecedents of anger are more helpful when brought into the communication. Therapists, like all human beings, get angry because they feel rejected, criticised, misunderstood, challenged or frustrated, which makes them feel fragile, incompetent, impotent, inadequate or vulnerable. These primary feelings can be carefully disclosed. For example, a typical intervention that is useful with patients possessing passive-aggressive features may sound like this: '*Look, I am doing my best, I am digging into my therapeutic resources and skills, but today I feel like I cannot be effective. It is like everything I do is ineffective and I am not able to give you anything useful. I acknowledge that it is frustrating to you, but it is important that I tell you about it. If I continue to try to find solutions to your problems that you end up not liking I wouldn't be helpful and my frustration would continue to mount. How do you feel about that? What do you think?*' From such a stance of open impotence, the therapist can become aware that she is not entirely responsible for the effectiveness of the therapy but that it is instead shared. If such a metacommunication is disclosed without resentment or criticism it will likely break a crystallised pattern in which the patient asks for care, but expects that the caregiver will then control and oppress, which leads the patient to consequently react by rebelling against the tyrant instead of accepting help. The therapist reacts automatically by trying to be helpful but instead is faced with another who is critical, angry and at times spiteful, which can lead to a sense of invalidation and then anger at not being valued for his therapeutic efforts.

We emphasise that it is of the utmost importance that the patient is invited to openly talk about any negative feelings toward the therapist. Of course, this does not mean authorising the patient to violate the boundaries, for example insulting the therapist, threatening her, despising her, refusing to pay the fee or interacting in a sarcastic or seductive manner. For example, the patient may state, '*All I want to do is go to bed with you. I don't understand why you don't accept this as the solution.*' If the patient refuses to respect the therapist after she gently invites the patient not to pursue this path, she should then redefine the boundaries by stating, '*I am sorry, but if you keep insulting me I cannot work with you. You have the right to think and communicate that I am not worthy, but if that is the case I will not be your therapist. If you find a way to express dissatisfaction in a different and more respectful manner, I am open to reflecting together about what is happening.*'

Relationship as a source of information

The therapist draws information from the therapy relationship in order to foster awareness of schemas. A key factor of change in patients with PD is the awareness of being driven by maladaptive interpersonal schemas (see Chapters 6 and 7). Therefore, the therapy relationship is a vantage point from which to observe maladaptive schemas in action (Freud, 1912; Luborsky and Crits-Christoph, 1990).

Bringing to the patient's attention how she is constructing the therapist in conformity to maladaptive schemas can be of great usefulness in promoting awareness of such schemas. This type of intervention must be performed with prudence and an open empirical stance, and the therapist must clearly understand that he is formulating a hypothesis which can be changed according to the patient's reaction or new evidence. The hypothesis about the pattern of transference can only be formulated out of vicious interpersonal cycles, in the absence of alliance ruptures or after they have been detected and repaired. For example, a patient says that she felt criticised by the therapist, which does not surprise the therapist due to previously detecting a schema, thanks to the analysis of narrative episodes, in which the patient is driven by a need for approval At this point the therapist must first promote differentiation until the patient feels safe and does not feel criticised by the therapist. Once the patient is relaxed and the schema is not active anymore, the therapist can suggest that the expectation of being criticised was schema-driven while the truth is that the therapist is benevolent.

It is important to be as precise as possible when matching everyday life episodes with therapist–patient events. The therapist may state, '*I guess the fact that you did not tell me that my decision to change our schedule was a problem for you is similar to moments in which you were unable to say "no" to your colleague who asked to use the job you did for his own personal interest. In both situations you put the other's interest before yours, avoiding any discussion because of your fear of hurting the other. But then you end up feeling angry and depressed. What do you think?'*

With such a formulation the patient can reflect on her own schema, provide feedback and correct it. We remember that in this moment the focus is not on healing the relationship, because it has already been restored, but gathering information from the relationship in order to enrich the shared formulation of the patient's functioning. It is therefore an intervention aimed at improving self-reflection, in particular awareness of the schema. We will describe this process in greater detail in Chapter 6. An example extracted from the therapy with Giulia helps us to better understand this process:

> Giulia repeatedly asked for appointments to be changed or for in-person sessions to be replaced by ones on the telephone and often arrived late. The therapist first examined his own reactions due to feeling irritated, neglected and manipulated by this elusive patient, and felt obligated to go along with her suggestions in the hope of pleasing her and maintaining the relationship. He had an inner drive to react by reproaching her and asking her to be more punctual and precise. He avoided enacting these tendencies and at the same time he asked himself if it was useful for the patient to become aware of how such behaviour was hampering her treatment. He deduced that simply ignoring the problem and granting Giulia the changes in appointments would leave her pathogenic schema of avoiding intimacy active in her transference and untouched.
>
> At that moment Giulia started a new love story, the relationship with her husband being in profound crisis. She described her lover as being in love with her and keen, right from the start, on making their relationship the only one she had. Giulia appeared frightened; she feared harming her family and her son, and felt guilty about indulging in these fantasies. Moreover, she had not made any decisions; she was in love with her lover but felt that any action would be premature. Vis-à-vis her lover's insistence she used semi-automatic defensive strategies by arriving to appointments late or avoiding them, and if she could not, she felt constrained.
>
> The therapist first validated her need for safety and a protective distance. Then he asked her to explore her associated memories (see Chapter 6), which included narratives of being courted, yet she attached no importance to the other's love or did not even notice it. She realised that she had never been attracted to men who sought her. She even felt that her marital relationship was constrictive and she had wanted to get out of it for years.
>
> The therapist advanced the idea that at the moment at which she obtained the intimacy she wished for she suddenly swung to a need for independence with the idea the other could be harshly critical and controlling. She then reacted by withdrawing from the relationship in order to regain her freedom. Giulia could see herself entirely in this reformulation of her schema.

At this point the therapist, on the basis of these agreed observations, noted that these tendencies were active in the therapeutic relationship too. In an ironic atmosphere Giulia and the therapist agreed that in therapy Giulia did everything possible to organise her appointments so that she did not feel obligated to always be present on the same day at the same time. The therapist openly declared that for him it was especially important not to make Giulia feel constricted but, at the same time, he felt that it was time to consider this pattern to be part of the problems to be tackled. Giulia agreed and the two of them began to negotiate the idea that in the future the therapist would be less often willing to change appointments or replace them with ones on the telephone. In the following sessions memories emerged of Giulia's mother always imposing her point of view and considering Giulia's worthless, and where only after signing up for university had the latter begun to make choices she felt to be her own when faced with her mother's disapproval. Her tendency to see the other as constrictive and tyrannical, and then to flee without confronting him/her openly, perhaps rooted in the relationship with her mother, thus appeared.

Conclusions

We showed how in MIT any moment of the therapy process happens in the context of the therapy relationship. Operations such as sharing, self-disclosure, promoting a positive atmosphere, preventing and repairing alliance ruptures and metacommunication permeate the session. In any moment the therapist swiftly shifts from improving metacognitive skills, fostering awareness of schemas, promoting change and treating symptoms, to a focus on the therapy relationship. In this process the relationship becomes a privileged source of knowledge about the patient's schemas, which is an intersubjective space where it is safer and easier to talk about mental states and a place to build new forms of relating in which maladaptive schemas are switched off while new and healthy ones are created. Most importantly, it is a place where communicating and understanding each other is easier than in daily life.

Chapter 6

Shared formulation of functioning

Enriching autobiographical memory, improving access to inner states and reconstructing schemas

Eliciting autobiographical memories

As part of a shared formulation of functioning, the first operation to be undertaken in MIT is to trace any mental states identifiable in patients' autobiographical memories (Dimaggio, Salvatore, Fiore et al., 2012). A therapist should be careful to avoid focusing the conversation on the abstract ideas, intellectualisations or generalised statements the patient brings. This must begin in the first appointment and autobiographical episodes should be encouraged continuously.

The only operations to be undertaken are seeking an optimal therapeutic relationship (see Chapter 5) and treating symptoms with strategies suited to the patient's metacognitive skills (see Chapter 10). This should continue until the therapist has gathered sufficiently clear and detailed narrative episodes and identified the dominant affects and thoughts. The therapist should avoid other operations aiming at change, such as encouraging a critical distance or trying more adaptive forms of functioning.

To elaborate, a patient says that she lives with a chronic sense of humiliation due to perceiving others as disrespectful. The therapist asks for more specific examples of when this has happened. In this case, the therapist could ask: *'Can you describe a situation in which someone made you feel humiliated?'* The therapist then explores the issue in greater detail by asking a question such as: *'Can you remember a precise moment in your day that would help me to better understand what happened?'* The therapist further inquires on the issue of humiliation by asking, *'Can you tell me about a situation in which you felt strongly humiliated? What happened to make you feel this way? When did it occur? Where were you? Who were you with? Did you communicate your humiliation to this person? How did you feel when you spoke?'* (Angus and McLeod, 2004; Hermans and Dimaggio, 2004; Luborsky and Crits-Christoph, 1990; Neimeyer, 2000). The patient's description of the environment can sometimes be very useful and at other times superfluous. The therapist should not merely obtain a story but also evoke emotions consistent with the recalled memories. Further discussion of stimulating emotional experiences will be addressed later.

The therapist should provide the patient with an explicit rationale for why it is necessary to evoke specific narrative episodes. The therapist should further explain that his aim is to better understand the patient and the patient's behaviours and develop a therapeutic relationship. The therapist should gently dissuade the patient from engaging in impersonal formulations (e.g. 'it was said that') in favour of the first or third person (e.g. 'He said that')

Many therapists fear that asking for specific episodes and thus stopping the flow of intellectualising and generalising can make a patient feel nervous, frustrated or as if the therapist is being intrusive. However, we believe that asking for examples in the form of narrative episodes is safe and leads a patient to believe that the therapist genuinely wants to understand, especially if the therapist has correctly outlined the rationale. If the patient displays evidence of withdrawal or becoming irritated, the therapist can switch the task to reflecting on how the patient feels when the therapist asks for more details. This simply refocuses the topic on the therapeutic relationship using metacommunication strategies (see Chapter 5).

Our experience using these strategies has been overwhelmingly positive. In some instances, patients who tend to intellectualise during MIT sessions eventually realise of their own accord that they are being abstract and will jokingly ask the therapist, '*You want me to give you an example now, don't you?*' Usually a therapist replies with a smile: '*Exactly!*'

Let us look at an example of how a therapist, noting an intellectualising narrative style, uses a cooperative attitude to point out to the patient that it is a problem:

Giulia was 34 years old and applied to our clinic because she was having difficulties with her partner. She lived with him and their five-year-old son and worked as a journalist. She had never before undertaken a course of psychotherapy. She described herself as '*intellectually active, anxious, generous, bossy, a bit pushy, sensitive and flexible*' and acknowledged that others called her '*tyrannical*'. She suffered from passive-aggressive disorder, had a below-threshold obsessive-compulsive disorder and narcissistic and dependent traits. She had a generalised anxiety disorder and hypochondria.

In session 1 the therapist noted her intellectualising style and made a continuous attempt to switch from abstract ideas to specific memories.

P: Let's say this year has been a strange one because in a certain sense it's been a year when I've had a crisis with my partner ... It's as if the lid had been taken off Pandora's box. With that off, so much came out ... perhaps because of this crisis with my partner too I've lived much more time out of the home than in it ... This is my way of reacting to things. If I've got problems with him, I try to intensify my relations with the friends of mine I get on well with ... or else I got myself another nice, self-gratifying situation I don't know how and so ...

T: Sorry, in what sense?

P: I've had this relationship that we can say still ...

T: Giulia, you have to excuse me if my tone seems mocking.

P: Of course, why not?

T: However, a situation … how did you say? A 'self-gratifying external situation'! Does that mean you've got an extramarital relationship?

P: [*smiles*] Yes, but I wallow in words! Let's say even more than one! But to tell you …

T: Which we now define as self-gratifying external situations! [*smiles*]

P: I don't know. You can use it too! [*smiles*]

T: I see, we've coined a new definition! But this does you credit, Giulia, with your work as a journalist.

Straight afterwards the therapist started to pose Giulia some specific questions, to which she gradually managed to reply.

A therapist tries to draw out the details of a narrative episode until all his questions – *Where? When? Who? What? What did you say to each other?* – have been adequately answered, to the extent that this is possible. To then access the cognitive-affective processes that led to the patient's problematic relationships and suffering the therapist asks: '*What did you feel and think at that moment? Can you remember what drove you to act like that?*'

In the following example we show how the therapist and patient can move from intellectualising to a specific narrative episode.

Arturo is the patient with paranoid and narcissistic traits previously described in Chapter 5. His therapist was afraid he might become violent towards others and there were moments when she feared for herself because she could sense his angry tension. However, his emotions did not surface spontaneously in his discourse. Therapy started with encouraging him to narrate episodes, through which it was then possible to explore his inner experience. Here is an extract from session 4:

P: It's as if that something that makes me want to act doesn't get triggered. I don't feel motivated to do it.

T: Help me understand this state of lack of motivation. What do you feel?

P: (*silence*) Hum, even I don't know. [*silence*] I don't know what to say because I've already tried [*to keep to a plan on his own*] and I mess up. I always go adrift at the end. I can't seem to keep to, to manage a programme, because I think there's no real goal.

T: Can you give me an example of a goal?

P: My boss gives me a job to do and so I know that it's that to be done and I get down to it. At the end of the day I have trouble giving myself an order, when there isn't one, because I'm left there to do sweet nothing.

> T: This is something new: having trouble giving oneself an order when the order doesn't come from outside. It's the first time you've said that. And this having trouble is as if it produced that sensation of being unmotivated, right?
>
> P: Yes. [*silence*]
>
> T: There's only that emotion or is there something else? When you realise you feel this thing, what do you experience?
>
> P: I couldn't say ... perhaps because I'm tired [*laughs*]
>
> T: What do you feel at this moment?
>
> P: Now that I'm talking about it, I feel this sense of lack of motivation, the usual work problem I have, which I can't manage to ... In a word I can't find a solution.
>
> T: In fact we find ourselves inside a problem that you don't have the power to solve, inside your firm, because it doesn't depend on you, but all this has some emotional consequences inside you. Can we find a specific moment during this week at which you managed to feel this thing more strongly?
>
> P: Probably Friday.
>
> T: When? Please, describe the moment and place to me exactly.
>
> P: A bit throughout the day and then it increased in the afternoon. At the end I was there doing sweet nothing and I could see that my colleagues were there talking about their work and I was saying to myself: 'What the hell am I doing here listening to this lot talking about what *they* have to do?'
>
> T: Was there one moment more difficult than the others?
>
> P: Yes. In the afternoon, towards two o'clock ...
>
> T: And where were you? ...
>
> P: In the office at my desk.
>
> T: And what were you doing?
>
> P: I was probably surfing at random on the Internet.
>
> We shall see later how, based on this scene, well-defined in terms of space and time, it became possible for the patient to access his emotions.

At the start of the session the patient was unable to access his inner state and could not provide a narrative, making it impossible to identify his inner experiences. As soon as a few narrative fragments appeared that were centred on his loss of motivation the therapist started to ask questions aimed at better understanding his inner state, i.e. she switched to working on metacognitive monitoring.

The collecting of narratives and knowledge of mental states are, for conceptual clarity, described as separate parts of the procedure but in fact they occur together and at the same time (see Figure 6.1). During the reconstruction of a story, the therapist should be posing questions about mental states. During the emergence of subjective experience, the therapist should be adding to the collection of episodes in which the patient experienced emotions.

In fact, the reactivation of autobiographical memory and improvement of metacognition are synergic processes. Clinical observations (see in particular Dimaggio,

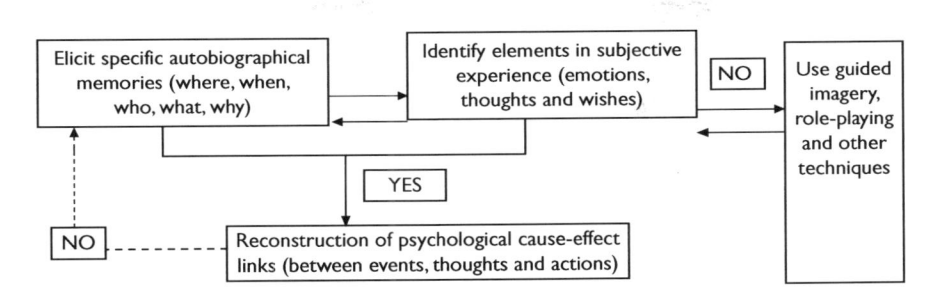

Figure 6.1 Promoting autobiographical memory and metacognitive monitoring.

Salvatore, Popolo et al., 2012), research on cognitive science (Ciaramelli, Bernardi and Moscovitch, 2013) and *neuroimaging* (Spreng and Grady, 2010; Spreng and Mar, 2012; Rabin and Rosenbaum, 2012; Whitehead, Marchant, Craik et al., 2009) show that there are neural links between brain areas underlying autobiographical memory and those devoted to metacognitive processes. This means that activating autobiographical memory 'switches on' mentalisation and vice versa.

Some PD patients need to be encouraged to switch from intellectualising and abstract concepts to autobiographical narratives throughout therapy, while others are better at it and overcome the problem after a few sessions. With some patients the problem is not only their intellectualising narrative style, but also a sincere lack of memories. In these cases the work consists in a true and proper rehabilitation of autobiographical memory. Instead of asking patients to recall memories from the past, the therapist should focus their attention on precise moments in the week following the session, i.e. *'In the days to come, try and pay attention to when you notice something that upsets you, specifically a problem that creates tension for you. Try to note what happened immediately before. Who were you with? What happened? Then let's try and recall this in the next session. It doesn't matter how much you recall or if we can see the link between the episode and what you felt. We can look into that together.'* Therefore, more than recalling the past, the patient is focused on attending to future events. Many patients gradually improve their ability to talk about themselves, after a bit of exercise. The therapist can promote improvement by the use of diaries and memos and encouraging the patient to focus attention on moments in which they feel there is something wrong. By relating these experiences in session, it builds upon the patient's ability to relate to the chronicle of their life, as opposed to merely commentating on it.

Improving monitoring: access to subjective experience

Narrative episodes are the terrain in which to search for subjective experience, but with some patients their difficulties in narrating are so severe that their subjective experience cannot be located in episodes from the past or between sessions, but rather in the flow of conversation during therapy. A therapist should start by showing interest in the contents of a patient's discourse, no matter how abstract it is, and try to get involved in the conversation. For example, a therapist could say, '*I'm very curious to hear what you think about contemporary architecture in our country*', or '*So you're a cinema lover. Tell me about the last film you enjoyed?*' During the flow of conversation a patient will display fluctuations in his emotional state and the therapist and patient should try to give these a name (i.e. '*It seems to me that while you were telling me about that building they've constructed you were irritated, almost angry, as if this hurt you personally, is that right?*' Once an emotion has been defined, it can be the key to evoking narrative episodes. For example, '*Can you recall any episodes in which someone intentionally did something that hurt you or stopped you from carrying out something you believed in?*'

Paying attention to a patient's non-verbal behaviour is critical. A therapist should consider expressive markers such as facial expressions, posture and tone of voice, which serve as clues for making hypotheses about underlying experience. The intervention could be, '*While you were telling me about spending the day on your own, you lowered your gaze, your voice almost cracked and I think you looked sad. Is that possible?*'

Therapists should be careful to avoid asking questions such as '*Why* did you act like that?' This question, often used in standard CBT, is not productive with PDs because it activates the semantic mode of reasoning. The *downward arrow technique* also should not be used at this stage because we are not trying to understand the logical, semantic reasoning leading to a particular action; this would again give communication an abstract, theoretical and rationalised form and remove the possibility of reconstructing the cognitive/affective processes.

Another access route to inner experience, again based on taking note of expressive behaviour, is through the collecting and pointing out of discrepancies between the behaviour manifested by a patient and the emotion he says he feels. For example, a patient might assert: '*I left and slammed the door*' but reply that he felt '*calm*'. In cases in which the affect and behaviour are incongruous, a therapist could intervene by pointing out the discrepancy non-judgementally. For example, '*So you're telling me that you left and slammed the door and you were evidently stirred by something, but then you say you were calm. I'm not able to fully understand. It seems to me there's something missing. Usually if we slam the door it's because we're angry and hurt. Is it possible you were driven by distress or anger?*'

A therapist should be cautious in proffering hypotheses about what emotions a patient might have felt and always ask for feedback. The therapist should always start with open questions, and only formulate hypotheses for the patient if the patient proves unable to describe his inner world, i.e. '*Is that really what you felt?*' '*Have I managed to grasp your inner world correctly?*' '*Do you feel my idea corresponds to what you feel and think?*'

If a patient is incapable of describing his mental states then the therapist can resort to a number of possibilities. First, the therapist can ask explicit suggestions like *'Is it possible you felt this?'* Second, the therapist could use their own mind as a model, i.e. *'If I had been in your shoes, I'd have felt this. Is it possible that you felt it?'* Third, if there is a pervasive problem with identifying emotions, some psycho-education in emotions can be useful. For example, a therapist can give a patient a list of emotions (see Basic Emotion List, Linehan, 1993) or the list of mental states typical of PD patients (Chapter 1) and ask him if he recognises any of the experiences listed as his own.

In the third session with Giulia her intellectualising style reappeared together with difficulty in describing her feelings and thoughts. The episode concerned anonymous phone calls she had received:

P: I reckon his girlfriend called me. There was this call with insults from his girlfriend, anonymous by the way, wasn't there? It was then that I started to take my distance [*from her lover*] and it was then that a crack opened up as it were. [*It will be clear later that this is between her and her lover.*]

T: How did you feel at that moment?

P: Very uneasy, very annoyed.

T: What do 'uneasy' and 'annoyed' mean? What emotions are they, Giulia?

P: At one moment fright, because in any case the nature of an anonymous phone call ... and then there wasn't just one call but a day full of calls.

T: Really? So fear, then?

P: Yes, fear. Let's say encroaching on a private space ... and then also a bit of intellectual contempt for the couple as a whole because in a certain sense they're a couple of intellectuals?

T: Contempt? By Giulia towards ...?

P: Caricature intellectuals because at the end of the day it's always the woman who's a whore and a man never has any responsibilities. It's easier for a woman to attack a woman than solve the problems with her partner ...

Giulia was talking in a theorising fashion. The therapist had difficulty grasping that she was accusing her lover's partner of attacking her instead of her partner because she was driven by the stereotype in which the cause of unfaithfulness is the woman. Her tendency to intellectualise continued strongly:

P: And so ... that's when I understood this aptitude of his for denying reality so that, and it's the same denial he uses when faced with a situation that is objectively unsustainable, because it's not getting infatuated for one evening that is compatible with your normal life. It's another love affair going on at the same time! I ... I'm not physically suited to bearing this stress caused by lies.

T: I haven't understood what 'denial' means.

P: From the phone call onwards I saw that it was as if he wasn't admitting the objective problems to himself ... the anxiety that he too undergoes from such a situation. He makes it sound easy, let's say. But feigning because in reality he's nervous, anxious and despairing when she leaves. It's more, how can I say, an artificial lack of worries than a real one, there you are ... and so from that point onwards it started diminishing to an ever greater extent.

T: You'll have to excuse me, Giulia.

P: Yes, yes, sorry. Perhaps it's difficult. Perhaps I'm making it more complicated because it's mixed up for me too.

T: Giulia ... You're very intelligent and you also make a refined use of reasoning ... I instead need to understand how you experience this ... because, otherwise, I'm not really in contact with Giulia, so that when I don't understand, I, a bit obsessively, ask you these questions ... in what way does he ... has he got a Christian name [*ironic*]?

P: Francesco.

T: In what way do Francesco, the things he does, the way in which he finds himself in this affair with Giulia give her a set of sensations leading her to ask herself: 'What am I doing here?' and to back off?

P: A bit of disappointment.

T: Disappointment, okay. A moment at which he does or says something that disappoints you.

P: The moment of the phone call.

T: From his partner?

P: From his partner, yes.

T: You feel disappointed by Francesco then.

P: Yes.

T: What leads you to be disappointed by him?

P: ... For him intellectually it must be unacceptable to think that his partner behaves in such a bestial manner, mustn't it? ... I reckon they talked about it and she denied it. But in a sort of game – how can I say? – a pre-established plot, he says 'You haven't by any chance telephoned?' and she says 'Are you crazy? I don't do such things'.

T: So at a certain point Francesco says, that is Giulia asks Francesco 'Francesco, sorry but have you spoken with your partner about this phone call she made?' He talks to her and says 'Yes, Giulia, I've spoken about it and ...?'

P: And she says it wasn't her.

T: And she says it wasn't her! At that point how did you react?

P: For a while I really backed off.

T: From Francesco?

P: Yes.

T: When you backed off you what were you driven by?

P: A tinge of disappointment in him.

T: So what is it that disappoints you about Francesco? I'd really like to understand the link between actions and disappointment.

P: The attempt to solve the question soothingly, which is by the way typical of so many men. This looking for me [*she means that Francesco looks for her*], but not as a specific striving towards me but as a despair-stopper.

T: Did you feel almost like a sort of treatment tool?

P: Exactly!

T: The real problem is not me. I mean it's not that you're concerned about me. It's that you're suffering because of her and want a bit of attention.

P: Yes, yes, so this …

T: Hum … Can you place it for me, Giulia? An example in which you had difficulty in …

P: Last night! These exchanges last night.

T: Can you tell me what you said to each other? The text messages?

P: I'll reconstruct exactly how it went, then.

T: Yes!

P: As banally as possible.

T: Absolutely!

P: … Well, we didn't speak on Monday and then yesterday evening I get this message in which he tells me it's been a rather tough day because of my not being present. Silvia [*Francesco's partner*] has come back, they've had a pleasant day together … however he tells me: 'I've been missing you very much' … I told him: 'I've suffered a lot because of your drama. I'm happy to hear you relieved.' He says: 'I'm not relieved. I'm still in despair about you leaving me' … And that's where we start arguing. I say: 'But how can you still think I can leave you?' …

T: But listen, Giulia, when you saw Francesco in despair when his partner wasn't there, how did you feel at that moment?

P: Uh, let's say … it's as if I had … You know the terminology they use for ratings? [laughs] His love was rated Triple A … At that point there was a down-rating!

T: You down-rated the value of his declarations of love!

P: To put it in a nutshell! [*laughs*]

T: [*laughs*] It's a very cute idea! Declarations of love not worth anything.

P: Exactly!

T: Like Greek government bonds!

P: And so I was saying to him: how can you now feel so bad about it again …

T: I'm thinking, Giulia … In this down-rating were there also your emotions of the feeling neglected, dropped, put in the background type?

P: Yes, yes … let's say that disorientation and then that looking for me in a rather shabby way, do you see? Yes, yes they for sure stimulated a part in which it gnaws at me and I let it be seen!

T: So, you felt neglected, put in the background, taken for granted and you got angry and said to him: 'Listen, baby, what do you want?'

P: Correct.

T: I was missing the emotional part, Giulia, where you were getting riled because you'd been …

P: You're clever because you can see my omissions!

At the end of this complex sequence Giulia was stimulated by the therapist's continuous questioning and managed to reconstruct the details of the episode, so that it was finally possible to understand that Giulia felt abandoned and neglected in favour of a rival and was as a consequence angry, something impossible to deduce at the start.

The goal of promoting monitoring is not only a cognitive awareness of one's inner world, but also an increase in affectivity (Pascual-Leone and Greenberg, 2007), especially if over-modulated. One of the main markers of therapeutic change is a within session variation in mental state (Dimaggio, Semerari, Carcione et al., 2007), but we can only talk of a true response to an intervention if a patient's affect changes as well. Often, instead, patients agree with their therapist but their affect remains the same. In such cases, a therapist can point out and draw attention to the discrepancy between a patient's description and what the patient experiences during sessions. There are several techniques available for increasing the emotional intensity of subjective experience in sessions.

A therapist can emotionally take part in the patient's place by saying something like, '*If I'd been you I'd have been very sad*', '*Is it possible you didn't get angry?*' An effective therapist is not only precise, careful and exact in his reconstructions but is also able to be present in the therapy room. Patients accept many of their therapist's observations if the therapist participates in the flesh and is able to transmit the sense of what he says and does fervently, passionately and incisively. In other words, interventions are more effective if a therapist makes himself a temporary vehicle for the patient's emotions and talks with a matching tone and posture, rather than distant or neutral ones.

We often use imagery techniques (Hackmann, Bennett-Levy and Holmes, 2011) in which patients are invited to go back in their imagination to a scene experienced in the past and gradually visualise all the details with an ever higher resolution. In practical terms, after asking patients to close their eyes and remove their attention from ourselves and our dialogue, we invite them to 'enter' the scene and describe it as if they were there, talking in the first person. As the imaginary immersion continues, the therapist leads the patient to focus on his bodily state, the colours and environmental details of the scene, the emotions felt, the other's expressions and the words and the way in which his emotional state changed with the flow of events. The more patients immerse themselves in the recalled scene and can again feel the warmth of the sun on their skin and smell the scents of where it took place, the more the affective channel is likely to be reactivated.[1]

After one year of therapy Monica, the patient with paranoid and obsessive-compulsive personality traits described in Chapter 5, told her therapist about a 'vague but strong sensation' that her father, at some moment in his infancy, must have had big emotional difficulties. This sensation did not, however, have any specific space-time coordinates and the therapist tried to find them by asking her to recall a scene occurring when she was about 14.

T: Close your eyes. Go back to that moment. Tell me what you see. Where are you at this moment?

P: I've gone back home from school.

T: Good, so you knock, your mum opens, you go in and ...?

P: I can't see Dad straight away because he's in the sitting room and the sitting room's behind a pillar.

T: Where's the pillar?

P: On the right.

T: Would you like to try and go there?

P: Yes. I go up to him. He's watching television.

T: Can you see him?

P: Yes, I can see him.

T: What position is he in? Is the television on?

P: Yes, it's on. He's there, dressed slovenly, on the sofa. He seems lifeless, wrapped up in himself.

Monica burst out crying. The therapist stood by her, listened to her and supported her and, when Monica was ready, he asked her what had happened. Monica said she was very upset because it was the first time she had seen her father fragile and listless, whereas she always remembered him to be energetic, cool, a winner.

In another session, a few months later, Monica talked about her father's death, occurring when she was 18. She had no doubt in asserting that she did not cry and would never have been able to let herself feel his loss.

P: Now I think about it, in fact I didn't really feel anything. I can remember the day of the funeral too. I was there and, as I always do, I tried to make sure everyone was OK.

T: Monica, it's as if you were detached from that situation. Do you feel up to going back to the day of the funeral?

P: I think so.

T: Let's try and go back there. Close your eyes. Is everything OK?

P: Yes.

T: Are you there?

P: Yes.

T: Who's there? A lot of people?

P: Yes, it's full of people.

T: Can you manage to see where your father is?

Monica could see the coffin, and for the first time in her life, she burst into heartfelt tears at the thought that her father was really dead. She was understandably upset, but also grateful because she realised these emotions had been bubbling under the surface and she had never allowed herself to feel them. There were a number of occasions when, within the therapeutic relationship, Monica and her therapist made ironic comments about how therapy was a 'hoax'. The patient came to sessions with everything under control and left in tears.

Let us reassure the reader – the goal of MIT is not to make patients suffer! What it involves is encouraging an access to distressing experiences that would otherwise remain present in the form of emotional experiences associated with hyper-arousal. After a year of therapy, Monica has started sleeping properly again and has overcome the depression linked to the loss of her mother. She again enjoys experiences

> in the past and the present; she can recall the smell of her mother's cooking and their cheerful conversations. She takes pleasure in describing the smell of the beer in a tasting course. She recovers her father's energy and uses it as a model when pursuing her professional ambitions.

Stimulating understanding of psychological cause and effect

Once specific autobiographical memories have been retrieved and there is access to a patient's inner state, it is time to probe chains of reasoning, i.e. in metacognitive terms, the relationship among variables. Of course this is an operation that in part occurs automatically on the surfacing of a patient's mental state. For example, the patient may be explaining that he felt angry because his partner rejected him. However, with PD patients, linking together cause and effect connnections between what occurs in their relationships and their reactions is not simple.

The psychological links needing to be reconstructed go in two directions, first in the event-antecedent-thought-emotion/behaviour direction and then emotion to thought (Greenberg, 2002). In line with what we know from neuroscience and experimental psychology about the influence of emotions and humour on thought (Damasio, 1994), a patient can enter an affective state with only a marginal awareness of the event triggering it and, via affect infusion or mood-induced reasoning processes (Bower, 1981; Forgas, 2002), the emotion can generate thoughts consistent with it.

The classical ABC-type links help in understanding how a patient puts together catastrophic intra-psychic chains. An abandoned narcissistic patient feeling a rapid heartbeat and thinking he is having a heart attack should be helped to grasp the link between the activating event (fast heartbeat), his catastrophic interpretation and his emotion (anxiety). What is of most note, however, in the treatment of PDs is to understand the psychological cause-effect links leading a narcissist to feel abandoned. These should once again be reconstructed on the basis of what goes on in the patient's mind while describing narrative episodes concerning his interpersonal relationships.

Once the patient has detailed a narrative episode, therapists should start with organising the material they have heard in accordance with the sequence typical of an interpersonal schema (see Chapters 2 and 4). At this point in therapy, it is not a question of reconstructing schemas, which, by definition, needs to recur to be defined as such. It is a question of starting out from the episode the patient has just narrated and summarising it out loud based on: (1) what event triggered it; (2) the wish/motivation/goal driving the patient; (3) understanding what the patient did or thought he did, to achieve his goal; (4) the other's response; and (5) understanding how the patient reacted to the other's response.

A typical summary organised like this would sound as follows: '*So your boss didn't accept reorganising the firm's database like you proposed [activating event].*

At that moment you felt the need to be recognised and for your work to be appreciated [wish], so you decided to talk with your colleagues in the hope of them helping you convince your boss that your idea was a good one [procedure for achieving the wish]. Your colleagues ignored you [other's response], and your reaction was to think that they were in alliance with your boss, which made you angry [self's response to other's response].'

Sometimes the psychological links are less obvious. When a patient is unable to establish any connections, the therapist can attempt to make this connection by using minimal theoretical inference and then inquire about the level of accuracy. For example, the therapist may suggest that a stomach ache may be due to anxiety over losing her job that a patient reported shortly before. Another example of a hypothesis offered by a therapist could be, '*You told me you enjoy your job and you're worried about losing it due to your firm cutting back on staff in the last two months. You mentioned your panic attacks began shortly after the firings began and on the day after your close colleague was fired, you had a particularly intense panic attack. Is it possible that your feelings of panic are triggered when you're frightened about losing your job, because it would confirm your belief about not being worth much?*'

One of the core aspects of MIT is the specific technique the therapist uses to perform this type of questioning, and it is important that the therapist starts with the wish. Formulations that are accurately encapsulating what the patient is trying to achieve will likely enable the patient to feel understood and accepted, and it communicates that the therapist is joined in the patient's pursuit of something worthy (Caspar and Ecker, 2008; Kramer, Rosciano, Pavlovic et al., 2011; Luborsky and Crits-Christoph, 1990).

Arturo had started therapy in an apathetic, empty and depressed state. At the start, the therapist had difficulty grasping the roots of the patient's depression, introversion and passivity. The therapist noticed the patient's facial expressions of frozen anger, and she occasionally felt frightened due to the potential of him becoming violent, which is not atypical of patients with paranoia. It was difficult for the therapist to understand the patient due to his tendency to be introverted and his difficulties in describing his inner world. A careful eliciting of a set of narrative episodes led the patient and therapist to a better understanding of the psychological cause and effect.

We saw how Arturo's unmotivated state was present in a situation in which he was sitting at his desk in the office. The therapist explored the various aspects of this experience:

T: Could you tell me what you felt sitting at your desk surfing on the Internet?
P: [*silenc/*) I think a bit nervy …
T: Can you explain that to me better?
P: Irritated, angry.
T: What were you thinking at that precise moment?

> *P*: Why should I be treated like that? They've got their work and I don't have any fucking work to do. I could be lending a hand, and I don't see why they won't involve me.
>
> At this point Arturo was capable of describing what provoked his emotions, which was something that he was unable to do in previous sessions. Once Arturo's inner world became clearer, he was able to communicate the anger he felt. He was also able to identify the origins of the anger, which allowed the therapist to feel less threatened and more empathetic.

The observation of a patient's non-verbal behaviour is important as well. For example, a therapist may notice that a patient lowers her eyes and begins to blush while the therapist is speaking about the poor marks her child received at school. In this moment it is important for the therapist to communicate his observations of the patient's non-verbal behaviours, and inquire about what is making her feel embarrassed. If the patient has difficulty understanding the meaning of the embarrassment she feels, the therapist can refer to previous session narratives and attempt an intervention. The therapist may say: '*So you went to the interview hoping that your son was doing well in school, because this would mean that you're a good mother and not a failure. When you learned he was performing poorly, it confirmed your belief that you're a bad mother, and you're embarrassed to be seen this way. Is that right?*'

One of the key aspects of therapy is understanding the psychological cause and effect relationships. Helping patients to identify these relationships is imperative because it allows them to begin to comprehend the pathogenic schemas that are causing them distress. The task can be challenging for a therapist and consequently it is important that the therapist has an adequate theoretical understanding of how a schema hinges on the *desire/procedure if… then … /other's response/self's response* structure, repeated practice and an ongoing focus on the wish driving the patient. Knowledge, practice and focus gradually enable the therapist to become more effective in formulating accurate hypotheses in a supportive and validating way.

Once a patient and therapist have jointly reconstructed the cognitive-affective processes, the next goal of therapy should be helping the patient understand that these processes likely represent stable meaning attribution forms. More specifically, therapists should focus on helping the patient understand that his or her beliefs are schemas rather than a reflection of reality. One of the main techniques adopted by MIT is evoking memories associated with the patient's narrated episodes.

Evoking associated memories to stimulate awareness of regularities

At this point in therapy a patient is getting close to an awareness of regularities or schemas. MIT attempts to ensure that this awareness originates from the patient rather than the interpretations of the therapist. Among the many similarities between MIT and mentalisation-based treatment (Bateman and Fonagy, 2004) there is the conviction that a therapist should not be perceived as too clever. For example, a therapist who makes associations for the patient, connects the patient's past with the present and the therapeutic relationship events with everyday life one is likely being too directive. It is important that the patient not feel compelled or forced to accept the ideas of the therapist because he will likely feel that the therapist is imposing his or her own ideas on what is, in the end, the patient's own inner world. Even if the associations proffered by a therapist are correct and the patient agrees with them, the patient will likely only gain an intellectual understanding lacking in emotional reactivation. It is most effective when the patient performs this task as independently as possible. If the association is formulated by the patient he will believe it is subjectively true, emotionally significant and, more importantly, he will feel it is his own. Working via the evoking of associated memories is more likely to lead to an affectively charged comprehension.

Many therapeutic approaches aim to systematically reconstruct life stories. Although this is not forbidden in MIT, it is suggested that reconstructing family history in detail is avoided due to the risk of obtaining a large quantity of information that may lead to preconceived ideas (*'he's behaving this way because it's as if he was relating with his mother in the situations where she was demanding with him'*). In fact, interpretations should be carefully avoided. If potentially important information seems to be missing from the patient's developmental history over the course of therapy, it can be investigated more systematically by the therapist.

In other words, it is important that a therapist tries to be as ingenuous as possible, and consequently ensures that the patient establishes the connections between episodes. The next step in MIT is for the therapist to summarise the narrative episode shared by the patient and identify any potential psychological cause-effect links. If the summary resonates with the patient, the therapist should ask him to recall another similar moment from his past (see Figure 6.2). The therapist should not select one specific aspect of the story for evoking associated memories. Instead, the therapist should allow the patient to freely connect with anything that he finds subjectively significant: anxiety due to rejection, anger due to a negative response or a tendency of introversion.

Let us begin with an example of how associated memories should be evoked, beginning with the first related episode. A therapist should summarise what has been narrated and identify any cause-effect links: '*You said that you wanted dinner to be ready for you when you got home, but your girlfriend was working at her desk instead of preparing dinner. You asked her why dinner wasn't ready and she replied that she hadn't had time and in your opinion she seemed tense and nervous. You felt abandoned and shut yourself in the bedroom, where your feelings vacillated between gloom and anger. Is that it?*' If the patient considers this a good reconstruction, the therapist can continue: '*Can you recall other memories, taking place at any moment in your life, when you desired a gesture of attention, or felt that someone's attention was unavailable? How about situations*

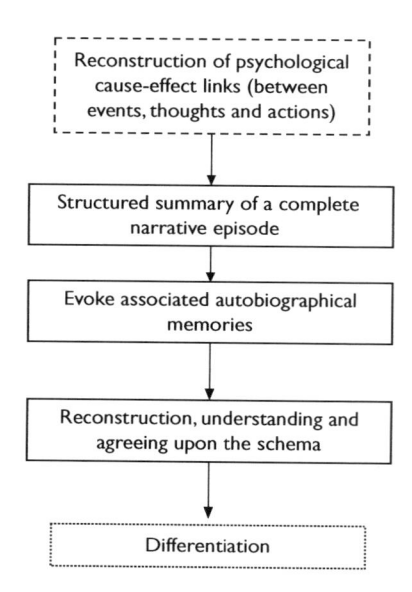

Figure 6.2 Reconstructing the schema.

when you clammed up and felt gloomy and angry?' Asking for more specific memories enables the patient to make connections between relational procedures. Memories of asking for attention, of angry protesting or of gloom because the other was felt to be preoccupied or distant are able to surface. If the therapist had, instead, asked: *'Can you recall other situations in which you got angry?'*, he would have blocked many mnemonic channels, which could have hidden precious memories consistent with the pathogenic schemas activated in therapy.

Associated memories should not necessarily refer to a patient's evolutionary developmental period. A therapist should utilise any memories that emerge in session: autobiographical memories are especially useful because they are windows for understanding how a person reconstructs events (see Chapter 1). A pathogenic schema is the structure around which the memories of relationships with parents, friends, colleagues and romantic partners are shaped. Therefore each episode is potentially a microscope for investigating the schema structure. Early memories have a particular value and can be an excellent process indicator. When early memories are used in session a patient is more likely to grasp a better understanding of the self and think: *'Wow, so I've been carrying this sense of abandonment since my mother used to leave me at a camp for two months during the summer, and I've never been able to get rid of it!'*

A clinician might expect memories evoked by association to have the same structure as the initial narrative episode, but this is not always the case. The initial narrative episode may portray a patient wishing for her efforts to be acknowledged by colleagues. The latter may portray the patient as indifferent or preferring someone else, and the patient's reported reaction may be resentful closing up. The associated memory may begin with a resentful closing up but it may not be linked to the theme of desiring approval. The patient may recall moments when she was seeking attention from her mother, but her mother was sorrowful and suffering with frequent headaches that led her to deny the patient's requests for attention. In the beginning of therapy the associated episode and the initial episode do not seem connected, but if the associated memory is explored more deeply, a new meaning may surface. For example, it may emerge that the patient always tried to earn top marks at school in the hope of pleasing her mother, who was only content when she was at the top of the class. This would suggest that the patient learned that she had to be perfect in order to treat her mother's chronic gloominess and consequently receive some attention. Therefore it is likely that the patient automatically perceives her colleagues' negative reactions to mean that she is imperfect, which exposes her to the danger of being symbolically rejected by a depressed and distant mother. Her colleagues' rejections thus activate a feeling of being abandoned that was previously unexpressed due to it being covered by her striving for perfectionism. The initial memory was therefore centred on her need for approval, while the associated memory was connoted by her unfulfilled wish to be cared for and her sense of being abandoned.

Reconstruction of the schema

Once the series of memories have been linked together by the patient, the goal of therapy shifts to the joint reconstruction of the schema. A therapist should explain to the patient that he has considered the patient's narratives and that he would like to jointly evaluate the possible similarities and/or recurring features present. This crucial task requires an increased level of participation from the patient, and therefore the therapist should be more diligent when asking for feedback.

Schema reconstructions are considered effective when patients are able to recognise the schemas as their own. Even a correct formulation can be rejected, which indicates that the schema has been poorly formulated or that a pathogenic interpersonal cycle has occurred. If the latter is true, the therapist will need to investigate and repair the relational damage before attempting a subsequent joint formulation (see Chapter 5).

A therapist should summarise the core elements of the collected episodes, and communicate any recurring themes he identifies. Episodes may be similar for many reasons including: the same wish is activated, the description of how the other responds is similar or because the patient has a tendency to react similarly in the different situations. If the therapist formulates the schema based on her patient's wish, the patient will likely perceive a greater level of empathy from the therapist. The therapist may say: '*You want this but you're afraid it can't be achieved*' or '*You wish for this but you're afraid that it can't be achieved, but it's as if in therapy you were guided by the hope that there is another, more positive outcome possible.*'

By using this particular statement, the therapist is communicating to a patient that there is a feasible way to overcome the patient's problems.

Once the therapist knows what interpersonal schema is likely to be underlying the episodes being narrated and considers the therapeutic relationship to be well-modulated, he can communicate his hypothesis to the patient. This formulation can also contain the procedures for shifting to a more adaptive schema and wish. For example, the therapist may say: '*You would tell your mother about something you had accomplished in the hope of receiving desired attention from her, but your mom would react harshly. Your mother's disdainful reaction left you feeling criticised, worthless and abandoned. Consequently, gaining approval by being valued and viewed positively became a more important life goal than being loved. This is why you began to act in a perfectionist manner.*'

However tactful, timely and empathetic a therapist may be, formulating a schema always involves the risk of the patient self-accusing: '*So there's something wrong with me.*' This is a well-known and manageable problem. When an MIT therapist provides any intervention the therapist should be aware of the possible consequences that the intervention may have on the therapeutic relationship. If the therapist interprets the patient as feeling criticised, the therapist should make it known: '*It is interesting that you feel criticised by yourself, and perhaps also by me. This makes me think that the negative idea you have of yourself is pervasive if simply identifying one of your tendencies leads you to place judgement on yourself. Do you feel that there was criticism or lack of hope in my tone?*' It is also important that the therapist inform the patient that the schema has been constructed since birth, and that the patient should not feel responsible. In addition, the therapist should instill hope by telling the patient that the schema will gradually become less powerful now that it has been discovered.

While formulating a schema it is possible that other elements in a patient's inner world come to the surface. As a patient gradually becomes aware of any elements recurring in his experience, other recollections should surface and these will contain new ideas and emotions to enrich the picture. In further analyses of the schema a therapist can take an active part and look himself for episodes narrated in previous sessions that appear linked. It is important for patients to make the first associations on their own, to acquire agency over their own thoughts; further associations can be a joint process, with a contribution by the therapist, so that patients get the idea that the latter has them in mind and considers them important.

The material emerging from the therapeutic relationship is precious for reconstructing schemas. The way that patients construct their relationship with the therapist is schema-dependent, and thus their pathogenic schema is activated and identifiable during therapy as well. The therapeutic relationship is an excellent source of information for understanding the patient's schematic functioning, but it is essential for the link between relational schemas activated in daily life and transference schemas activated in therapy are only proposed once the therapist has regulated the relationship. This avoids making it seem that any difficulties in the relationship depend solely on the patient's problems.

In Chapter 5 we described how the therapist in the case of Fulvio (self-employed, 44 years old, with avoidant PD and dependent and depressive traits) had stopped asking him to show himself in public to overcome his social phobia because he realised that if the patient complied with his requests the patient would feel a restriction of independence, which he described as how his mother made him feel in his narratives. Fulvio relaxed and decided he would show himself in public when he was less anxious. Once a good relational atmosphere had been re-established, the therapist used what had occurred in the relationship to more clearly formulate the patient's pathogenic schema with him: '*It was important for me to let you choose whether to show yourself or not. Your opinion is more significant than mine. I'd like to reflect further with you on what was happening: if I had continued to insist, after you'd shown me that you didn't want to do it, could I have ended up behaving like your mother, who didn't respect what you wanted?*' The therapist was guided by the non-verbal behaviour he saw and when he felt free to choose not to show himself, Fulvio not only felt unburdened of his anxiety linked to social exposure but also gave clear signs of relief at feeling free to choose. At this point he acknowledged that this formulation was probably correct and considered the hypothesis that he was driven by a schema where he sought independence and the other blocked him, imposed his/her own goals and criticised him. He also grasped that this schema was getting activated during therapy even if he acknowledged that the therapist had never imposed anything, and instead had always respected Fulvio's independence. He therefore felt respected and understood in his schema relating to the managing of dominance-submission, and two months later began exercises showing himself in public, which proved to be successful.

Jointly identifying that there are recurring events with recognisable sequences is often accompanied by the patient moving toward differentiation: '*So it's me who tends to always see these things!?*' In any case the terrain is now ready for promoting awareness that suffering and problems are generated more by how the patient constructs her relational world than by external events, i.e. for differentiating, as we shall see in the next chapter.

The formulation of the schema does not denote the end of therapy. It is likely that after the formulation, the patient and therapist will become used to talking about the schemas. For example, the patient may state, '*My schema has been reactivated*', and the therapist may reply, '*So, you acted based on your schema.*' In this case it is probably that the patient and therapist are simply replacing old theories with new and possibly more precise ones. In fact, this is an intellectualisation. Once the schemas have been identified, in subsequent sessions one should look for recent narrative episodes in which they seem to become reactivated. Passing from theory, '*The schema has become reactivated*', to narrative, '*The usual things occurred. I was at work and it happened to me that ...*', makes it possible to continue to focus on living and vivid experiences. In this example the schema is likely activated but attention is placed on the narrative, which makes it possible to see discrepant elements and the healthy parts of self. These elements indicate that the schema is being activated and in the course of being processed and modified. In other words, once the schema has been identified, a therapist should continuously test it by recourse to autobiographical memories.

When a patient has reached an awareness that there are recurring schemas underlying his suffering and relational problems, the joint formulation of functioning is complete. If other pathogenic areas surface they should be investigated using the procedure outlined in this chapter. This is the point at which a patient and therapist should take steps to plan change based on the promoting of differentiation and access to the patient's healthy parts.

Note

1   Techniques requiring a patient to adopt other roles are also capable of increasing the level of emotional experience. *Role play* is one of these. While a patient takes on the role he has been assigned, he physically relives the experience and this re-experience provides more accessible material for reflecting on the self. *The two chair technique* is also useful – originating from the Emotion Focused Therapy school (Greenberg, 2002) and recently adapted for avoidant personality disorder (Pos, 2014). For space reasons we are not going to describe these techniques.

Chapter 7

Promoting differentiation

Differentiating is the understanding that the ideas we have of ourselves, as well as our expectations of how others will respond to our wishes, largely depend on our schematic constructions of events and consequently do not reflect events accurately. More specifically, differentiating is the process of altering maladaptive cognitions. For example, the subjective idea *'Others will criticise and reject me if I look for appreciation because I'm not worth much'* can be modified to the more realistic idea *'I realise I tend to think I'm not worth much in other people's eyes, but this is not necessarily true.'*

Guiding a patient to differentiate, i.e. to adopt a perspective from which to consider his own beliefs and reactions to events, which are subjective rather than mirroring reality, is a fundamental step in psychotherapy. Cognitive psychotherapy orientations emphasise promoting a critical distance (Hollon and Beck, 1979) or *defusion* (Hayes and Strosahl, 2004; Blackledge, 2007) which is a similar process. Differentiation is an essential step toward structural change, and it allows patients to construct more adaptive self-views, understand the perspectives of others in a more evolved way and engage in behavioural experiments aimed at overcoming avoidances and exploring new relational areas of life,.

A psychotherapy patient can achieve differentiation in a variety of ways. The most classic is to acquire a true and proper critical distance, which is historically one of the principle factors of change in CBT. Patients revise their beliefs by considering the empirical evidence that is available to them. A possible example of a patient using empirical evidence to alter their beliefs is: *'I thought I was inept, with others always criticising me, but I've discovered it isn't true and that I'm worth something.'* It is important that MIT therapists do not promote a critical distance as the main form of differentiation because it is often difficult for PD patients to modify their beliefs. For similar reasons, therapists should be cautious of using this therapeutic technique prematurely in the course of therapy. A second, and more frequently used, MIT differentiation technique is to help patients become aware of more favourable self-images, which are often dormant on the borders of consciousness. For example, a therapist should try to help patients acknowledge more adaptive concepts, such as *'I generally think I'm not worth anything, but I realise that there are situations in which I feel effective and capable. I do have a more favourable opinion of myself.'*

A third differentiating technique used by MIT therapists is to help patients understand that their developmental histories influence their current beliefs and that their beliefs are often not a reflection of reality. This form of differentiating does not involve becoming aware of the inaccuracy of one's ideas in the here and now, but rather the understanding that one selectively pays attention to the stimuli that support their beliefs formulated during development. For example, an individual may discover that he is sensitive to the feelings of abandonment because he often felt this way when he sought attention from others while growing up. This new understanding may be portrayed by a patient saying, '*When I feel fragile I often believe that others will humiliate me, and now I realise that this is what happened to me while I was growing up; when I displayed my fears, my parents would accuse me of being weak.*' Schema reconstruction procedures, which occur after collecting many similarly themed narrative episodes, aim to acquire differentiation in this way because it helps patients identify the historical regularities of how they relate to others.

A fourth form of differentiation occurs when a patient does not call into question the truth value of his belief but instead realises that his emotional response is subjective and could be less intense or completely different than it is currently (Ellis, 1962). A therapist should not attempt to convince a patient that his perception of being humiliated is unfounded, or that the patient's emotional response of anger and shame is inappropriate. Instead, a therapist should try to help the patient understand that his reaction to a particular event is comprehensible, but that the intensity of his emotional response is a subjective factor that is able to be modulated. It is important that the therapist helps the patient metacognitively ask himself: '*Must I necessarily react like this when I feel humiliated?*', '*Why do I allow others' words provoke these distressing emotions?*' or '*Rejection has always hurt me, but can I respond differently to avoid suffering or perceiving this distress as insurmountable?*' (Ellis, 1962). Metacognitive questions of this sort are useful for promoting agency over one's affects in addition to differentiation. Patients begin to discover that their perceptions are subjective and that their emotional responses are also manageable.

Romina, 37 years old, was a highly functioning classics teacher who suffered from paranoid PD with obsessive-compulsive traits. She recalled many narrative episodes in which she perceived her fiancé as being unfaithful to her and flirting with other women in her presence. She was prone to identifying instances when her colleagues formulated relationships from which she was excluded, left her out of important decisions and ganged up on her. This provoked a mixture of ill-defined distress and anger in her. Her typical reaction involved feeling offended and resentful protest; however, she feared that her reactions would lead others to abandon her. The therapist did not call into question the truth of her perceptions or the appropriateness of her resentful and critical reaction, even if Romina herself recognised that her reactions may be problematical. He instead highlighted an instance when Romina identified that the intensity of her feelings of being hurt and aggrieved varied depending on how she felt that day. In this instance there was a focus Romina acquiring a detailed knowledge of her inner state rather than helping her take a critical distance from her representations of others as being derisive and dominating. More specifically, over the course of her therapy, Romina became increasingly more aware of her paranoid and vulnerable state, which consisted of a fear of being controlled and subjugated by others and abandonment. Together, the therapist and Romina learned that her underlying distressful state modulated her attention towards others' derisive actions and her degree of emotional reactivity. Romina gained benefit from this intervention and immediately felt some relief from her vulnerable state. Thinking about the situations in which others excluded her or made fun of her became less distressing, she immediately began to feel a greater connection to others and this helped her to feel more involved in important work decisions.

The last form of differentiating consists of discovering that there are fluctuations in the degree of certainty in one's convictions. For example, when a patient believes his idea is 100 per cent true outside of session when he is immersed in a problematic situation, but in sessions begins to believe that it is likely only 80 per cent true, he is communicating that his idea is a hypothesis as reality does not admit degrees of truth.[1]

When to promote differentiation

As mentioned previously, helping a patient to differentiate is a key element of MIT and the first step in accessing the healthy parts of the self (see Chapter 8). The prerequisite to beginning to promote differentiation is for a patient to achieve an awareness of the recurring, schema-driven forms relating to his own life experiences. This awareness can be achieved *after* evoking associated memories (see Chapters 4 and 6). However, differentiation should be promoted *before* other forms of change occur (see Figure 7.1 below). In MIT a patient must achieve awareness of his tendency to be driven by rigid interpersonal schemas before embarking on behavioural experiments, constructing new ways to manage relational problems, acquiring more effective social skills or achieving a broader and more sophisticated theory of others' minds.

If a patient has not achieved the ability to differentiate, other attempts toward change should to be avoided (see Chapter 4, and Figures 4.1 and 4.2). More specifically, if a patient is asked to tackle a feared situation (e.g. understanding the perspective of another with whom he is in conflict) before differentiating, he will likely be unsuccessful. For example, a patient must become aware of schemas which represent the other as one who neglects and abandons to understand that his partner is not disinterested in him, but instead is just tired from a day of work and looking after their child. The patient may reflect: '*I realise I feel abandoned, and that it is typical for me to feel this way. What could have caused my wife to appear unapproachable other than the idea that she does not care about me?'* It is important that the patient begin by questioning whether the feeling of abandonment is accurate, and then subsequently explore alternative hypotheses about the other's intentions. For example, the patient may think, *'I now realise that my wife seemed unapproachable because she was exhausted by looking after our daughter all day, not because she does not care about me.'*

It is important that a therapist makes sure the patient is aware of his schemas before implementing more advanced interventions. For example, it would be detrimental to prematurely ask the patient to take the perspective of the other because he may question, *'Why is my therapist asking me to justify the other who is abandoning me?'* Therefore, a therapist should not suggest that the patient's negative perceptions of others may be misrepresented without the patient first acquiring a critical distance from his pathogenic schemas. Harmful interventions include: *'You tend to choose people like that'*, *'You tend to ask for help in a plaintive way and this is why others withdraw.'* It is possible that a patient understands that his negative perceptions of others' behaviours are inaccurate, but he may be unaware of how to change them. The patient may also feel incapable of changing his schemas and consequently believe that others will abandon him. Suggesting that the other has left because of the patient's schemas and subsequent behaviours would confirm that his idea of deserving abandonment is well-founded. To reiterate, the therapist should not suggest that the patient is responsible for others' negative reactions until he has an adequate understanding of his pathogenic schemas and experienced positive states that will help support him,

---

With Arturo, the paranoid patient with narcissistic traits described in Chapter 6, prematurely attempting to promote more favourable views of others was unproductive. In the following extract, Arturo complains about feeling marginalised by others at work, which he reacted to by alternating between anger and fantasies of revenge and abulia and withdrawal. The therapist responds by suggesting that others would react differently if he were more open. This intervention was formulated without helping the patient to reconstruct his narrative on the basis of his desire for approval and his expectations about others' reactions. Moreover, the patient had not first been invited to evoke associated memories that could lead him to understand that his perception of not being supported was a typical way of interpreting events and likely inaccurate. The ineffective intervention is demonstrated below.

T: And could you tell me what you felt at that moment, sitting at your desk surfing on the Internet?

P: [*silence*] … I think a bit annoyed …

T: What were you thinking?

P: Why should I be treated like that? … These people have got their work … I've got nothing to do … I could be of help, in my small way, in what they're doing too and I don't see why I shouldn't be involved.

T: And at that moment were your colleagues not paying you any attention?

P: No. But in any case I didn't do anything to let them see I was irritated.

T: In your opinion, do your colleagues realise how much effort you put forth?

P: In my opinion, no ... then at 3:30 I left ... saying, 'Anyhow it's pointless my being here ... There's nothing to do.' I said it out loud [*laughs*] and I left.

T: Did you speak directly to anyone?

P: No, I just said it, addressed to everybody and nobody.

T: And when you said this did you notice any reaction from your colleagues?

P: [*silence*] I believe there was some reaction ... They heard these words and stopped for a second ... But they didn't do anything ... Nobody said anything.

T: Did you try to tackle this problem with them directly?

P: Yes ... with one of them, before Christmas. I believe he talked about it, and after that I was given something to do ... But not much, all said ...

T: How would you like the world to be ... With your colleagues giving you a hand?

P: Yes ... It ought to be a bit different. There are tasks where they know I might have the right skills and they could start saying, 'We can get him involved more regularly' ... in such a way that my boss gets influenced in my favour.

T: Would you do that for a colleague?

P: I don't know ... Now that I'm in this situation I'd probably do something ... But if I hadn't experienced it I don't know ... Perhaps they haven't ever experienced this situation, and they don't realise ...

T: What is stopping you from approaching them? When you tell me about these things...When I picture the scenes you narrate to me ... I imagine you as always being a bit on your own ...

P: A bit, yes ... But what's stopping me from approaching them is that they're in a completely different situation. They're integrated, they've got their work to do and their own business to look after, but not me ... This makes me feel a thousand light years away from them ... There are some of them, in my opinion, that don't understand me at all ... In fact, perhaps they think I'm getting special treatment, given that I'm there doing fuck all from morning to night.

T: I ask myself, what would happen if you talked about yourself a bit more ... told your colleagues about the effort involved in doing nothing ... Also you said another thing that struck me, that is that your uneasiness can't be seen.

P: In my opinion, they can see it but don't understand ... Every so often I say something, that I'm pissed off ...

T: Seeing anger and seeing suffering are different things ... If they could see your effort ... how do you think they'd react? They see the anger.

P: [*silence*] Why should they react?

T: I don't know ... Let's stop a second ... It's as if you told me that, if you're angry, the others can react, but if you were to express distress or sorrow, the others wouldn't react ... so that anger can be expressed ...

P: I don't believe it changes much ... I've got the feeling that if I expressed distress, they'd feel uneasy and would try to get away from the uneasiness. [*silence*]

The therapist asks Arturo several times to imagine what the others may think and to explore the idea that if he behaved differently, he might generate other reactions. Although at certain moments Arturo is less angry because he realises that others can have different experiences and as a result realises that their actions are not driven by evil intentions, his underlying paranoid belief that others cannot understand him does not alter and his anger resurfaces. The interventions aimed at reinforcing the theory of the mind and believing that acting differently will produce change were ineffective. At the end of the extract Arturo foresees that expressing negative emotions will lead others to withdraw. Therefore he persists in making schema-dependent attributions in which he longs for the attention and support of others, while the others remain distant and abandon him.

As we shall see later, one of the most effective ways to promote differentiation is through the therapeutic relationship. More specifically, the therapy session allows differentiation to involve the formulation of alternative hypotheses of the mind of the other, the therapist. This is possible because in session the other is actually present, as well as a dialogue related to the mental contents of the patient and the other, which allows any problems to be identified and processed on the spot. Increasing a patient's ability to see things from another perspective, and promoting a critical distance from his ideas about relationships to enable his mind to be open to alternative constructions of self and others, requires the following carefully shaped procedures.

Strategies for promoting differentiation

The process we have termed *shared formulation of functioning* is aimed at preparing differentiation (see Figure 7.1).

Up to this point in treatment, a patient has gathered a number of autobiographical memories and has identified what she thinks and feels and what motivates her actions. Her therapist has constructed a summary portraying how her psychological suffering derives from failure to achieve one or more wishes. The therapist's instigation has

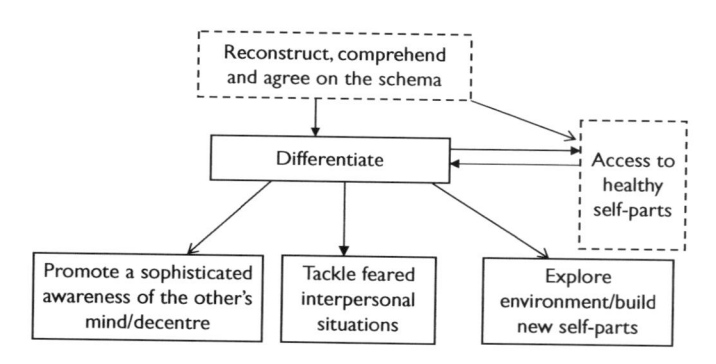

Figure 7.1 When to promote differentiation.

enabled the patient to evoke memories linked to the first wish she has been unable to obtain, which was retrieved from her network of associated memories. Due to the memories being similar, the therapist has sufficient material to suggest to the patient that since the relationship pattern is repeated over time, with different persons and in different circumstances, it is likely an internalised interpersonal schema. At this point, differentiating means creating a critical distance from one's pathogenic schemas.

As mentioned previously, the five ways to differentiate include:

1   changing his idea because it is discovered that it is wrong;
2   finding that he has ideas about himself and others that are different from his schema-dependent beliefs;
3   grasping that the schemas are rooted in his life history and therefore should not be taken as reliable guides for understanding current reality;
4   acquiring awareness of his mind's power to modulate or tolerate psychological distress;
5   understanding the degree to which he believes an idea is accurate and realising that as our state of mind changes, the degree of certainty changes as well.

Which form of differentiation is used depends on the quality of the therapeutic relationship, the amount that the schema is egodystonic, the intensity of the negative affects linked to the schema, the pervasiveness of the schema and the strength of the patient's metacognitive beliefs related to the opportuneness and importance of believing in the schema. For example, if a schema is egosyntonic or of the *coping* type, and the patient considers it necessary and useful, differentiation should be promoted cautiously. More specifically, the process of differentiation should begin by helping her understand that her emotional response is subjective, and that the degree of belief in an interpretation of others' intentions varies in line with the context and one's inner state.

If a patient feels others to be threatening and is convinced that reacting angrily by punishing them is a good method for handling the danger, differentiation should not be forced prematurely. It is important that the therapist refrain from asking the patient to consider that his expectation is unrealistic. Instead, the therapist should ask how much the patient believes his perception of danger to be true, how convinced the patient is that he will succumb by reacting in a revengeful manner and why the patient believes the actions of others produce such intense distress. It is essential for a clinician to promote differentiation in the form of a true and proper critical distance, i.e. '*I think this but I realise that things look differently when considered from another perspective,*' especially if a schema is egosyntonic.

A clinician should work on differentiation at the same time as promoting access to healthy parts (Figure 7.1) (see Chapter 8). The two operations are synergistic: taking a critical distance from one's pathogenic schemas makes it possible to see healthy and adaptive self-parts, while also allowing access to positive experiences which assist the patient in seeing that pathogenic schemas may not correspond to facts.

We will now describe the strategies used in MIT to help a patient differentiate.

Differentiating in the therapeutic relationship

The therapeutic relationship is an optimal setting to show a patient that his ideas about others and about himself may not correspond with reality. Metacommunication strategies related to this process were discussed in Chapter 5, but let's consider some important technical aspects. One can use the therapeutic relationship in various ways to promote a critical distance. The therapist can ask: *'How do you feel I'm reacting? Am I doing or saying something that is giving you the idea that I too could reject, criticise or harm you?'* A clinician should not insist on showing how his own point of view is different from the one the patient ascribes to him, but instead invite the patient to freely explore her own mind. This stimulates the perception that thinking about the therapist's mind is a safe, authorised and feasible operation. In fact, similar patients often have histories involving adults who refused to reveal or discuss their own states of mind, rendering the exploration of the other's mind as risky or pointless.

If a patient notices that his therapist is reacting differently from expected, a first seed of differentiation has been sown. However, a patient often stresses that the relationship with the therapist is special, with the latter possessing unique understanding and accepting qualities which others will not display. An effective reply to this objection by a therapist consists in inviting the patient to focus on the subjective reaction he experiences when faced with his therapist's benevolent attitude. The intervention would sound like this: *'I realise that this may be considered a somewhat artificial situation; however, try to linger over what you feel. While you feel understood by me, accepted, not abandoned, you endorsed feeling a positive emotion, which was apparent to me as well. I may be perceived as being well-disposed towards you due to my professional role, but what you experience is true; it's you. You have the ability to feel appreciated, accepted, and valued. In your inner world there is a more benevolent view of yourself, and at least a specialised relationship is capable of bringing it to light. Our work now is to see if we can manage to ensure that you feel this outside our sessions, and with other people.'*

As we saw in Chapter 5, the therapeutic relationship, like all relationships, can be a terrain for activating pathogenic interpersonal schemas and a therapist can contribute to triggering and maintaining a dysfunctional interpersonal cycle. The interventions a therapist performs to extricate herself from this cycle are occasions that a patient can exploit for differentiating. For example, if a therapist invites a patient to express what she feels and thinks about him – *'Do I see you've clammed up? Is it possible you don't trust me? Are you afraid I could control or reject you if I knew what was passing through your mind? Have I done or said something that gave you this impression?'* – she will realise that her expectation about being challenged, attacked and abandoned has turned out to be at odds with what has happened in sessions. Moreover, if a therapist manages to maintain a cooperative, non-competitive atmosphere, a patient can differentiate in other ways as well. For example, a patient can begin to understand that communication can make it possible to feel accepted and appreciated, even if the relationship is initially based on a lack of mutual recognition and incomprehension. Thus a therapist can use what occurs in session to formulate experiments involving outside relationships. One may ask: '*Is it possible to recreate similar relational conditions between one session and the next?*', '*Can one try to negotiate and find solutions when there are misunderstandings, abandonments and mutual hostilities present?*' According to pathogenic schemas it is not possible, but events occurring in sessions show that there is another way. All of the techniques involving differentiation via the therapeutic relationship aim at promoting a true and proper critical distance: '*I've got a schema, but I realise that things can be different.*'

Demonstrating the recurring nature of narratives: the schema as an inner structure

A therapist should summarise a patient's narrative episodes and take note of interactional patterns throughout the patient's life. The therapist can identify that although the contexts and people he interacts with have differed throughout his life, the wish activated in the patient, others' responses to the patient and the patient's responses to others are recurring. At this point in therapy the patient is in a position to see that the repetition is due to inner, structural elements. After linking many various episodes, he is now capable of realising that that whatever the context and the people he interacts with, he tends to anticipate his wish will fail.

In one session, Arturo described how a work colleague had insulted him by telling him that something he had written sounded like it came from a stupid child. Unlike in the past, Arturo did not react violently and instead he tried to ask for an explanation in the hope of correcting the sentence. The colleague continued to deride him and when Arturo calmly insisted for an explanation a second time, the colleague ordered him to be quiet and threatened to hit him. Arturo felt strong and capable, and he replied that if confronted, he would accept the challenge. The colleague gradually became frightened and submissive. Arturo had no intention of arriving at physical blows; rather his goal was to explain himself and correct his mistake. The therapist validated Arturo's self-control and his ability to not dwell on his angry state. She then asked him what memories he could recall of being in similar situations in which he felt humiliated due to having written something poorly, as well as how he felt when he was not given the option of making a correction. He immediately thought of his father deriding him and imposing his own social success values on him while the patient was in the process of choosing a university course. After his recollection, Arturo realised that his reactiveness to criticism did not depend solely on current reality, i.e. the insult received, but also on the fact that historically he had never felt listened to or supported. This lack of support significantly affected him, to the extent that he stopped pursuing the goals that meant the most to him.

This form of differentiation is particularly effective if the memories recalled by association are linked to early developmental history, as was true in Arturo's case. In these moments it is the patient who gets to say: '*So, it's as if I was having a reckoning with my mother (or my father or other significant figures).*'

Differentiation regarding cognitive/affective self-representation: promoting agency over mental states

Even after collecting associated memories, some patients persist in believing in that their schemas are accurate, especially those relating to others. They may believe that they have simply encountered others, such as their relatives, who are not capable of meeting their wishes, and that there is someone who they have not met yet who is capable of respecting, loving or caring for them exactly as they wish. Consequently, they continue to consider their reactions of anger, resentment, withdrawal, shame or fear to be realistic. Such patients have ego-syntonic schemas or coping procedures that they consider irrevocable. In these cases, promoting differentiation regarding the entirety of the schema should be avoided. For example, one should not question a paranoid individual's idea that others are threatening. Instead, the patient's narrative episodes should be explored until egodystonic core schemas emerge. For example, a patient can be led to not dwell on his revengeful anger towards malevolent others, but instead reflect upon the sense of vulnerability he experiences when in their presence by evoking distant episodes when they felt this way. At this point in therapy, he should be invited to think about the possibility of feeling vulnerable as subjective and therefore amenable to change. In the beginning stages of this intervention it is important that the therapist not attempt to discuss the patient's main belief that others are threatening and hostile. Prior to implementing these interventions, the therapist should work on validating the patient, and perhaps using self-disclosure in the hope of creating a strong therapeutic alliance.

In the case of Romina, the paranoid PD patient described earlier, her therapist used a *self-disclosure*: '*I can understand you. I realise that feeling misunderstood by someone who imposes his will on you is a very distressing experience. I would feel like that too. What strikes me is that once this suffering state has been activated the emotion you feel is intense and pervasive, and it conditions your behaviour and won't leave your mind. Your reaction is, at least partly, comprehensible and justified; however, you do have power over it. It's a mental state, something you're able to change. If a person disregards your point of view and tries to crush it, you can feel humiliated. I can understand that. I too have memories similar to yours, where my point of view was ignored and my wishes were not listened to or respected. Although your reaction of feeling humiliated is automatic and understandable, the intensity and persistence of the emotion is under your control. The level of distress you experience depends much more on your belief of being incapable of criticism.*'

The goal with patients who negatively react to the idea that their constructions of others are based on schemas rather than on reality is to help them recognise that their emotional reactions are subjective. More specifically, the aim is for patients to strengthen their agency over their mental states and to understand that an emotion is an inner response that the other can only evoke but has no power over the intensity and duration.

> Eva was a 38-year-old commercial artist and had a dependent and depressive PD. She was excessively critical of herself and others, had obsessive-compulsive traits and displayed passive-aggressive behaviour. She endorsed feeling constantly invalidated by her mother, who systematically criticised her when she was a child. Her goal was to convince her mother to behave differently; she thought this was the only way for her to feel better. The therapist intervened as follows: '*Look, I can understand your mom had a negative impact on you due to her behaviours. I can understand you because I have similar memories, but it's an idea you've been exploring for a long time now and you haven't got any benefit from it. Trying to change your mom has proved to be useless and frustrating for you.*' Until now the therapist had not called into question the interpretation the patient gave of her mother. He also validated the patient by showing comprehension and using self-disclosure to let the patient know that he has had similar experiences. Later on the therapist attempted to direct Eva's focus of attention from her mother's behaviour to her own reactions to that behaviour. He asked, '*Eva, why do you take your mother's opinion so personally? Why do you necessarily have to feel humiliated and unrecognised, and at times even ugly and clumsy, if your mother criticises you? I can understand these emotions arise inside of you, but there's no reason they should persist.*' The therapist also stressed that Eva was reacting not so much to her 'real' mother as to her internalised mother, a critical figure inside of her that she had made her own. Eva responded positively to these interventions and gradually became aware that she had the power to abandon the automatic feelings of humiliation and instead act in line with her own wishes and inclinations when she was being criticised.

Some patients my struggle with ruminative fantasies that they are unable to take a critical distance from, and consequently they may spend a lot of time in session dwelling on them. Continuous rumination inhibits the patient from responding to interventions like those described above. In this situation the therapist is encouraged to politely point out that only one idea seems to interest the patient and that there is no room in sessions for talking about anything else or any other perspective (Lysaker and Buck, 2010). The therapist can also mention that he has no space for intervening if the patient will not attempt to think about events from another perspective.

Evaluating the degree of certainty in a belief

Another technique that is available is evaluating the degree of certainty in a patient's belief. This technique can be implemented when a patient displays ego-syntonic or coping schemas and has positive metacognitive beliefs about the usefulness of these schemas. In such cases a clinician can explore the degree of the patient's conviction, i.e. the intensity with which the patient believes his metabelief to be realistic (Wells, 2008). First and foremost the therapist should clearly identify and summarise the patient's metabelief: '*It seems that you think others will deceive you if you ask for help and it appears that you think that you're right to be on guard because this will stop you from being duped.*' A patient should then be asked how convinced he is that his belief is accurate: '*You told me that when your partner didn't answer the phone you thought she was being unfaithful to you. How much did you believe this, on a scale from 1 per cent to 100 per cent?*' The patient may reply that the degree of conviction was 100 per cent. However, if the episode continues to be explored, the patient may recall other instances of interaction in which his partner was attentive and present. At this point the therapist can ask the patient: '*At this moment, talking with me here, how convinced are you that your girlfriend didn't answer the phone because she was being unfaithful to you?*' The patient may reply '80 per cent'. The switch from total certainty (100 per cent) to high probability (80 per cent) is enough of a window to allow the therapist to show the patient that what may be initially perceived as an objective truth may instead be a subjective sensation and not a mirror image of reality. Once a patient forms a metabelief that his conviction may not be true, his certainty about a pathogenic idea has been corroded and there is now room for further forms of differentiation.

> Giulia talks about making twenty phone calls per day to her son's pediatrician due to being worried about his health. When the therapist asks her how convinced she is that it is right to behave in this alarmed fashion regarding her son's health, she replies: '*I was 100 per cent convinced, but now talking here with you, I am a bit less convinced. Let's say 70 per cent.*' At this point the therapist does not rationally refute the legitimacy of the patient's behaviour but instead helps her understand that she is not talking about a truth but rather a subjective belief. Giulia's controlling behaviour regarding her son's health becomes less frequent after this realisation.

Differentiating using healthy self-aspects as an observation point

This is one of the differentiation strategies most used by MIT and for this reason we will describe it in greater detail. During conversation, patients will access healthy self-parts on their own accord or as guided by their therapist. Among the collection of associated memories or in the descriptions of recent episodes emerge fragments of episodes or whole memories, which are discrepant from the schematic representations of self and others. For example, a patient may describe their success in a work situation while actually feeling inept and unable to be independent when faced with superior and critical others. Stimulating access to these healthy, schema-discrepant self-parts during conversation is one of the main techniques used in MIT for encouraging differentiation. Here we will discuss how accessing healthy self-parts encourages differentiation but we will cover this therapeutic mechanism in greater detail in Chapter 8. A therapist should pay great attention when patients display health, well-being and adaptation and describe themselves and the other in more favourable ways and then relate the narrative extracts to wishes they hope to be satisfied. A therapist should readily take advantage of these 'sparkling moments' (White and Epston, 1990) or 'innovative moments' (Gonçalves, Ribeiro, Mendes et al., 2011; Gonçalves, Mendes, Cruz et al., 2012) and point them out to the patient.

The aim is to identify these narrative episodes before they escape conscious reflection and to keep them in working memory for as long as possible. Keeping these narrative episodes in consciousness can be difficult due to their overwhelming power over the patient's schema-dependent images. It is important to note that the goal of this technique is not to make a patient doubt that her negative beliefs are true, but to help her discover that in these situations her view of self and other is different from what she usually thinks and expects. She discovers she is describing herself as active and able, accepted and appreciated, and capable of joy, whereas in many other moments she thought her life was one of endless gloom. The therapist should validate this arising state with clear communicational markers: his tone of voice, his posture and any emphasis employed should clearly convey the sense that what has emerged deserves attention and support. It is essential for a patient to experience affect that is consistent with the positive representation, even if only present at a low level of intensity, when she is describing her adaptive self-parts. It is important that the therapist's words are consistent with the patient's emotional experience, and if the patient's positive affect is barely present, the therapist's should remain more impressed and communicate this so that it is more likely remembered by the patient. Achieving the patient's focus on these positive mental states creates the conditions for them to become stable.

At this point the therapist should ask the patient to use this vantage point for considering her usual point of view. The intervention sounds as follows: *'Now you've just told me how you felt satisfied with what you'd done, and that your employer expressed appreciation. This is different from the idea that you usually have about not performing well at work and that others disparage what you do. While you were talking to me about what you'd done I saw in your face, and heard in your voice that you were content. Looking at yourself from this perspective, what do you think about your usual ideas? Is the person talking to me now not the same person who thinks you are not worth anything? What is this more favourable perspective of yours due to? Furthermore, what is stopping you from being aware of these positive moments in your daily life?'*

These interventions often turn out to be effective due to the patient being caught right in the heat of the moment of accessing her healthy self-parts. In these moments her dysfunctional beliefs and pathogenic schemas are incongruous with this adaptive representation and the affect associated with it and consequently believing in them becomes particularly difficult. In other words a patient can find it easier to differentiate if guided in this way.

In her first session, Lucia, the graphic designer suffering from avoidant and depressive PD described in Chapter 5, said she lacked stimuli and was apathetic, gloomy and sad. She described feeling tormented by distress by the idea of her partner gambling or attempting suicide. She endorsed feeling guilty about thinking of leaving him and indicated that she would only feel alright if he got better but she felt powerless to help him. Lucia's sole goal was to look after him, though she was convinced that her malaise was contributing to his. She was tormented by the idea that she was no longer enjoying life and she was worried there was no escape from the monotony.

To help Lucia to differentiate, the therapist pointed out to her that her eyes sparkled each time she spoke of her work and he continued to stress that her posture and facial expressions were congruous with the well-being she hoped for each time the patient described positive life events. After hearing the patient describe numerous positive situations, he asked her to keep track of any good moments that she experienced throughout the following week using a method similar to the CBT self-observation diaries used for depression (Beck, 2011). In the following session Lucia began by reviewing a long list of positive moments she had experienced: physical exercise in the morning, a 'good breakfast', listening to the radio in the car and opening-up the office when her colleagues still had not arrived. Acknowledging and accepting that she experienced good moments led to a crack in the patient's depressed and powerless self-image. The therapist helped Lucia realise that well-being was achievable by setting independent goals, pursuing them and drawing pleasure from them, and that the belief that her partner needed to get better in order for her to feel a sense of well-being was not as imperative as she initially thought.

Conversational strategies aimed at promoting a sense of sharing in topics of joint interest (see Chapter 5) are also very useful in accessing healthy parts of the patient. When a dialogue involves questions arousing the interest of both, the patient is more likely to access memories involving pleasure, enthusiasm, relaxation, satisfaction, playfulness, curiosity and competence. The therapist can use these sensations as a lever to help the patient adopt a critical distance from his current beliefs. Once a patient has experienced a positive *arousal* linked to adaptive representations it is imperative that he spend a significant amount of time in this affective state in session. The longer he experiences this positive arousal the more likely he will recall the related dialogue between one session and the next and to cultivate the positive representation at home and work and with his friends. This persistent, positive recollection will slowly strengthen and as a result his pathogenic schemas will become gradually less true and pervasive.

Eva felt constantly criticised by her mother and also felt pitiless toward herself. At the end of her second year of therapy she told her therapist that she was a good cook. The therapist emphasised the healthy self-part that the patient identified by asking her to show him some photos of the various stages in the preparation of a sumptuous Christmas dinner so that he could learn more about her talent. They looked at the photos together and lingered over the aromas of the food, the stages of preparation to bake the cake, the reactions of the guests and so on. While describing the scene, the patient's eyes were filled with joy. The therapist's intervention was as follows:

T: I'm struck because you're constantly telling me that you're feeling down, unmotivated and worthless and that you often feel criticised and rejected, but while you were describing yourself cook I could feel the energy and industry that encompassed you. You liked it, and felt confident in what you were doing and like others appreciated you in that moment.

P: Yes, in fact. Indeed … would you like me to also tell you about how I did the roast ham [*smiles*]?

At this point Eva showed him a series of photos taken at various stages in the preparation of the ham and told a story in which the main character was the ham. The therapist looked at the photos with her, feeling curious and not without a certain weakness from hunger! Then he commented:

T: At this moment while you're recalling this scene you feel good. Is that correct, Eva? It's visible that you put a lot of passion into it, and that you enjoy telling me about it.

P: Yes, it's true.

At this point, the therapist should try to anchor the patient to the positive and affectively charged observing self and then ask: '*Good, but from this position what do you think of that other you? The worthless one, without any qualities or motivation?*' If the patient suffers from a PD he will quickly be overwhelmed by his pathological mental state and will try to play down the positive experience that was just recalled. He may find arguments to minimise or circumscribe it or relative details that reduce its significance. The therapist should respond to this self-sabotage by attempting to focus the patient's attention to the recent shift in his mental states and to underline how easily the patient's pathogenic mental state has regained the upper hand. The necessity of remaining in this positive mental state for as long as possible should also be emphasised, and it should be communicated that the positive mental states, like the negative states, are not truths but rather they are ways of reacting that can be managed and modulated. It is important to stress that the problem for PDs is not that the representations of self and other are not false or unrealistic, but that these representations are pervasive, impermeable to alternative views, rigidly used and accompanied by an intense and distressing emotional echo which generates maladaptive actions.

From a clinical point of view, we should expect that in the early stages of therapy it will be difficult for the patient to acquire a lasting positive state due to it quickly being replaced by a negative one. Negative states are somatically engraved in procedural memory and consequently they are a type of mental automatism. The co-presence of the two states and the awareness of the sudden shift between the two is an important therapeutic factor.

While Eva was describing the Christmas dinner, her face began to darken as she remembered a negative comment her mother made about how Eva was dressed. Eva shared her frustration by stating, '*How is it possible that she always needs to judge and criticise me?*' The patient immediately reverted to the state she felt when the criticism was originally received. Her global of feeling acceptance and approval from others permeated her story about the dinner. In one of the patient's mental states (that regarding her relationship with her guests) the self was seen as effective and charged with positive affects and the other was seen as validating and full of appreciation. In the other mental state (that regarding her relationship with her mother) the self wished for acceptance and approval but the other was seen as critical. In this state the self's reaction was depression and loss of initiative and the patient thought, '*So what's the point of doing it? I don't feel like it. I could just drop everything and quit.*' These thoughts represent a loss of agency, personal efficacy and motivation, and the dominant emotion was anger due to the injustice that was suffered. This strong feeling of anger was a reaction of the healthy part of the self which felt it deserved appreciation and positive opinions. At this point in the session the therapist pointed out to Eva that her mind was fluctuating between one state and another, and that when one was felt to be true, the other seemed to disappear and vice versa. As Eva began to see this shift between mental states, she started to realise that the negative image and the resulting depression were not the only refrain in her life which she had initially thought at the beginning of the session. Her access to the positive state she entered into while cooking was proof that her idea about life being monotonous and like an endless tunnel was not realistic. The therapist did not confute her belief; it was the patient who realised the irrationality of this belief through the direct realisation of having alternative self-images.

Eva's narrative shows that interventions of this kind, in which a patient is asked to use the perspective of a mental state to reflect critically on the pathogenic beliefs typical of his negative states, are also implicitly aimed at promoting integration. The patient may realise, '*One part of me feels passive and powerless, and the other part of me feels capable of enjoying life and has initiative.*' We will return to this in greater detail in Chapter 9.

Use of experiments for strengthening only partially acquired differentiation

In the next chapter we will discuss the next stage of therapy that is implemented once some associated memories are recalled and differentiation has been promoted.

The therapy contract should be renegotiated, and the patient should be asked to engage in experiments to overcome avoidances and to construct new ways of thinking, feeling and relating. These experiments have the aim of further reinforcing differentiation. As sessions progress, patients begin to understand that their view of events is subjective, contrary to what they previously believed. However, patients are often incapable of acting in accordance with this new view between therapy sessions. Their pathogenic schema has therefore been temporarily set aside at a cognitive level, but procedurally it continues to dictate action. The real change in perspective begins when differentiation is fully achieved and this involves emotional and behavioural changes. Only when a patient manages to act differently from his schema can we say that it has been replaced by alternative views or at least possesses less power and pervasiveness. When planning behavioural experiments with the patient, it is important that the therapist communicate to the patient that the initial goal is not so much to produce change but to remove any remaining maladaptive schemas.

During an experiment the patient typically experiences a mixture of old thoughts and emotions that are often supported by distressing mental states and flashes of more favourable ones. The therapist and patient should process what happened during the experiment as well as how the patient thought and felt. Together they should evaluate the patient's vacillations between the patient's world view that is typical of PD and another perspective. This process of evaluation helps stimulate differentiation further. During the experiment patients often find that they have acquired more effective forms of coping, which constitutes another part of differentiation: '*I thought I was incapable of replying calmly and firmly to my boss's pressure. I thought I'd fall to pieces or react angrily, but instead I managed to only feel a bit uneasy and afraid of breaking down. I felt I had something valid to say, and I said it calmly and was listened to.*' This use of experimentation, which is a common technique in CBT's rational-emotional therapy, encourages the reviewing of beliefs, i.e. *empirical disputing*: a patient has an idea which he has already partly criticised and uses the results of the experiment to evaluate how much his pathogenic idea holds or whether there are alternative views of reality (Ellis, 1962).

True and proper disputing

A therapist may progress to the classic disputing procedure typical of CBT (Beck, 2011) when the following conditions are met: the atmosphere in a therapeutic relationship is not conflictual, affective markers indicate that the negative affect linked to the schema is not particularly powerful, no protective mechanisms have been activated and there are no metacognitive beliefs suggesting to the patient that it is legitimate but also important to believe in the schema. A therapist may bring to the patient's attention any discrepancies between what he is saying and what emerges from looking differently at his narrative episodes or the therapist can use a classic CBT technique and ask the patient to assume the burden of proof in regard to the accuracy of his beliefs.

> Eva described to her therapist that she had been feeling isolated due to not spending time with others unless she initiated the social gathering. The therapist responded by listing a number of people who had initiated contact with the patient during the past week. The list included a wooer, a colleague asking her for advice and another colleague offering her a job – all of whom the patient seemed not to be considering. He thus directly confuted her schema which did not stand up to the challenge of reality. This intervention helped Eva realise that she had not been noticing any of the signals indicating that others had shown interest in her.

Of all the procedures for promoting differentiation, *disputing* is the one we suggest using least often and most cautiously. Recall that schemas are more than just beliefs; they are emotionally marked representations that can be thought of as produced inside the body during development, making it difficult for a patient to deem them wrong or dysfunctional. Furthermore, only in some cases are ideas about self and others in relationships manifestly false, meaning that more often it is a question of rigid perspectives and a tendency to see things from only one angle. Occasionally a patient's interpretation of events is implausible and he does not display a particular attachment to his beliefs. In these instances it is appropriate for the therapist to invite the patient to think about how unrealistic his ideas are and inquire about any proof that he has to support them. Due to the patient not having a strong attachment to his beliefs, this challenge is unlikely to deteriorate the therapeutic relationship. The disputing technique is more appropriate for the advanced stages of treatment when differentiation has already been partially achieved through the techniques previously suggested.

As therapy progresses a patient will become aware of certain situations that have been repeated throughout his life and he will also have come to the realisation that he has over-intense emotional reactions to these events. In session the patient will occasionally communicate that he understands that these are subjective representations and not reality but that he reverts to a schema-dependent way of thinking under stress. The therapist can summarise what has been achieved in therapy so far and communicate to the patient that although his progress has been temporarily lost they can work together in its restoration. The therapist should then invite the patient to provide evidence to support his beliefs to patiently portray that it is not enough only to state that the schema-dependent idea is true.

What to do once differentiation is acquired?

Acquiring an initial capacity to differentiate and acknowledging the subjective nature of suffering is the cornerstone of therapeutic change. Practically all other changes require differentiation for them to reach fruition. Once a patient begins to become aware that his perception is only one view of the world and consequently not reality, it is possible to progress to more advanced phases of treatment such as: building well-being via an access to, and the exercise of alternative views of, self with other which is free from schemas, forming an accurate and decentred theory of the other's mind and using it to solve relational problems, and creating a comprehensive self-image by combining one's various facets into a coherent whole. We shall describe these operations in subsequent chapters.

Note

1 It is important to note that the forms of differentiation described here are examples of particular interpersonal relationship schema-dependent beliefs. There are, however, other subjects of differentiation such as catastrophic beliefs typical of anxiety disorders or thought-action fusion beliefs typical in obsessive-compulsive disorder. There is also the lack of differentiation of the dissociative type when a patient is unable to distinguish in which state of consciousness an experience occurs: *'Is it a memory? A dream? Did it really happen or have I invented it?'* We are not going to dwell on promoting these types of differentiation because they are not specific to the PD discussed here, but we refer the reader to additional resources specific to CBT (Beck, 2005; Shafran and Rachman, 2004) and dissociative disorder therapies (Van der Hart, Nijenhuis and Steele, 2006).

Chapter 8

Construction of new self-aspects

Access to self-parts, exploration, increase in agency, overcoming avoidances

Some important aspects of PD therapy include learning to question, distancing from pathogenic schemas and constructing new self-images and narratives to guide one towards adaptation and self-achievement (Livesley, 2003). The latter goal is more difficult to accomplish and usually requires more time. It involves identifying our desires, reacquiring a sense of agency, building new interpersonal schemas that will guide our actions and anticipate that our wishes can be achieved and, finally, trying to achieve the most important things we guard in our hearts. At this stage our world map gets larger. By exploring new situations, starting new relationships and experimenting with new ways of thinking and behaving, patients encounter experiences they never have before, get to know aspects of the world formerly unknown to them, reinforce skills never before used or developed, and exercise abilities they did not think they had or could acquire.

This constructing task starts at a very precise point in the sequences of interventions proposed by MIT, where patients are beginning to differentiate and become aware that the obstacles to their self-achievement and well-being depend mostly on how they reconstruct events. At the same time, they are beginning to access their healthy self-parts and positive subjective experiences such as relaxing, playing, feelings of attunement, mutual help and activeness. A therapist should help a patient to take note of, enlarge on and recall these adaptive aspects that are charged with positive emotions (Frederickson, 2001; Greenberg, 2002) (see Figure 8.1).

Once a patient has started to differentiate and become aware of his positive self-aspects, it is time to reformulate the therapeutic contract. Once patients are aware they are being driven by schemas that cause suffering and the expectation of negative responses from others, many patients typically ask, '*So is it me who tends to think I'm not worth anything and expects others to be nicer to me, with even the slightest negative sign being enough for me to feel discouraged or offended? I can see I'm made like that, but ... and now, to feel better, what should I do?*' This is a question that can sometimes make a therapist go into a cold panic.

This chapter is an attempt to offer techniques for replying to this question. We shall see, in the following order, how to: (1) help patients access self-parts during sessions; (2) reformulate the therapeutic contract in order to promote

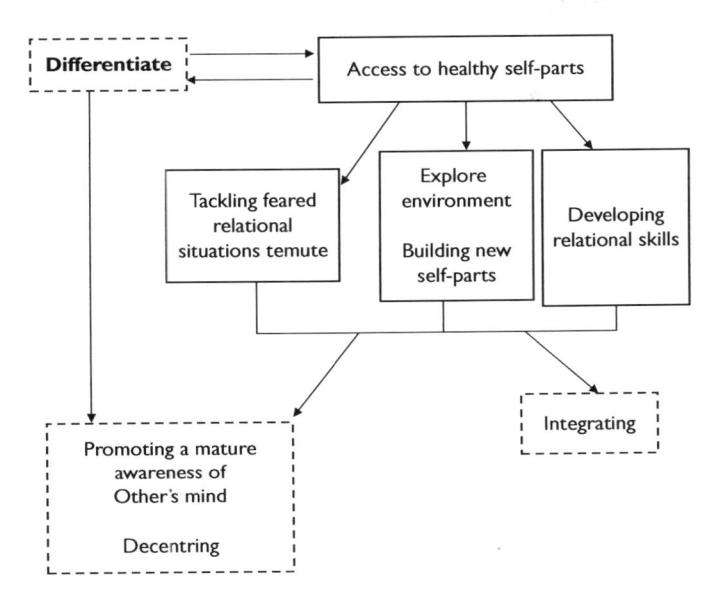

Figure 8.1 Access to healthy self-parts.

change between one session and the next; (3) activate the exploratory system, promote agency and help patients to use their own wishes as action guides; (4) programme behavioural experiments and review patients' experiences in session while they undertake new actions in their daily life; (5) enrich the system of self-representations with the elements surfacing during explorations.

The change process at this point in a therapy is based especially on an *experiment planning – exploration of new areas in the world – reflection* cycle (Dimaggio, Popolo, Carcione et al., in press).

The planning – experiment – reflection cycle

The building of self-parts is a cyclical learning process. The cycle starts when patients have identified, taken note of and memorised their healthy parts in session. The stages in the cycle are: (1) *planning* new forms of behaviour while making forecasts about the types of experiences a patient will encounter and the social consequences of this; (2) *behavioural exposure/exploration*, that is adopting new forms of behaviour driven by thoughts and emotions stimulating well-being, adaptation and widening of social relations; (3) *ongoing reflection* during sessions about the new experiences until they are *integrated* into the self-system (Gonçalves, Matos and Santos, 2009; Stiles, 2011).

A patient with avoidant PD may find he wants a romantic relationship to satisfy his sexual desires and also to reinforce his self-esteem and not feel like an outcast.

The necessary condition for turning the actual search for a partner in a patient's daily life into a therapeutic goal is for the patient to have, in session, experienced situations of self-efficacy in which his self-esteem was good. One needs to salvage those moments of hope at which he dreamed about a girl and wanted her and, if in the past he has had relationships, however short, recall the positive moments in which he experienced emotions, involvement and romantic dreams. Such memories will help the patient desire the girl and feel like he is capable of attracting her. At this point planning starts. Is the patient interested in a specific girl? Does he not know any girls and thus needs to go to places where he can meet someone? It is necessary to pinpoint any intermediate goals. What places to go to? Does he have any friends who could help by introducing him to a girl?

Once the planning has been done, the patient should try to turn the plans into action. This is the *behavioural experiment/exposure* stage, involving a true and proper exploration of territory and which we will describe later. In the sessions that follow, the patient and therapist should use the exploration as a new narrative episode to be investigated: this is the *reflection* stage. What happened? What did the patient feel and experience while he was calling his friend about going out or while talking to the girl at the pub? Did he have recognisable experiences, traceable to his schema, or did he experience pleasure, self-efficacy and confidence? We shall now describe the various aspects of building new self-parts point by point.

Accessing healthy parts in session

The best way of showing a PD patient that she is capable of feeling confident, competent, relaxed and enthusiastic is to catch her while she is experiencing such feelings. As we showed in Chapter 5, a therapist should pay continuous attention to any non-verbal signals and to the contents of the patient's discourse, and, as soon as the latter shows recognisable indications of positive states and talks about himself in schema-discrepant ways, point this out to him. In this way the patient does not need to be convinced or his pathogenic beliefs debated to make him differentiate; it is enough to get him to pay attention to what he is feeling at that moment and link his sensorial experience with metacognitive reflections.

The aim of these interventions is not simply to promote awareness but to stimulate a true and proper shift in mental state. Once the patient has noticed his positive state, the therapist should see that he passes as much of the session as possible in this state. This helps to interrupt the ruminant circuits in the patient's negative states, with the favourable experience remaining in working memory long enough to be memorised. As we would recall, one of the reasons PDs persist is due to the activation of affect-dependent cognitive processes. A profitable strategy is to interrupt these processes by exploiting the change in affect, which then generates cognitions congruent with it. In this way, we are applying the principles of the *broaden-and-build* theory of positive emotions (Frederickson, 2001). People experiencing positive emotions are more confident, motivated to achieve plans, capable of blocking stress and apt to solve problems creatively. With PD patients, furthermore, if they improve their mood and affective experience quality in session, the therapeutic alliance becomes stronger and the outcome better (McMain, Links, Guimond et al., 2013; Richardson-Vejlgaard, Broudy, Brodsky et al., 2013). The more we manage to get patients to remain in positive states, the more we are making it possible for them to activate adaptive forms of functioning.

The access to positive states has a second function: programming change between sessions. During positive or schema-discrepant states, positive self-representations and desires surface. A therapist can programme behavioural change based on these, as we shall see after a description of how to reformulate the therapeutic contract.

Accessing healthy self-parts was a core element in the therapy of Lucia, the commercial artist suffering from avoidant and depressive PD, described in Chapter 5.

> Lucia started her earliest sessions feeling disheartened, discouraged and depressed. The idea that her boyfriend might from one moment to the next become depressed or go gambling crippled her and made her angry. Finding herself being angry made her feel guilty; in this she could see exactly the same relationship that there was between her depressed father and her mother, who criticised him for being passive. She felt powerless to exit from the pattern she had learned and criticised herself because her anger was harming her partner. However, during their conversations the therapist constantly asked her to focus on those moments in which she did not feel distressed. The therapist was reconstructing Lucia's schema and pointed out to her that she was driven by the wish to be independent and creative but was blocked by the idea that, if she were to pursue it, she would harm the other and feel guilty. She feared being alone and losing the other and for this reason repressed any activity that might give her relief or pleasure.
>
> The therapist demonstrated to Lucia that she was unable to imagine being alright separately from the other and asked her to consider making her well-being a therapy goal, even if her partner continued to have problems, as she did not have the power to cure him and self-sacrifice was unnecessary. At the same time, she pointed out that feeling better would perhaps have some indirect beneficial effects on her partner. With some difficulty, Lucia was able to see these were reasonable goals but at the same time she admitted that it was very difficult for her to pursue them. At this point the therapist asked her to yield, in session, to fantasies about what she would like to do if on her own. Although with much difficulty and guilty feelings, Lucia managed to confess that, when she was young, she did rock-climbing. While recalling the sensations climbing gave her, she changed expression, smiling with her head upright and her eyes sparkling with energy. The therapist immediately pointed out this change and told her that at that moment she looked better. Lucia was taken aback and felt guilty. The therapist insisted. She validated the guilty feelings and showed Lucia that they indicated how important her partner was for her, but also stressed that there was a vital aspect of herself that did not deserve to be left to disappear.
>
> A few sessions later, in the context of the exploration driven by her attempt to achieve her desires, Lucia accessed another old love of hers, painting. Starting in

adolescence Lucia used to paint for hours on end. She copied old masters and, as she grew up, developed her own personal style. She recalled that her father never gave her his approval and pointed out every little flaw without ever praising her for the quality of her works or encouraging her to continue. Over the years Lucia painted hundreds of copies of Renaissance and Flemish paintings and numerous abstract works. She bitterly confessed that she had not painted for some years and there were only some almost invisible traces left of this love of hers. The therapist empathetically attuned with her bitterness and confessed to Lucia that she was sorry too because she also loved painting. She, however, pointed out that behind this bitterness there was love, culture and skill and that Lucia still had a faint desire to paint. She asked Lucia if she could see some photos or reproductions of her works. Lucia had an old book and brought it to one of the next sessions. In the part about experiments aimed at achieving patients' wishes, we shall go back to seeing how Lucia's therapy evolved after accessing her desires and positive states in session.

Reformulation of the therapeutic contract

It has been known for some time that the formulation of the therapeutic contract is a fundamental element in PD therapy (Clarkin, Yeomans and Kernberg, 1999; Linehan, 1993; Links, Mercer and Novick, in press). Here we point out that the contract should be updated and renegotiated on an ongoing basis during therapy. As a patient gradually progresses, the goals change and the therapist should never assume that what he believes are reasonable, desirable and necessary goals appear the same way to the patient. Additionally, he should not take for granted if the patient wants or feels capable of undertaking the actions necessary for achieving his own well-being. Forgetting to redefine what was agreed about mutual goals and tasks is often a cause of alliance ruptures, reduction in the patient's agency and frustration for the therapist. A mistake often made by therapists is to insist that the patient do what they themselves consider useful, with the reaction being one of opposition or alarm, very frequent in all the PDS treated here. A therapist should always perceive when he is proceeding without an agreement so that he stops and renegotiates the contract.

We will summarise the preconditions indicating that the therapeutic contract needs to be reformulated. At this stage a patient has a good self-reflectivity, to the extent that she has started to perceive that she is driven by pathogenic schemas and is able to differentiate. Her differentiation is, however, still unstable; between one session and the next she realises she often falls back into her negative states and in these situations finds it difficult to keep up the differentiation she has achieved. At the same time her professional and relational lives may not be satisfying; she is either out of work, working a job below her skill level or not in line with her interests, or has accepted something out of pure necessity. She has few or no friends, her romantic relationships are either zero or problematic and she may not yet have untied herself from her parents. At the same time, as we have just seen, she has accessed positive aspects of experience and realises she has some unachieved wishes.

At this point there needs to be a small revolution in the therapy framework. The therapist should now point out that well-being depends gradually more on the actions carried out by the patient between sessions rather than on what happens during a session. The therapeutic dialogue is still reflecting on any new material emerging in order to interpret it and combine it in the patient's identity, but the real engine for change becomes what the patient does in his daily life. Of course, the therapist should underscore that in any distress, stress or relapse situations he will always be present, close and supportive, and ready to deepen his knowledge of the patient's inner world and enhance regulation of his mental states. The new, shared goal will be for the patient to live a richer and more fulfilling life by having new experiences, learning new skills and building new meanings. In order to do this, she will need to focus on what she desires, wants and hopes for herself and on what she feels to be intimate and personal (Dimaggio, Salvatore, Fiore et al., 2012; Hayes, Strosahl and Wilson, 2011; Padesky and Mooney, 2012). Once these aspects have been identified, one can think about sustainable ways of trying to achieve them by programming true and proper behavioural experiments.

The therapist should explain that the goal of the experiments is, first and foremost, to produce new experience sources that can then be the subject of reflection in session and that the new meanings emerging will be the basis for formulating further plans and behavioural experiments. We shall, therefore, describe how to activate a sort of new *actions/reflections/further new actions* cycle, a path aimed at enriching the patient's inner and relational world (Gonçalves, Matos and Santos, 2009).

Courteously and supportively the therapist should explain:

- Although the patient has partly taken a critical distance from his schemas, there are still avoidance mechanisms leaving the schemas untouched at a procedural level so that they still dictate action. Without overcoming avoidances, the pathogenic schemas will continue their harmful action, while tackling them will reduce the potency of these structures.
- Well-being depends on activity (agency) (Stiles, 2011), projectuality and self-achievement and without pursuing one's own goals and desiderata it will be difficult to achieve it.
- Social life is complex and difficult to understand. The exercise of reflecting on minds in the act of competing, courting, caregiving and asking for help is the tool that can open up knowledge of one's own mind and others' minds, and of how others react when we practice new parts of ourselves.

It is a question of explaining to patients that, without leaving their house and meeting others, they will not lose their sense of solitude and alienation, without any professional plans their sense of inefficacy will not truly shrink, and without experiencing independence their sensation of being fragile and at others' mercy will not diminish. We can, instead, feel satisfied if we pursue goals we feel to be ours, which we believe in and which excite us.

In MIT the therapeutic contract does not get formulated or reformulated at some defined moment but gets re-discussed at each turning point. If new aspects of the patient surface that require restarting the work from narrative episodes to understanding schemas, the therapist can suggest part of the sessions be focused on continuing exploration and other parts to increasing awareness of the patient's inner world. Here is what a typical reformulation of the contract sounds like:

'Good. Now we've grasped that you feel clumsy, inadequate and full of shame and, because of this, you avoid meeting people whom you might like and to whom you could bond. We know this is how you see yourself and not how you really are. On the other hand, you've got a huge fear about attracting attention because you wouldn't know how to behave in new situations and the fear you have of being criticised and seeming ridiculous is still strong. This means that a part of you is anchored to the idea that you're ridiculous and others could criticise or humiliate you. Furthermore you have difficulty imagining how others might react if you did today what you've been avoiding for years in the past. For treatment to be useful, we need to try to do something outside sessions and increase social contacts. You said you have some old friends you'd like to get in contact with, but you're afraid of being rejected. We could start by telephoning the one you felt closest to you. If the call goes okay, you could think about suggesting going out for a pizza together or meeting up on a Friday evening. Would you agree to doing something like that or do you have other, more acceptable and feasible ideas than the one I've just proposed to you? I would stress that this is not my aim. I don't think that if you do it you'll be a good patient and otherwise I'll be disappointed. We've worked well together, things are changing and I only wanted to share with you the realistic expectation that to change further we'll need to try doing something new, obviously cautiously and gradually, when you're ready and with respect for your fears. Let's try and see how you can restart a social life, go out with friends and meet a girl, which is perhaps your strongest wish at present. If you feel up to trying, let's think together how. If it's too much, let's think about doing things you consider more feasible. If you can't manage to take new paths, I'll always be with you, listening to you attentively and carefully, but I just need to remind you that like this it's going to be difficult for us to truly overcome the problems that are still making you suffer. Do you feel up to trying this together? Are we agreed and shall we together decide the next move to make?'

During this chapter we will describe first how the experiments should be planned in a *planning–experiment–reflection* cycle. Then we will describe the goals at which the experiments are aimed, from overcoming avoidances to the activation of the exploratory system in order to construct self-parts syntonic with one's own wishes.

Activating the exploratory system and carrying out behavioural experiments

The core factor in change is the activation of the exploratory system (Panksepp, 1998), with which a patient becomes curious about the world and gradually passes from understanding what has driven her life hitherto to discovering how her life could be if she acted differently and explored places unknown to her. The goals to pursue at this stage vary depending on the patient's main problem, as do the obstacles to tackle and the rationale with which the experiment is programmed.

The patient may:

- avoid feared situations and thus deny herself new experiences and self-achievement opportunities. If this is the problem, the patient's goal should be *to tackle avoidances* and expose herself to the feared relational situations;
- lack agency and access her wishes with difficulty. In this case she does not act adaptively because she has difficulty identifying the inner sources of her actions and feels prevented from taking control of her life. If this is the problem, the patient's goal should be to access her desires and strengthen agency;
- know what she wants and be quite confident in the possibility of achieving it, but lack a map to guide her and the necessary skills. If this is the problem, the goal should be *to create the right context for learning these new skills* and enrich the patients' relationship repertoire.

Table 8.1. is a schematic representation of the problems encountered and the related treatment goals.

While exploring new relationships, a patient practices her theory of mind and decentring skills. The schema-dependent perspectives from which she reads others' intentions, thoughts and emotions have by now shown that they are the result of stereotypes or attentional biases. She knows she is more likely to notice certain thoughts or intentions or see them where they do not exist and react while ignoring other cues not relevant to her schemas. In encounters occurring at the exploration stage, patients can build up alternative interpretations, notice the richness of emotions and ideas and the complexity driving others, and grasp that they see the world from a different perspective that does not always include them. We shall

Table 8.1 Planning exploration according to type of problem

Patient problem	Treatment goals
Massive avoidances and impossibility of having new experiences	Tackling the avoidances with exposure to feared situations
Lack of agency	Promotion of access to wishes and strengthening of the ability to choose independently
Lack of the necessary skills for achieving one's wishes	Building of the necessary skills and formation of new interpersonal schemas

describe the theory of mind-broadening and decentring perspective-building operations in detail in Chapter 9 but would point out that they are interwoven with the exploration stage discussed here.

Tackling avoidances/exposure to feared situations

The focus of these experiments is the fact that a patient often *fears* the other's negative response. It is therefore a process similar to that occurring in CBT for anxiety disorders, for example social phobia (Clark and Beck, 2010). Many PD patients fear others' reactions and avoid exposure, which restricts their social life. A person with avoidant PD withdraws from social exposure for fear of criticism. A person with dependent features fears that if he becomes independent, he will displease the other who will abandon him, and therefore avoids any action the other will disapprove of. A patient with paranoid PD fears humiliation or aggression and isolates herself. A man with narcissism is convinced he is not supported and chillily closes himself up in an ivory tower. As soon as a patient with obsessive-compulsive PD feels like relaxing or enjoying life, he judges himself to be selfish and immoral and is convinced he is depriving others of something he owes them, so that he consequently feels guilty and blocks any activities providing him with well-being.

In their different ways these are all operations for forestalling the arising of negative affects evoked by forecasts about the consequences of one's actions. There does not need to be a 'real' other to restrain behaviour; sometimes the forecasts a patient makes inside him are enough. An obsessive-compulsive PD patient fears being judged and even self-criticism, that is an internalised critical other, is enough to block him when, for example, he is anticipating relaxing on holiday. Patients may possess a cognitive awareness that these fears are substantially the result of schemas and are therefore unfounded, but the schemas are encoded at a procedural and automatic level from which they dictate behaviour. Thus, even if patients say they can understand that they do not really fear criticism or being abandoned, they avoid exposure.

To challenge these residual fears and the procedural part of their schemas, which is the most solid one, patients need exposure. With exposure they can see that their fears are unfounded, they have mastery skills and others do not react as in their negative expectations. While tackling a feared situation, a patient has a chance to access the pleasurable aspects of experience. For example, when a patient with avoidant PD and social phobia overcomes her fear of looking ridiculous because she sweats and goes to a dinner, she enjoys the pleasure of the convivial company. An avoidant young man afraid of intimacy when courting a woman then discovers the beauty of romance and sex. A dependent woman acting independently discovers a sense of efficacy and positive self-esteem.

Organising exposures to feared situations follows CBT principles for phobias. Goals (*planning*) should be defined and the therapist and patient should jointly choose those fears that she can envision most easily. There should then be an agreement on the forms and timing of the exposure. The patient undertakes the experiment (*behavioural exposure*) and, in the next session, the new narrative episode should be picked through in detail, while observing the inner experience correlated to it by focusing on how the patient ascribes meaning to what happened (*reflection*).

After a year and a half of therapy Fulvio, the patient with avoidant PD, dependent and depressive traits and social phobia described in Chapter 5, had improved. His phobic symptoms had diminished, his mood was better and he felt more free. His perfectionism had become less extreme and he was now more capable of enjoying life; there were numerous episodes related by him where he played with his daughters while paying less attention to their performance at school and in sports. In his social relationships he still found it difficult to express his own point of view when he disagreed with others. He felt restrained by his fear of being belittled and by the idea that if he asserted himself, he would be harming others, be considered arrogant and feel guilty. Over a number of months his relationship with his partner in the consulting firm became central. Fulvio described his partner, a cousin, as being unreliable and incapable of meeting deadlines. For this reason he had to do the majority of the work and often had to make up for his partner's failings. The firm's profits were, however, shared 50–50, which he found more and more unfair. Initially Fulvio did not want to tackle the problem and had decided to leave the situation just as it was, to avoid hurting his cousin and feeling guilty. At the same time, he did not wish to close down the firm because he did not want to work alone and was afraid he couldn't manage all the responsibilities.

Initially, there were no conditions for reformulating the therapeutic contract. The therapist could only help Fulvio to accept and modulate his inevitable negative feelings deriving from the conflictual relationship with his partner. Fulvio was aware of how laborious this would be and that he was choosing to put up with a frustrating situation. In the months that followed, however, he related numerous episodes in which he felt hindered and sometimes exploited by his cousin and that the excess of work he was taking on due to his cousin's deficiencies was hard to bear.

The therapist asked Fulvio how much he still felt inclined to modulate these feelings, which meant enduring a stressful and tiring psychological task. Fulvio realised his original plan was not fostering his own well-being. A joint decision was then made to reformulate the therapeutic contract: he was to confront his cousin and raise the question with him. The potential consequences were that he would suffer anticipatory anxiety, be afraid of not controlling his anger and fear breaking up their relationship, thus leading to his fear of not being able to run the firm on his own. To avoid making the experiment too constrictive, he was free to choose the moment for the discussion, even if it was several months later (*planning*). The occasion turned out to be when the offices were to be refurbished. His cousin, in Fulvio's words, was immobile and this forced Fulvio to do the manual job of putting the files back in place and to climb over his cousin's binders still strewn along the corridor. In a moment of anger, Fulvio recalled what had been said in session and realised it was the right moment to confront his partner. At this point, he went into the cousin's room and told him what he thought firmly and angrily but without exploding.

Surprisingly, his cousin reacted by taking full responsibility and acknowledging his limitations. Fulvio temporarily obtained more cooperation and felt relieved (*exploration/behavioural experiment*). In session, Fulvio and the therapist went back over the episode and he realised he was able to handle conflicts and felt more capable of doing things on his own. He started to overcome his sense of guilt and found he was entitled to have the recognition he deserved without being stopped by mental images of harming others (*reflection*).

The *planning/exploration/reflection* cycle continued during the following months and Fulvio often changed his behaviour and expressed his point of view firmly and decisively, while feeling proud and realising he was able to convince people without hurting them. He still had problems enjoying the fruits of his good work because he was afraid this would make him vain, but he gradually managed to appreciate what he was doing and accept compliments.

Access to wishes: exploring the territory/ promoting independence and agency

These experiments focus on a patient's wishes, and consequently the work involves promoting *agency* and consolidating identity. Accessing one's own wishes, pursuing them, experiencing a sense of agency instead of passivity and conforming to the norm and acting independently by following one's own preferences, emotions and values are at the heart of regaining health in PD therapy. The world starts to take the shape no longer of a source of danger and frustration but of a new territory to explore and investigate.

This part of the treatment is consistent with Acceptance and Commitment Therapy (ACT) (Hayes, Strosahl and Wilson, 2011), which asks patients to focus on their own values and undertake actions in line with their values to overcome their malaise and pursue self-achievement. The difference between ACT and MIT is that MIT does not focus so much on personal values which, in our opinion, risk being expressed in an abstract, intellectualising fashion and sometimes represent merely forms of coping. In MIT, patients are instead asked to act on the basis of more authentic desires emerging in their autobiographical memories. In this way, we try to help patients become more in touch with their embodied motivations, emotionally laden and closer to the nuclei on which identity is founded.

For example, a person might state that he is driven by the value of being a good father and wants to devote himself more to his children whom he feels he has been neglecting. Such a wish might not be a basic motivation but a coping strategy using moral perfectionism in order to avoid feeling unworthy.

The analysis of his narrative episodes might indicate that the patient is already spending time with his children at the expense of some creative activities he stopped doing some time ago due to guilty feelings, as he is profoundly convinced that, if he does something gratifying to himself, people close to him will suffer.

In this case the therapy goal is paradoxically to devote himself *less* to his children and to balance his parental duties with activities aimed at self-achievement.

In her second and third months of therapy, Lucia started sessions in a pessimistic state. She was worried about her inability to carry out what had been suggested in session. Her therapist asked her to describe her days. The picture emerging was different. Lucia had spoken about the idea of doing rock-climbing and her partner reacted badly and accused her of wanting to spend time without him. The therapist immediately pointed out that this was a sign of progress: inside her she had nevertheless kept the wish to go rock-climbing and she had spoken about it with her partner. Although faced with a negative response, her sense of guilt was less intense and her idea about joining a mountaineering club had not gone away. The therapist pointed out to Lucia that, while she spoke, she displayed more anger than guilt and the idea of rock-climbing made her seem more lively and active. Lucia objected that if her partner's mental health did not improve, there was no hope. At the same time, however, she declared: '*These mechanisms of mine paralyse me.*' The therapist insisted that this awareness also represented progress; Lucia was no longer saying '*I'm not able to do anything, I'm restricted and powerless*' and realised she had internalised mechanisms on which she was working during therapy.

As the conversation continued, Lucia related that she had still not gone to see the mountaineering club but had visited its website which she liked, and she was still taken by the idea of going there in person. These were all signs that she was starting to sustain in her mind the path that goes from acknowledging a wish to its planning and carrying out, i.e. the *planning and behavioural exposure* stages. The *reflection* in session part showed that, thanks to the attempt to make her healthy parts emerge, Lucia had acquired a greater critical distance from her pathogenic schemas. Between the sessions that followed she went out together with her partner and together with some relatives (something that had not happened for years), and they had a pleasant evening. She brought the book with her paintings to therapy. The therapist was keen to look at them – she too had been an amateur painter – and found she admired the quality of the work. Lucia displayed a technique of a professional level and an uncommon taste and artistic knowledge, qualities that she knew she had, as could be seen from the flash of pride in her face when she talked about her works but which she underrated. She was touched when the therapist encouraged her to pick up her brushes again. At the same time, she was overcome by a wave of bitterness when she remembered how, as an adolescent, her mother never expressed any positive comments when she looked at Lucia's paintings but instead pointed out the slightest mistakes.

As can be seen from this excerpt, exploration aimed at promoting actions consistent with wishes, together with differentiation, is the prelude to building a more integrated self-image. Various strands of one's personal history become integrated into a richly nuanced picture, in which hopes, bitterness, memories and opportunities cohabit in conscious reflection, whereas previously the mind did not manage to keep them together. In Chapter 9 we shall see how to reinforce this work.

Building new skills

The focus of these experiments is what the patient *lacks*; the goal is the creation of new tools for finding one's way in relationships. This involves :

- constructing tools for tackling new social situations, such as enrolling in a course, obtaining a driver's licence, taking on a business activity or learning new skills (cooking, using the computer, etc.);
- widening one's repertoire of social skills, such as relating with peers, courting a person in whom one is interested, expressing an idea assertively, calming a conflict and so on;
- widening one's repertoire of self-other schemas via the exercise of new skills.

This part is generally complementary to the first two forms of activation of the exploratory system, that is overcoming avoidances and pursuing wishes. When patients have to tackle feared situations, they ask themselves: 'But how am I going to …?'. They find they wish for something but do not know what to do to pursue it. A clinician has the task of helping them to sustain their curiosity and their exploring with suitable tools. The building of skills can take place in individual sessions, as we will show with a few clinical examples, or by complementing individual therapy with some specific modules.

Promoting skills in individual sessions

The moment at which to promote new skills in individual sessions is typically in a motivational context that lies between the exploratory system (Bowlby, 1988; Panksepp, 1998) and fear of the unknown. The patient wants to learn but is afraid of the new world opening up before him and of failing. This can cause paralysis and the lack of skills can block actions. Attachment therefore becomes reactivated in this stage, but in a more physiological way. The patient feels the fear of the unknown that grabs persons when they separate from reference figures in order to explore terrains new to them. The therapist can allay this fear by supplying knowledge rendering the world less unknown and the skills to facilitate the exploration, with a reasonable hope that this will calm the patient.

At this stage, it is appropriate for a therapist to provide information about how to carry out the activities foreseen, to explain the expected consequences in a detailed and reassuring way and to teach the patient about what is lacking for acting independently. If this is done at the appropriate moment and in the correct form, the patient is likely to use what he has learned and continue to act and explore in an independent manner, taking on the therapist's teaching.

As can be seen from the above, providing skills is interwoven with other therapy steps. With the re-emerging of pathogenic schemas, differentiation should be promoted, not on a cognitive level, but in session by providing procedures and skills to reinforce a favourable, schema-discrepant self-view.

Tiziano, the patient described in Chapter 1, displayed a serious social isolation. He had previously been diagnosed with schizophrenia and was taking neuroleptics. However, the diagnosis was incorrect and had led to pessimism and inappropriate drug treatment (neuroleptics in full doses). Tiziano turned out to be suffering from avoidant PD with sub-threshold obsessive-compulsive and paranoid PDs and a total of 20 SCID-II criteria complied with OCD and social phobia. After a few months of MIT, the neuroleptic therapy was suspended without any negative consequence.

Tiziano's social withdrawal was serious. He had never had a girlfriend, did not work and had no plans. This was inconsistent with his intelligence; Tiziano had a diploma and an above-average intellect, particularly in the logical-verbal area. Over several months of combined individual and family therapy, he made rapid progress. His self-esteem improved, his anxiety diminished and his fear about being crazy disappeared. He started to want to be independent. A core question was cooking his own lunch, given that food was one of the principal causes of the mutual accusations Tiziano and his mother launched at each other. In a family session, it was negotiated that the patient should become more independent in the managing of his food but he had no idea about how to prepare a meal. The two therapists acted as models, explaining to him how they themselves had learned to cook by trial and error. There was a fun atmosphere as they described some simple recipes which aroused Tiziano's curiosity and gave him a sense of self-efficacy as he saw he was able to do them. In the months that followed, he started to cook on his own, even if only sporadically.

Similarly, for the first time in about fifteen years, he started fantasising about finding a job. In family therapy, the therapists first worked, successfully, on lowering his parents' expectations, which were unrealistic with regard to the time needed to find a job, and on getting them to be less critical towards him for being passive. This resulted in the patient feeling less judged and oppressed and therefore created a situation in which he could independently express his wish to work. In individual sessions, however, it appeared difficult for him to find his bearings. Tiziano had never explored his inner world to seek out plans for his future. It gradually emerged that he preferred literary matters and work in that sphere. However, he had no professional qualifications and did not know how or where to give vent to this generic vocation. The individual therapist suggested he carry out some online vocational guidance tests. Tiziano was curious but unsure as he did not know how to do this. As she saw Tiziano was interested but disoriented, the therapist proposed they look for a test together in session. In this way, once he returned home and got seized by his negative mental states involving passivity and low self-esteem, he would not give up looking. Tiziano accepted and was visibly relieved by the idea of getting help. The therapist conducted a search on the Internet, describing each step out loud with Tiziano noting everything. When he got home, he repeated the procedure on his own but hit a problem and stopped. He posed the problem in session and this time asked if he could use the computer himself. With Tiziano at the keyboard the two of them quickly solved the problem and Tiziano became capable of doing the vocational guidance test.

At the same time, agency should be strengthened and self-reflectivity perfected, by increasing access to wishes and integrating the emerging parts in the patient's self-image.

Anya was 22 and suffered from serious avoidant, dependent and paranoid PDs. She felt incapable, inept and ashamed of herself, and sought help from reference figures she saw as stronger and more competent, but by which she felt dominated and crushed. She spoke of repeated past experiences with men abusing her. She reported receiving sexual advances from a teacher on a vocational guidance course she was following. She was not prepared to respond to them but remained still and frozen while he touched her, afraid that, if she repelled him, he would make her fail the course as he had threatened.

In session, it surfaced that part of her submissiveness was due to a limited self-esteem, fed in turn by the idea that she was incapable of studying and grasping the subject matter. The therapist saw that Anya not only had a self-esteem problem but also a difficulty in organising herself when it came to studying. At that point she decided to complement the work on personality – where Anya was reflecting on the origins of her negative self-image vis-à-vis dominant and abusing others – with a course on improving study methods, a sphere in which the therapist was also skilled. Thus several sessions were devoted to looking at strategies for learning better, with the therapist helping Anya to grasp which subject matter she should study for the examination and which not; she then explained to her how to draw up hierarchies of importance regarding the material to be studied. They worked together at how to organise class notes and match them with a text. Initially Anya felt frightened; she collated material but was not sure she was doing it correctly and asked the therapist to do it for her. The first time, the therapist showed Anya the task step by step. In the next session she started by doing the collation of the notes and a book and as soon as Anya showed she had understood, asked her to continue. After a short while, the patient became more skilled, sure of herself and capable of organising herself alone. This process had a positive influence on the therapeutic relationship. Anya built up a functional dependency relationship with the therapist; she needed help and received it from a figure that, instead of dominating her, stimulated her independence. Meanwhile, she acquired skills that consolidated her self-esteem and made her more independent and less in need. Some months later she passed the examination and obtained the diploma.

Using additional forms of treatment

We would recall that MIT is integrative, in that it takes advantage of techniques coming from other, predominately cognitive-behavioural therapies and uses them in accordance with each case formulation. At this stage in therapy we would, therefore, invite the use of tools such as assertiveness training (O'Donohue and Fisher, 2009; Vavrichek, 2012), skills training for patients with comorbid social phobia (Herbert, Guadiano, Rheingold et al., 2005), skills training for developing more general social skills (Greene and Burleson, 2003) or problem-solving training (Chang, D'Zurilla and Sanna 2004). With regard to skills training, there is already a protocol for promoting social skills based on a growing understanding of mental states, which is applied to psychotic patients (Metacognitive Oriented Social Skills Training (MOSST)) (Ottavi, D'Alia, Lysaker et al., 2013). In MOSST, patients first relate a narrative episode and then in a group they are assisted in putting together a picture as metacognitively sophisticated as possible of what they themselves and others think and feel. Later they carry out role-play exercises in which they exercise the skill in question and try to use their knowledge of mental states effectively.

A similar approach can be used with PD patients with histories of profound inhibition and social isolation, with prevailingly avoidant, dependent, obsessive-compulsive and paranoid features and schizoid traits. It involves using group sessions to first promote mentalisation skills, in particular theory of the other's mind, and then use mentalistic awareness to simulate behaviour aimed at solving conflicts, cooperating or achieving goals.

On the other hand, MIT is not an eclectic therapy; the decision-making procedures it uses are binding. This means that the same intervention can be highly appropriate if administered at the right moment or strongly advised against if there are no relational and metacognitive conditions for it to be of benefit.

Let us imagine a dependent patient unable to express her own point of view through fear of the others' reaction, which would expose her to the risk of being abandoned. One might think that assertiveness training would be useful. In MIT it can be recommended but only if a patient has first understood her pathogenic schemas, that is that her suffering is due to her fear of being abandoned and believing that her image of herself as incapable of managing on her own and deserving to be abandoned. She needs to have started grasping that this is a hypothesis, and to have accessed parts of herself in which she feels competent, efficient and worthy of upholding her own point of view. At the same time, lack of practice can make it difficult for her to convincingly express her own ideas in public. Assertiveness training can thus provide her with the tools for upholding her new, pathology-free self-images in her relational world.

The same training, if proposed at an early stage in treatment, without the above-mentioned requisites, is to be strongly discouraged. At best a patient would mechanically learn skills that she would then not feel as her own, dominated as she is by negative self-images that she experiences as the truth.

Group therapy is another situation in which to build new skills. In MIT-oriented groups (which for reasons of space we do not describe in this book), patients exercise their communication skills during relational exchanges and, as well as increasing their knowledge of self and of others' minds, train at new exchanges in which they exercise reciprocity, turn-taking, mutual caregiving and social play.

We include here only one example, taken from an MIT-oriented group psychotherapy session, in which a patient was helped in learning how to court a woman through role play.

Giorgio was a 25-year-old engineer suffering from obsessive-compulsive and paranoid PD, obsessive-compulsive disorder and dysmorphophobia, as he saw his body to be horrid and deformed. He had never had a girlfriend and had difficulty masturbating because he had intrusive thoughts about making love and he found this disgusting. During the months prior to the pretend play we are going to describe, he had displayed delirious beliefs about sexual relations in a group session. He believed that love did not exist, that young couples in love were just following a script as a social pretence and that women were cold, threatening and distant and never truly interested in men. The therapist barely managed to get him to understand that this was a bizarre and falsifiable idea and Giorgio began to realise that the idea was based on the stiff relationship between his parents and the coldness his mother had always shown towards him. Once he had acquired differentiation, at least at intervals, Giorgio displayed suffering because he longed for a woman but did not know how to approach her.

During a group session, the therapist invited him to choose a girl from the group and pretend to court her. His first attempt was clumsy but the atmosphere among the group was merry. Giorgio was received with a mixture of warmth, support and kindly making fun of him, and he let himself get involved in this. The patient chosen as his courting partner gave some feedback: she found Giorgio likeable but his strategy was not effective. The whole group provided suggestions about how to be more seductive, how to personalise an advance and what words to choose. After two or three attempts, in the midst of embarrassment and laughter, Giorgio changed tack and managed to be passionate and direct and effective, which provoked a positive reaction in the woman and all the others. A few sessions later he invited a woman he liked to go out with him and started his first romantic relationship.

Conclusions

Exploring one's environment, overcoming the fears preventing a satisfying social life, pursuing one's own interests and inclinations and putting together new skills are vital PD therapy goals. In this chapter we have shown that in order to achieve these, a patient needs to have acquired a good self-reflectivity so that he is able to differentiate, the therapeutic contract needs to have been reformulated and the patient needs consciously to have decided to undertake new actions between one session and the next in order to try to live a life richer in self-achievement opportunities. We have shown how change occurs through a planning–exploration–reflection cycle.

The ultimate goal of this work is not behavioural change. Behavioural change is instrumental for enriching identity, thanks to the new experiences patients have while engaging in and succeeding in the operations described above. Patients exercising new skills, following their own inclinations, and overcoming fears not only mitigate the impact of the automatisms underlying pathogenic schemas, but also generate new schemas and widen their cognitive map of the world. They rewrite their self-narrative and complement the images that are the source of their problems and suffering with more favourable and sophisticated representations, capable of leading them towards satisfaction and adaptation. Combining the newly acquired self-parts in one's identity is, however, a complex task, both cognitively and emotionally.

At the same time, by moving in the world as never before, patients meet others and have to confront other's minds. The work described here is interwoven, therefore, with the need to understand others in a mature and nuanced fashion, and to form an integrated view of self, combining what *works* with what *does not work*, who one *was* with who *one is becoming*. In the next chapter we will describe how to move patients to integrate and understand the complexities of others' minds.

Chapter 9

Promoting the understanding of the other's mind and integration

In this chapter we will outline the advanced steps a therapist should implement in MIT once a patient is managing to differentiate (see Chapter 7), has had at least partial access to his healthy parts and is exploring new forms of acting, feeling and thinking (see Chapters 7 and 8). At this point in therapy one can pursue other goals such as helping the patient to arrive at a more sophisticated, realistic and decentred idea of the other's mind, to grasp his own personal contribution in the creation of the dysfunctional interpersonal cycles that are established in relationships, to form an integrated self-image which includes the passing between one mental state and another and his own changes as contexts alter over the course of treatment, and to facilitate the development of an identity based on an awareness of individual qualities, limits and preferences. In the paragraphs that follow we will present the specific MIT techniques aimed at promoting, firstly, a sophisticated theory of the other's mind and the acquisition of a decentred point of view, and then a more integrated image of the self with others.

Promoting the understanding of others' minds and decentring

In Chapter 3 we thoroughly discussed the process of understanding others' minds and decentring. Before getting to the heart of the intervention we shall describe the treatment implications of problems specific to this area, the most important of which is in regard to the timing of the interventions. More specifically, if a patient has serious difficulties understanding others, a therapist may be tempted to intervene too early by promoting, for example, a patient's empathetic skills or correcting her attributional biases. From an MIT point of view this is a mistake. For example, a patient diagnosed with paranoid PD may feel indignant due to the ridicule he receives from his colleagues. In this situation a therapist is likely to feel driven to make him consider alternative and more favourable hypotheses about his colleagues' intentions in the hope of relieving his feelings of resentment, but the most likely result is that the patient will feel like the therapist is allying with the others or, at best, does not feel understood. A patient with avoidant PD may present as seriously depressed because she has no social relations and is sure that others judge her to be unlikeable. In this case the therapist may intervene by looking for evidence that the patient is less at the centre of others' attention than she perceives and that others judge her more favourably as well. Due to the premature implementation of the intervention, the patient often reacts sceptically and does not engage in the behavioural experiments necessary for disproving her pathogenic idea.

The tendency for a therapist to prematurely attempt to redirect the patient's perceptions of the other's mind is all the stronger the more convinced the therapist is that a dysfunction is the source of subjective suffering and a potential source of harm for the patient or for others. He might predict that the paranoid patient mentioned previously will become increasingly more angry and veer toward a retaliation that could cause him to be dismissed or even make him dangerous to others. If, however, a therapist worries about others, his interventions are likely to sound critical to the patient. The therapist of the patient with avoidant PD might instead imagine her entering a cycle of depression and isolation that could trigger latent suicidal ideation. Considering the scenarios above, the therapist may be pulled to react by oscillating between a sense of alarm and urgency in regard to avoiding harm to patients and others, and a subtle hostility towards patients and their tendency to characterise others negatively and stereotypically.

For the therapeutic work to proceed effectively, however, one needs to abstain from such interventions. The patient who isolates herself due to the fear of others' opinions and the patient who becomes angry with his colleagues because he is convinced that they are mocking him are driven by schema-dependent attributions and letting go of these attributions involves great risks. If a patient believed another to be harmless, when instead the latter really intended to be contemptuous, the patient would feel battered and humiliated. If the patient considered him kind when the latter was in reality critical and judgemental, he would expose himself to the risk of confirming his idea that his self is inept.

In this sense, coping behaviours such as isolation, avoiding relationships or reactive aggressiveness are necessary, because trying to persuade a patient that the other is different than originally perceived can alarm or make him feel misunderstood or criticised. He may also feel pressured into relinquishing indispensable safety mechanisms and thus paradoxically become more alarmed. For this reason, interventions focused on a more sophisticated and decentred understanding of others' minds should be attempted only after patients have grasped that they are driven by a schema and have started to take a critical distance from their underlying negative self-image (see Chapters 6 and 7).

Interventions regarding others' minds can be schematically expressed as follows: '*You had the idea that you were inept. You believed it strongly and therefore were convinced that others would mock, humiliate and criticise you. Now we have seen that this is a schema of yours and that this is not necessarily the way things are. You have begun to believe that you are worth more. On the basis of this, should we try and see if you are able to see different signals when interacting with others? Could we explore the idea that others are not criticising or judging you, and if they have a hostile look that this is not necessarily directed toward you?'* The interventions we are going to describe are quite likely to be effective and constitute an indispensable part of treatment when communicated like above, as they are the moment when a patient opens up to the idea that others are richer and more unpredictable and interesting than he once thought in the past. They represent an opportunity to experience more varied and open social relationships. And, furthermore, any requests at this point from the therapist to put oneself in others' shoes should be less risky for the therapeutic relationship, given that the patient will likely not feel either misunderstood or criticised by the former, nor will he likely be frightened by the idea of putting himself in others' shoes.

There are various ways in which a therapist can help patients to understand others' minds in a more sophisticated and decentred manner:

- via the therapeutic relationship;
- by encouraging them to use their memories of the therapeutic relationship between sessions, and in particular in moments when they feel pulled to interpret the other's mind stereotypically;
- by using imaginary exercises aimed at exploring the other's mind in a more sophisticated way;
- by using diagrams depicting how the other's mind works;
- via role play.

During this chapter we are going to describe each of these intervention strategies in detail. Moreover, the task of exploration, described in Chapter 8, leads patients to increased exchanges with others. During the behavioural interventions patients are asked to adopt others' perspectives immediately after acquiring a critical distance from their schema.

Promoting a sophisticated and decentred understanding of the therapist's mind

The other's mind 'closest to hand' for a patient, and in a context with less emotional stress than in daily relationships, is the therapist's. When a patient imagines what his therapist is thinking and feeling and why, his ideas are inevitably conditioned by his dysfunctional interpersonal schemas. At this stage in therapy any discrepancies between the representations a patient has about his therapist's intentions and the flow of thoughts in the therapist's mind can emerge. To effectively use the therapeutic relationship as a tool, the therapist must first show the patient that his perceptions are schema-dependent and then, after promoting differentiation, help him to identify alternative hypotheses about what the therapist really feels and thinks. In certain respects this is a real-life exercise promoting both differentiation and theory of mind.

Carmine was 21 years old and suffered from paranoid PD with below threshold avoidant and schizotypal PD. He lived on a college campus far from his home. He left his hometown because he was convinced that others from the town could 'read' signs of him being 'an idiot'. Owing to this sense of worthlessness he obtained his school diploma with great difficulty and – subsequently – it led to a gradual increase in social isolation and his decision to enroll in a religious college in the provincial capital. However, here too he soon became convinced that others judged him mercilessly. In social settings, such as parties with the representatives of the college and other guests, his self-centred and persecutory perception of the other's mind led him to stay completely silent or, if someone spoke to him, to almost not reply and to look down at the ground. These were the moments when Carmine's emotional suffering, composed of shame and a sense of worthlessness, reached its greatest intensity.

The therapist and patient managed to reconstruct his main dysfunctional schema, which was largely constructed by his relationship with his parents who used to continuously judge and humiliate him when the patient wished to be loved. The patient's self responded by feeling vulnerable and worthless, and withdrew from relationships to protect itself from humiliation. This schema became particularly evident in the therapeutic relationship; for example, on one occasion when the therapist praised Carmine for his punctuality and the scrupulousness in relation to his therapy, the therapist noticed a sudden change in the patient's facial expression. The therapist brought this detail to Carmine's attention, and together they managed to discover that the praise had made him think that the therapist thought he was an idiot because he found it necessary to praise him 'like a child'.

The therapist responded by calmly explaining to Carmine that the praise had been spontaneous and that he does not consider him an idiot or childish. He then reminded the patient of the schema that they had reconstructed in the earlier stages of the therapy and redirected the patient to the diagram that they had constructed. Carmine acknowledged that he had assimilated the therapist to his father, who had on several occasions mockingly said '*Well done, you'll certainly go a long way in life with that brain*' to underscore his mistakes. Due to the positive shift in Carmine's ability to differentiate schema and reality, the therapist implemented a more advanced intervention aimed at understanding the other's mind by using the therapeutic relationship.

This particular intervention has many goals. The therapist and patient begin by investigating the signals that led the patient to read the other's mind dysfunctionally. Specific to the issue of the patient imagining a negative opinion from the therapist, the therapist may respond by stating, '*Once again we have seen how feeling that others judge you as an idiot stems from experiences of your past. At this present moment, between you and me, what do you think could induce me to consider you an idiot? Is there something in my facial expression or my tone of voice that suggests it to you?*' This question is nearly rhetorical due to the patient now being able to differentiate and focus his attention on real signals, and consequently he will probably no longer be able to find concrete pretexts which he can identify as negative signals. Not surprisingly, Carmine smiled and responded that he had been wrong. On this basis, the therapist asked him: '*Can you try and identify some alternative hypotheses about what I truly felt and thought when I praised you, and what I currently am feeling and thinking?*' As a result of this intervention, Carmine was able to appreciate the therapist's authentically positive opinion and his sincere gesture of offering care.

As portrayed above, when a patient is able and inclined to differentiate or recovers an ability to differentiate which was momentarily rendered ineffective by a high level of arousal, interventions aimed at encouraging alternative hypotheses about the other's mind, starting with the therapist's, are often beneficial. The following extract depicts a session occurring at the end of Carmine's first year of therapy and demonstrates the work that was executed to help him understand the therapist's mind in a more sophisticated, realistic and decentred manner. As the previous session was ending, Carmine quickly mentioned an episode in which, during a lunch with his schoolmates and the college officials, he had found the courage to contribute in a discussion typical of students, but immediately became inhibited by the impression that he was being judged negatively. In the session we report below, the therapist works on promoting an understanding of the other's mind within the therapeutic relationship:

> *P*: Now, while I'm speaking, I think I'm too … I don't know, too negative and that you think I'm a fool.
> *T*: So, if I've understood you correctly, while you were speaking you thought you were acting like a fool or an idiot, and thought that I was thinking the same thing about you?!
> *P*: … about being one who doesn't care about the person he's with.
> *T*: Ah, a bit like that scene from dinner that you talked about last time. Where you thought the others were thinking that you were being too pushy, and that you weren't following the rules of conversation or caring about the others. So again you are feeling like a fool. A bit like a child wanting to intervene in grown-ups' talk.
> *P*: [*pause*] … Yes!
> *T*: I'm glad you expressed this concern because you are giving me a chance to tell you exactly what's passing through my mind. To be sincere, I was thinking that you were presenting yourself very well and were being very respectful toward me. I didn't think you were expressing stupidity at all. After you shared your concern I was thinking that you're becoming good at identifying these thoughts. Before you felt only an oppressive suffering and were unable to endure my gaze. Instead, you are now able to bear it well, and you can identify what you feel and express this openly. Very good! That's the way! I hope you don't still think I have a negative opinion of you!
> *P*: No, no. [*laughs*]
> *T*: Can you manage to see this? Do you have a sense of what I just said?
> *P*: Yes, I think so. Perhaps it's true.
> *T*: That is, joking apart, what am I thinking about you at this moment?
> *P*: [*smiles*] No, alright, you in fact seem satisfied with me.

With a validating and cordial emphasis the therapist should then ask patients to explore their mind and help them discover that the contents are different from their expectations (Bateman and Fonagy, 2004). They should also begin to work on encouraging the transposition of this skill to relationships outside of therapy as well. The therapist in the scenario above began to work toward this goal by stating, '*Ah, a bit like that scene from dinner that you talked about last time. Where you thought the others were thinking that you were being too pushy, and that you weren't following the rules of conversation or caring about the others.*' We will discuss interventions specifically directed at this aspect later.

Using a more nuanced awareness of the therapist's mind to understand others

Using the interpersonal processes of the therapeutic relationship helps patients begin to construct a representation of the other that is different than their usual one. What patients learn from the therapeutic relationship will create the foundation for patients constructing alternative representations of the minds of persons with whom they interact on a daily basis. The therapist should begin by building a bridge between the therapeutic relationship and external interactions in the hope of improving the patient's ability to differentiate between his guesses related to others' intentions and the actual ideas and emotions that others have. If a patient has managed to differentiate with the therapist's mind as a model, she will be able to carry out a similar operation with other minds. This idea is depicted in the following extract, which was drawn from the session subsequent to that just portrayed:

> T: Do any other episode similar to the one with me last week come to mind?
> P: [*pause*] Uh, perhaps at dinner the other evening, but I can't remember it very well.
> T: Okay, can you recall the other people who were there with you?
> P: Antonio, Marco and someone else named Carmine.
> T: Okay. And where were you?
> P: In the refectory.
> T: Very good. We almost have all of the details comprising the scene. What were you doing?
> P: I was talking with Marco, but I can't remember what about.
> T: Don't worry, perhaps it'll come to mind. We can see the scene more or less, and know you were talking with Marco. While you were conversing with Marco did you get that nasty feeling of shame which is linked to the sensation that others were judging you negatively?
> P: Yes, yes.
> T: I understand. And I know how nasty that feeling can be. I've seen it in live action here between you and me. But listen, might it not be that at that moment, while you were talking with Marco and were convinced he was judging you negatively, there was something present that was similar to what happened a little while ago between the two of us? When you had the strong sensation that I was judging you very negatively and instead I had something completely different in my head.
> P: Uh, perhaps, I think undoubtedly yes.

At this point a therapist can try to implement the first exercise in exploring alternative hypotheses about the other's mind in the same way as he has done with his therapist. More specifically, the therapist can help the patient assess whether others outside of the therapeutic relationship have different intentions to those the patient typically ascribes to them. The intervention consists of entrusting the patient with a task involving observation of the other over the course of interactions. More specifically, the therapist asks the patient to notice and inspect signals in the other, such as facial expressions. After having, for example, recognised that the other is plausibly more sad than angry, as formerly guessed, the therapist invites the patient to identify a number of hypotheses regarding the beliefs and motives underlying the emotion.

Another useful indicator to use in this situation is prior knowledge of the other, such as his habitual way of being or history. For example, if the other is best characterised as gentle and cordial, though a bit anxious, the patient could consider that the other is not judging him severely, but may instead be worried about personal matters. The patient can use this prior knowledge to identify alternative intentions and mental states that are likely behind the other avoiding eye contact. An important part of this section of the intervention is to promote logical reasoning related to the functioning of the other's mind. With Carmine, for example, the therapist returned to the college lunch episode that he previously mentioned. After asking him to recall the other diners' facial expressions, the therapist asked him to identify what they were thinking when he started speaking. Carmine managed to arrive at the idea that some of them probably did not judge him to be stupid at all, but were in fact 'content' to see him more at ease. It is important to note that it is helpful to train more severe patients who have difficulty decoding facial expressions in facial expression recognition tasks to facilitate tasks involving the observation of the other's non-verbal signals (Ekman, 2003; Ekman and Rosenberg, 2005; Ekman, Wallace and Friesen, 2009).

Earlier we discussed how understanding the other's mind and decentring can be stimulated by helping patients read their therapist's mind more realistically. We described this type of intervention first but that does not imply that it should necessarily be the first or only intervention. Instead, therapists should use an array of interventions that directly stimulate the above-mentioned functions. They should, however, be careful to ensure that any progress previously achieved does not become lost. In particular, it is important to stress that over long periods of time in therapy differentiation has many ups and downs. When interacting and thinking about others while under stress, patients are likely to resort to schema-driven attributions that they believe as true. If necessary therapists should reconsolidate differentiation as in the following extract taken from a later session with Carmine:

> T: This seems to be one of those situations where you tend to think that the person you are with thinks badly of you. While working together we have discovered that you often have this sensation when you're judging yourself to be stupid and you feel ashamed, which is typical of your schema. Could the same thing have happened this time?
>
> P: I think undoubtedly yes.
>
> T: Don't worry, Carmine. It's normal for this tendency to occasionally get triggered automatically. When it happens, we just have to become aware of it and remember that it is not the reality. As time passes this will happen to you less and less.
>
> P: Okay.

Once patients provide positive feedback after interventions that are aimed at consolidating awareness of a schema and differentiation the therapist can promote a more nuanced theory of the other's mind.

Guided imagery exercises for promoting and maintaining understanding of the other's mind and decentring

Guided imagery exercises stimulate patients to view others from new perspectives. When faced with a narrative episode in which a patient interprets the meaning of the other's action or expression in a non-decentred or schema-driven way – '*When she looked at me and smiled, I got the feeling she had a negative opinion of me*' – a therapist should first try to elicit a detailed memory of the interaction. The therapist can do so by asking the patient to focus her attention on the picture of the other's face, expressive nuances and tone of voice. He should then propose an imaginary exercise focusing on the reading of the other's mind, as in the following extract from Carmine's therapy:

> T: Would you like to do an exercise together? It involves using guided imagery to get an idea of what else could have driven Antonio to look and smile at you.
>
> P: Yes.
>
> T: Okay, try to close your eyes and go back to that scene. Are you doing it?
>
> P: Yes.
>
> T: Stop at the picture of Antonio looking at you and smiling. Can you see him?
>
> P: Yes, I can picture him in my mind.
>
> T: Very good, Carmine. Now try to imagine what's going through Antonio's mind as he smiles. But, while doing this, try not to think that Antonio has Carmine in front of him. That is, imagine just Antonio's personal motives that might induce him to smile. Try to put yourself completely in his shoes while keeping the picture of his smiling face in your mind. Am I managing to explain myself?

P: I think so. I think I'm managing to do it.

T: Antonio smiling. Just think about Antonio smiling like he smiled to you in that scene, but now you're not present. Concentrate.

P: Yes.

T: What's passing through Antonio's mind as he smiles?

P: That he's okay, he's happy.

T: At this moment does he seem to be a strict person, one who judges and criticises? A bad person?

P: No, no.

T: Try now to imagine that you're with him and he has that same smile, that expression we've imagined up to now.

P: Okay.

T: How do you feel while you're in front of Antonio now?

P: At ease.

T: Untroubled?

P: Yes.

T: At this moment could Antonio be happy to see you and not be judging you?

P: Yes, I think so.

T: Do you see? This exercise has been very interesting because it has shown us that when imagining Antonio with that same smile, but without you being with him, you thought he was kind and satisfied. When you placed yourself back into the scene you perceived his smile differently. You felt at ease and untroubled with another smiling at you cordially. This is an example of how your sensation of what the other is thinking often risks being not very objective, as if it was guided by your state of mind at that moment, whereas to grasp the other's real intentions we perhaps need to take our shoes off and put ourselves in the other's. What do you say?

P: I think undoubtedly yes.

Representing the other's mind in a graph

Asking patients to represent the other's mind in graph form can help to increase their understanding of it. A typical tool is a 'pie graph'. This type of graph is commonly used in CBT for anxiety disorders (Wells, 2008). Its purpose is to block catastrophic or unrealistic attributions by stimulating alternative evaluations of events. It involves a therapist helping patients to give less importance to their negative evaluations and accompany them with other, more reasonable ones, with an estimation of the probability of each of them. In this way patients are trained to consider multiple hypotheses with a varying degree of probability when ascribing meaning to events.

When applying this to understanding the other's mind and decentring, the therapist should first identify the moment in a narrative episode when the patient has made self-centred or schema-driven attributions about the other's mind. They should then establish the patient's degree of conviction about the truth of these attributions by asking him to give each a percentage score. Finally, the therapist should help the patient create a list of potential alternative explanations for the event. Some of these explanations can be suggested by the therapist, but it is essential that the therapist ask the patient for feedback about how much he considers them valid. The therapist should then ask the patient to ascribe a percentage score to the probability of each of these alternative evaluations. The patient should then draw a pie chart, with the width of each of the 'slices' corresponding to the percentages ascribed. The task can be rendered more fun by asking the patient to draw a cartoon with the head of a stylised person and various possible thoughts that the patient and therapist try to ascribe to the other. The patient generally ends up realising that he needs to consider alternative hypotheses, including those which are more decentred or neutral.

Marcello was a 36-year-old patient and his initial diagnosis was obsessive-compulsive and avoidant PD. An extract from a session during his second year of therapy exemplifies the technique described above. The therapist and patient were focused on a narrative episode depicting the patient feeling criticised by his boss:

T: What made you think he considered you inept?
P: He had this disgusted look on his face while we were by the coffee machine and I had just told him that I needed a few more days to finish the report.
T: Disgusted in the sense of …? How would we define it? Really disgusted?
P: Yes.
T: Disgust is like this [*mimes*]. Was it like this, with the corners of the mouth turned down?
P: Yes, yes. Quite like that.
T: Has he made this facial expression with you on other occasions that you can recall?
P: No, I must say that we have a great underlying mutual esteem.
T: Shall we do an exercise? First of all, let's establish how convinced you are that your boss's facial expression was linked to his thinking that you were inept. From 0 to 100 how convinced are you?
P: Well, I'd say 90 per cent.
T: Now we get to the heart of the exercise. Shall we take into consideration some other possible reasons for why your boss might have had that disgusted expression? Does anything come to mind?
P: I wouldn't know. Who knows, he could have had an argument with his wife [*smiles*].
T: Yes, absolutely, the typical morning in-front-of-the-coffee-pot-argument-with-wife face [*they laugh*]. Some other hypotheses?
P: He could have been in a generally bad mood.
T: Perfect. This too is reasonable. Anything else?
P: Tiredness?!
T: Let's take note of this hypothesis too. More?

P: Nothing else really comes to mind.

T: What do you think about his being worried about having too much work to do, and perhaps the delay in the report too, but without this necessarily involving him thinking you were inept?

P: Could be.

After collecting a sufficient set of hypotheses, the therapist proceeded with the true and proper representation in graph form:

T: Okay, we have a list of alternative possibilities to the boss thinking Marcello is inept: (1) argument with his wife; (2) bad mood; (3) tiredness; (4) general worry about work without thinking Marcello is inept. Do they tally?

P: Yes.

T: Now I'm going to draw a graph to get a view of them all together. The circle is like a pie. The whole pie is the totality of the alternatives we have identified. Now, let's give a percentage to each of them. Let's start with the first: how true do you think it could be that your boss argued with his wife?

P: Let's say 20 per cent.

T: How possible is it that he was in a bad mood?

P: Well, this is similar to the first alternative. If he had argued with his wife, he probably would not have been in a good mood [*smiles*].

T: [*smiles*] Sure, you're right, but could it have been for other reasons other than his wife?

P: Sure. I'm joking. Let's say 10 per cent.

T: Good. How possible is it that he was tired?

P: In fact it's a difficult period for everyone in the office – 40 per cent.

T: How much for being worried about work, but without this involving thinking that Antonio is inept?

P: It's not impossible. Perhaps 20 per cent.

T: There's now only room for 10 per cent.

P: Yes, I can see that.

T: Look at this graph. Can you see how your initial interpretation has ended-up in the smallest slice? If you again consider all of the alternatives, how much do you now believe that your boss thought you were inept?

P: Looking at it now, it seems very unlikely.

The aim of this intervention, like those of the others described previously and of the one that follows, is not to promote a positive and well-disposed view of the other's mind so much as to increase a patient's ability to formulate alternative hypotheses. It is similar to the interventions proposed by Bateman and Fonagy (2004) to stimulate an awareness in patients suffering from borderline PD of the complexity of others' minds, beginning with the therapist, and thus of the need to consider various perspectives when interpreting others' intentions.

Role play

During role play the therapist helps the patient to adopt a particular behaviour in session to handle a difficult situation. This technique, aimed at a knowledge of others' theories of mind and decentring in the context of the individual therapies[1] of patients with PDs, is put into practice as follows. The therapist gathers the details of a relational episode when the patient has made a schema-driven interpretation of the other's mind, leading to a dysfunctional behaviour such as closing-up, mistrust or aggressiveness. Without commenting on the patient's behaviour, the therapist proposes to role play the scene that was just recalled. The role playing is split into two parts. In the first part the patient plays himself while the therapist plays the other. This role assignment calls for the patient to look for elements in the situation, such as the other's verbal and non-verbal behaviour, that could justify the interpretation of the other's mind that arose during the episode. When recalling the scene in the different emotional atmosphere of the session a patient is able to directly access alternative readings of the other's mind. It is often the second part of the intervention when such readings emerge more spontaneously. In this second part the patient plays the other's role while the therapist plays the patient and tries to enact the latter's behaviour as accurately as possible. During this part of the simulation, the patient is asked to take on an unusual role. One possibility is that the patient resorts to 'identification' in order to understand the other who he is playing.[2] By experiencing the other's emotions and embodying the latter as if the emotions were his own, a patient is more likely to be able to comprehend the other's point of view. Moreover, by playing both roles one after the other – with perhaps new interpretations arising during the second role assignment – he may intuitively realise that his own perspective of the other's mind has changed.

In certain cases role play does not promote a better comprehension of the other's mind. The exercise is nevertheless useful because it boosts differentiation. More specifically, the patient becomes aware of how difficult it is for him to put himself in another's shoes, which is still considered an increase in insight into his own problems.

Role play proved useful in treating Rino, a 28-year-old clerk suffering from paranoid PD with significant schizoid traits, who sought therapy for a severe depression. He displayed a limited ability to decentre which had caused repeated angry outbursts against his work colleagues, who he perceived as evil-minded and ostracising. Rino verbally attacked the personnel manager, a friend of his outside of work, because he was convinced that the manager wanted to create problems for him about his holiday entitlement. Over the course of his therapy Rino grasped that he has a tendency to become aggressive and vindictive when he fears a significant other (e.g. his friends, mother and therapist) perceives him as unlikeable. He could not stop himself, however, from attacking his best friend when the latter arrived late for an appointment because he interpreted the other's lateness as a confirmation that he despised him.

In a session during Rino's second year of therapy the therapist proposed some role playing based on one of the episodes where he attacked his friend. For the first segment of the role play Rino played himself, which did not lead to any alternative readings of the other's mind. Consequently, Rino continued to feel unlikeable in the other's eyes and again became angry. During the second part the therapist simulated Rino's behaviour while the latter played his friend. When the therapist, addressing Rino, raised his voice like Rino himself had described shortly before, the patient went pale. The therapist promptly stopped the game and asked him how he had felt at the moment he became pale. Rino indicated that he felt humiliated and attacked in an almost physical fashion, whereas in reality he had nothing to reproach himself for at that moment. He thus intuitively grasped his friend's perspective who likely felt unfairly attacked by him. On this basis the therapist asked Rino to reflect on possible alternative motivations underlying his friend's lateness. Among the various hypotheses identified by Rino he included that his friend may simply be '*someone who's always late*', which demonstrated an increase in his ability to decentre. 'Someone who's always late' was still an attribution with a generic quality but it was enough to put him at ease and make him think that his friend's behaviour was not addressed personally towards him.

Promoting the understanding of dysfunctional interpersonal cycles

A dysfunctional interpersonal cycle (see Chapters 1 and 5) is a relational process in which expectations of one of the participants evoke aversive responses from the other, often confirming the subject's initial negative expectations. The cycle often arises from expectations, schemas and procedures of both of the participants that mutually trigger reactions reinforcing maladaptive expectations and behaviours in each of them.

At moments where he had to enter a dialogue with another, Carmine was driven by a desire to be appreciated. Consequently, he became convinced that the other was judging him severely and thus entered a state of shame. As a result, he had difficulty replying to the other's questions, did not make adequate eye contact and took on a surly expression; this attitude led the other to become irritated or feel rejected, and therefore to stiffen and back off. Carmine perceived this behaviour as a confirmation of the other's tendency to judge him negatively and this increased the shame he often felt.

For a patient to understand the functioning of this cycle and see that it occurs in the interpersonal dynamics in which he is involved, his understanding of the other's mind needs to have improved. This increase in skill level allows the patient to understand the difference between a schema-driven interpretation of the other's mind and a more realistic and decentred one. The more limited and egocentric a patient's perception of the other's mind, the more powerful an interpersonal cycle can be. During the same therapy period from which the previous extracts were taken, the therapist used the diagram explaining Carmine's schema to help him understand that a schema-dependent reading of the other's mind influences the interaction and contributes the triggering of pathogenic interpersonal cycles:

T: I'd like to share a general impression of mine that I can show you using a diagram on the blackboard. This helps us to organise our ideas and understand that there's a link between your schema, which we've seen often leads you to feel ashamed, and what automatically occurs many times when you interact with others [*the therapist accompanies this verbal intervention with a diagram drawn on the blackboard*]. Do you remember how we described Carmine's negative schema? That deep down Carmine wishes to be accepted and liked, but feels that on the other side there's a strict and pitiless judge, which consequently makes him feel at fault and ashamed. Now let's ask ourselves, what happens when you interact with a person you hold in high esteem? Perhaps with me?

P: I feel ashamed and it's me who has a very negative opinion of myself.

T: Excellent ... A bit like we saw last time, you paste this opinion into the other's head and in the end the result is that you don't look him in the eye, stay quiet and withdraw. Does this correspond to how you experience such interactions?

P: Yes, I'd say so.

T: At this point how might the other react when he sees these expressions? Think about it for a moment!

P: ... Perhaps he thinks I'm annoyed with him.

T: Exactly, very good. Let's write that. That's exactly right. Or possibly that you even despise him!

P: Oh dear!

When Carmine realised that he tended to initiate this cycle every time he started a dialogue with the cycle became significantly less pervasive. As we have seen, moreover, thanks to the therapist's explicit advice Carmine learned to modify his behaviour substantially by maintaining an increase in eye contact, avoiding a surly expression and adopting a collaborative attitude in appropriate contexts. In the following extract, taken from the same period in his therapy, we see the effects of this intervention:

P: While I was coming here I passed by the refectory and saw Angelo.

T: Okay, and what happened?

P: He said, 'Where are you going?' and I replied. At the beginning of the conversation I couldn't manage to look him in the eyes, but then periodically I tried to look up and see what was in his gaze ...

T: Magnificent. You remembered what we'd said and you avoided becoming blocked or inhibited. Am I right? What did you notice in his look and tone of voice? Something positive?

P: Yes, that perhaps he saw me as being a bit down but perhaps he didn't criticise me ... Maybe a bit worried. I don't know.

Promoting integration

The term *integration* embraces a series of metacognitive operations, such as the ability to reconcile contrasting representations of the self and other, to recognise small changes of how one's way of feeling and thinking is evolving, and to understand that the new parts of the self emerging during therapy have become assimilated – through a constructive exchange with the environment – into new, more adaptive interpersonal schemas (Dimaggio, Semerari, Carcione et al., 2007; Dimaggio, Hermans and Lysaker, 2010; Stiles, 2011). Consequently, interventions for promoting integration should also take various forms (Salvatore, Popolo, Dimaggio, in press), which we are going to describe collectively in the following section of this chapter (see Chapter 2).

Integration interventions are therefore aimed at helping patients to:

- integrate different, and often contradictory, self-other representations. With regard to this aspect of interaction, MIT intervenes primarily by stimulating patients to explicitly acknowledge their different representations of self, other and the relationship at the moment they arise together or successively. Additionally, the intervention takes advantage of a revised and more detailed diagram which corrects the one that was created at the end of assessment (see Chapters 3 and 5);
- identify new self-parts emerging in therapy and integrate them into their identity. Interventions focused on this goal generally consist of asking patients to reflect on how they have been changing over the course of their therapy; graphs modifying the diagram based on the shared formulation of functioning can be helpful;
- acquire an integrated perspective on how their treatment is evolving, so that they have a sense of how much they have achieved during their therapy. This intervention generally takes the form of a *reformulation letter*.

In the remainder of this chapter we will describe each of these integration interventions in detail.

Interventions focused on integration of self-other representations

The aim of the work on this aspect of integration is to show patients in a validating manner that they are driven by multiple, differing and often contradictory images of self, other and their relationship. As we proposed at the end of assessment (see Chapter 3), the therapist and patient should draw a diagram together of the patient's main schema or schemas and also include the way his states of mind depend on them. Based on what the patient has achieved so far, the therapist should return attention to the schema diagram to discuss with the patient how the schemas, alone or alternating with other schemas, cause an alternating between self-other representations that the patient is unable to keep integrated or perceives as being incompatible.

Sandra was a 24-year-old patient who suffered from obsessive-compulsive and dependent PD as well as a not otherwise specified eating disorder. At the beginning of her therapy she was limiting calorie consumption and consequently lost approximately 22 pounds and had amenorrhea. She was also a dancer and would practise for hours while ignoring any signs of tiredness.

One of the first narrative episodes that Sandra shared involved a dance lesson where she felt she was fainting because she had not eaten and was very tired. She did not have the courage to share how she was feeling to the teacher because she feared she would be perceived as irresponsible and insufficiently committed. Thanks to an exploration of associated memories, Sandra remembered another episode dating back to when she was about eight years old. She recalled eating a dish with a particular relish and her father 'shot her down' by telling her that it was part of her responsibilities to have an impeccable physical appearance, and that she should never give her neighbour the impression that she did not know how to control her instincts. Sandra and her therapist identified that on both occasions, with her teacher and with her father, she felt she was to blame and saw herself as '*a good for nothing*' and '*a disappointment*' due to her actions being driven by her most natural desires and needs. When asked by the therapist to recall other episodes when a similar view of herself had manifested, Sandra remembered that as an adolescent she had been in despair one evening because she felt an enormous need to vent her feelings to her father, obtain his support and give her a hug. When she mustered the courage to share her feelings with her father, she immediately felt '*paralysed by his strict look*' and uncompassionate response.

Sandra therefore seemed to have a schema which is typical of obsessive-compulsive PD. Her self wished to be understood and supported in its desires and needs but the other does not comprehend and instead criticises and reminds her of her moral duties. The self's response is to feel guilty (e.g. '*I shouldn't have thought about not going to school*'), and suppresses its request to be understood by increasing its commitment to duties (e.g. dancing, physical fitness) and becoming perfectionistic to alleviate the level of guilt experienced. As a result, Sandra feels lonely, sad and overburdened, feelings that are in turn suppressed, not accepted and viewed as signs of moral weakness. At the moment of its formulation the therapist and Sandra called this the 'responsibility schema' (see Figure 9.1).

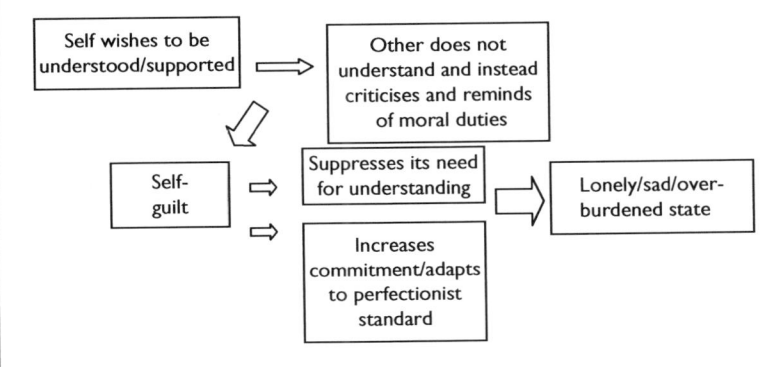

Figure 9.1 Sandra: responsibility schema.

Dysfunctional aspects emerged in Sandra's romantic relationships as well. Her last boyfriend, who she had broken up with one year prior to therapy, had once taken her to visit some caves. Sandra recalled that this experience had involved several *'causes of unease'* for her. Even if she felt happy at the idea of her boyfriend wanting to share this experience with her, she felt cold and became bored. Back home this state of boredom *'got bigger'* to the extent that it became *'a sort of irritation and then anger'* which she felt for several days. Sandra recalled spontaneously that this same strange anger had surfaced many times during her relationship with a previous boyfriend too, especially when she had stopped dancing because *'one evening he said that dancing stole too much time from things they could do together'*. She recalled that at that moment stopping dancing was *'automatic'* and did not cause her any regrets. She did not perceive it as a distressing experience, but after a few days she felt that same anger and was *'unmanageable at home with her parents'*. With the therapist's help, Sandra began to realise that she tended to comply with the others' wishes in her romantic relationships out of fear of losing the latter's attention and love, and consequently abandoned her own wishes which caused a sense of sadness and anger. With the help of her therapist she was soon able to conceptualise these emotions as a feeling of constraint. Thanks to this realisation she was able to recall a prototypical episode from her childhood. Her mother was a very religious woman, and early on in Sandra's childhood she started taking her to Sunday services and on various trips of a religious nature. On one occasion, when she was nine years old, Sandra told her that she wanted to go on a school trip rather than come with her to mass. Her mother communicated to Sandra that she was very disappointed and hurt by her request and did not speak to her for several hours. Out of fear of losing her mother's love forever, Sandra told her that she would willingly give up the school trip. She felt *'reborn'* when her mother hugged her and from that moment on she never made any other similar requests.

It was therefore possible to identify a second dysfunctional schema. Sandra's self wishing that its desires be seen and validated and its independence respected, yet the other (for example, her mother) responding by feeling disappointed and hurt, and denying her love and attention. Sandra then responds by feeling unloveable and frightened by the idea of losing attention and love, and consequently her self stops pursuing its own independent plans so as to continue to ensure the closeness of the other. This schema was termed the 'dependence schema' (see Figure 9.2).

At an advanced stage in her therapy the therapist worked on the integration of the various self-parts forming as a result of the combination of her schemas. He retraced various narrative episodes they had already analysed together and showed Sandra that in the relationship with her current partner she vacillated seamlessly from one schema to another. Using the diagrams that the therapist reconstructed, he pointed out that Sandra's 'dependence schema' becomes activated in various situations. For example, Sandra had stopped expressing her desire to spend time with her girl-friends, even though it left her feeling lonely and restless, because she was convinced that this would disappoint her partner and induce him to leave her. The therapist used the diagram to show Sandra that this mental state almost always led to a shift toward the 'responsibility schema' which was evidenced, for example, by Sandra wishing

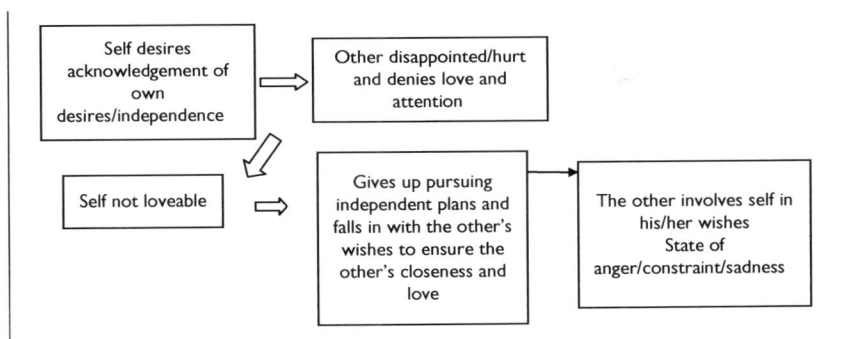

Figure 9.2 Sandra: dependence schema.

for her partner's help and understanding, and Sandra feeling an increased sense of sadness and loneliness when he did not provide this to her. She fully recognised herself in this reconstruction and this stimulated a realisation that her behaviour, previously inexplicable to Sandra, acquired consistency (see Figure 9.3).

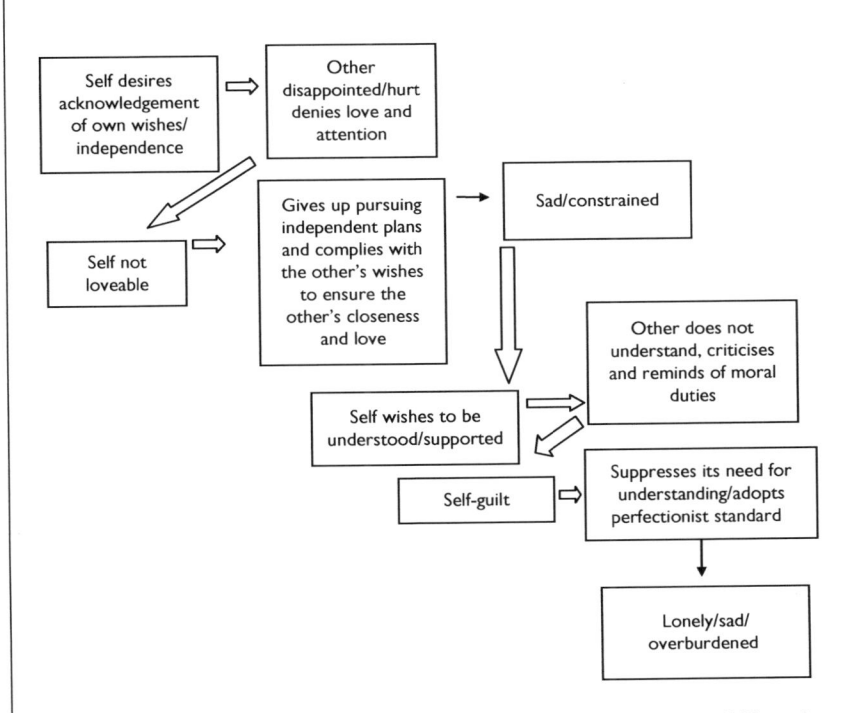

Figure 9.3 Sandra: interaction between dependence schema and responsibility schema.

Another aim of integration interventions is for patients to understand that representations of the other can vary as contexts and emotional states alter, and that every person is an entity with many facets (Bromberg, 1988; Hermans and Dimaggio, 2004; Stiles, 2011) that need to be integrated into a coherent whole. Grasping that in certain situations a partner seems distant and concentrated on himself and in others loving and attentive which leads to the instability of the relationship can be useful for acquiring an integrated image of the other which embraces both aspects and favours their acceptance. The intervention should begin with the analysis of a narrative episode that is centred on an interpersonal interaction, for example with a partner. The therapist should formulate interventions promoting the integration of contradictory aspects of the self and other with this sort of structure: '*In this episode we're seeing how angry you became with your wife, because you felt she was concentrating on herself and incapable of comprehending the importance of your work. We've seen that you often wish to be appreciated for your special worth, and expect the other to either acknowledge it or compete with you by hindering or not paying you due attention. In the first case you feel effective and strong, and in the second angry and vindictive. In your relationship with your wife, you also seem to vacillate between these two positions. A little while ago you angrily described her as inattentive and even envious of your successes, while at other times you told me how she has made you feel important and admired. Like during that dinner with your business partners, she remarked in front of everyone on how hard you'd been working on the project you'd been assigned. The way in which you describe your wife seems to vary according to the expectation you have of her at each moment, and it's difficult to see her as a person who is both neglecting and accepting. It seems that you swing between these two ideas, which also correspond to incompatible ways of seeing yourself and the other. Together we've examined many episodes when you describe your wife in a variety of ways. What do you think about it now when we're talking about it calmly? Is your wife the one person or the other? Or is she a woman with several nuances? Is one of the two impressions more predominant with the other in the background, or can you also see aspects which perhaps we haven't ever paid attention to?*'

An indirect consequence of this type of intervention regarding the integration of self and other representations is that a patient can acquire a more mature view of interpersonal relationships, as in Elisa's case:

> Elisa was a 27-year-old patient who suffered from obsessive-compulsive, narcissistic and passive-aggressive PD, with prominent perfectionist and pessimist traits. At the start of her therapy she was vacillating between situations where she felt nervous and detached from or in love and perceived as important to her romantic partner. When Elisa felt nervous and detached she questioned her love for him in absolutist terms and was prey to worrying about continuing their relationship. In a joint formulation of her functioning, the therapist and Elisa reconstructed her core dysfunctional schema, which consisted of the self wishing for recognition of its special worth from another, who if he acknowledged it, put the self in a position of

importance and 'perfection'. If the other, instead, did not acknowledge this special worth but was hypercritical about her mistakes, as when Elisa's father did not speak to her for days because of a poor mark, the self perceived itself as a failure and worthless. The therapist helped Elisa to focus on the opposing self- and other-representations in the relationship with her boyfriend and to understand the rules that prompted the alternation between them. More specifically, at an advanced therapy stage, the therapist helped Elisa to understand that the periods of devitalised detachment, in which she doubted whether to continue the relationship, were triggered by her boyfriend's behaviour that she wrongly interpreted as a rejection, as when he passed an afternoon silently watching football matches on TV. This helped her understand that in reality she still loved her boyfriend, whether her worth was acknowledged or not. Consequently, her worries diminished and then disappeared (Dimaggio, Carcione, Salvatore et al., 2011).

Interventions to stimulate the recognition of new emerging self-parts and their integration into the patient's identity

At an advanced treatment stage, patients often realise that they are thinking and acting in new ways but do not recognise themselves and consequently feel surprised, confused and puzzled. The therapeutic intervention regarding this aspect of integration consists of helping the patient become aware of the signs of the new emerging self-parts and give them a name or stress their importance. This work starts during the therapeutic conversation when, basing himself on a narrative episode, the therapist first warmly stresses the positive aspects emerging and then summarises the most significant change elements with specific interventions. For example, the therapist may say, '*The episode we are examining is very important because it is one of the situations where in the past, when interacting with others, you felt the target of a negative opinion and were seized by a sense of shame that led you to withdraw as fast as you could. This time, in a situation where you were exposed in the same way, you initially experienced the same shame but did not allow this feeling to lead you to flight. You were able to stop and take your time, and then you even managed to reduce your shame to the point of making a joke. Thanks to this shift in behaviour you were able to realise that the people around you were kind, and considered you witty and likeable. You see, we can consider this part of you, a part of you that can bear shame and manage to interact with others with jocularity. This is a new part of you, which is an important and creative result of your therapy.*'

Advanced stages of MIT feature interventions entail therapists trying to offer patients a view of how they are changing as good results are obtained. Therapists also help patients integrate the new aspects of themselves in their overall self-image. The intervention regarding this aspect of integration can be reinforced with a representation in graph form that modifies the diagram based on the shared formulation of functioning. A diagram provides precious assistance in giving patients an evocative picture of how their therapeutic change is tangible. It is a signal to them that, even if their schema still exists, there are new, *non-schema-driven* self-parts that are making their way to the surface.

At an advanced stage in Sandra's therapy, her therapist proposed behavioural experiments similar to those described in Chapter 8. One of the areas covered by the experiments was promoting the satisfaction of her own wishes within significant relationships. A fundamental goal was to challenge a series of schema-dependent cognitions, such as

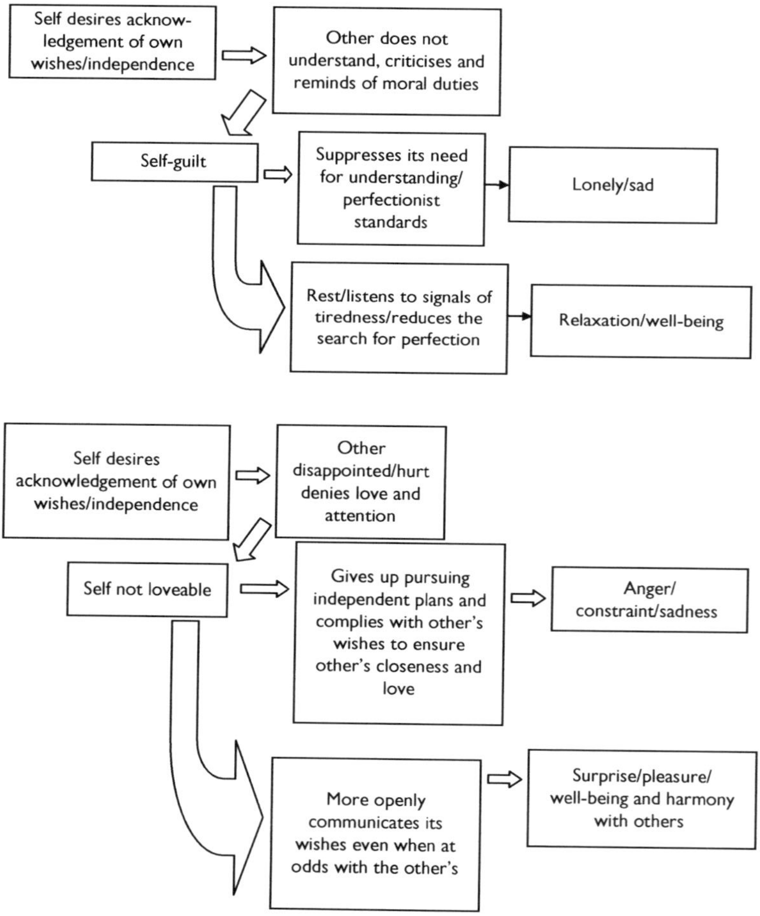

Figure 9.4 Modification of the diagram showing the joint formulation of functioning with stress on the new parts emerging in Sandra after two years of therapy.

'*I fear that if I say I won't go to the cinema, he'll leave me*', through the programming of pattern-breaking behaviours like '*I'll try not going and see if it happens.*'

A second goal was for Sandra to become more focused on her own wishes and use them to guide her choices and behave more assertively. As a result, during a session from the second year of therapy, Sandra described that her partner had again proposed that they visit a cave and when she remembered the therapist's face and reassuring words as well as recalling the diagram they had drawn up together, she politely refused and explained the reasons behind her decision. She felt relieved when her partner cancelled the trip due to preferring to spend the weekend with her instead. This new and pleasant sensation surprised and disoriented her.

The therapist proposed other behavioural experiments to reduce the strength of her perfectionistic standards and to help her feel pleasure when she ate or danced. The agreed tasks included that she should stop weighing her food and grant herself a day or two's rest from training every time she even vaguely registered a sense of tiredness. Thanks to these experiments, for the first time Sandra managed to feel a sense of relief and physical relaxation. During one session the therapist explicitly praised her for her strong commitment to the experiments and highlighted the progress she had made. The therapist then revisited the diagram depicting her responsibility and dependence schemas, and together they made some adjustments (see Figure 9.4). Thanks to this reconstruction in diagram form, Sandra managed to understand that the sense of relief she felt in various circumstances with her boyfriend and regarding food and training was a sign of a significant inner maturation.

Summary of case evolution in letter form

Reformulation letters written at the end of a therapy, commonly used in cognitive analytic therapy (Ryle and Kerr, 2002) and mentalisation-based therapy (Bateman and Fonagy, 2004), help patients achieve a general sense of the course of their therapy. Therapists can use the letters to show patients that the schema-discrepant self-parts surfacing during therapy are now getting consolidated in the form of new, functional and adaptive schemas. Below is the new reformulation letter the therapist delivered to Sandra.

Dear Sandra

The aim of this letter is to help you focus on the progress you've made after two and a half years of therapy. First of all, I congratulate you on your commitment. The progress you have made is largely due to your constancy and to the sincerity with which you've been able to call yourself into question over time. The first important result we achieved together was an improvement in your ability to read your emotions, as well as the meaning events have for you. Thanks to this we have been able to identify the schemas that drove your thoughts and behaviours, which we together labelled the 'responsibility schema' and the 'dependence schema'. By identifying these forms of functioning we were able to understand that you suffered when external events reactivated these schemas. You then acquired the ability to separate yourself from the schemas and interpret others' intentions more realistically. Then you started to challenge these schemas with small experiments. In this, let me say, you were really good, because these experiments went in the direction of gradually entering your most troublesome areas and exposing yourself to the anxiety that any of us would feel if asked to adopt views and behaviours different from what is usual and safe, risking moral criticism or rejection. Here we saw a Sandra who manages to openly communicate her wishes to her partner without gratifying him, and who understands that she does not need to mould herself to the other's wishes, and that she does not deserve to be abandoned. A Sandra who deserves to grant herself a little rest – and, why not? – a nice pizza, when she feels tired, doesn't want to train or would simply like a pizza! In this way you challenged the idea that if you're not perfect you'll be considered immorally at fault and blameworthy, or even unloveable. Well, all this hard work has repaid you and now we can say that a new part of Sandra, which together we called 'Loveable Sandra', has been born and that it's set in a new schema, a different and creative way of seeing the world. This represents a substantial modification of the dependence schema. In this new schema the other responds with love and attention to Sandra's wish to see her desires acknowledged, without this involving the loss of the other's closeness. As a result, Sandra feels lovable for who she is, and free to acknowledge and negotiate her needs and to express her point of view in a significant relationship. This new schema is linked to a radical improvement in your ability to identify your wishes and communicate them in a relationship. Now when, for example, you feel a sense of constraint in the relationship with your boyfriend, you are able to stand back and observe it. You are able to understand that it depends on a failure to express your own wishes and you communicate them effectively. Your tendency to control what you eat has also diminished, thanks to together dismantling your tendency to feel exaggeratedly responsible, which was supported by the responsibility schema. And lastly, and this is the most important thing, thanks to all this you're able to live your life as something that can give you pleasure, and no longer just as a laborious 'training'.

Sandra very emotionally told the therapist that the letter had helped her to place an even greater focus on her change. A month later the therapist proposed that Sandra should start getting ready to terminate from therapy. Before stopping therapy completely, the therapist planned a step-down phase (one session every two weeks) for three months, and then a follow-up period with one session per month. Sandra willingly accepted.

If we go back over the principal steps in the letter, it is possible to list the most important principles guiding the creation of a reformulation letter. Before reading the letter out loud, as occurs in cognitive analytic therapy (Ryle and Kerr, 2002), the therapist should explain that it is a view of the therapy from his point of view, and that he is reading it out loud to get the patient's point of view and correct it until it is in tune with the latter's perception of the change in him/her. Generally the patient's corrections are marginal, given that this is a tool often used at the end of successful therapies. The therapist should also ask for feedback about the impact of the letter on the therapeutic relationship. For example, how does the therapist appear to the patient while reconstructing the therapy?

The letter should:

- have a sharing tone;
- include a concise report of the fundamental steps in the therapeutic path undertaken by the patient;
- focus on a description of the new schemas and on how the initial ones have been modified while using the same style and language as the shared formulation of functioning from the initial stage of the therapy,
- be written with an openly validating style, consisting in particular in acknowledging the patient's commitment to the therapy and his/her real contribution to the achievement of the result.

Conclusions

In the advanced stages of a therapy the goal is to promote metacognitively more complex operations, such as:

- understanding in a sophisticated manner, which is rich in nuances and, if possible, decentred, what drives others to feel and act;
- forming an integrated and consistent self-image;
- understanding that others have numerous aspects which sometimes make them seem like different people to us, but that behind any changes hide individual persons whom the patient can now appraise in their entirety.

These operations should be rigorously carried out only after patients have started to take on a critical distance from their schemas. If this were not the case, the forming of new ideas about the self and others would be blocked by the power of the schemas to trace every discrepant element back to themselves. When patients acquire the ability to see others in a new way, change their ideas and accept that they are composed of multiple self-aspects that still form a whole, a range of possibilities for acting more adaptively on the social scene opens up before them. Decentring and integrating skills will be useful for some metacognitive mastery operations described in the next chapter.

Notes

1. For more details about how role play has also recently been used as a tool for promoting an increase in metacognitive and social skills in patients with schizophrenia see Ottavi, D'Alia, Lysaker et al., 2013)
2. Embodied simulation processes (Gallese and Lakoff, 2005) rooted in neural functioning have control precedence over reasoning when we are called to 'put ourselves in the other's shoes'. This part of role play tends to trigger and facilitate these simulation processes.

Chapter 10

Treating symptoms and promoting mastery of relational problems

The metacognitive skills that patients manage to employ and the quality of their therapeutic relationship guide MIT interventions in two crucial aspects of PD: treating symptoms and mastery of subjective suffering and promoting interpersonal problem-solving skills.

In this chapter, we discuss how metacognition and the therapeutic relationship guide therapists when treating symptoms and solving relational problems. The better the metacognition, the more ample and flexible the strategies and techniques a clinician can adopt. The quality of a therapeutic relationship tells a clinician whether to continue working on symptoms and problems or interrupt this until the relationship is restored.

This chapter is divided into three parts. In the first we show how MIT uses techniques of a mainly cognitive-behavioural type for the treatment of symptoms in PD. We would stress that the techniques used correspond to forms of mastery for the handling of intrapsychical problems and subjective suffering (see Chapter 2). In the second part we show how to promote mastery strategies in the relational domain while taking advantage of any increase in metacognitive skills. In the third part we will describe two clinical cases involving PD patients with serious symptoms. The cases show how MIT operates by oscillating between treating a patient's personality to treating symptoms in a context where it promotes growing metacognitive skills and regulates the therapeutic relationship and how, as metacognition improves, it changes strategies. The two cases constitute syntheses of typical MIT therapy, which at the end of the book the reader will be able to see in its entirety.

PART I TREATING SYMPTOMS

Treating PD necessarily includes working to reduce the associated symptoms. The high rate of co-occurrence between anxiety disorders and PD is well-known: 52 per cent for obsessive-compulsive disorder, 48 per cent for social phobia, 47 per cent for generalised anxiety and 41–47 per cent for panic disorder respectively without and with agoraphobia (Friborg, Martinussen, Kaiser et al., 2013). Even mood disorders display significant rates of co-occurrence with PDs: 51 per cent for the unipolar types and between 29 and 40 per cent for bipolar disorder (Krishnan, 2005; George, Miklowitz, Richards et al., 2003). The occurrence of eating disorders in young adults predicts a tendency to depressive relapses (Sheets, Duncan, Bjornsson et al., 2013).

Eating disorders associated with obsessive-compulsive and borderline PDs (Sansone, Levitt and Sansone, 2006) are also frequently found. Generally, three personality sub-types linked to eating disorders tend to emerge: high functioning/perfectionist, dysregulated and hyper-controlled/constrained, the last with avoidance features (Thompson-Brenner and Westen, 2005). Thompson-Brenner, Eddy, Satir and colleagues (2008) found that the avoidant-depressive personality sub-type, corresponding to hyper-controlled, was an indicator of poor family and school functioning in a sample of adolescents with eating disorders. Among adolescents with eating disorders, Gazzillo, Lingiardi, Peloso and colleagues (2013) identified the hyper-controlled/constrained sub-type, with emotional suppression tendency to avoid situations evoking emotions and difficulty describing themselves and others, which are characteristics of many of the PDs described in this book.

It is, therefore, essential for an MIT clinician to have a solid knowledge of the most advanced and scientifically validated psychotherapeutic techniques to be able to treat these disorders effectively. For these reasons, and in line with its scientific and cultural roots, MIT mainly uses the repertoire of cognitive-behavioural techniques, even if it is open to absorbing those used by other approaches where they have been shown to be empirically well-grounded.

When treating symptoms in MIT, there are two principles to be followed:

1   Interventions should be based on the quality of the therapeutic relationship. If the latter is dysfunctional, the work on symptoms should be interrupted and the intervention shift to re-establishing relationship quality (see Chapter 5).
2   The intervention should be tuned to the metacognitive skill profile that a patient possesses at that point in a session. If the latter possesses limited self-reflectivity, one should use mainly behavioural strategies, whereas if his metacognitive skills are well-developed, symptoms can be treated by using gradually more complex cognitive techniques.

Symptomatic disorders are very often the reason PD patients seek therapy. PD psychotherapy should necessarily include strategies for treating symptoms (Millon, 1999), especially because the more a PD is serious end widespread, the greater the intensity of the subjective distress and the more numerous the co-diagnoses (Dimaggio, Carcione, Nicolò et al., 2013; Seivewright, Tyrer and Johnson, 2004).

PD patients respond to treatments aimed at certain symptoms like depression similarly to patients without PD (De Bolle, De Fruyt, Quilty et al., 2011), but come to therapy with greater subjective suffering than the latter and at the end of treatment have more symptoms (Unger, Hoffmann, Köhler et al., 2013).

Furthermore, Unger and colleagues found that the results for patients with co-occurrence of symptomatic and personality disorders are less consistent over time and at follow-up, part of the benefit is lost. For obsessive-compulsive disorder the presence of schizotypal, paranoid and narcissistic PD and the presence of two or more PDs was linked to a worse treatment outcome (Thiel, Hertenstein, Nissen et al., 2013). When the focus of therapy is PD, symptoms tend to recede before the core personality disorder, but at the end of treatment they are still strong (Livesley, 2003).

The interweaving between an interpersonal dysfunction and symptoms has an impact on treatment. Treating the underlying PD, in particular the interpersonal problems that are its trademark (Leichsenring, Salzer, Beutel et al., 2013), does not solve symptoms. Instead, it requires a tailored intervention (Thiel, Hertenstein, Nissen et al., 2013). As we have seen, patients ask straight away for relief from symptoms and, if the therapy is capable of providing it, this improves the patient's mood and strengthens the alliance. Thanks to this symptomatic intervention collateral effect, it is easier to treat the PD.

Even if it helps to reduce symptoms by operating on the roots of the relational processes triggering and exacerbating them, treating personality alone will not make the symptoms disappear. Clinical experience and research on psychopathology show that symptoms depend only partly on relational problems. The latter are also supported by intrapsychical maintenance mechanisms. OCD, for example, can be triggered by pathogenic interpersonal schemas where the self-image is negative, imperfect, loathsome and deserving of rejection in the eyes of critical, rejecting and neglecting others (Doron and Kyrios, 2005; Frost and Steketee, 1997); however, if obsessive behaviour persists, this is mostly due to cognitive-affective maintenance processes (Baptista, Magna, McKay et al., 2011; Calkins, Berman and Wilhelm, 2013), behavioural reinforcements and a neurobiological substratum (Murphy, Moya, Fox et al., 2013). Without specifically tackling these maintenance processes, symptoms diminish only partly.

The example of eating disorders is still more striking, as there is often a serious PD underlying it (Cassin and Von Ranson, 2005; Claes, Vandereycken, Luyten et al., 2006; Wonderlich, Lilenfeld, Riso et al., 2005; Lavender, Wonderlich, Crosby et al., 2013). A patient with anorexia starting therapy dangerously underweight cannot be treated for PD unless first kept alive with medical treatment and helped to renourish herself. The treatment of the mechanisms involving her personality which led the patient to use restrictive eating behaviour as a dysfunctional coping strategy comes later when the patient has started to regain weight.

The patients described here therefore display an interweaving between personality dysfunction and symptoms, which necessarily requires shifting the focus between the former and the latter in a strategically orientated manner (Shahar and Davidson, 2009). The combined focus on symptoms and personality is necessary also because PD has a toxic effect on symptom treatment: the presence of a PD makes it more difficult to establish and maintain a good working alliance.

Patients can be less willing to do homework. Furthermore, for such patients embodying the role of someone cared for by the therapist, it can in itself become problematic. They can construct the attachment figure in anticipation as threatening, constrictive, tyrannical, critical and so on, which leads them not to cooperate in carrying out the tasks needed to reduce their symptoms. Moreover, patients can pass in the same session from complaining about anxiety or obsessions to describing failures in their interpersonal or professional spheres and thus interrupt the work needed for calming their symptoms.

Another problem is comorbidity involving patients displaying multiple disorders simultaneously. One patient we describe later suffered from OCD, social phobia, eating disorder and depression. Comorbidity makes it impossible to follow a particular procedure as it requires case-specific decisions (Shahar and Davidson, 2009; Westen, Novotny and Thompson-Brenner, 2004). There is little sense in treating symptoms in a sequence, given that in a particular session one problem may be more urgent from the patient's point of view. Forcing him to tackle a problem different from the one distressing him and for which he is asking for an intervention would undermine the alliance and the forming of a cooperative atmosphere.

Lastly, symptoms are multi-determined and supported by complex psychopathological mechanisms and having access to a range of techniques helps to attack them from several points of view. An example of how a symptom responds to various attack strategies comes from a study on social phobia. Although patients respond well to both cognitive-behavioural and psychodynamic treatments, CBT turned out to be significantly superior in treating social anxiety and interpersonal problems (Leichensring, Salzer, Beutel et al., 2013; Canton, Scott and Glue, 2012). CBT for social phobia typically applies *cognitive restructuring* and *in vivo exposure* to anxiety-provoking social situations. Patients are taught to identify and challenge their dysfunctional beliefs about their social skills and their assumptions of being negatively judged by others. The exposures constitute an opportunity to confront generally avoided situations and put into practice new *social skills* learned in therapy via role play, imaginary-exposures and specific social skills training. Lastly, CBT teaches socially anxious patients anxiety management techniques (Clark and Beck, 2010). Psychodynamic therapy tackles the underlying personality structure within the therapeutic relationship using a formulation – consistent with that used in MIT – based on CCRT (see Chapter 3). It aims to help patients modify the conflictual relationship theme leading them to fear others' opinions and to distance themselves from others. There are different paths leading to the same result, which is the reduction of social phobia and improvement of implicit and explicit self-esteem (Ritter, Leichsenring, Strauss et al., 2013). A clinician knowing them both is able to find the best way to treat a specific patient, who can respond differently to the various techniques. In general, the cognitive-behavioural approach to treating symptoms nevertheless remains the one with the most evidence-based literature supporting its efficacy (Roth and Fonagy, 2005).

To summarise, MIT has several principles when working on symptoms in a PD therapy context:

- treating PD and regulating the alliance increase compliance with symptomatic treatment and a good outcome (Castonguay, Schut, Aikens et al. 2004; Costantino, Marnell, Haile et al., 2008);
- at the same time, effectively treating symptoms restores a patient's confidence and stimulates the building of alliance and compliance with PD treatment;
- treating symptoms with specific and continuously updated techniques is indispensable but, since symptoms are multi-determined, they should be tackled via multiple access routes. In any case, it is not practical to use symptom treatment procedures mechanically without making use of their interweaving (Shahar and Davidson, 2009).

Using these principles, we are going to subdivide patients into three groups, based on their levels of metacognitive functioning.

The first group has poor self-reflective skills, in particular limited awareness of emotions and the role emotions play in mediating events, thoughts and behaviours. This group has difficulty understanding others and ascribes thoughts to them in accordance with generalisations and stereotypes or constructs them in a schema-dependent manner.

The second group has intermediate self-reflective skills and grasps what causes emotions and what emotions provoke. These patients start to differentiate, that is to take a critical distance from one's interpersonal schemas, but this skill is ephemeral and fluctuating and usually only present in session. This group defines others with a minimum of sensitiveness, even if rarely managing to interpret others by detaching themselves from their own perspective.

The third group has high self-reflective skills, differentiates fairly consistently except under stress and is aware that, if one remains tied to dysfunctional interpretations, it is due to the pressure of emotions that makes it difficult to regulate. Others are understood quite well and their point of view is grasped even when different from one's own, but this ability to understand others is temporarily hampered when under stress.

Based on this subdivision we are going to show how MIT adopts interventions and techniques for treating symptoms, handling suffering and improving mastery in relationships in line with metacognitive skills.

Symptom and subjective suffering intervention procedures

MIT procedures for treating symptoms start with knowing the factors that trigger the symptoms and the dysfunctional cognitive-affective processes maintaining them. Choosing psychotherapeutic techniques is a complex process that takes into consideration:

- the level of metacognitive skills currently displayed by a patient;
- therapeutic relationship quality;
- evidence supporting the various techniques for particular symptoms;
- the clinician having greater mastery of one technique over another if their efficacy is equal;
- the consistency of the technique with the personalised formulation of a patient's symptoms.

When a patient considers a symptom to be the priority, this should be tackled first. Treatment of a symptom should be interrupted if:

1. ruptures in the alliance occur (in this case one should start working on the therapeutic relationship (see Chapter 5));
2. a patient changes the conversation of his own free will (in this case one should start working on interpersonal or existential problems);
3. enough space has been conceded to treatment of symptoms and, after agreeing with the patient, the clinician considers it necessary to tackle areas relating to personality.

The techniques initially chosen to treat a symptom can gradually be replaced by others if the patient no longer responds to a particular type of technique or if the patient's metacognitive skills have improved to the extent that it becomes possible to accompany or replace the techniques with others requiring greater metacognitive skills.

We are now going to explain how symptom treatment is interwoven with that of PD. We group the techniques with the level of self-reflective skills a patient manages to employ at that moment in therapy. We also use understanding the other's mind as an important parameter.

Poor emotional awareness and limited understanding of the other's mind

Symptom treatment here is directed towards patients with difficulty identifying their inner states and, in particular, poor emotional monitoring and an inability to understand the antecedents to events or the way in which emotions are triggered by thoughts and in turn influence those same thoughts and behaviour. Such patients display symptoms but are unable to put together complex ABC (*antecedent-beliefs-consequence*, or event-thought-emotion-behaviour) or TR (thought recording) (Beck, 2011) causal chains, or grasp how interpersonal events cause suffering. In this case, mainly psychoeducational and behavioural interventions are recommended.

First, one needs to adopt a listening and non-critical stance, empathise with the distress caused by the symptoms and place value on the patient's underlying emotional experience, reminding her that anxiety, sadness and anger are basic human emotions. At the same time, it is indispensable to adopt a normalising and soothing attitude; in this way a patient learns from the therapist's words that his disorder is well-known, widespread and treatable, and that often it is merely an extreme and distressing expression of universal forms of functioning.

With patients with limited self-reflectivity, it is essential to explain the symptom maintenance model as typically seen in CBT. To arrive at a joint case-conceptualisation, the clinician should look for narrative episodes in which the symptom appeared. After finding an episode, the intervention should start with this kind of observation: '*So we can see the same sequence of events either on the bus or at the supermarket: you feel a tingling in your arm, you immediately think it's a heart attack and you're afraid. This makes your heart beat even faster and this tachycardia confirms to you that you're undergoing a heart attack. At this point you panic. After the most recent episodes of this type you decided to avoid going on the bus and to supermarkets and you're now strongly convinced that it's better to avoid places where you can't see an exit.*'

It is now time to start psychoeducating the patient about the symptom. Using simple diagrams, one should explain that it is caused by cognitive-affective processes and often maintained by dysfunctional behaviour, for example avoidance, which reinforces the patient's tendency to believe her catastrophic ideas to be true because it prevents them being disproved on the basis of experience.

In *panic disorder*, for example, a patient needs to be taught about the nature and physiological characteristics of her anxiety and panic, describe the nature of the unpleasant physical sensations she experiences and the vicious cycles supporting her disorder (Clark, 1986; Clark and Beck, 2010), explain what stimuli triggered her panic and highlight the erroneous catastrophic interpretations and enacting responses involving avoidance and safety-seeking. With this, it is possible to point out the core role played by erroneous catastrophic interpretations of physical symptoms in giving rise to and maintaining panic. It helps a patient grasp how much her involvement is active and decisive in triggering an attack and making it persist. An attack is the result of a process continuously reinforced by many aspects over which a patient has more control than she believes.

Following this, the patient could benefit from basic cognitive interventions aimed at weakening her erroneous catastrophic interpretations and the threat, fear and danger schemas underlying her physical or mental states. The patient could also benefit from classical behavioural techniques like *interoceptive exposures* (Clark and Beck, 2010; Lee, Noda, Nakano et al., 2006), which are true and proper in-session experiments designed to disprove the dysfunctional catastrophic convictions supporting her disorder.

For example, should a patient be convinced that the dizziness felt during her anxiety attacks is a sign that she is about to faint, the therapist should get her to carry out in session some simple hyperventilation exercises (that is increasing the frequency and deepness of one's breathing) to induce an excess of oxygen in the brain and, thus, an innocuous sensation of dizziness. Doing this experiment several times will show the patient that the dizziness she notices in given circumstances are caused by a hyperoxygenation triggered by the way she breathes when anxious and that she will not, therefore, faint. Getting the patient to induce the symptoms of her own free will means not only disproving the mistaken convictions underlying them but also interrupting her habit of shunning and avoiding them due to the fact that she considers them dangerous.

With patients with limited self-reflectivity *relaxation techniques* (such as autogenic training or progressive muscular relaxation) (Schultz and Luthe, 1959), *breathing training* (such as diaphragmatic breathing) and *anxiety management* techniques not aimed at treating panic disorder can contribute to reducing arousal and stress levels which play a part in maintaining symptoms. Cognitively more complex interventions aimed at altering patients' convictions about their physical sensations being unbearable or uncontrollable and belief in their vulnerability/ fragility should be postponed.

According to the cognitive model (Clark and Beck, 2010), anxiety is a response to an internal or external stimulus triggering the idea that a threat is present. This model is more consistent with a diathesis-stress perspective where particular situations or signals (*stress*) activate an anxiety response in individuals with a propensity towards easily detecting threat (*diathesis*). In many cases, main life events, traumas or continuous adversities contribute to anxiety. In others, the precipitating factors are not as dramatic and are in the normal life event range, such as an increase in workplace stress or an uncertain medical test outcome for a minor disease. Therapy includes an explanation of these processes too. Furthermore, the reduction of avoidance and other dysfunctional safety-seeking behaviour and the promotion of individual tolerance of psychical unease through *in vivo exposure* will be tackled at a later stage.

In the case of *patients with depression* and poor self-reflectivity, an empathetic listening stance is particularly necessary given the levels of subjective distress, sense of failure and their self-accusations. After explaining the nature of his depression to a patient, he can benefit, as a first step, from advice to activate himself from a behavioural point of view by performing physical activity (Carek, Laibstain, Carek et al., 2011; Beck, 2011) or adjusting his sleeping-waking routine (Salgado-Delgado, Tapia Osorio, Saderi et al., 2011). This part of the intervention should be accompanied by an evoking of narrative episodes, which will progressively lead the patient to understand that his depression – we would recall that we are talking about depression in a PD context – depends on negative expectations about relationships.

At this level, behavioural activation (Dimidjian, Barrera, Martell et al., 2011) is one of the most important goals for depressed patients. Many no longer carry out a number of activities from which they drew a sense of mastery and pleasure and, at the same time, the majority of patients make increased use of certain behaviours (staying in bed, watching TV) that maintain or increase negative mood. The simplest and quickest way to activate these patients from a behavioural point of view is to review their daily routine and then, using forms for *planning and self-monitoring pleasurable activities*, together plan potential tasks that can be performed at home such us phoning friends or finding places to go.

While planning, a therapist needs to be careful to alternate short periods of activity with other, longer ones involving relaxation or rest and to ask patients to recognise their merit every time they keep to the plan. Particular attention needs to be given to anticipating responses to the possible automatic thoughts that depressed patients very often utilise and which could interfere with the carrying out of activities or the gaining of a sense of pleasure or mastery deriving from them (Beck, 2011).

Another aspect that can be taken into consideration at this stage is the tendency of depressed patients to assess themselves negatively and minimise, or even forget, their positive qualities. *Positive self-assertion diaries* are very useful tools in this respect and do not require high metacognitive skills as they are simple daily (mental or written) lists of the positive things patients are doing or the things for which they deserve recognition. Taking up pleasurable activities again can also be the subject of these self-assertion diaries.

In addition, motivational notes in the form of *coping cards* (Beck, 2011) can be used. With depressed patients with limited self-reflectivity, it is possible to introduce certain concepts relating to *cognitive attentional syndrome* (CAS) (Wells, 2008), from which they are probably suffering, even if the treatment and assessment of it in personal meaning terms is going to be the subject of more advanced therapy stages.

CAS is a particular pattern of response to internal experiences that maintains a negative emotion and reinforces dysfunctional beliefs/ideas. The pattern features rumination, worry, threat monitoring and maladaptive coping strategies.[1] At this stage, one should explain to a patient what is supporting the CAS, that is: (1) positive metacognitive beliefs about the need to ruminate as a means for overcoming depressive emotions and responding to problems; (2) negative metacognitive beliefs about the uncontrollability of the rumination, the self's psychological vulnerability and the danger of depressive experiences.

Patients with *eating disorders* with limited self-reflectivity can gain advantage from psychoeducational interventions regarding correct eating or the physical consequences associated with a persistence of their problematic eating behaviour (Vandereycken, Aerts and Dierckx, 2013). Techniques originating from *enhanced transdiagnostic CBT for eating disorders* (CBT-E) (Fairburn, 2008), such as *eating self-monitoring* with which it is possible to promote a greater awareness of one's way of eating, a *weekly weighing* exclusively in session with the goal of reassuring patients about the real size of any variations in weight, eliminating compulsive *weight checking* or removing the avoidance of weight checking, *regular eating* to promote eating that is planned time-wise and well distributed over the span of a day and *body shape checking* reduction procedures, can be employed. In addition, the intervention should touch on any *self-imposed eating rules*, such as eating only in the morning, not eating in front of others, not eating more than person X, not eating before digesting the previous meal and so on, by showing that they do not have the hoped-for effects. A therapist can plan behavioural experiments (in vivo exposures) where patients have to break one of their self-imposed rules, for example by drinking a glass of milk at break-time and not at breakfast, discovering that the actual consequences are different from those feared and, thus, progressively reducing compliance with the rule.

With regard to patients with anorexia's guiding rule, 'avoid almost all food', one can use the *food inoculation training* technique, similar to systematic desensitisation using food as a phobic stimulus. Briefly, this technique foresees the drawing up, in agreement with the patient, of a list of foods subdivided into four groups with different degrees of difficulty in consumption, from low to very high. Every two or three sessions there is a 'food negotiation' at the end of which a foodstuff is chosen at a suitable level of difficulty and the quantity of it gets increased or it gets introduced into the patient's diet. The planning of its consumption involves *when* exactly the chosen food should be consumed, *where* and *in whose presence*, in what *quantities* (generally very small) and how the *consequences* in terms of guilt feelings, brooding or obsessions are to be tackled.

In the case of eating disorders, we would stress in particular that any technical interventions should be constantly assessed on the basis of therapeutic relationship quality: how does the patient construct her therapist while he is explaining to her that her self-imposed eating rules are harmful, ineffective and irrational? Is an interpersonal cycle being activated, where the therapist is seen as threatening, invalidating or tyrannical? If something like this occurs, the work on symptoms should be interrupted and, as a procedure, one should work on the therapeutic relationship until these problematical processes have been solved and the working alliance re-established.

In the case of underweight patients, a therapist should stimulate a motivation for change, by sounding out the patient's ambitions and projects and trying to suggest that a reasonable weight is physiologically necessary for the achievement of the patient's academic, professional or existential goals (Fairburn, 2008).

Only when the patient's self-reflective skills have improved is it possible to work on identifying particular links between eating behaviours and extra-eating events, situations or occurrences, on the over-evaluation of appearance and weight as indicators of personal worth, on mood-correlated changes in eating and on features such as perfectionism, low self-esteem and interpersonal problems, as we are going to show later.

Lastly we are going to look at how to treat *obsessive-compulsive disorder* if self-reflective skills are minimal. If a patient has pervasive compulsions, one should primarily opt for mostly behavioural strategies such as *exposure and response prevention* (ERP) (Marks, 1975; Taylor, 2002) requiring limited self-reflection. ERP is a formalised procedure aimed at making patients experience their obsessions, by exposing the patient to them and preventing them from resorting to compulsions or safety procedures like distraction, thought control, avoidance or seeking reassurance. It is a very effective technique applicable to any kind of obsession. If, for example, the patient is bothered by the idea of pushing someone under a subway train, he has to expose himself to a situation evoking this impulse by standing on a subway platform. If his obsession is a terrifying scene, like hurting someone he loves, he has to expose himself to this scene by mentally concentrating on it, describing it in detail or exposing himself to objects or situations evoking it. If his obsession is a doubt, 'I'm not gay, am I?' or 'I'm not a pedophile, am I?', he has to expose himself to the doubt by trying not to take it into consideration: not looking for information confirming or disproving the doubt, not monitoring his body looking for signs of sexual excitement when in the presence of certain types of people and so on; he, therefore, has to try and behave as if the doubt was meaningless.

The ERP procedure is not merely a behavioural strategy as its possible action mechanisms include not only habituation, extinction and counter-conditioning, but also cognitive changes relating to a person's self-efficacy and forecasts of danger and expectations of success when faced with the feared stimulus (Tryon, 2005). It is, in any case, a technique not requiring high self-reflective skills and it can, consequently, be proposed to patients with limited emotional awareness.

When patients possess adequate self-reflectivity, then more cognitive strategies aimed at contrasting erroneous interpretations of intrusive thoughts suffering from biases such as thought-action fusion, excessive sense of responsibility, overestimation of threats and danger, and intolerance of uncertainty (see later) can be used.

Claudia was a 37-year-old clerk suffering from OCD, with predominant cleaning rituals. She washed her body hundreds of times a day, and was constantly cleaning her home and changing her bed sheets. Her self-reflectivity was so poor that at the start of therapy her SCID-II interview did not find any PD, a false negative as became clear during therapy.

The rituals were complex: she washed her hands three times after every contact with an object. Her romantic relationship was passing through a crisis because her partner was exhausted by the rituals. She managed to keep her job, because the rituals were less frequent at her workplace, due to her sense of duty as a result of which, even if she felt the impulse to wash herself, she did not leave her desk. Her metacognitive dysfunction was serious: she had no emotional awareness. Her therapist asked her what emotion she felt when she saw something dirty or felt dirty but her only reply was: '*It annoys me and I need to wash myself.*' The therapist suggested that it was disgust or fear of being contaminated, two emotions typical of OCD, but Claudia was unable to pinpoint them and grasp what compelled her to wash herself. She was, however, motivated to change and cooperate. Bearing in mind the good alliance and the serious metacognitive dysfunction, an ERP programme appeared suitable and Claudia started on this. In just a few sessions she obtained good results and the washing diminished significantly.

In MIT, an improvement in a symptom in PD patients has a double significance: it is both a therapy goal per se and by reducing the coping behaviours linked to the symptom, it makes it possible for the patients to remain longer in the mental states preceding the dysfunctional coping – washing herself in the case of the patient described above – and thus improve metacognition. We shall see later that, when Claudia refrained from washing, she could observe her mental state for longer and discovered aspects of her inner world that later made it possible to diagnose a complex PD. Claudia arrived at grasping that, when she saw herself as being dirty, her self-image was that she was unpleasant and the dominant emotions were disgust and shame. We will see later that the symptom was treated on a different basis and then work began on her personality.

During the therapy stages in which a patient has limited awareness of the antecedents of a symptom, one can also promote mindfulness. It is, moreover, possible to suggest to a patient that he take part in a mindfulness-based stress reduction (MBSR) programme (Kabat-Zinn, 1990; Grossman, Niemann, Schmidt et al., 2004). Mindfulness is the English translation of the word *sati* in the Pali language, which means 'aware attention' or 'bare attention' and is a form of meditation consisting of 'paying attention in a particular way: on purpose, in the present moment, and nonjudgmentally' (Kabat-Zinn, 1994: 63).

A core mechanism through which mindfulness unfolds its effects is to be found in teaching a patient an attitude involving a continuous and non-judgemental observation of the sensations and thoughts correlated with his disorders set against the carrying out of attempts at flight or avoidance behaviours. MBSR adopts a relatively intensive training in mindfulness meditation. The goals of an MBSR programme include profound and positive changes in attitude, behaviour and perception of oneself, others and the world (Kabat-Zinn, 1994).

Adequate relating of variables and fluctuating differentiation – initial understanding of the other's mind

When patients become capable of putting together psychological causal chains, there is a greater range of techniques that can be used.

In the case of *panic disorder*, a patient is capable of saying what produces his suffering, identifying the situational and/or relational antecedents leading to the raising of arousal, and in what ways certain automatic thoughts lead to catastrophically interpreting signs of high arousal (Beck, 2011). Let us consider the example of a patient with avoidant PD, social phobia and hypochondria, who at the start of therapy was frightened that her stomach ache was a sign of a serious illness. During treatment she arrived at grasping that the stomach ache was a neurovegetative expression of her anxiety about being humiliated in public. Understanding this provided an alternative and plausible explanation for her stomach ache that rendered her hypochondriacal interpretation less credible and made it possible to shift the focus of her treatment to the interpersonal schemas underlying her avoidant PD and social phobia.

Patients with an adequate relating of variables are, therefore, capable of fully carrying out an ABC, that is to grasp that a situational antecedent produces an automatic thought, which in turn triggers distressing emotions and dysfunctional behaviours. In session, a therapist can adopt practically the full range of advanced techniques available in the various forms of CBT (Beck, 2011).

With panic disorder (Clark and Beck, 2010), cognitively more complex interventions are possible at this point in a therapy. These interventions are aimed at remoulding patients' convictions about physical sensations being unbearable or uncontrollable and the core self-images of vulnerability/fragility when faced with others who criticise, abandon and interfere with their independence. One can start to show that the anxiety is triggered by events activating pathogenic interpersonal schemas, in which, for example, the self is fragile, the other will abandon it and the self will find itself weak and incapable of handling the feared danger alone. At the same time, one should work at promoting the emergence of more adaptive self-images, such as strong, capable and independent (see Chapter 8).

At this stage, a patient's individual tolerance of the physical sensations and subjective anxiety can be promoted by pushing him to become aware of how capable he is of managing and accepting physical symptoms, even more oppressive ones *not* linked to anxiety. One can lastly invite the patient to reduce avoidance and other safety-seeking behaviours through a *graded in vivo exposure*.[2] This involves gradually exposing patients to feared situations and helping them to tolerate the foreseeable increase in anxiety until their spontaneous disinflation. This procedure promotes the extinction of the fear response and an increase in the personal experiencing of success. Experiencing effective mastery and success are then used to balance the negative images the patient carries in his memory and uses in an automatic manner.

With regard to *depressed* patients with an adequate relating of variables, it is possible to fully explore their negative view of self, the world and the future, intrinsically linked to ideas of loss (Beck and Alford, 2008). Patients will be able to grasp that their suffering derives from the idea of a failure to achieve goals in the interpersonal domain (see Chapter 1) such as the wish to be successful or the expectation that others will consider them incapable. At this stage, it is possible to promote differentiation and help the patient understand that, even if an external event, such as the breaking up of an important romantic relationship or losing a job, is a cause of suffering for any human being, the persistence of this suffering depends on one's schema-dependent inclinations. We have described how to promote this awareness in detail in Chapter 7. Patients' self-perceptions of guilt and ineptness, together with their pessimistic forecasts about the future, can also begin to be traced to maladaptive interpersonal schemas.

With reference to depressed patients, in the presence of CAS and its features such as ruminating, worry, threat monitoring and maladaptive coping, metacognitive therapy (MCT) principles (MCT) (Papageorgiou and Wells, 2003) can be applied. The clinician can adopt *attentional training, detached mindfulness* and questioning positive and negative metacognitions using classic *disputing* procedures.

Attentional training (ATT) is a procedure lasting approximately twelve minutes per session and is composed of three categories of auditory attention exercises involving selective attention (five minutes), attentional commutation (five minutes) and split attention (two minutes). Patients are asked to concentrate visually on a fixed point and to remain like this for the whole exercise. Sounds are then added (at least three sounds concurrently inside the room and four to six sounds outside the room) to be identified and located ideally from a spatial point of view. Patients are told to treat any inner intrusions of thoughts or sensations (*triggers*) as 'noise'. The aim is not for patients to suppress or avoid paying attention to inner events but to learn to control them more flexibly by reducing their *self-focus* and shifting their attention from themselves to the external environment.

Detached mindfulness is a form of information processing that can be promoted via a series of exercises and which is to be applied to patients' cognitive and affective reactions, which generally triggers their worries. Rather than questioning the validity of their negative thoughts, therapists encourage patients to detach themselves from the thoughts triggering the ruminating while keeping an objective awareness of them. Compared to mindfulness, detached mindfulness does not involve an attentional anchoring to breathing or to the present moment but a detached and non-conceptual observation of one's flow of consciousness, without objectives or evaluations.

In the case of eating disorders, the increase in metacognitive skills makes it possible to treat the main disorder-maintenance mechanisms. The patient can begin discovering how she overestimates the importance of appearance and weight, and see the schema-dependent character of their expectations. At this stage, patients can be helped in grasping how distressing relational events triggers dysfunctional eating behaviours. A patient can, for example, arrive at the understanding that a binge took place after an episode where she felt criticised by a parent or abandoned by a boyfriend. The therapist can help her see that the self's response to the other's response was to feel incapable, inept and undeserving, and to use food to calm herself down (see Sandra's case described in Chapter 9).

A therapist and a patient with anorexia should work together so that the latter understands that she overestimates the negative consequences of consuming food. Work in MIT on schemas helps a patient see how this overestimating depends on internalised interpersonal schemas.

Lastly, as analysed in Chapter 8, a therapist can programme interventions to boost a patient's participation in activities in which she feels self-efficacious and can use her positive self-aspects to find her way in society in a way that brings satisfaction and achievement (Fairburn, 2008). The pinpointing of these activities can be the outcome of a short *brainstorming* procedure and, if any obstacles arise, one can resort to a classical *problem-solving* procedure.

With patients suffering from *OCD* (Abramovitz, 2009; Clark, 2012) but possessing an adequate relating of variables it becomes possible, through cognitive restructuring, to dispute the principal beliefs causing and feeding obsessive thoughts, that is:

- inflated responsibility, in the form of a bias leading patients to think that, if they have a minimal influence on the outcome of a negative event, this is the same as being totally responsible for it;
- overestimating the risk that a feared event will take place;
- ascribing an exaggerated importance to thoughts and the belief that one needs to absolutely exercise control over them to maintain one's mental health or behave conforming to norms;
- thought-action fusion, which is the belief that thinking about things is the same as doing them;
- perfectionism and intolerance of uncertainty.

At this stage in their therapy, OCD patients can grasp that their symptoms depend on the schema as follows:

1   *'I expect appreciation.'*
2   *'If I do something of my own accord, the other criticises me or gets harmed.'*
3   *'I feel undeserving and to blame.'*
4   *'I must improve, because if I'm perfect, I'll avoid the criticism and will not do harm to others.'*

Once patients grasp the underlying interpersonal schema, one can work on helping them to differentiate and promoting the idea that one can be imperfect but still be accepted and not cause harm. This dismantles some mechanisms maintaining symptoms.

For almost all the symptomatic disorders considered here, if differentiation improves (see Chapter 7), therapists can boost it using imagery rescripting techniques (Hackmann, Bennett-Levy and Holmes, 2011) or video-feedback (Rodebaugh, Heimberg, Schultz et al., 2010). For example, a patient suffering from social phobia might begin to grasp that he suffers because historically he has put together the idea of being inept vis-à-vis critical others. At the same time, contact with others still generates suffering, because the patient continues to be tormented by intrusive images where others humiliate him. His therapist can ask him to imagine a scene where he fears he behaved ridiculously and go back over it while imagining he behaved more effectively. The patient can, for example, arrive at the moment in which he became paralysed by shame and think of ways to overcome it by finding strategies for re-establishing communication. At the end of the exercise, the therapist can help the patient consider the idea that being ridiculous in others' eyes is not necessarily true. The patient discovers he has resources, including an ability to respond to difficult situations suitably and effectively. Interventions regarding metacognitive beliefs (Wells, 2008) can be useful, in which the brooding processes and the positive and negative beliefs underlying them are explained.

These patients, with a good relating of variables and fluctuating differentiation skills, are perfect candidates for a mindfulness programme aimed at taking a critical distance from interpersonal schemas (Ottavi, Passarella, Pasinetti et al., in press), which we will describe below.

Good self-reflectivity and understanding of other's mind

At this point in treatment, a patient has a clear awareness of his schemas and has acquired a certain degree of critical distance from them. He also understands others in a sophisticated and decentred manner. Under stress, activated by relational contexts and life situations to which they are vulnerable, such patients typically have moments where self-reflectivity declines and they understand the other's mindless flexibly. At such moments, a therapist can start working again and for as long as necessary on re-establishing optimal metacognitive functioning and promptly use this understanding of mental functioning to see with the patient how a problematical relational context triggered symptoms.

Among symptom treatment techniques, a therapist is now free to choose the most appropriate. These are the advanced stages of therapy, where the interweaving between the treatment of symptoms and the PD is strong. A patient will typically have effectively used behavioural interventions, knows the causes triggering a symptom and knows how to take critical distance from maladaptive beliefs. At the same time, he is aware of the relational problem exacerbating it. In this case, metacognitively complex reasoning can be added to the repertoire.

In the case of *health anxiety*, a therapist can reconstruct the relational *trigger* of a symptom together with the patient and form the following chain: a problematic relational event occurs – *'the other is abandoning me'*; the patient's neurovegetative alarm system gets activated, he feels anxious *and* displays signs of high arousal; and the patient interprets this somatic signal catastrophically – *'I've got a nasty illness.'* The patient has already performed strategies typically effective for health anxiety and the associated rumination in the form of postposition of worry and the reduction of physical checks and of asking for advice (Taylor and Gordon, 2004) with partial success. In addition, he is now able to shift attention from the symptom to the relational problem, for example rejection sensitivity. He is able to focus on the distressing scene and differentiate in various ways: he can grasp that he indeed feared abandonment but that it was neither real nor impending. He can understand that, when he sees himself as being abandoned, he believes he will never again be loved and that this is unrealistic, as he recalls previous interpersonal relationships where he was loved. He can grasp that the other is not really abandoning him but tends to temporarily break away when he feels under stress or pressure and then seeks the relationship again of his own accord. All these evaluations, by affecting the roots of the increase in arousal (the fear of being abandoned), have the power to soothe distress and thus deprive the hypochondriacal symptom of another source from which it draws, that is hyper-arousal.

In the case of *eating disorders*, the links between symptoms and perfectionism and how this can be a form of dysfunctional relational coping should be explored. The patient can use the now sophisticated understanding of others' minds as a leverage to have the patient grasp that her interpreting others' communication as signs of rejection and abandonment are schema-driven interpretation biases. The patient can be helped to interpret others in a more sophisticated and decentred way (see Chapter 9), which further reduces residual factors triggering eating symptoms.

Similar operations are possible with *anxiety disorders*. Through dialogue a patient will arrive at interpreting symptoms as follows: '*I became anxious after I felt rejected by my girlfriend*'; '*Wishing for closeness and expecting to be rejected is one of my life themes*'; '*When I feel rejected, I become alarmed and then I forget that the alarm arises from my fear of being abandoned and I start to think I'm ill because I experience palpitations, feel itchy and out of breath, and have a stomach ache or headache*'; '*Now I'm able to focus on the underlying problem, which is being abandoned. I know I fear it, but it usually doesn't happen. I'm stronger and capable of bearing others not being there more than I thought. My girlfriend isn't leaving me; she's just annoyed, tired or down in the dumps for her own reasons, which I can now see clearly.*'

At the end of the day, what helps patients with good reflective skills to dismantle their residual symptoms is understanding that the origins of their anxiety, depressive, eating or obsessive symptoms lie in part in their underlying interpersonal goals of being frustrated (see Chapters 1 and 3).

Lastly, we would recall that with patients possessing strong metacognition, a clinician finds it easy to take the various techniques and choose those that work, including the simpler ones. A patient with good metacognition can be aware why he develops obsessions, hypochondria or anxiety, and remember that, if he does physical exercise, relaxes or meditates, the symptom goes away.

PART 2 PROMOTING MASTERY IN THE RELATIONAL DOMAIN

PD patients behave on the social scene in ways that prevent them from solving their problems, placating conflicts or reducing the negative emotions associated with relationships (Carcione, Semerari, Nicolò et al., 2011). MIT procedures for promoting interpersonal mastery are based on the assumption that PD patients should be helped to master and solve relational problems due to adequate communicational strategies. They also need to learn how to overcome distress linked to relationships.

The strategies a clinician suggests for mastering interpersonal problems should also be consistent with patients' metacognitive skills, as they generally increase during treatment. For example, a patient could seek help from a friend merely to hear his voice and, therefore, with a minimal reading of his mind. Later in therapy he can ask the same friend after having formed a very well-structured idea of how and why this person, with his skills, attitudes and knowledge, will be able to help.

The criteria guiding an intervention for promoting interpersonal mastery and regulating the states of mind associated with relationships are:

- tackling relational problems if they are a priority for the patient;
- in the case of alliance ruptures switching to working on the therapeutic relationship; and
- re-evaluating and replacing the mastery strategies employed as the patient's metacognitive skills increase.

Poor emotional awareness and limited understanding of the other's mind

PD patients with poor metacognitive skills suffer from often serious relational problems that cause them dismay and leave them without solutions. Rejection sensitivity can lead to depression or outbursts of anger, and fear of criticism can lead to anxiety. It is difficult to manage interpersonal relationships with poor metacognitive skills, but patients can still be offered some simple suggestions about how to tackle their problems.

A patient may be depressed because he fears abandonment or is obsessively jealous and tends to incessantly telephone his partner to ask for reassurance, which exacerbates the relational problem. He has poor self-reflective skills to describe his problem: he expresses an emotion as best he can, as tension, irritation or agitation, and cannot grasp which behaviour by the other triggers his unease. In this case, one can ask the patient to try to abstain from problematic behaviour such as repeatedly telephoning and use distraction strategies, for example physical exercise. It is enough if the patient knows he is suffering and that, by avoiding telephoning and doing other things, he will feel better, without in any way reasoning about why he expects his partner to abandon or be unfaithful to him. He does not even need to understand why incessant telephoning harms the relationship by making the other feel oppressed or irritated; it is enough if he understands that doing physical exercise is more beneficial than telephoning.

Even only abstaining voluntarily from dysfunctional behaviour, without using distraction strategies, can be a valid alternative, with the clinician suggesting to the patient that he try to not activate automatisms in the relational domain. A patient might tend to verbally attack others by whom he feels criticised. It is sufficient if he says he feels 'bad' – even without knowing how to better express the emotions he feels when faced with the criticism – and is aware, even if for only generally moral or social opportunity reasons, that his aggressive behaviour is dysfunctional: '*It's not good to be aggressive. I don't like it.*' It is also sufficient if he has a non-specific awareness that his behaviour could have undesired consequences: '*If I'm aggressive, I could have problems.*' At this level he does not need an understanding of why such behaviour produces reactions that may bounce back and cause him problems. It is sufficient he possesses the intention to stop his problematic behaviour.

If a patient – typically with narcissistic or paranoid vulnerabilities that lead him to behave aggressively – knows that his aggressive verbal behaviour is problematic and risky, the therapist can suggest avoiding the conditions triggering conflicts. One can plan together strategies involving the patient shifting his attention when he realises that he is activating his problematic behaviour. Work on promoting a minimum of self-reflectivity, which postpones or blocks the activation of dysfunctional behaviour, is often useful. The therapist can suggest: '*When you realise you are about to attack, shift your attention if you can from whatever wrong the other has done you and from the fact that he deserves to be insulted, and focus on your inner world. What do you feel at that moment? What thoughts and emotions are making you edgy? Just simply shifting attention from the other to yourself will probably make your fantasy of harming the other less strong or important.*' As a clinician promotes self-reflectivity, he is laying the foundations for finding out the causes underlying conflicts and making them a treatment focus.

Adequate relating variables and unstable differentiation – acceptable understanding of the other's mind with no decentration

In the relational domain, patients have managed to grasp that symptoms are sustained by stressful relational events, so that, for example, a closing up by the patient laden with gloom and hostility, seen as inexplicable at the start of therapy, follows from being left by a partner or criticised by reference figures.

Understanding the other's mind includes making acceptable and plausible descriptions of what he thinks and feels, and to a certain extent why, but attributions are usually egocentric and schema-dependent. A patient can grasp that the other is gloomy and hostile, but cannot arrive at understanding that the latter's anger is not directed at him. At this level, he is not aware of the impact his own behaviour has on the other; if the other closes up, it is not because he is not interested in the patient but because he feels tired by the repeated criticisms and accusations directed at him by the patient himself.

A patient is, for example, aware that he wishes to be appreciated, vacillating between thinking he is inept and has some worth and being paralysed by the idea that the other will humiliate him. A therapist can work on supplying the patient with tools for reinforcing his positive self-image, on the assumption that the patient is no longer prey to solely negative ideas that he treats as true.

In Chapter 8, we described how a therapist started a study method improvement programme with Anya, the patient with avoidant, dependent and paranoid PD. This programme was aimed at acquiring new skills but was, at the same time, a relational domain mastery strategy. In fact, Anya was tempted to react by leaving the course or verbally attacking the people by whom she felt threatened and abused. Both strategies would have had negative effects on her professional aspirations. Anya was not asked to understand why she was so inclined towards negative opinions or why she became paralysed when faced with unwelcome sexual advances. It was merely suggested that she use an anxiety modulation strategy, capable of increasing her sense of self-efficacy. All this was performed in the context of a therapeutic relationship in which the therapist cordially pointed out that she had the right not to submit to the advances and could allow herself to repel the other. The goal was not to convince Anya that she could have confidence in herself or that the other would not attack her, but simply that the therapist was on her side, thus sowing the seeds for a corrective emotional experience. Due to the combination of this validating attitude by the therapist and the effectiveness of the learning strategy, Anya responded positively. At this point, she started to grasp that her compliant submission arose from the idea that she was worthless and therefore had to ingratiate herself with the other, as she would otherwise be rejected and would fail. At the same time, she started to grasp that the other would not have the chance to put his threats into action because he would expose himself to his harassment becoming public knowledge. Owing, therefore, to her increased sense of efficacy, her self-reflectivity and understanding of the other's mind improved and, thanks to this, Anya was able to continue going to her courses while feeling less anxious, as she avoided exposure to any intimate moments with the teacher. She no longer had any need for aggressive behaviour, as she managed to maintain a safe distance and thus not expose herself to the harassment.

Going back to the general principles regulating shifts between symptom treatment and work on the therapeutic relationship, a clinician needs to be ready to gather any signals of ruptures in the relationship and interrupt the work on symptoms in order to repair them. The shift to working on the therapeutic relationship is accompanied almost automatically by a return to working on the underlying PD. If, in fact, a rupture is successfully repaired, the patient will understand that the schemas activated with the therapist are reproductions of his own stable structures. At this stage, a patient has the metacognitive skills needed for more complex shifts.

When a patient has developed metacognitive skills, including starting to differentiate – at least in session – and perceives the other in a not exclusively schema-dependent way, he can benefit from various types of programmes for managing relational problems, for example interpersonal efficacy training for social phobia (Beidel and Turner, 2007), assertiveness training (O'Donohue and

In Chapter 5 we described how Fulvio, the patient suffering from avoidant PD with dependent and depressive traits, showed signs of stress at the idea of exposure in order to overcome his social phobia. Instead of insisting on proposing exposure, the therapist scrutinised what was happening in session and, together with the patient, reconstructed how Fulvio saw the task as being constrictive, in line with recollections of his mother forcing him to do things against his will. The therapist therefore agreed with Fulvio that his wish for independence should be satisfied before alleviating symptoms and postponed the exposures. He only reminded Fulvio that they would monitor together the symptom trend, because there was the risk that not tackling it would, in the long term, represent behavioural avoidance. Fulvio agreed and a few months later he started an exposure programme, which led to the disappearance of social phobia after one year of treatment.

Fisher, 2009; Vavrichek, 2012) or anger management training (Faupel, Herrick and Sharp, 2011).

We would recall a fundamental aspect of MIT: the same training can be particularly suitable if a patient has sufficient metacognitive skills, but useless and harmful if administered without the patient being able to see the significance of it. A patient with avoidant or dependent PD and social phobia should not be exposed to group training for improving interpersonal skills at the start of therapy when she is not able to adopt a critical distance from her interpersonal schemas. Confronting the others would activate the pathogenic schemas from which she is not capable of standing back. The learning of skills would be mechanical and would not be absorbed by her. On the other hand, when a patient is capable of saying: '*I've always feared that I'm worthless and the others will mock me. Now I realise I'm worth something and can provoke positive reactions, but I don't have a good idea about how to behave in company. I've lived too long in isolation*', then specific training can provide him with exactly those skills that he needs for moving competently with others. If a dependent patient with passive-aggressive traits who vacillates between submission and stubborn opposition receives assertiveness training at the start of therapy, she is unlikely to benefit from it. At a certain point in her therapy, she can arrive at describing her functioning as follows: '*I wish to be independent, but I expect others to constrain me and be tyrannical. I realise I learned this from my family; my parents always forced me to fit in with their ideas and they didn't even listen to me. I can see that others are often simply affirming their point of view and don't want to subjugate me. Maybe they hold to their ideas as much as I do to mine. Now I'd like to expound my ideas during discussions, but I tend to speak humbly, to avoid any confrontations, or else to become hostile and polemical. I know neither of these strategies works but I don't know any alternatives.*' With this degree of self-reflectivity, assertiveness training becomes a gymnasium where patients try out functional ways of expressing themselves in an effective manner without clashing with others.

Strong self-reflectivity and understanding of the other's mind

At advanced stages of therapy, patients arrive at perceiving that human relations are complex and there are often no perfect solutions, misunderstandings and conflicts are part of life and there are frustrations waiting around every corner. Patients can now be helped to use their understanding of themselves and others to solve problems differently. An accurate knowledge of others' minds will lead a patient and therapist to carefully select the persons most capable of providing help.

Therapists can help patients become aware of their weaknesses, accept them and thus avoid vicious cycles. For example, a patient with narcissism reacting angrily when others block him will arrive at saying to himself: *'I want to be supported, but many people don't do it. They may not do it because they're inept, because they're not interested, or simply because they've got other things to do. I feel a tinge of anger in these circumstances; I know it will never disappear completely, but I acknowledge it and know how to control it, and, when it surfaces, there's something I can do to be calm. Then, once I'm calm, I'm able to talk with my colleagues, beg their pardon, or cooperate.'*

Bianca was 39 years old and suffered from dependent and passive-aggressive PD. For the last six years she with involved in a relationship with a partner whom she described as rancorous, jealous, irate and contemptuous every time he felt abandoned or neglected. When faced with his criticisms, Bianca entered states of despair; a prey to anguish and anger, she tried to urgently re-establish contact, with the result of exacerbating the conflict. At an advanced stage in her treatment, her therapist asked her how involved she was with her partner and she replied that she loved him. The reasonable certainty that, notwithstanding Bianca's schema-dependent interpretations, her partner had problematic personality characteristics, led the therapist to rewrite the contract as follows: *'Bianca, you love your husband and are choosing consciously to have a relationship with him. On the other hand, you expect he behaves in ways that are outside his reaches. He's probably a difficult person, who will continue to often react by closing up, offending you or threatening to leave you. We've seen that it's useless to continue protesting or compulsively trying to achieve reconciliation. I believe that, if you want to have a good relationship with your partner, you'll have to accept that this is likely to be complex, tough, and sometimes distressing and, at the same time, you have the power to make it better. This would require you choosing to understand how you can influence yourself and him as the therapy goal, so as to promote communication, reduce the intensity of your harmful relational cycles and promote mutual closeness and understanding. Do you feel up to going in this direction?'*

Bianca burst into tears and remained in a gloomy state for the following week, struck by the knowledge of how realistic the therapist's observations were. She accepted working on changing the course of the relationship. The first goal was for Bianca to recall how, every time her partner threatened to leave her, she saw him as distant and then sought him out. Thanks to this memory, rich in a sophisticated knowledge of her husband's mind, Bianca stopped compulsive looking for closeness and forgiveness whenever he criticised her and started to patiently wait in silence for him to re-approach her. She tolerated the distress thanks to her memory that the abandonment she feared was not true. Her partner systematically re-approached her and asked for forgiveness. Bianca then started to seize the moments in which her partner was most open to dialogue and only at such moments did she point out to him that his accusations wounded and humiliated her, something that he accepted and which made him behave in a kinder and more respectful way. The relationship progressively became more intimate and cooperative and less conflictual.

Thanks to their deeper knowledge of their own and others' minds, therapists can help patients interact strategically and avoid pointless clashes.

Metacognitive-oriented mindfulness-based training

Recently, as part of MIT, a mindfulness-based programme, designed for the treatment of symptoms and brooding over interpersonal problems with the PD patients described here, has been drawn up and is called *metacognitive-interpersonal mindfulness-based training* (Ottavi, Passarella, Pasinetti et al., in press). The authors have devised a new mindfulness-based procedure involving specific techniques and we are evaluating its efficacy. The programme is tailored for patients at advanced stages of therapy who are aware of being driven by pathogenic interpersonal schemas and have started to differentiate but, weighed down by the negative emotions evoked by their relationships, worry about themes involving being abandoned or humiliated, about limited personal worth, and so on. At this point, patients and therapists know that the former's understanding of their psychological functioning has by now reached a sufficient level to let any remaining efforts be concentrated on spending as little time as possible worrying. Mindfulness is the tool of choice in these cases; our adaptation is not limited to helping patients stand back from their mental states and shift their attention, for example, to their breathing or to encouraging a compassionate attitude towards themselves.

The programme includes specific exercises during the meditation group in which patients first recall a problematic autobiographical memory and re-experience the related negative emotion (Ottavi, Passarella, Pasinetti et al., in press). They then recall the distressing state dominating them linked to the relationship, for example: '*I shall never be appreciated by others and, when I try to expound my point of view, I'll be told to shut up and become humiliated.'* They also recall that their representation in question is schema-driven. After this, patients perform group exercises that help them gently shift their attention elsewhere from this specific thought. They become further aware that they suffer from ideas generated by pathogenic schemas and consider them ever more ideas and not reality, in a context in which they realise they have power over ideas, can remove them from their minds and not allow themselves to be influenced by them.

At this point in the programme, therapists should propose working on *imagery rescripting*. In their minds, patients revisit their problematic scenes, but their therapist asks them to change the scene outcome. For example, a patient returns to a scene where she felt despised and then tries to imagine that the other is kind and will respond promptly to her request that he not persist in criticising, or evokes in her mind pictures of a self that meets others who appreciate and give her support. Between one session and the next, patients are asked to carry out this exercise and foster an observational detachment from their distressing interpersonal themes and form kinder interpersonal representations.

PART 3 THE INTERWEAVING AMONG SYMPTOMS, MANAGING OF RELATIONAL PROBLEMS AND TREATMENT OF PD: TWO CLINICAL CASES

To provide examples of how the treatment of PD and symptoms, and the managing of relational problems are interweaved, we report two clinical cases here. We can see how the exploring of life events preceding a symptom is a window towards understanding the PD. In fact, narrative episodes preceding the aggravation of a symptom often involve relational problems and therefore, once explored, therapy can shift to trying to understand the interpersonal schema nesting in an episode and then working on it with the procedures described in this book.

Angelo was 35 years old and suffered from narcissistic PD with avoidant, obsessive-compulsive, passive-aggressive and paranoid traits. He met 21 SCID-II criteria. He suffered from somatoform disorder, with urinary and faecal incontinence, which was found to be psychogenic after numerous neurological consultations and diagnostic tests. He also suffered from muscular tension, tremors, difficulties digesting, nausea and chronic asthenia. The incontinence caused him uncontrollable anxiety and to soothe it he abused alcohol and indulged in promiscuous sexual behaviour. At the start of his therapy, he had pronounced metacognitive difficulties, not recognising his own emotions and almost believing that he did not have any; consequently he interpreted signs of arousal as signals of an illness, that is incontinence. He was involved in a romantic relationship for eight years with which he was unsatisfied. He worked only now and then, doing manual work well below his abilities (see Dimaggio, Valeri, Ottavi et al., 2014, for the full therapy description).

Angelo was diffident, defeatist and critical towards his therapist, who reacted by feeling hurt and angry and in turn criticised the patient for not cooperating. At this point, Angelo considered the therapist an adversary to be convinced – he did not believe that his incontinence had psychogenic roots, did not let her speak and he dictated the agenda for each session. Her supervisor helped the therapist to understand that Angelo activated in her a need for recognition when faced with critical and invalidating figures who provoked anger. The therapist acknowledged that this was a life theme of hers and she managed to modulate her anger and interrupt the *competitive cycles* preventing alliance building.

Once the therapeutic relationship had been modulated, the therapist proposed that, in order to better understand how Angelo functioned, they could explore his relational narrative episodes and determine if there were psychological antecedents for the somatisation while also accepting that Angelo could be right and that the symptom was not psychogenic. At the start, Angelo broke the alliance. When the therapist asked him for narrative episodes, he felt subjugated and reacted with hostility and disdainful criticisms. After validating Angelo's sentiments, the therapist pointed out to him how important it was for him to keep control of his therapy. At the same time she explained that she was asking for specific episodes because she was driven by the wish to know him and considered that exploring episodes brought her closer to his experiences without obliging her to resort to abstract psychological theories which would not give her a picture of who Angelo really was. Angelo felt both supported in his need for independence and relieved that the therapist did not want to '*play at being a psychologist*'.

At the same time, the therapist proposed to Angelo that they work on reassessing his catastrophic beliefs about incontinence: Angelo said he was constantly a prey to his stimulus and was never able to control it, driven as he was by hyper-generalising and catastrophising cognitive biases. Given that he was unaware of his emotions but capable of describing his cognitive processes accurately, the therapist suggested he keep a diary in which to write down the number of times he felt '*an urgent need to go to the toilet*' and the thoughts and states of mind experienced before feeling the stimulus, while urinating or defecating, and immediately afterwards. The diary had a dual purpose: on the one hand, it served to empirically evaluate the frequency of the episodes and, on the other, it aimed to promote metacognition by generating a constant focusing on his inner world. Angelo accepted and immediately discovered that he was overestimating the times he felt the stimulus to defecate and this reassured him. The stimulus was only present in problematic situations and less intense and more controllable in non-problematic situations. He also realised that his urgent need to urinate was activated when he was tense as a result of problematical interactions with others. At the same time, by observing his non-verbal behaviour while he related the episodes, the therapist was able to point out to Angelo that, when he expressed anger or shame, he felt the stimulus to urinate or defecate more urgently and isolated himself, unaware, however, that this avoidance was triggered by his fear of criticism. At this point Angelo started, even if only temporarily, to divert his attention from symptoms and to think about the distress he felt when he saw himself criticised or abandoned. The symptoms had therefore improved at this point, thanks both to the re-evaluation of the frequency of the incontinence episodes, which led to a decrease in his anticipatory anxiety, and to the understanding of the antecedent events, which led Angelo to worry less about his incontinence and concentrate on his relational difficulties.

When reconstructing the episodes, it became clear that, as soon as Angelo felt others to be distant, he became sure that he was being rejected forever and, as he did not differentiate, he was incapable of grasping that he feared being abandoned without any good reasons. At the same time he did not decentre, as he was prone to seeing rejection even when there were no signs to justify this, and was incapable of putting himself in the other's shoes and grasping that the latter was unavailable because he was tired or taken up by his own problems.

It was then possible to reconstruct his interpersonal schemas. His first wish was to be recognised as special; the response from the Other (for example, his father) was disinterest, underrating and domination; the Self's responses to the Other's response were: (1) underrated and incapable, with a consequent collapse in self-esteem (in this state his emotion was anxiety, which activated his incontinence, and in certain situations Angelo soothed his anxiety with compulsive sex); (2) capable but unjustly unrecognised by another who neglected him, and angry. The Other responded to this anger by backing off and this made Angelo feel lost, which activated a new schema linked to attachment.

The second wish was to be loved and the Other's response was rejection. The Self responded by feeling unloved due to insufficient worth, which led him to pursue perfectionist standards with the idea that, if the Other understood his exceptional worth, he would necessarily love him. Faced with a lack of response in the form of admiration or love and in line with the typical narcissistic PD schemas, Angelo closed himself disdainfully and resentfully in an ivory tower.

At this point in therapy, the focus shifted to treating his PD and focusing on how problems in this domain were worsening symptoms. Angelo began to tackle relationships with an exploratory goal (see Chapter 8) to test whether the pathogenic schemas corresponded to the truth and to build more satisfying relationships. During new episodes emerging over the course of the behavioural experiments, he became aware that when he felt ignored, the stimulus to urinate increased.

Moreover, he noticed signals inconsistent with the schemas, as he discovered that some people were interested in him without admiring him, or he found himself participating in others' conversations. In both cases, the stimulus to urinate was less intense and more controllable.

In the subsequent sessions other memories surfaced, linked to promiscuous sex and alcohol abuse. The typical antecedent of this impulsive behaviour was: Angelo wished to be loved and admired, looked for signs of appreciation and admiration and felt the other to be distant and critical. In one episode, Angelo told his father about some work that he did that went well. His father reacted coldly and instead shifted the topic to his own professional successes, thus belittling his son's work choices. In response, Angelo oscillated between inefficacy and anger, and had an outburst of rage that made his father back away. At this point he felt alone, abandoned and in despair. Once his rage diminished, gloominess took over and to soothe himself Angelo drank and then had sex with a prostitute.

Thanks to his understanding of the schema and how dysfunctional coping was a reaction to his gloominess and to the underrating, the therapist suggested that at similar moments Angelo could use more effective mastery strategies to soothe himself, in particular relaxing and concentrating on his work.

The need-for-esteem-and-admiration theme also emerged in his romantic relationship. When he tried to achieve a goal, he sensed he had little ability to achieve it and felt ineffective; he then sought support from his girlfriend who was represented as being unwilling to help and he *reacted* with scorn, considering her imperfect and defective. He consequently became cold and withdrew from the relationship.

Finally, it emerged that at the root of his need for admiration and support, there was a core lack of agency. Angelo was pervaded by impotence preventing him from committing himself to achieving goals, was driven by a vague ambition but without any real contact with what he desired, and thus found himself confused and paralysed, which fed impotence and a sense of incapability. The therapist helped him to recall memories where he had a good personal worth and stimulated his contact with his desires, in which he discovered he had a sincere enthusiasm for his work, and he began to let himself be motivated while seeking admiration and support less.

The therapist's validating and sharing attitude was beneficial, but it also had some side effects. As soon as Angelo saw the therapist as being warm and caring, he automatically and unconsciously was seized by memories in which she had neglected him or tried to impose her ideas on him. We would recall that this is typical of narcissistic PD therapies: when a patient feels cared for, schemas become activated in which the other is intrusive, controlling, invalidating or dominant, and thus paradoxically the relational problems increase.

The picture of the therapist Angelo constructed swung between two extremes: on the one hand, he depicted her as warm and supportive in an idealised way, the antithesis of the invalidating figures from his family; on the other, in a schema-consistent manner, he imagined she would underrate, abandon and dominate him and reacted angrily and contemptuously, declaring himself to be superior and more 'illuminated'. The therapist had to ask her supervisor again for help in order to overcome the difficulties caused by this combination of hyper-involvement, low self-esteem and anger, and thus managed to arrive more stably in a dimension of solid personal worth. At this point she told the patient of her displeasure at not being given the necessary confidence and explained that this aspect was an obstacle to the promotion of the therapeutic process. This reflection on the relationship fostered an exit from the cycle and stimulated Angelo to grasp that he could trigger negative reactions when he challenged the other. At the same time, the therapist, while avoiding both competing and submitting, started to offer him a model in which one can be confident in one's own worth without either yielding to a tyrant or being at war.

Overall, Angelo understood his convictions about relationships were based on ideas learned during development and started to behave differently. He then switched from the idea: '*I will only be accepted if perfect*' to '*I was convinced I would only be accepted if perfect, but I can hope to be appreciated for who I am.'* The symptom continued to occur, but his ability to grasp the relational antecedents of it rendered it progressively more controllable and less intense.

Thanks to the combination of acquiring a critical distance from his schemas, the reduction of symptoms and avoidances, the improvement in his access to his wishes and the reinforcement of his agency, Angelo began to successfully pursue professional goals more in line with his abilities and inclinations. He broke up with his girlfriend after perceiving that he did not love her and had chosen her because he considered her true to his family's ideal woman model. His alcohol abuse disappeared and his promiscuous sexual behaviour drastically diminished.

Claudia, the patient with OCD described at the start of this chapter, progressively improved with regard to her narrative and metacognitive skills. This resulted in the SCID-II carried out after one year of therapy showing a diagnosis of obsessive-compulsive, dependent PD and below threshold avoidant PD. As well as OCD, the patient suffered from bulimia nervosa, social phobia and major depression. We shall now describe the therapeutic process.

After four months of psychotherapy, her OCD, which was treated with ERP, had improved and her descriptions of her inner states were more fluent. She also began taking Sertraline, which further reduced the number of times she washed herself and improved her mood. At that moment, the therapeutic relationship was good and the therapist had a validating and curious stance, which favoured the investigation of her inner states in a non-judging atmosphere, probably forestalling the activation of pathogenic schemas in which Claudia might have felt invalidated.

Focusing on the antecedents of her symptomatic relapses made it possible for her to evoke an initial, prototypical episode, preceding the explosion of OCD. Claudia was in a subway train after just moving to Rome and she was attending a university. The train was full of people, and she felt herself squashed by many people and experienced a sensation of dirtiness and disgust even within herself. She started to wash herself in an attempt to clean herself, without alleviating these sensations. The therapist asked her if this sensation of being dirty and the need to keep clean reminded her of other episodes (see Chapter 6 for the eliciting of associated memories). Claudia thought about how anxious her parents were and the therapist asked her for specific memories. Claudia recalled an episode where she had gone to the sea with friends and returned home slightly late. Her mother and father were very worried that something horrible had happened to her. Claudia felt guilty about making her loved ones suffer and she began to worry. With the episodes collected, it was possible to formulate her pathogenic interpersonal schema: Claudia wished to be independent but, when she acted in accordance with her wishes (enjoying herself at the sea with her friends), the Other reacted by feeling frightened and harmed. Claudia reacted to this response from the Other with strong guilt feelings about being disgusting and harmful; the Self's response to the Other's response included a tendency to distance herself from relationships to avoid making loved ones suffer and then also to avoid experiencing the sensation of being '*disgusted at oneself*'. Her worrying was activated by this idea and led her to avoid relationships in order to not expose others to the risk of suffering. She gradually ended up having only two friends whom she saw rarely.

Thanks to reconstructing all these memories, Claudia grasped that there was a symbolic attempt to free herself of the idea that she was dirty, disgusting and harmful underlying her symptom. She thus began to differentiate and comprehend that this idea was not true but the result of her development history. Furthermore, she recalled that her sister often checked the gas, doors and windows in their home and her mother cleaned it continuously. Her OCD improved further and Claudia now only had a shower in the evening.

After she had reconstructed and comprehended her interpersonal schema, it was important to create positive experiences. Thanks to the improvement in metacognitive monitoring, Claudia realised she was depressed mainly because she was living a life with limited amusement or friendships. She began to relish the wish to spend her free time in the company of friends. However, another obstacle emerged: social phobia. In spite of starting to differentiate, her fear of being judged was intense, and also her proneness to feeling ashamed, with strong tendencies towards avoidance. The therapist's first step was to ask Claudia to focus her attention on the positive events occurring between sessions and to put together ABCs aimed at eliciting positive emotions and thoughts. The purpose was to show Claudia that in her life there was room for pleasure and that maybe she was already having pleasurable experiences without realising it.

In fact, in the next session Claudia spoke about how, following up her wish to have social relations and nice experiences, she had decided to go out with some female colleagues, hugged them and also tried on some clothes while going shopping with them. These anticipatory images gave her calmness, joy, a sense of inclusion in the group, freedom and enjoyment. The therapist validated these emerging positive states strongly and told Claudia that she herself had qualities that she did not recall when it was necessary. At this point, residual pictures of a disgusting self vis-à-vis a critical other surfaced, preventing a complete solution of her social phobia. The therapist took advantage of Claudia's access to positive affects and of her wish for relationships and planned an exposure programme with her. The goal was to block the remaining power of her expectations that others would criticise, reject or leave her because she was dirty. Claudia thus began this exposure by going out ever more often with her colleagues, looking for new friends on the Internet for conversation and fun, and by talking about hobbies she had rediscovered such as reading, the cinema or walking in the country. Her depictions of critical others did not emerge and, thanks to her stable focus on her positive affects and kind pictures of the self, they were easily removed from her mind and treated as not true. Overall, this work improved her mood and social phobia.

Her OCD persisted but was less intense and, especially, took the form of worry. Thanks to her stable access to affectively loaded and positive self-representations, the therapist, who kept a validating attitude, was able to point out to Claudia that her remaining problem was her difficulty in recalling positive mental pictures outside of sessions. She suggested she use *flashcards* where she could write down her qualities to act as a replacement memory in situations in which the negative brooding took hold of her. This led to a further improvement in her mood and what remained of her social phobia, by combating the now rare moments where Claudia went back to becoming a prey to worry.

One year from the start of her therapy, Claudia related that during the previous days she experienced bulimia episodes with purging, a disorder from which she had suffered in the past. While reconstructing the antecedents of the symptom, she remembered years before she had moments free of rituals. At that time, the problem was linked to her affective relationships: after having a nice time with her partner, the partner left and she felt lonely, lost, frustrated and confused. Her sensation was that she had forever lost the happiness she had just experienced. At this point, she could not tolerate the negative emotion and she binged to combat her sensation of emptiness and experience the satisfaction of feeling full of food. A short while after the binge, however, feelings of guilt and disgust with herself emerged, and she saw herself as being ugly and fat to the point of resorting to purging.

The therapist recalled that a few months earlier, Claudia's boyfriend had left her, a separation for which she had not displayed any suffering. The therapist hypothesised that, since Claudia was currently experiencing positive emotions again, her fear of losing, reactivated by the sense of affective loss, was emerging. Claudia began to grasp that she was again desperate at the idea that being abandoned would destroy the well-being she had only just acquired and started to realise that, as soon as moments of well-being surfaced, she became prey to intrusive images of being abandoned without hope. She nostalgically thought about her ex-boyfriend and, seized by despair, she binged.

At the start, the treatment of her bulimia was difficult. Claudia had a moment of despair: on the one hand, she was disheartened by the reappearance of an old symptom, and on the other, being abandoned confirmed the core image of the self as being disgusting and doomed to be rejected. The therapist explained that the symptom had reappeared precisely because she had remade contact with states of well-being and was, therefore, part of a positive therapy trend. Claudia did not react and stayed in a state of despair. The therapist tried again to overcome this moment of disheartedness and concentrated on recovering the positive memories of a few weeks before. In session, they immediately reconstructed the valid path taken together, and between one session and the next, Claudia again resorted to flashcards to remind her of her positive self-aspects, even if she responded only temporarily and plunged back again into states of despair and unworthiness. The therapist switched to investigating the therapeutic relationship. Claudia said she felt the therapist to be validating, supportive, understanding and warm, but, on the other hand, she was convinced that her unworthiness was true and obvious to such an extent that even the therapist would end up seeing her as such. At this point, there were the relational conditions suggesting the use of *self-disclosure*. The therapist recalled a distressing episode from her own past in which, when faced with being left by a partner, she suffered on account of a short period of binging to combat her moments of emptiness and solitude. The therapist possessed a good affective modulation, successfully overcame the symptomatic episode, and was thus able to disclose it without the risk of having to face disturbing personal memories in session. This self-disclosure immediately provided relief to Claudia, who felt understood, welcomed, less lonely and not judged. She did not consider the therapist's behaviour to be shameful and immediately accepted it without judging it. It was also easier, while she listened to the therapist's story about what led her to binge, for her to recognise herself in it and reconstruct the reasoning and emotional processes activating her own dysfunctional eating behaviour.

After this self-disclosure Claudia improved rapidly. She started using the flashcards again and found it much easier to pick up her positive self-images again. Using the flashcards also helped her to improve metacognitive monitoring and understand the antecedents of her binging more quickly. In fact, some flashcards summarised her chains of reasoning preceding the binging, as reconstructed in session.

Another role played by the flashcards was as a memo about strategies for mastering distress due to the fear of being abandoned. As alternatives to her binging, Claudia could resort to activities that were amusing and that she considered pleasing and satisfying, like reading a good article, going shopping, walking in the country or calling a friend to go out for dinner or drinks. Claudia was learning to combat her states of emptiness with pleasant experiences she sought intentionally.

After about one and a half years of therapy, her symptoms had improved significantly. Claudia had become more aware of her problem-solving skills, had rediscovered the desire to have social relationships and was happy to go out with her friends. She no longer treated her pathogenic interpersonal schemas as exclusively true; she often considered them to be hypotheses and combined them with alternative self-views based on positive images.

Conclusions

PD therapy and the treating of the associated relational problems are constantly interlinked with the treatment of symptoms. When a patient's metacognitive skills improve, there is an increase in the range of techniques for treating symptoms and of strategies for mastering relational problems available to the clinician and patient. In this chapter, we have proposed a first guide to treating symptoms with MIT for patients suffering from PD, but in the future it will be necessary to provide more specific indications about treating some of the symptoms most frequently co-occurring such as OCD, eating disorders, anxiety and mood disorders. Each of these symptoms responds to different techniques, and how to switch from a technique to working on the PD is the next MIT goal. Here we have tried to demonstrate if a patient's metacognition is poor, therapists should adopt solution strategies that are mainly behavioural or involve attention shifting. Then, as the patient's knowledge of his own and others' minds improves, it is possible to employ many other cognitive and metacognitive techniques. With this first attempt, we trust we have shown how MIT aims to maximise clinical effectiveness by adopting the repertoire of tools offered by therapeutic practices that are acknowledged as valid within a theoretically coherent treatment framework, attentive to the individual case formulation while continuously regulating the therapeutic relationship.

Notes

1   *Rumination* is a voluntary and active coping strategy consisting of repetitive thoughts aimed at understanding the reasons for one's gloominess and finding ways to manage disturbing thoughts and emotions. Rumination seeks answers to questions such as *'Why do I feel like this?'*, *'What does it mean?'*, *'How can I feel better?'*

 Worry is a voluntary and active coping strategy aimed at anticipating a danger and planning strategies to avoid or tackle it. Worry seeks answers to questions such as *'What if my depression never ends?'*, *'What should I do with my future?'*, *'What if this symptom is again a sign of illness?'*

 Threat monitoring takes the form of focusing on the depression symptoms and changes in mood. Patients monitor energy levels or go looking for signs of tiredness when trying to assess the gravity of their problem and their ability to tackle it.

 Maladaptive coping behaviours include the avoidance of activities and social contact, substance abuse and self-directed punishment or harm to try to regulate mood.

2   Since many individuals with panic disorder display at least slight forms of agoraphobic avoidance, graded *in vivo* exposure is an essential component of CBT for panic disorder. The technique involves the patient drawing up a list of situations he finds difficult to face and ranking them, on the basis of an assessment of the anxious responses they evoke, from 0 (no fear) to 100 (extreme fear).

 After identifying and ranking the most feared situations, the patient is asked to progressively expose himself to them and remain in the selected situation long enough (specifically from 30 to 60 minutes, up to a maximum of 90 minutes) to notice that the level of anxiety diminishes on its own. During the exposure, the patient is asked to observe and accept his growing level of anxiety rather than divert attention and to eliminate any habitually used protection behaviours (requests for reassurance, rituals, etc.).

 Behavioural manuals on graded *in vivo* exposure recommend daily sessions five days a week and for periods of three to four weeks, until the initially identified situations become completely manageable by the patient.

Chapter 11

Comparison of metacognitive interpersonal therapy and cognitive behavioural therapies

MIT is an integrative therapy, feeding on influences originating from many different sources, from narrative constructivism (Neimeyer, 2000) to relational psychoanalysis (Mitchell, 1988; Safran and Muran, 2000) and psychodynamic-orientated therapies developed for treating PDs (Bateman and Fonagy, 2004). It is, however, historically part of the cognitive behavioural therapy family, with which it displays some fundamental points of contact and distinctive elements. It is useful to describe the similarities and differences when compared with standard cognitive behavioural therapy (CBT) (Beck, 2011; Newman, 2012), and more specifically the number of recent cognitivist approaches for PDS (Padesky and Mooney, 2012; Young, Klosko and Weishaar, 2003).

The focus on metacognitive dysfunctions

In comparison to the CBT family, including the new forms developed for treating PDS, MIT pays unique attention to patients' metacognitive dysfunctions. On the basis of the assumption that one of the core elements in personality disorder is a difficulty in identifying mental states, thinking about them and using this knowledge to solve relational problems, MIT has developed a series of specific techniques and ways of working on the therapeutic relationship that is deliberately adapted for promoting metacognition. Furthermore, MIT continuously bears in mind that metacognitive difficulties constitute a barrier to treatment and the entire intervention framework described in this book takes account of this.

Cognitive behavioural approaches pay less attention to this aspect, even if there are references (especially among the so-called third-generation approaches) to similar concepts such as *metacognitive awareness* (Segal, Teasdale and Williams, 2002; Herbert and Forman, 2011), *emotional awareness* (Lane, 2000; Lane and Schwartz, 1987), *mindfulness* (Kabat-Zinn, 1994; Segal, Teasdale and Williams, 2002) and *detached mindfulness* (Wells, 2005).

Moreover, certain classic CBT interventions, starting with the psycho-educational ones regarding emotions, also aim to overcome patients' alexithymia.

More formally and with specific reference to PDS, *dialectical-behaviour therapy* (DBT) (Linehan, 1993) explicitly addresses patients' difficulty in getting to know their own affects. In its description of borderline PD, this is a metacognitive dysfunction feature related to emotional monitoring. DBT promotes *mindfulness* as a process regulating one's attention towards one's mental states and uses modalities to mitigate any tendencies towards impulsiveness and emotional reactivity. In any case, MIT is the only cognitive behavioural therapy to pay particular attention to the entire range of metacognitive skills and to have built treatment around them.

Promotion of differentiation

Another core point in the comparison between MIT and CBT concerns the modalities with which to promote differentiation. As we saw in Chapter 7, helping patients to differentiate is a fundamental turning point in psychotherapy. Differentiation is adopting a perspective from which the patient can view their beliefs and reactions to events, which are typically more subjective than they are accurate. Cognitive psychotherapies talk about promoting a critical distance or *cognitive distancing* (Hollon and Beck, 1979) and, more recently, *cognitive defusion* (Hayes and Strosahl, 2004; Blackledge, 2007) or *reperceiving* (Shapiro, Carlson, Astin et al., 2006).

The main difference between MIT and standard CBT in this regard lies in the fact that CBT promotes differentiation composed of the rational and empirical confutation of pathogenic convictions, such as automatic thoughts, intermediate beliefs and core beliefs. In other words, CBT aims at inducing a revision of a patient's dysfunctional beliefs in light of empirical evidence or their logical untenability. In third-wave cognitive behavioural approaches such as mindfulness-based stress reduction (MBSR), or acceptance and commitment therapy (ACT), there is, instead, forms of promoting differentiation based on what is considered 'decentring' from thoughts (Segal et al., 2002), physical sensations and other emotional states (Baer, 2010). We would point out that the term decentring is used differently in the mindfulness school than what we describe in metacognition. Mindfulness uses it to define a critical distance from one's thoughts, whereas in metacognition it indicates an ability to understand that others see the world from a different perspective from one's own (see Chapter 2).

Because of PD patients' unyielding and often egosyntonic beliefs, MIT considers it opportune to primarily promote other forms of differentiation such as the following:

- An awareness that there are alternative and more positive self-images alongside the negative one. This form of differentiation corresponds to what CBT does when, alongside negative core beliefs, it identifies and highlights the more adaptive ones that a patient already possesses and becomes activated in non-problematical contexts.
- An understanding by patients that they selectively pay attention to signals they received during development and are likely to echo them. CBT also

aims to comprehend the way a dysfunctional belief is rooted in development history. However, MIT and CBT approach this goal in radically different ways. While already at the psycho-education stage, CBT therapists explain to patients that their core beliefs generate systematic biases in the processing of information and have been constructed during their life history, a history that the therapists systematically put together during assessment. In MIT, this work involving the early construction of life histories and psycho-education about core beliefs is avoided. Therapists help patients link the present and past during conversation on the basis of associations among autobiographical memories that patients carry out partly on their own. In other words, therapists do not explain to patients that their beliefs are rooted in their life history. Instead, they aim at encouraging patients' ability to link their own various life episodes and grasp that there are regularities, showing that present convictions have been generated in earlier periods in their lives;

- A comprehension that the intensity of emotional responses is a subjective factor that can be modulated, however well-founded or reasonable the underlying cognitive beliefs (see Chapter 7). This detachment from one's emotional reactions is characteristic of rational emotive behaviour therapy too (Ellis, 1962) and is the core of mindfulness.

Overall, none of the differentiating strategies for MIT is unique or taken on its own; each of them can be retraced to strategies adopted by the various cognitive behavioural schools. The way MIT puts them into practice is a distinctive feature, because it depends on a formulation of patients' functioning at a specific moment in their therapy, on the type of pathogenic interpersonal schemas activated by them and on an evaluation of their metacognitive dysfunctions.

Nature and characteristics of schemas

MIT focuses mainly on *interpersonal* schemas. The reason is that it assumes that the principal problems in PDS come from how patients represent their relationships with others to themselves. In MIT, the self-image is not the sole interest. The focus is on how, in a situation in which he is driven by a wish connected to his relationship experiences, a patient with a problematic self-image expects the other to respond. To give an example, it is not enough to tell patients that they have a *vulnerable* self-image. One needs to understand how they expect the other to respond. It is one thing to feel vulnerable and expect the other to ideally save and help us; it is another, vis-à-vis that same vulnerable self-image, to think that the other is taking advantage of us, and yet another to expect that he will despise us for the weakness we have displayed. A self-representation is important depending on how a patient expects the other to respond. MIT uses a formulation of interpersonal schemas consistent with the core conflictual relational theme (CCRT) (Luborsky and Crits-Christoph, 1990).

The structure of a schema essentially includes:

- a wish, for example, being cared for or appreciated;
- a wish-related self-image;
- the response expected from the other; and
- the Self's response to the other's response.

In Chapters 1 and 3, there is a detailed description of the form taken by interpersonal schemas and the typical contents in PDS.

In CBT (Beck, 2011), schemas are conceived as cognitive structures containing basic individual beliefs and assumptions that shape patients' perception of events and their response to these. More specifically, in Beck's model, schemas include three types of beliefs that play a role in individual responses. These are *strategic beliefs*, that is assumptions about what is needed to survive or to reduce distressing experiences, *conditional beliefs* known as 'if … then' procedures imposing specific responses to certain stimuli, and *unconditional beliefs* consisting of chronic assumptions about the self, others and the world. For example, a patient with paranoid PD could have the strategic belief *'don't trust anyone'*, the conditional belief, *'if I always keep on guard, I'll be able to protect myself'* and the unconditional belief *'I'm a victim and the others threaten me'* (Rafaeli, 2009).

The biggest differences compared to MIT schemas are the absence of certain elements (such as a wish) and the greater emphasis given to the self-image (core image of self) rather than to the response expected from the Other, and to the Self's response to the Other's response. Nevertheless, conditional strategic beliefs correspond to a great extent to procedures in MIT for activating a desired response from the other or forms of coping for dealing with a feared response; in CBT there is also a reference to chronic assumptions about others and about the world as founding elements to schemas (in MIT, this is the response expected from the other). CBT also ascribes great importance to so-called 'compensatory strategies', consisting of repeated modalities with which individuals manage their core beliefs and which are similar to 'Self's responses to the response expected from the Other'. For example, a patient believing that others are hostile could use compensatory strategies involving avoidance or excessive dependence or yieldingness. In CBT for PDS, patients receive help, in this sense, to understand that they are overutilising or underutilising certain compensatory strategies.

Schema modes, from schema focused therapy (Young, Klosko and Weishaar, 2003), are even more similar to those conceptualised in MIT, in that their theoretical formulation contains self-images, images of the other and forms of coping (responses by the self to the other's response). What differentiates them from MIT schemas is that there is not a systematic focusing on the wish when a schema is converted to a formula. Young's theory does not clearly assert that schemas become activated in the context of a wish that a person attempts to satisfy.

The formulation offered to a patient can sound different too. MIT does not involve stating: '*You've got an inadequacy schema, on account of which you tend to avoid taking on risks at work because you're afraid about cutting a poor figure*', but instead: '*You wish to be appreciated and held in regard. You feel your boss does not appreciate you and at this point the idea that you're worthless resurfaces, and to protect yourself from any more criticism you don't take the risk of doing more challenging work, which would gain you more recognition.*'

MIT considers a formulation that does not start from an identification of the patient's wish could be seen as too critical, whereas an emphasis on his wish conveys the message that the work to be done will consist of finding new ways to achieve something to which aspiring is legitimate, human and easily agreed on.

Beyond schema contents, an important difference between CBT and MIT is that the main goal of change in CBT is to dismantle dysfunctional and erroneous beliefs. In MIT, the goal is not so much to confute schemas or consider them wrong or unrealistic in themselves, but to point out that they are recurring and maladaptive and especially used as a compulsive form of handling suffering.

Destructuring pathology parts versus constructing healthy parts

In MIT, the emphasis is on constructing healthy parts more than breaking down the pathological parts of a personality. The main goal is for patients to pursue wishes they feel are theirs and which can provide a foundation for their identity, as well as constructing new schemas and skills making it possible for them to move more agilely, flexibly and effectively around society. In this, MIT is similar to several recent therapies for PDS, such as strength-based cognitive therapy (Padesky and Mooney, 2012), schema focused therapy (Young, Klosko and Weishaar, 2003) or applications of acceptance and commitment therapy (Hayes, Strosahl and Wilson, 2011; Cameron, Reed and Gaudiano, 2014). In CBT, part of the work is directed at this goal. Procedures designed to develop new core beliefs through behavioural experiments or *acting as if* (Beck, 2011) aim at constructing or reactivating healthy self parts as part of better adaptation.

Conceptualising patients and their problems in continuous evolution

Case formulation in MIT is based on identifying what emotions a patient experiences in significant interpersonal relationships and understanding what dysfunctional interpersonal schemas are driving his social actions. The search for information in MIT is mainly carried out through an accurate reconstruction of recent and past autobiographical episodes involving interpersonal relationships.

During case formulation, the therapist and patient work at accurately identifying and naming the emotions felt by the patient during these autobiographical memories or narrative episodes and grasping what relational events triggered them and the behaviours ensuing them. A precious source of information is a patient's non-verbal behaviour in session.

In MIT, as we have highlighted, the starting point for the formulation is systematically the wish, that is the plan pursued by a patient in the interpersonal domain, and the way in which she tends to foresee that this wish (e.g. being loved, independent or successful) will be frustrated or fail. Formulating on the basis of the patient's wish or plans is common to both MIT and cognitive/integrative therapies based on plan analysis (Caspar and Ecker, 2008; Kramer, Berthoud and Keller, 2014).

Standard CBT also considers an accurate conceptualisation to be a milestone in an effective treatment. This is a vital link between the initial diagnostic assessment stage and the therapeutic plan (Newman, 2012). It includes schemas (the dysfunctional beliefs portending relational problems in a patient's current life), together with the factors predisposing, precipitating (such as traumatic events or shifts in social role) and perpetuating a disorder, including cultural and social elements from the context to which patients belong (Newman, 2012). The patient's strengths and resources are important. Lastly, CBT clinicians also pay attention to the adaptive and maladaptive, affective and behavioural cognitive mechanisms patients have developed to tackle their dysfunctional beliefs, and point out, over the course of the sessions, that the underlying elements of the conceptualisation – core beliefs, assumptions and coping strategies – are linked to each other explaining present problems and can be traced back to developmental history.

Emphasis on present moment: attention to life history

In MIT, the therapist does not investigate patients' life stories in a systematic and organised manner. This does not mean lack of interest in the historical origins of schemas but, simply, that we consider psychopathology more relevant than aetiology. If a dysfunctional schema is operating today and causing harm, it is important to understand its structure so as to dismantle it; reconstructing a life history is relevant if it contributes to this process.

Past memories naturally have an extremely important role, because they help us see that ideas about relationships are rooted in a history rather than being truths. The therapist should promote associative links between recent and past episodes by asking patients to return to moments in their memory, in whatever life period they take place, that they feel to be similar to recent relational episodes.

Should a patient have difficulty recalling remote episodes, the focus should stay on the present – especially the therapeutic relationship – or can even shift to the future by asking the patient to pay attention to what occurs between the present session and the next, and to report any narrative episodes at the next appointment. In brief, the goal is not to reconstruct the patient's life history in detail, but to have material rooted in autobiographical memories with which one can obtain a formulation of the patient's psychological functioning as close as possible to her subjective experience.

In CBT, even if she directs her attention to the present and to the problem a patient is complaining about in the here and now, the clinician also reconstructs the factors underlying the development of dysfunctional schemas relating to the self, others and the world based on the hypothesis that, thanks to this reconstruction, the therapist and patient will better grasp the phenomena involved in the disorder and make meaning out of it. The CBT model for PDs can be considered biosocial: it looks for the origins of personality problems in the mutual interaction between temperament and childhood experiences (especially those involving caregivers' emotional availability) and, from an aetiological point of view, considers the processes creating internal working models of relationships, a sense of identity and sense of personal worth to be of core importance (Davidson, 2008).

For these reasons, a CBT clinician engages in a systematic reconstruction of a patient's life history and a search for significant childhood and adolescent experiences that could have represented predisposing or vulnerability factors in regard to the specific disorder displayed by the patient. She assesses the attachment style to the caregiver, explores primary and secondary socialisation experiences and relationships with peers at important ages like adolescence, and looks for traumatic events. In general, much more than for symptom disorders, she pays attention to all the distal and proximal variables that may have contributed to the development and continuation of the dysfunctional patterns displayed by a patient, including the compensation strategies he uses and the coping styles he most commonly adopts (Beck, Freeman and Davis, 2004).

Techniques for modifying thoughts, mood and behaviour

MIT is an integrative model using cognitive behavioural techniques and mindfulness, is interpersonal and emotion-focused, and in general adopts the 'what works' principle (Livesley, 2003). Overall, MIT uses the same techniques utilised in the various types of CBT, including the third wave. The difference is that these techniques are used following iterative procedures (see Chapters 4 and 10) which, in circumstances where the techniques adopted are unable to be effective because of relational problems or limited awareness of mental states, foresees a rapid switch to working on the therapeutic relationship or a return to improving metacognition.

CBT uses cognitive restructuring, behaviour modification techniques, exposure, psycho-education and skills training techniques (Linehan, 1993), based on the assumption that PDS are maintained by a combination of dysfunctional beliefs about the Self and Others, contextual and environmental factors reinforcing problematic behaviour and skills deficits hampering an adaptive response. Although there is less scientific literature about the efficacy of cognitive behavioural techniques with PDS than symptomatic disorders, they are nevertheless formulated and flexible enough to tackle the pervasive hampering of functioning commonly seen in PD patients (Matusiewicz, Christopher, Banducci et al., 2010).

As we showed in Chapters 8 and 10, MIT also adopts cognitive behavioural techniques aimed at change, such as behavioural exposure and construction of social skills, although it is as part of the treatment rationale described in this book.

Cooperation and active participation by patients

A disposition towards a mutually agreed and conscious construction of the therapeutic project is the point at which MIT is probably most aligned with CBT. Right from the start in MIT, the therapist underscores that the therapeutic task is shared and that, from time to time, the hypotheses formulated will be discussed until both agree on how to proceed towards change. The therapist also explains that the diagnostic hypotheses and conceptualisations proposed represent an 'attempt' to understand the patient's psychological functioning, the validity of which will need to be confirmed by feedback. In MIT, moreover, as a patient's metacognitive skills improve, the therapy goals are altered. Each change takes place through a renegotiation of the therapeutic contract. The therapist points out to the patient the progress he has made, assesses together with the patient the problems to be tackled, and asks if the latter agrees in considering them therapy goals. Once the goals have been agreed, there is a renegotiation of mutual roles, tasks and commitments.

In CBT, cooperation *by* patients and *with* patients is highly formalised. Clinicians and patients decide what to tackle in each session, establish the agenda and discuss what to do between one session and the next as homework. The goal is to get patients to take a more active part in sessions, through deciding what topics to talk about, finding episodes since the previous session that activated their dysfunctional beliefs, summarising the important points in them and thinking up personalised homework (Beck, 2011).

In CBT, therapist-patient agreement on diagnosis, case formulation and treatment plan represents a key element in a therapy. A clinician should foster this by actively and gradually working at informing a patient about what he is learning as the information arises. This cooperative process of joint case formulation has been described by Padesky as working elbow to elbow with the patient (Kuyken, Padesky and Dudley, 2009). Finally, CBT places strong emphasis on identifying therapeutic goals and agreeing on them with patients, an element that MIT has absorbed in its entirety.

Therapeutic relationship and alliance

MIT has been developed in particular for treating often serious cases of patients suffering from PD (Dimaggio, Semerari, Carcione et al., 2007). For this reason, the therapist is aware that problems will emerge at an early stage in the therapeutic relationship. As a result, right from the earliest moments of contact with a new patient, he works on building a good relationship, pays constant attention to any potential ruptures in the alliance and, when appropriate, uses any tools suitable for repairing them (Dimaggio, Carcione, Salvatore et al., 2010; see Chapter 5). In this way, he tries to restore as soon as possible an optimal quality to the therapeutic relationship which is indispensible for an effective treatment programme.

The relationship is not only a treatment tool but also a source of information and the object of treatment itself. Therapists think over what happens in session in order to acquire elements regarding patients' recurring forms of relational functioning. Repairing and preventing ruptures serves, moreover, to maintain a well-modulated emotional atmosphere that patients can slowly internalise and use as a model for beneficial and functioning relationships. A good, internalised, therapeutic relationship can be transported to outside sessions and applied to day-to-day relationships.

Therapists always acknowledge they play a role in the good or poor quality of the relationship and feel involved in and responsible for the human interaction underway. This prevents them from embodying an authoritarian stance or trying to raise themselves up as a model to be imitated.

MIT, moreover, pays the utmost attention to rupture markers in session. When therapists catch signals of a potential rupture in the therapeutic relationship in a patient's verbal or non-verbal attitude or extra-session actions, they give absolute priority to these over any other contents. The intervention focus automatically becomes exploring the relational problem and treating the relationship.

Standard CBT also bears in mind that PD patients enter treatment with a disposition laden with pervasive negative forecasts about others and the world (*They'll mistreat me. They'll reject me. I'll always be a failure*) and, therefore, with a set of negative forecasts about therapy and the therapist (Beck, Freeman and Davis, 2004).

CBT also, therefore, pays attention to therapist–patient relationship issues (Strauss, Hayes, Johnson et al., 2006) and to so-called 'transference', a concept used to refer to those situations in which patients display an extreme and persistent erroneous appraisal of the therapist based on their previous experiences in significant relationships, rather than on the clinician's real behaviour. According to standard CBT, this phenomenon is nothing but the (cognitive) result of the hyper-generalisation performed by patients of the beliefs they acquired in relationships with significant others.

According to CBT, one of the main signs there is a problem in the therapeutic relationship is a lack of cooperation or a limited compliance by patients to commit themselves to therapy activities (Beck, Freeman and Davis, 2004).

When difficulties arise within the therapeutic relationship, generally revealed by intense emotional reactions, a CBT therapist includes this in the case conceptualisation and does not adopt a defensive attitude, but takes advantage of the occasion for working on pinpointing the patient's underlying expectations, beliefs, and interpersonal strategies, based on the hypothesis that these play an important role in the patient's problems *outside* therapy (Beck, Freeman and Davis, 2004).

The clinician resorts to all his interpersonal skills to tackle the problem and proposes himself as a model of honesty, openness, flexibility, and optimism about repairs in the therapeutic relationship (Beck, 2005), and asks the patient for feedback about the relationship so that treatment can continue (Burns, 2011).

With regard to countertransference, CBT considers it an indicator of the problematical psychological impact a patient has on others, including the therapist (Newman, 2012). This is unlike MIT (see Chapter 5), which sees it also as a window to the therapist's psyche.

When patients have difficult interpersonal relationships driven by their dysfunctional convictions, others often respond with a *fight/flight/freeze* reaction, that is either by opposing them or trying to reduce or avoid contact. Such problematic interpersonal scenarios can activate a patient's unloveable, abandoned, mistrusting, dependent and vulnerable-to-danger schemas. A competent CBT therapist does everything possible *not* to respond along attack/flight lines, even when faced with patients expressing disapproval or anger. To stay calm and reflective when faced with a patient's complaints, accusations or silence, a therapist must be strongly motivated to empathetically understand the patient's reactions, express this understanding, conceptualise the problem and work on finding an effective solution.

Overall, what differentiates MIT from CBT is a frequent explicit reflection about the therapeutic relationship, which is a core characteristic of the former.

Patients learn long term to be their own therapists: the role of psycho-education

Although sharing with CBT the aim of teaching patients how to be their own therapists, MIT pursues this goal with the creation of new cognitive affective styles, which, often born within the therapeutic relationship, lead patients to ascribe new meanings to events.

To be her own therapist, a patient needs to understand her disorder. In MIT, we follow this goal by ensuring that the formulation of the patient's psychological functioning is agreed at every step (see Chapter 6). Patient and therapist work together to reconstruct the former's pathogenic interpersonal schemas through an analysis of autobiographical memories, with the patient acknowledging their pernicious effect and taking a critical distance from them between one session and another. MIT, therefore, more than teaching patients what disorder they suffer from, aims at helping them to understand their mechanisms and finding joint solutions.

Although the emphasis is especially on a joint formulation of each specific case, some MIT interventions are of a psycho-educational nature. If necessary, the therapist explains what an emotion is, what role it has in adaptation and why it is important to activate autobiographical forms of reasoning rather than use semantic generalisations. The therapist also explains how to proceed in therapy and, at more advanced stages, offers patients ideas on how to behave more suitably in relationships with others and with a greater hope of success.

Standard CBT is to some extent more educational as it aims to teach patients to be their own therapists, not only promoting a profound understanding of the pathogenic mechanisms underlying their psychical disorders but also providing information on the functioning of the human mind in general. In fact, from the earliest sessions, the therapist demonstrates the cognitive model to the patient (e.g. how automatic thoughts influence emotions and behaviour and how intermediate and basic beliefs feed such automatic thoughts). Immediately afterwards, as in the CBT procedures for almost all symptom disorders, the stage involving psycho-education about the patient's disorder is launched and the main components underlying its birth and maintenance are explained.

Moreover, in consideration of the deficits found in PDs in many areas of functioning, CBT adopts psycho-educational skills training (social skills training, anger management, conversational skills) by which individual difficulties can be identified, information provided on the various skills (such as speaking in public, asking for a date, making a compliment, accepting a criticism and so on), examples given of specific behaviour (modelling) and simulated in-session exposure exercises (role play) carried out. After collecting the patient's feedback, there is an agreement on how to put into practice a specific target behaviour in a certain extra-session context with the aim of generalising the acquisition of the skill (Stanley, Bundy, Beberman et al., 2001).

However, this precious psycho-educational skills training is often used by MIT, even if used according to the parameters defined by the procedures outlined throughout this volume (see Chapter 10).

Duration of therapy and frequency of sessions

Given the complex nature of PD psychopathological case histories, MIT requires time to produce any appreciable clinical improvements. This is done while achieving a partial or complete restoration of a patient's global functioning. When the disorders are more serious, even more time is necessary. In general, after assessment, an approximate period (which can be from two to three years) is agreed with patients, while stressing, however, that this is only an indication in principle. The reasons for such a long period are then explained and the patient's feedback on this is noted.

Given that MIT adopts the CBT repertoire of techniques for reducing the symptoms associated with PDS, early improvements in symptoms can occur in a short time – from a few weeks to two or three months – whereas stabilising any improvement in symptoms requires more time and, even more so, a change in personality structure. It is, therefore, explained to patients that their therapy will entail the treatment of schemas that have taken years to crystallise and that the process, which will involve first understanding their structure and then reducing their power, will require time.

With regard to MIT session frequency, these are initially on a weekly basis and when necessary can be twice weekly. When a therapy is going positively and both parties agree that the patient has changed and stably acquired, at least partly, some fundamental skills, one can switch to fortnightly sessions for a few months, with a further reduction in frequency in the months that follow. When therapy is over, periodical follow-up sessions are planned approximately every three months.

CBT treatments for PDS last between six and twelve months (McMain, Links, Gnam et al., 2009) to two to three years (Giesen-Bloo, van Dyck, Spinhoven et al., 2006). Van Bilsen and Thomson (2011) report an average therapy duration with patients suffering from PDS of no less than two years. Session frequency is normally weekly. The CBT literature mainly concerns borderline disorder, not dealt with in this book. A more appropriate reference point for a comparison with non-borderline PD therapies is the recent schema therapy trial of a two-year duration. In the first year the sessions were scheduled weekly, for a total of 40, and in the second year, ten booster sessions took place (Bamelis, Evers and Arntz, 2012; Bamelis, Evers and Spinhoven et al., 2014).

MIT may seem excessively long compared to other cognitive therapies for PDS. We consider the problem not to be excessive length but the unrealistic idea that PD therapies can be truly effective in a short time. A careful reading of efficacy studies regarding PDS – almost exclusively focused on borderline PD – shows that at the end of treatment patients still display serious symptoms and have substantial social and relational dysfunctions (Bateman and Fonagy, 2009; McMain, Links, Gnam et al., 2009).

The efficacy studies on other PDS present a more optimistic picture (Matusiewicz, Christopher, Banducci et al., 2010), but it is necessary to define the goal: if it is an improvement in symptoms and relations, one or two years can be enough; if it is a return to conditions of well-being and good social functioning, it likely needs to be longer.

Session structure

MIT follows procedures that are iterative and less organised than in CBT. These guide a therapist through treatment of symptoms, handling of the therapeutic relationship, improvement in metacognition, understanding old schemas and forming or giving room to more adaptive ones. The agenda, or the order of priority to be applied to the elements to be tackled, almost always starts from what a patient considers the main problem. The criterion defining priority is emotional importance: the choice is to deal with the topic the patient feels to be most important in that session or at that moment in a session. In MIT, therapists never impose priorities and, when assessing the need to tackle a particular topic, they negotiate this with the patient (see Lysaker, Buck, Leonhardt et al., 2014, for a similar example in metacognition-oriented therapies for psychosis).

In CBT, the structure of therapy sessions is quite similar for the various disorders, but interventions can vary considerably from patient to patient, especially with PDS. Establishing the agenda is a well-organised and core aspect; doing this in a cooperative manner together with the patient is one of the particular features of this approach.

A clinician then proceeds to check the patient's mood, symptoms and experiences over the previous week, sets the session agenda in a cooperative manner, looks for feedback on the previous session, checks any homework, discusses the questions put in the agenda, sets new homework, makes frequent summaries and asks for feedback at the end of each session (Beck, 2011). The data and information gathered at the end of the session are the basis for those that follow (Persons, 2008).

The way in which CBT for PDS is organised does not entail anything automatic or impersonally mechanical. The relationship with the patient and the latter's cognitive emotional contents remain the main focus of interest and CBT therapists should have a flexible response to what a patient brings to sessions (Padesky and Mooney, 2012).

Homework and bibliotherapy

In cases of comorbidity with symptom disorders, MIT assigns homework characteristic of the cognitive behavioural procedures typical of those disorders and explains the link between the task and expected improvement to the patient. In general, in the initial part of therapy, patients are asked to observe, and possibly record, what happens in their daily lives with the aim of saving recent narrative episodes on which to work. The primary aim of homework in MIT during the so-called shared formulation of functioning stage (see Chapters 4 and 6) is to place a patient in a condition to collect emotional information useful for exploring his underlying interpersonal schemas and enriching them. Homework then becomes the very core of therapy once the stage promoting change has started, which involves constructing healthy self-parts (see Chapter 8).

If a patient does not do her homework, whether this involves the treatment of her personality or the solution of her symptoms (see Chapters 8 and 10), her therapist does not put pressure on her but tries to explore what is making it so difficult to do it. Without seeming critical, the therapist points out that the road to health depends more on the work between one session and another than on the work done in session, and leaves the patient the final responsibility on this question.

Homework constitutes one of the hallmarks of CBT and is considered a key mechanism for promoting change. The goals in CBT are wide-ranging: it makes it possible to practise skills and techniques learned in session and bring about new ways of thinking and behaving in real life, and represents a way of learning through experience by which a patient becomes, over time, his own therapist.

A CBT therapist selects homework carefully in order to make it accepted by the patient. She displays a cooperative attitude when she assigns it and provides an explanation in a logical form of its rationale. Moreover, she looks at how likely it is that the patient will do it, through a check on the latter's comprehension and ability to do it, involving giving some of the homework directly in session.

CBT therapists also help patients develop realistic expectations about homework, tackle the negative thoughts patients have after doing it and conceptualise the reasons why patients have difficulties doing it. For high resistance patients, CBT foresees a less authoritarian way of assigning homework by, for example, letting them directly choose a task from a list proposed by the therapist (Dobson, 2001).

MIT does not usually use *bibliotherapy* in the strict sense, that is suggesting informative books to patients with the idea that they can constitute self-help tools. MIT prefers that any extra-session assistance be constituted more by relationship 'prostheses', that is by 'extensions' of the relational climate in session, such as memoranda or summaries written by the therapist, recordings of sessions with explanations by the clinician, coping cards created directly on the patient's smartphone, and so on.

Furthermore, various research (Newman, 2000; Reeves and Stace, 2005; O'Donohue and Cummings, 2011) has found that it is better to avoid using bibliotherapy in PDS where there is emotional avoidance and interpersonal discomfort.

Notwithstanding this, MIT therapists, like CBT therapists, can recommend books or movies with the aim of increasing the sense of mutual understanding and mentalising on a topic. For example, suggesting to a narcissistic-avoidant patient that he watch *Good Will Hunting* and devoting a session to talking about it helps to increase mutual understanding on the question of the sense of omnipotence as a way of tackling distress and fragility.

The film or book thus become an emotionally marked metaphor to use in session to comprehend the universality of a problematic question, increase mutual understanding (the patient feels that the therapist understands him deep down and talks the same language as him) and lay the foundations for alternative schemas. If it is a patient herself that asks for didactic or illustrative material about her disorder or the therapeutic process, MIT therapists accept the request and suggest appropriate reading.

The picture emerging from this comparison is that, although it remains an integrative therapy, MIT shares several fundamental assumptions with the CBT family, in particular the idea that formulation of functioning and construction of the therapeutic project must be explicit and mutually agreed. In the same way, even if it has not emerged in this chapter, the stance adopted by CBT, which is to formulate a clear model open to empirical checks, has been absorbed by MIT. As we hinted already in the introduction, one of our aims in writing this manual was to provide a guide to treatment rendering it reproducible, reliable and testable in efficacy trials. This is what we shall try to carry out in the next few years. To assess the ability of MIT to generate clinical and statistically significant change, a pilot non-controlled efficacy trial lasting two years is currently underway, with a six-month follow-up. Other outcome studies are in the planning phase in different countries, both in Europe and in the USA.

Diagnostic instruments usually adopted in MIT

In parallel to the first interviews, a series of tests and tasks are administered for diagnostic and research purposes. The tests are typically not administered by the treating clinician, who instead discusses the results with patients who have a desire to increase their understanding of their own psychological functioning. The results are not discussed in a systematic way, that is the clinician neither is obliged to discuss the results of any of the tasks nor to give a full description of the results of a PD assessment. The information is given on the basis of what the patient is willing to learn and on his or her schemas and metacognitive capacities. For example, it is pointless to explain to a patient that he or she suffers from three PDs and meets 35 criteria in total! Instead, the clinician should only provide information that is helpful in assisting the patient in better understanding his or her own functioning in a way that allows for better treatment engagement.

For example, in the case of a patient with a severe PD who is unaware of her maladaptive interpersonal schemas and is unable to describe her inner states, it is useful to review the results of an alexithymia test in the hope of helping her figure out that she has difficulty understanding feelings and that this can be an early treatment target.

A possible test battery to administer to potential MIT patients may include:

Personality disorder

- Structured Clinical Interview for DSM-IV Axis II (SCID-II) (First, Gibbon, Spitzer et al., 1997)
- Millon Clinical Multiaxial Inventory (MCMI-III) (Millon, Millon, Davis et al., 2009)

Interpersonal schemas and interpersonal relationships

Though the best way to assess interpersonal schemas in MIT is the analysis of patient discourses and the patterns occurring within the therapy relationship, the following can be adopted to quickly assess maladaptive schemas:

- Young Schema Questionnaire (YSQ, L-3) (Young and Brown, 2003)

To assess problems in interpersonal relationships:

- Inventory of Interpersonal Problems (IIP-32) (Horowitz, Alden, Wiggins et al., 2000)

Though not described here, instruments to assess working models of attachment may also be used.

Metacognition

The assessment of metacognitive dysfunctions include:

- Metacognition Assessment Scale – Revised (MAS-R) (Carcione, Dimaggio, Conti et al., 2010) as applied to one of the first therapy sessions or to a semi-structured interview.
- Advanced Picture Sequencing Task (Dimaggio and Brüne, 2012, unpublished).

Aspects of the metacognitive systems (see Chapter 2) include emotional awareness (both of the self and others) and regulation, as well as theory of others' minds. Related measures include:

Emotional awareness and regulation

- Toronto Alexithymia Scale – 20 (TAS-20) (Bagby, Parker and Taylor, 1994)
- Bermond-Vorst Alexithymia Questionnaire (BVAQ) (Vorst and Bermond, 2001)
- Difficulties in Emotion Regulation Scale (DERS) (Gratz and Roemer, 2004)
- Emotional Inhibition Scale (EIS) (Kellner, 1986)
- Emotional Regulation Questionnaire (Gross and John, 2003)
- Emotional Intelligence Test (MSCEIT) (Mayer, Salovey and Caruso, 2001)
- Bell-Lysaker Emotional Recognition Task (BLERT) (Bell, Bryson and Lysaker, 1997) is a traditional measure of affect recognition. Participants are presented with video segments and asked to correctly identify two positive, four negative and one neutral affect portrayed by an actor in a video. Scores are available for the number of correctly identified affects, ranging from 0 to 21, with high scores reflecting greater affect recognition. Categorical stability of measurement over five months (Kappa = 0.93) and discriminant validity among community, substance abuse and schizophrenia samples has been demonstrated elsewhere (Bell, Bryson and Lysaker, 1997). Assessment with healthy controls has tended to suggest that they attain a total score of 17 or higher.

Symptoms

- Symptom Checklist-90-R (SCL-90 R) (Derogatis, 1994) measuring global symptomatology
- Beck Depression Inventory-II (BDI-II) (Beck, Steer and Brown, 1996)
- State-Trait Anxiety Inventory (STAI-Y, form-Y) (Spielberger, Gorssuch, Lushene et al., 1983)

Possible co-occurring symptoms can be assessed with specific tools. Examples are, in the case of obsessive-compulsive disorder: Y-BOCS (Goodman, Price, Rasmussen, 1989); in the case of eating disorders: EDI-3 (Garner, 2004).

List of instruments

We briefly describe the characteristics and psychometric properties of the above-listed instruments.

SCID-II

Structured Clinical Interview for DSM-IV Axis II
(First, Gibbon, Spitzer et al., 1997)

SCID-II is a semi-structured interview developed by First, Gibbon, Spitzer and coworkers (1997) to assess the PD listed in DSM-IV (APA, 2000), plus depressive and passive-aggressive disorders (then listed in Appendix B). The first portion of the interview consists of a 119-item questionnaire with yes/no answers, and the latter portion consists of a clinical interview comprised of open-ended questions aimed at investigating maladaptive behaviours, cognitions and coping styles. Usually the questionnaire is administered in the screening phase and then only the items to which the patient answered 'yes' are investigated in the interview.

The interview can rate each answer with 1, 2 or 3. One is given when the features described in the criterion are absent or false. Two means that the person meets the criterion partially or does not provident sufficient examples that suggest a stable feature. Three means that the item describes a stable person's character-istic, which is present in different areas.

All the criteria are then recorded in a table allowing for chart categorical diagno-sis (presence or absence of one of more full-blown PD). It also allows for dimen-sional assessment both in terms of the number of criteria met for each disorder and the overall number of criteria met. The last is a relevant index of a patient's severity, beyond the presence of any specific diagnosis. The presence of two sub-threshold disorders, or meeting at least ten overall criteria, allows for the diagnosis of person-ality disorder not otherwise specified (PDNOS). Usually the interview is adminis-tered to the patients only, but other persons may be involved in case there is need for additional information. In the Centre of Metacognitive Interpersonal Therapy in Rome, the SCID-II is then reviewed after a consultation between the interviewer and the treating clinician until consensus is reached. It often happens that criteria not present in the interview are then evident in the first sessions and those are then added to the final diagnosis. SCID II has a satisfactory internal consistency, from 0.71 to 0.94, and test-retest reliability indicators varying from 0.48 to 0.98 for categorical diagnoses and from 0.90 to 0.94 for dimensional judgements.

MCMI-III

Millon Clinical Multiaxial Inventory
(Millon, Millon, Davis et al., 2009)

The MCMI-III is a self-report personality inventory (Millon, Millon, Davis et al., 2009). It has been widely used and validated, and is considered reliable and easy to apply. The interview usually requires around 25 minutes to complete. The patient answers true or false to 175 items. It measures both personality problems and symptoms. Fourteen scales measure PD both clinically relevant and extremely severe. Three scales measure rigid and maladaptive personality styles. Six scales measure symptom disorders such as anxiety, somatisation, mood disorders and so on. Three scales evaluate severe clinical syndromes such as thought disorders or delusions. It is important to note that specific subscales evaluate the validity of the protocol.

YSQ

Young Schema Questionnaire
(Young and Brown, 2003)

The extended version of the Young Schema Questionnaire (YSQ, L-3) (Young and Brown, 2003) is a 232-item self-report measure that asks the patient to describe on a 6-point Likert scale (from 1= completely false to 6 = perfectly describes me) some characteristic of the self and others. Items are chosen in order to evaluate the 18 schemas hypothesised as underpinning psychopathology. A shortened version (YSQ, S-3) (Young and Brown, 2003) uses 90-items and has been demonstrated as having similar psychometric properties (Stopa, Thorne, Waters et al., 2001). The YSQ is widely used and has been translated into many languages.

Test-retest reliability is good (0.50 to 0.82) and internal consistency is high (α = 0.83 to 0.96) (Schmidt, Joiner, Young et al., 1995). Convergent and discriminant validity have been established in the measure of self-esteem (Rosenberg, 1965), cognitive vulnerability to depression (Beck, Steer and Brown, 1996) and assessment of PD (Personality Diagnostic Questionnaire – Revised) (Hyler, Skodol, Oldham et al., 1992).

IIP-32

Inventory of Interpersonal Problems
(Horowitz, Alden, Wiggins et al., 2000)

The IIP-32 is a 32-item self-report instrument that measures distress arising from interpersonal sources. The measure comprises eight sub-scales. The sub-scales enable examinees to describe the kinds of interpersonal problems that have been most salient in their recent experiences across diverse interpersonal situations:

- *Domineering/controlling.* A high score indicates that the person finds it difficult to relax and not take control over other people. People with high scores have described themselves as too controlling or manipulative.
- *Vindictive/self-centred.* A high score indicates problems of hostile dominance. The person readily experiences and expresses anger and irritability, is preoccupied with getting revenge and fights too much with other people.
- *Cold/distant.* A high score indicates minimal feelings of affection for and little connection with other people.
- *Socially avoidant.* A high score indicates feelings of anxiety, timidity or embarrassment in the presence of other people.
- *Non-assertive.* A high score indicates a severe lack of self-confidence, low self-esteem and severe reluctance to assert oneself over other people.
- *Exploitable.* A high score indicates excessive readiness to yield in a friendly way to the influence of others.
- *Overly nurturant.* A high score indicates a strong tendency to empathise with others in need and nurture them, even when doing so requires the person to sacrifice one's own needs for the sake of those who seem to be in need.
- *Intrusive/needy.* A high score indicates a need to be both friendly and controlling. People with high scores describe themselves as excessively friendly, outgoing and sociable to an extreme degree that others experience as excessively intrusive into their affairs.

Patients are asked to rate the degree of suffering linked to any item on a 0–4 point Likert scale. Both a total score and scores for the 8 sub-scales are obtained. Mean scores are 40<T<60. T>70 indicates high interpersonal distress. The IIP-32 has been shown to possess high internal consistency, reliability and validity, and high test-retest reliability (Soldz, Budman, Demby et al., 1995).

MAS-R

Metacognition Assessment Scale – Revised
(Carcione, Dimaggio, Conti et al., 2010)
    The MAS-R is based on the idea that metacognition is made of semi-independent sub-functions. Its goal is to evaluate the metacognitive capacities that patients display in their personal narratives. It can be applied to transcripts or videotapes of sessions, and semi-structured interviews and assessments, and can be repeated over time in order to explore whether metacognitive functioning changes according to therapy effects or is generally stable or amenable to modifications. The MAS-R requires training and practice in order to be reliably scored. The scale is divided into three sections, which taps into the abilities:

- reflecting on own mental states (*understanding own mind/UM*);
- reflecting on the mental states of the other (*understanding others' mind/ UOM*)/*decententration/D*;
- facing psychological suffering and interpersonal problems due to an understanding of underlying mental states (*Mastery – M*).

Each sub-scale is then made of different functions, as portrayed in Table A.1.

When applied to therapy transcripts every session is divided into three parts equal in terms of number of therapist/patient speaking turns. Then each part is considered a unit of scoring. In the case of semi-structured interviews, the full interview is the scoring unit. Each item is rated according to a 1–5 point scale. First the rater evaluates if a specific sub-function (e.g. emotional identification in the self) has been portrayed. If not, a non-engaged (NE) is marked. If the function described by the item is active, then a score from 1 to 5 is given. Scores are given according to how much during one unit any sub-function (item) is: (1) used by the patient; (2) articulated and nuanced; (3) properly used and spontaneously offered as opposed to requiring probing by the interviewer. In addition, the Mastery sub-scale also requires raters to evaluate whether an individual's responding is (4) adaptive, i.e. the strategy used is appropriate for the problem to be solved with some consideration of associated costs and benefits to the individual.

Final scores can be calculated for (1) the MAS-R total and (2) for any sub-scale; (3) analyses can be performed at a single-item level, for example when exploring correlations with symptoms or interpersonal functioning; (4) an index of metacognitive engagement can also be calculated considering the ratio of engaged/not engaged items.

A-PST

Advanced Picture Sequencing Task
(Dimaggio and Brüne, 2012; Brüne, Dimaggio and Edel, 2013)

The A-PST is a theory of mind task developed in order to avoid the ceiling effects that simpler tasks often have when applied to persons with disorders such as

Table A.1

Understanding own mind	Understanding others' minds	Mastery
1. MONITORING	1. MONITORING	First-level strategies
Cognitive identification	*Cognitive identification*	
Emotional identification	*Emotional identification*	
Relating variables	*Relating variables*	Second-level strategies
2. DIFFERENTIATION	2. DECENTRATION	Third-level strategies
3. INTEGRATION		

schizophrenia or autism. It assesses the patient's ability to correctly rearrange a story divided into vignettes by the understanding of the sequence and the mental states of the protagonists. It consists of eight stories about social interactions among two or more persons. The stories were written in order to make patients deal with emotional-arousing situations, therefore avoiding neutral material. The stories tap into interpersonal motives which are usually problematic for patients with PD and develop around themes such as attachment, social rank, social threat, group inclusion, cooperation and sexuality. The task is divided in two parts. First, seven vignettes are presented in random order and the patient is asked to correctly sequence them. Then four alternative endings are presented and the patient is asked to choose one. The endings are categorised into four domains: 'antisocial', 'socially avoidant', 'prosocial/cooperative' and 'disorganised/bizarre', and there is no correct final choice. After the sequencing is completed the patient is asked to describe the mental states (cognitions and affects) of the characters. Two scores are given, one for the sequencing and one, in a 0–2 scale, for the quality of mentalistic attributions. A score of 0 suggests poor or absent descriptions of mental states or wrong ascriptions (e.g. the patient says the character is sad while the situation and the character's facial expression indicate anger); 1 involves some ability to describe mental states but patients tend to describe just a few nuances or provide repetitive descriptions of a state, or there is poor ability to describe the evolution of the mental states of the characters as the story unfolds; 2 means ability to describe different mental states, make correct attributions and catch the evolution of the mental state during the story.

DERS

Difficulties in Emotion Regulation Scale
(Gratz and Roemer, 2004)

The DERS is a 36-item self-report questionnaire developed by Gratz and Roemer (2004) to assess clinically relevant difficulties in emotion regulation, particularly with regard to negative or distressing emotions.

Factor analysis suggests that there are six specific sub-scales present, which indicates the existence of six corresponding dimensions or facets of emotion dysregulation:

- *non-acceptance* – non-acceptance of emotional responses;
- *goals* – difficulties engaging in goal-directed behaviour when emotionally upset;
- *impulse* – impulse control difficulties when distressed;
- *awareness* – lack of emotional awareness;
- *strategies* – limited access to a wide range of emotion regulation strategies;
- *clarity* – lack of emotional clarity.

Subscales scores are obtained by summing each corresponding item. It is important to pay attention to items with reverse scoring.

Participants are asked to indicate how often each item applies to them on a scale ranging from 1 (almost never) to 5 (almost always). Scores are summed to provide a comprehensive assessment of general emotion dysregulation (i.e. the DERS total score). Sub-scale scores are obtained by summing each corresponding item, paying attention to those that have reverse scoring. Higher scores on the DERS indicate greater difficulties in emotion regulation, whiler higher scores on each sub-scale indicate difficulties in any specific dimension.

The DERS has demonstrated an internal consistency of 0.93, a test-retest reliability of 0.88 during a four- to eight-week period and a clear factor structure (Gratz and Roemer, 2004). Furthermore, it has been found to be related to several criterion variables (e.g. experiential avoidance and self-harm) and to behavioural measures of emotion dysregulation (Gratz, Rosenthal, Tull et al., 2006). Other empirical findings suggest a good construct validity and a high internal consistency with both clinical and non-clinical samples. The DERS has also demonstrated sensitivity to changes corresponding to successful therapeutic outcomes (Gratz, Rosenthal, Tull et al., 2006).

EIS

Emotional Inhibition Scale
(Kellner, 1986, in Grandi, Sirri, Wise et al., 2011)

The EIS is a 16-item self-report instrument developed by Kellner (1981, as mentioned in Grandi, Sirri, Wise et al., 2011) to assess the conscious inhibition of emotional states. It consists of 16 items, each scored on a five-point Likert scale ranging from 'no' to 'always'. The EIS includes four sub-scales: *verbal inhibition, timidity, disguise of feelings* and *self-control*. Participants rank each item on a five-point Likert scale. It requires up to 15 minutes to be administered. Higher scores indicate timidity, introversion and emotional over-control.

MSCEIT

Mayer-Salovey-Caruso Emotional Intelligence Test
(Mayer, Salovey and Caruso, 2001)

The MSCEIT is a widely used scale assessing emotional intelligence as measured through a series of tasks involving emotionally related problem-solving. Tasks consists of verbal material, identification of facial expressions, association of emotions to images representing real or abstract scenes, and finding solutions for interpersonally challenging situations.

MSCEIT is comprised of 141 items, which are divided into four areas: *emotional perception, facilitation of thought, emotional understanding* and *emotional regulation*. These are divided into the two areas *experiential* and *strategic*. MSCEIT can be administered individually or in groups, using both paper-and-pencil and online processes. There is no time limit but usually requires around 45 minutes to complete. MSCEIT is highly reliable at the level of the four sub-scales (da 0.74 a 0.89), the areas (experiential = 0.90, strategic = 0.85) and total (0.91).

BLERT

Bell-Lysaker Emotional Recognition Task
(Bell, Bryson and Lysaker, 1997)

The BLERT is a traditional measure of affect recognition. Participants are presented with video segments and asked to correctly identify two positive, four negative and one neutral affect portrayed by an actor in a video. Scores are available for the number of correctly identified affects, ranging from 0 to 21, with high scores reflecting greater affect recognition. Categorical stability of measurement over five months (Kappa = 0.93) and discriminant validity among community, substance abuse and schizophrenia samples has been demonstrated elsewhere. Assessment with healthy controls has tended to suggest that they attain a total score of 17 or higher.

TAS-20

Toronto Alexithymia Scale TAS-20
(Bagby, Parker and Taylor, 1994)

Alexithymia means 'no words for feelings' (Sifneos, 1973) and is described as a difficulty in identifying and verbalising one's own emotional states, and a tendency not to include emotions in one's own cognitive evaluations, while preferring to focus on information coming from the external environment.

The TAS-20 is a self-report instrument used to measure alexithymia. It includes 20 items that are rated on a five-point Likert scale ranging from 1 = 'strongly disagree' to 5 = 'strongly agree'. The items are summed to produce a total score out of 100, with lower scores indicating better outcomes. The TAS-20 also includes three sub-scales that evaluate different dimensions of alexithymia: (1) difficulty describing feelings; (2) difficulty identifying feelings; and (3) externally oriented thinking. It has been evaluated by confirmatory factor-analytic procedures in 19 different countries (Parker, Taylor and Bagby, 2003). Based on a college student sample, Bagby, Parker and Taylor (1994) found that the TAS-20 had good internal consistency for the total score, with Cronbach's alpha = 0.81 and acceptable internal consistency for the factor scores (difficulty identifying feelings, 0.78; difficulty describing feelings, 0.75; externally oriented thinking, 0.66). Test-retest reliability over three weeks was 0.77 for the total score. A more recent psychometric investigation with a large sample of community participants also found that the TAS-20 had good internal reliabilities for total and factor scores, with all coefficient alphas greater than 0.70 (Parker, Taylor and Bagby, 2003). TAS-20 scores have good correlations with observer ratings of alexithymia (e.g. Bagby, Parker and Taylor, 1994). The alexithymic status of an individual can also be categorised based on the use of cut-offs for the

TAS-20 total score (Bagby, Parker and Taylor, 1994): Scores less than or equal to 51 reflect non-alexithymia, scores of 52 to 60 reflect possible alexithymia and scores of 61 or greater reflect full alexithymia.

BVAQ

Bermond-Vorst Alexithymia Questionnaire
(Vorst and Bermond, 2001)

The Bermond-Vorst Alexithymia Questionnaire is a 40-item self-report measure developed by Vorst and Bermond (2001) to assess the alexithymia construct, defined as a combination of five specific traits: emotionalising, fantasising, identifying, analysing and verbalising. This self-report measure was designed to examine five putative facets as described previously and two putative dimensions of alexithymia. Each sub-scale ('identifying', 'describing', 'analysing', 'fantasising' and 'emotionalising') consist of eight items which are measured on a five-point Likert scale. The BVAQ exhibits a second-order factor structure consisting of two sub-scales ('fantasising' and 'emotionalising') constituting an affective dimension and three sub-scales ('identifying', 'describing' and 'analysing') comprising a cognitive dimension. The total score of the BVAQ-40 ranges from 40 to 200 points, with high scores indicating greater proneness to alexithymia. Regarding its psychometric properties, Cronbach's alpha coefficients range from 0.67 to 0.87 for each of the five subscales (Vorst and Bermond, 2001). The validity of the BVAQ is acceptable (Vorst and Bermond, 2001).

BDI-II

Beck Depression Inventory-II
(Beck, Steer and Brown, 1996)

BDI-II is a 21-item measure assessing depression over the previous two weeks. Higher scores suggest more depression experienced. Beck, Steer and Brown (1996) reported a mean score of 14.55 for non-patient female university students. One-week test-retest reliability in a mixed gender sample of outpatients was 0.93. Here, internal consistency was 0.79 at pre-test and 0.85 at post-test. Items refer to the typical symptoms of patients with depression, including sadness, pessimism, failure, loss of pleasure, guilt, low self-esteem, self-criticism, suicidal ideation, crying, agitation, loss of interest, indecisiveness, feelings of worthlessness, loss of energy, irregular sleeping patterns, irritability, changes in appetite, difficulty concentrating, fatigue and sexual dysfunction. Depression can be thought of as having two components: the affective component (e.g. mood) and the physical or 'somatic' component (e.g. loss of appetite). The BDI-II reflects this and can be separated into two sub-scales. The purpose of the sub-scales are to help determine the primary cause of a patient's depression.

The affective sub-scale contains: pessimism, past failures, guilty feelings, punishment feelings, self-dislike, self-criticalness, suicidal thoughts or wishes, and worthlessness. The somatic sub-scale consists of the other 13 items: sadness, loss of pleasure, crying, agitation, loss of interest, indecisiveness, loss of energy, change in sleep patterns, irritability, change in appetite, concentration difficulties, tiredness and/or fatigue, and loss of interest in sex. The two subscales were moderately correlated at 0.57, suggesting that the physical and psychological aspects of depression are related rather than totally distinct.

Time to complete this test is about 10 minutes. Each answer is scored on a scale value of 0 to 3. The cutoffs used differ from the original: 0–13: minimal depression; 14–19: mild depression; 20–28: moderate depression; and 29–63: severe depression.

STAI-Y

State-Trait Anxiety Inventory (form-Y)
(Spielberger, Gorssuch, Lushene et al.1983)

The STAI-Y is a self-report instrument measuring state-anxiety, or anxiety about an event, and trait-anxiety, or anxiety level as a personal characteristic (STAI T-Anxiety Scale, STAI S-Anxiety Scale). The STAI-Y has no limits on time, takes about 10 minutes to complete and can be administered individually or in groups. All items are rated on a four-point scale. The four-point scale for S-anxiety is as follows: (1) not at all; (2) somewhat; (3) moderately so; (4) very much so. The four-point scale for T-anxiety is as follows: (1) almost never; (2) sometimes; (3) often; (4) almost always. For some items the scores must be reversed when scored. Scores range from 20 to 80, with higher scores correlating with greater anxiety. Internal consistency is very good for both state anxiety (from 0.91 to 0.95) and trait anxiety (from 0.85 to 0.90), with a good test-retest reliability indicator of 0.49 for state anxiety and 0.82 for trait anxiety (Spielberger, Gorssuch, Lushene et al., 1983).

SCL-90-R

Symptom Checklist-90-Revised
(Derogatis, 1983)

SCL-90-R is a widely used self-report measure that assesses psychiatric symptom distress. The 90 items in this measure are rated on a scale ranging from 0 = 'not at all' to 4 = 'extremely' and ask about the degree of symptom distress in the past seven days. Higher scores are indicative of greater symptom distress. The instrument yields a global severity index that reflects overall psychological distress. Internal consistency reliability has been found to be good to excellent for the nine dimensions, with alpha coefficients ranging between 0.77 and 0.90. The measure has also demonstrated good to excellent test-retest reliability, with coefficients ranging from 0.78 to 0.90 over a two-week period.

ERQ

Emotion Regulation Questionnaire
(Gross and John, 2003)

ERQ is a 10-item self-report measure consisting of two commonly used regulatory strategies, including one employed prior to the full activation of an emotional response (antecedent-focused cognitive reappraisal) and one employed after the emotional response has been generated (response-focused suppression of expression). Suppression is regarded as consuming more mental resources and less efficient than reappraisal.

Items are rated on a seven-point Likert scale, ranging from 1 (strongly disagree) to 7 (strongly agree). The ERQ has good internal consistency and has demonstrated strong convergent-discriminant and predictive validity.

References

Abramowitz, J. S. (2009) *Getting Over OCD: A 10-Step Workbook for Taking Back Your Life*. New York: Guilford Press.

Adler, J. M., Chin, E. D., Kolisetty, A. P. and Oltmanss, T. F. (2012) 'The distinguishing characteristics of narrative identity in adults with features of borderline personality disorder: an empirical investigation', *Journal of Personality Disorders*, 26: 498–512.

Allen, J. G., Fonagy, P. and Bateman, A. W. (2008) *Mentalizing in Clinical Practice*. Arlington, VA: American Psychiatric Publishing.

American Psychiatric Association (2000) *Diagnostic and Statistical Manual of Mental Disorders*, 4th edn, text revision (DSM-IV-TR). Washington, DC: APA.

American Psychiatric Association (2013) *Diagnostic and Statistical Manual of Mental Disorders*, 5th edn (DSM-5). Arlington, VA: APA.

Ames, D. R. (2004) 'Inside the mind-reader's toolkit: projection and stereotyping in mental state inference', *Journal of Personality and Social Psychology*, 87: 340–53.

Angus, L. and McLeod, J. (2004) *The Handbook of Narrative and Psychotherapy: Practice, Theory and Research*. Thousand Oaks, CA: Sage.

Arntz, A., Klokman, J. and Sieswerda, S. (2005) 'An experimental test of the schema mode model of borderline personality disorder', *Journal of Behavior Therapy*, 36: 226–39.

Aspland, H., Llewelyn, S., Hardy, G. E., Barkham, M. and Stiles, W. B. (2008) 'Alliance ruptures and rupture resolution in cognitive-behavior therapy: a preliminary task analysis', *Psychotherapy Research*, 18: 699–710.

Ayearst, L. E., Flett, G. L. and Hewitt, P. L. (2012) 'Where is multidimensional perfectionism in DSM-5? A question posed to the DSM-5 personality and personality disorders work group', *Personality Disorders: Theory, Research, and Treatment*, 3: 458–69.

Baer, R. A. (2010) *Assessing Mindfulness and Acceptance Processes in Clients: Illuminating the Theory and Practice of Change*. Oakland, CA: New Harbinger.

Bagby, R. M., Parker, J. D. and Taylor, G. J. (1994) 'The twenty-item Toronto Alexithymia Scale-I. Item selection and cross-validation of the factor structure', *Journal of Psychosomatic Research*, 38: 23–32.

Bamelis, L. L. M., Evers, S. M. A. A. and Arntz, A. (2012) 'Design of a multicentered randomized controlled trial on the clinical and cost effectiveness of schema therapy for personality disorders', *BMC Public Health*, 12: 75.

Bamelis, L. L. M., Evers, S. M. A. A., Spinhoven, P. and Arntz, A. (2014) 'Results of a multicenter randomized controlled trial of the clinical effectiveness of schema therapy for personality disorders', *American Journal of Psychiatry*, 171: 305–22.

Bamelis, L. L. M., Renner, F., Heidkamp, D. and Arntz, A. (2011) 'Extended schema mode conceptualizations for specific personality disorders: an empirical study', *Journal of Personality Disorders*, 25: 41–58.

Baptista, M. N., Magna, L. A., McKay, D. and Del-Porto, J. A. (2011) 'Assessment of obsessive beliefs: comparing individuals with obsessive-compulsive disorder to a medical sample', *Journal of Behavior Therapy and Experimental Psychiatry*, 42: 1–5.

Baron-Cohen, S., Leslie, A. and Frith, U. (1985) 'Does the autistic child have a "theory of mind"?', *Cognition*, 21: 37–46.

Basile, B., Mancini, F., Macaluso, E., Caltagirone, C., Frackowiak, R. S. and Bozzali, M. (2011) 'Deontological and altruistic guilt: evidence for distinct neurobiological substrates', *Human Brain Mapping*, 32: 229–39.

Bateman, A. and Fonagy, P. (2004) *Psychotherapy for Borderline Personality Disorder: Mentalization Based Treatment*. Oxford: Oxford University Press.

Bateman, A. W. and Fonagy, P. (2009) 'Randomly controlled trial of outpatient mentalizing-based therapy versus structured clinical management for borderline personality disorder', *American Journal of Psychiatry*, 166: 1355–64.

Beck, A. T. (2005) *Anxiety Disorders and Phobias: A Cognitive Perspective*. New York: Basic Books.

Beck, A. T. and Alford, B. A. (2008) *Depression: Causes and Treatment*, 2nd edn. Philadelphia, PA: University of Pennsylvania Press.

Beck, A. T. and Steer, R. A. (1993) *Beck Anxiety Inventory Manual*. Boston, MA: Harcourt Brace.

Beck, A. T., Baruch, E., Balter, J. M., Steer, R. A. and Warman, D. M. (2004) 'A new instrument for measuring insight: the Beck Cognitive Insight Scale', *Schizophrenia Research*, 68: 319–29.

Beck, A. T., Freeman, A. and Davis, D. D. (2004) *Cognitive Therapy of Personality Disorders*. New York: Guilford Press.

Beck, A. T., Steer, R. A. and Brown, G. K. (1996) *BDI-II, Beck Depression Inventory: Manual*, 2nd edn. Boston, MA: Harcourt Brace.

Beck, J. G. and Shipherd, J. C. (1997) 'Repeated exposure to interoceptive cues: does habituation of fear occur in panic disorder patients? A preliminary report', *Behaviour Research and Therapy*, 35: 551–7.

Beck, J. S. (2011) *Cognitive Behavior Therapy: Basics and Beyond*, 2nd edn. New York: Guilford Press.

Beidel, D. C. and Turner, S. M. (2007) *Shy Children, Phobic Adults: Nature and Treatment of Social Anxiety Disorder*. Washington, DC: American Psychological Association.

Bell, M. D., Bryson, G. J. and Lysaker, P. H. (1997) 'Positive and negative affect recognition in schizophrenia: a comparison with substance abuse and normal control subjects', *Psychiatry Research*, 73: 73–82.

Bender, D. S. (2005) 'The therapeutic alliance in the treatment of personality disorders', *Journal of Psychiatric Practice*, 11: 73–87.

Betan, E., Heim, A. K., Conklin, C. Z. and Westen, D. (2005) 'Countertransference phenomena and personality pathology in clinical practice: an empirical investigation', *American Journal of Psychiatry*, 162: 890–8.

Blackledge, J. T. (2007) 'Disrupting verbal processes: cognitive defusion in acceptance and commitment therapy and other mindfulness-based psychotherapies', *Psychological Record*, 57: 555–76.

Borkovec, T. D., Alcaine, O. and Behar, E. (2004) 'Avoidance theory of worry and generalized anxiety disorder', in R. G. Heimberg, C. L. Turk and D. S. Mennin (eds), *Generalized Anxiety Disorder: Advances in Research and Practice.* New York: Guilford Press, pp. 77–108.

Borkovec, T. D., Robinson, E., Pruzinsky, T. and DePree, J. A. (1983) 'Preliminary exploration of worry: some characteristics and processes', *Behaviour Research and Therapy,* 21: 9–16.

Bower, G. H. (1981) 'Mood and memory', *American Psychologist,* 36: 129–48.

Bowlby, J. (1988) *A Secure Base: Clinical Applications of Attachment Theory.* London: Routledge.

Bressi, C., Taylor, G. J., Parker, J. D. A., Bressi, S., Brambilla, V., Aguglia, E., Allegranti, S., Brieger, P., Ehrt, U. and Marneros, A. (2003) 'Frequency of comorbid personality disorders in bipolar and unipolar affective disorders', *Comprehensive Psychiatry,* 44: 28–34.

Bromberg, P. (1988) *Standing in the Spaces. Essays on Clinical Process, Trauma and Dissociation.* Hillsdale, NJ: Analytic Press.

Brüne, M., Abdel-Hamid, M., Lehmkämper, C. and Sonntag, C. (2007) 'Mental state attribution, neurocognitive functioning, and psychopathology: what predicts poor social competence in schizophrenia best?', *Schizophrenia Research,* 92: 151–9.

Brüne, M., Dimaggio, G. and Edel, M.-A. (2013) 'Mentalization-based group therapy for inpatients with borderline personality disorder: preliminary findings', *Clinical Neuropsychiatry,* 10: 196–201.

Calkins, A. W., Berman, N. C. and Wilhelm, S. (2013) 'Recent advances in research on cognition and emotion in OCD: a review', *Current Psychiatry Report,* 15 (5): 357.

Cameron, A., Reed, K. P. and Gaudiano, B. A. (2014) 'Addressing treatment motivation in borderline personality disorder: rationale for incorporating values-based exercises into dialectical behavior therapy', *Journal of Contemporary Psychotherapy,* 44: 109–16.

Canton, J., Scott, K. M. and Glue, P. (2012) 'Optimal treatment of social phobia: systematic review and meta-analysis', *Neuropsychiatric Disease and Treatment,* 8: 203–15.

Carcione, A., Dimaggio, G., Conti, L., Fiore, D., Nicolò, G. and Semerari, A. (2010) 'Metacognition Assessment Scale-R, scoring manual V.4.0'. Unpublished manuscript.

Carcione, A., Semerari, A., Nicolò, G., Pedone, R., Popolo, R., Conti, L., Fiore, D., Procacci, M. and Dimaggio, G. (2011) 'Metacognitive mastery dysfunctions in personality disorder psychotherapy', *Psychiatry Research,* 190: 60–71.

Carek, P. J., Laibstain, S. E. and Carek, S. M. (2011) 'Exercise for the treatment of depression and anxiety', *International Journal of Psychiatry in Medicine,* 41: 15–28.

Caspar, F. and Ecker, S. (2008) 'Treatment of an avoidant patient with comorbid psychopathology: a plan analysis perspective', *Journal of Clinical Psychology: In Session,* 64: 139–53.

Cassin, S. E. and Von Ranson, K. M. (2005) 'Personality and eating disorders: a decade in review', *Clinical Psychology Review,* 25: 895–916.

Castonguay, L. G., Schut, A. J., Aikins, D., Constantino, M. J., Laurenceau, J. P., Bologh, L. and Burns, D. D. (2004) 'Repairing alliance ruptures in cognitive therapy: a preliminary investigation of an integrative therapy for depression', *Journal of Psychotherapy Integration,* 14: 4–20.

Chang, E. C., D'Zurilla, T. J. and Sanna, L. J. (2004) *Social Problem Solving: Theory, Research, and Training.* Washington, DC: American Psychological Association.

Ciaramelli, E., Bernardi, F. and Moscovitch, M. (2013) 'Individualized Theory of Mind (iToM): when memory modulates empathy', *Frontiers in Psychology,* 4: 4.

Claes, L., Vandereycken, W., Luyten, P., Soenens, B., Pieters, G. and Vertommen, H. (2006) 'Personality prototypes in eating disorders based on the big five model', *Journal of Personality Disorders*, 20 (4): 401–16.

Clark, D. A. (2012) *Cognitive-Behavioral Therapy for OCD*. New York: Guilford Press.

Clark, D. A. and Beck, A. T. (2010) *Cognitive Therapy of Anxiety Disorders: Science and Practice*. New York: Guilford Press.

Clark, D. M. (1986) 'A cognitive approach to panic', *Behaviour Research and Therapy*, 24 (4): 461–70.

Clarkin, J. F., Yeomans, F. E. and Kernberg, O. F. (1999) *Psychotherapy for Borderline Personality*. New Yor: Wiley.

Cloninger, C. R. (1994) 'Temperament and personality', *Current Opinion in Neurobiology*, 4: 166–73.

Colli, A., Tanzilli, A., Dimaggio, G. and Lingiardi, V. (2014) 'Patient personality and therapist responses: an empirical investigation', *American Journal of Psychiatry*, 171 (1): 102–8.

Constantino, M. J., Marnell, M. E., Haile, A. J., Arnow, B., Kanther-Sista, S. N., Wolman, K. and Zappert, L. (2008) 'Integrative cognitive therapy for depression: a randomized pilot comparison', *Psychotherapy: Theory, Research, Practice and Training*, 45: 122–34.

Crits-Christoph, P., Connolly Gibbons, M. B. C., Crits-Christoph, K., Narducci, J., Schamberger, M. and Gallop, R. (2006) 'Can therapists be trained to improve their alliances? A preliminary study of alliance-fostering psychotherapy', *Psychotherapy Research*, 16 (3): 268–81.

Damasio, A. (1994) *Decartes' Error: Emotion Reason and Human Brain*. New York: Putnam.

Davidson, K. M. (2008) 'Cognitive-behavioural therapy for personality disorders', *Psychiatry*, 7 (3): 117–20.

De Bolle, M., De Fruyt, F., Quilty, L.C., Rolland, J.P., Decuyper, M. and Bagby, R. M. (2011) 'Does personality disorder co-morbidity impact treatment outcome for patients with major depression? A multi-level analysis', *Journal of Personality Disorders*, 25 (1): 1–15.

Derogatis, L. R. (1994) *Symptom Checklist-90-R: Administration, Scoring, and Procedures Manual*, 3rd edn. Minneapolis, MN: National Computer Systems.

Dimaggio, G. (2011) 'Impoverished self-narrative and impaired self-reflection as targets for the psychotherapy of personality disorders', *Journal of Contemporary Psychotherapy*, 41: 165–74.

Dimaggio, G. (2012) 'Narcissistic personality disorder: rethinking what we know', *Psychiatric Times*, 29: 17–25.

Dimaggio, G. and Attinà, G. (2012) 'Metacognitive interpersonal therapy for narcissistic personality disorders with perfectionistic features: the case of Leonardo', *Journal of Clinical Psychology: In-Session*, 68: 922–34.

Dimaggio, G. and Brüne, M. (2012) 'Advanced Mentalising Picture Sequencing Task'. Unpublished material. Rome: Bochum.

Dimaggio, G. and Lysaker, P. H. (eds) (2010) *Metacognition and Severe Adult Mental Disorders: From Basic Research to Treatment*. London: Routledge.

Dimaggio, G., Attinà, G., Popolo, R. and Salvatore, G. (2012) 'Personality disorders with over-regulation of emotions and poor self-reflectivity: the case of a man with avoidant and not-otherwise specified PD, social phobia and dysthymia treated with metacognitive interpersonal therapy', *Personality and Mental Health*, 6: 156–62.

Dimaggio, G., Carcione, A., Conti, M. L., Nicolò, G., Fiore, D., Pedone, R., Popolo, R., Procacci, M. and Semerari, A. (2009) 'Impaired decentration in Personality Disorder: a series of single cases analysed with the Metacognition Assessment Scale', *Clinical Psychology and Psychotherapy*, 16 (5): 450–62.

Dimaggio, G., Carcione, A., Nicolò, G., Lysaker, P. H., d'Angerio, S., Conti, M. L., Fiore, D., Pedone, R., Procacci, M., Popolo, R. and Semerari, A. (2013) 'Differences between axes depend on where you set the bar. Associations among symptoms, interpersonal relationship and alexithymia with number of personality disorder criteria', *Journal of Personality Disorders*, 27: 371–82.

Dimaggio, G., Carcione, A., Petrilli, M., Procacci, M., Semerari, A. and Nicolò, G. (2005) 'States of mind organization in personality disorders. Typical states and the triggering of inter-state shifts', *Clinical Psychology and Psychotherapy*, 12: 346–59.

Dimaggio, G., Carcione, A., Salvatore, G., Nicolò, G., Sisto, A. and Semerari, A. (2011) 'Progressively increasing metacognition through a step-by-step procedure in a case of obsessive-compulsive personality disorder treated with metacognitive interpersonal therapy', *Psychology and Psychotherapy: Theory, Research and Practice*, 84: 70–83.

Dimaggio, G., Carcione, A., Salvatore, G., Semerari, A. and Nicolò, G. (2010) 'A rational model for maximizing the effect of regulating therapy relationship in personality disorders', *Psychology and Psychotherapy: Theory, Research and Practice*, 83: 363–84.

Dimaggio, G., Hermans, H. J. M. and Lysaker, P. H. (2010) 'Health and adaptation in a multiple self: the role of absence of dialogue and poor metacognition in clinical populations', *Theory and Psychology*, 20: 379–99.

Dimaggio, G., Lysaker, P. H., Carcione, A., Nicolò, G. and Semerari, A. (2008) 'Know yourself and you shall know the other ... to a certain extent. Multiple paths of influence of self-reflection on mindreading', *Consciousness and Cognition*, 17: 778–89.

Dimaggio, G., Nicolò, G., Fiore, R., Pedone, R., Popolo, R., Centenero, E., Semerari, A. and Carcione, A. (2008) 'States of minds in narcissistic personality disorder. Three psychotherapy patients analysed through the Grid of Problematic States', *Psychotherapy Research*, 18: 466–80.

Dimaggio, G., Popolo, R., Carcione, A. and Salvatore, G. (in press) 'Accessing autobiographical memories and promoting metacognition in the inhibited-constricted personality disorder', in J. W. Livesley, G. Dimaggio and J. F. Clarkin (eds), *Integrated Modular Treatment for Personality Disorders*. New York: Guilford Press.

Dimaggio, G., Popolo, R., Fiore, D., Carcione, A. and Salvatore, G. (in press) 'Enriching self-narratives in patients with personality disorders: advanced phases of treatment', in J. W. Livesley, G. Dimaggio and J. F. Clarkin (eds), *Integrated Modular Treatment for Personality Disorders*. New York: Guilford Press.

Dimaggio, G., Procacci, M., Nicolò, G., Popolo, R., Semerari, A., Carcione, A. and Lysaker, P. H. (2007) 'Poor metacognition in narcissistic and avoidant personality disorders: analysis of four psychotherapy patients', *Clinical Psychology and Psychotherapy*, 14: 386–401.

Dimaggio, G., Salvatore, G., Fiore, D., Carcione, A., Nicolò, G. and Semerari, A. (2012) 'General principles for treating the overconstricted personality disorder. Toward operationalizing technique', *Journal of Personality Disorders*, 26: 63–83.

Dimaggio, G., Salvatore, G., Montano, A., Lysaker, P. H., Buonocore, L., Carlucci, S., Disturco, N., Bianchi, L., Santini, F., Baca, E., Galasso, V., Carabelli, F., Ottavi, P., Attinà, G., Marini, M., Catania, D., D'Urzo, M., Imbimbo, A., Olivieri, D., Borzì, R. and Popolo, R. (2012) *Poor Affect Recognition and Regulation in Personality Disorders: Preliminary*

Data from an Outpatient Sample of Treatment-Seeking Adults. Paper presented at the conference of the European Association for Behavioral and Cognitive Therapies, Geneva, July.

Dimaggio, G., Salvatore, G., Nicolò, G., Fiore, D. and Procacci, M. (2010) 'Enhancing mental state understanding in over-constricted personality disorder using metacognitive interpersonal therapy', in G. Dimaggio and P. H. Lysaker (eds), *Metacognition and Severe Adult Mental Disorders. From Research to Treatment.* London: Routledge, pp. 247–68.

Dimaggio, G., Salvatore, G., Popolo, R. and Lysaker, P. H. (2012) 'Autobiographical memory dysfunctions and poor understanding of mental states in personality disorders and schizophrenia: clinical implications', *Frontiers in Cognition*, 3: 529.

Dimaggio, G., Semerari, A., Carcione, A., Nicolò, G. and Procacci, M. (2007) *Psychotherapy of Personality Disorders: Metacognition, States of Mind and Interpersonal Cycles.* London: Routledge.

Dimaggio, G., Semerari, A., Falcone, M., Nicolò, G., Carcione, A. and Procacci, M. (2002) 'Metacognition, states of mind, cognitive biases and interpersonal cycles. Proposal for an integrated model of Narcissism', *Journal of Psychotherapy Integration*, 12: 421–51.

Dimaggio, G., Valeri, S., Ottavi, P., Popolo, R., Salvatore, G. and Montano, A. (2014) 'Adopting metacognitive interpersonal therapy to treat narcissistic personality disorder with severe somatization', *Journal of Contemporary Psychotherapy*, 44: 85–95.

Dimaggio, G., Vanheule, S., Lysaker, P. H., Carcione, A. and Nicolò, G. (2009) 'Impaired self-reflection in psychiatric disorders among adults: a proposal for the existence of a network of semi-independent functions', *Consciousness and Cognition*, 18: 653–64.

Dimidjian, S., Barrera Jr, M., Martell, C., Muñoz, R. F. and Lewinsohn, P. M. (2011) 'The origins and current status of behavioural activation treatments for depression', *Annual Review of Clinical Psychology*, 7: 1–38.

Dobson, K. S. (2001) *Handbook of Cognitive-Behavioral Therapies*, 2nd edn. New York: Guilford Press.

Doron, G. and Kyrios, M. (2005) 'Obsessive compulsive disorder: a review of possible specific internal representations within a broader cognitive theory', *Clinical Psychology Review*, 25: 415–32.

Ekman, P. (2003) *Emotions Revealed: Recognizing Faces and Feelings to Improve Communication and Emotional Life*, 2nd edn. New York: Owl Books.

Ekman, P. and Rosenberg, L. R. (2005) *What the Face Reveals: Basic and Applied Studies of Spontaneous Expression Using the Facial Action Coding System (FACS)*, Series in Affective Science. Oxford: Oxford University Press.

Ekman, P., Wallace, V. and Friesen (2009) *Unmasking the Face: A Guide to Recognizing Emotions from Facial Clues.* Englewood Cliffs, NJ: Prentice Hall.

Ellis, A. (1962) *Reason And Emotion In Psychotherapy.* New York: Lyle Stuart.

Fairburn, C. G. (2008) 'Eating disorders: the transdiagnostic view and the cognitive behavioral theory', in C. G. Fairburn (ed.), *Cognitive Behavior Therapy and Eating Disorders.* New York: Guilford Press, pp. 7–22.

Fan, Y., Wonneberger, C., Enzi, B., de Greck, M., Ulrich, C., Tempelmann, C., Bogerts, B., Doering, S. and Northoff, G. (2011) 'The narcissistic self and its psychological and neural correlates: an exploratory fMRI study', *Psychological Medicine*, 41: 1641–50.

Farber, B. A. (2006) *Self-disclosure in Psychotherapy.* New York: Guilford.

Farina, B. and Liotti, G. (2013) 'Does a dissociative psychopathological dimension exist? A review on dissociative processes and symptoms in developmental trauma spectrum disorders', *Clinical Neuropsychiatry*, 10: 11–18.

Faupel, A., Herrick, E. and Sharp, P. (2011) *Anger Management: A Practical Guide*. New York: Routledge.

First, M. B., Gibbon, M., Spitzer, R. L., Williams, J. B. W. and Benjamin, L. S. (1997) *Structured Clinical Interview for DSM-IV Axis II Personality Disorders (SCID-II)*. Washington, DC: American Psychiatric Press.

Fitzpatrick, S., Sherry, S. B., Hartling, N., Hewitt, P. L., Flett, G. L. and Sherry, D. (2011) 'Narcissism, perfectionism, and interest in cosmetic surgery', *Plastic and Reconstructive Surgery*, 127: 176e–177e.

Fonagy, P., Gergely, G., Jurist, E. L. and Target, M. (2002) *Affect Regulation, Mentalization, and the Development of the Self*. London: Other Press.

Forgas, J. P. (2002) 'Feeling and doing: the role of affect in interpersonal behavior', *Psychological Inquiry*, 9: 205–10.

Fredrickson, B. L. (2001) 'The role of positive emotions in positive psychology: the broaden and-build theory of positive emotions', *American Psychologist*, 56: 218–26.

Freud, S. (1912) 'The dynamics of transference', in J. Strachey (ed.) (1961) *Standard Edition of the Complete Works of Sigmund Freud*, Vol. 12. London: Hogarth Press, pp. 99–108.

Friborg, O., Martinussen, M., Kaiser, S., Overgård, K.T. and Rosenvinge, J. H. (2013) 'Comorbidity of personality disorders in anxiety disorders: a meta-analysis of 30 years of research', *Journal of Affective Disorders*, 145: 143–55.

Frijda, N. H. (1986) *The Emotions*. London: Cambridge University Press.

Frith, C. D. (1992) *The Cognitive Neuropsychology of Schizophrenia*. Hove: Lawrence Erlbaum.

Frost, R. O. and Steketee, G. (1997) Perfectionism in obsessive-compulsive disorder patients', *Behaviour Research and Therapy*, 35: 291–6.

Frost, R. O., Marten, P., Lahart, C. and Rosenblate, R. (1990) 'The dimensions of perfectionism', *Cognitive Therapy and Research*, 14: 449–68.

Gallese, V. and Lakoff, G. (2005) 'The brain's concepts: the role of the sensory-motor system in reason and language', *Cognitive Neuropsychology*, 22: 455–79.

Garner, D. M. (2004) *Eating Disorder Inventory-3. Professional Manual*. Lutz, FL: Psychological Assessment Resources.

Gazzillo, F., Lingiardi, V., Peloso, A., Giordani, S., Vesco, S., Zanna, V., Filippucci, L. and Vicari, S. (2013) 'Personality subtypes in adolescents with anorexia nervosa', *Comprehensive Psychiatry*, 54: 702–12.

George, E. L., Miklowitz, D. J., Richards, J. A., Simoneau, T. L. and Taylor, D. O. (2003) 'The comorbidity of bipolar disorder and axis II personality disorders: prevalence and clinical correlates', *Bipolar Disorder*, 5: 115–22.

Giesen-Bloo, J., van Dyck, R., Spinhoven, P., van Tilberg, W., Dirksen, C., van Asselt, T., Kremers, I., Nardort, M. and Arntz, A. (2006) 'Outpatient psychotherapy for borderline personality disorder: randomized trial of schema-focused therapy vs transference-focused therapy', *Archives of General Psychiatry*, 63: 649–58.

Gilbert, P. (1989) *Human Nature and Suffering*. London and New York: Psychology Press/ Guilford Press.

Gilbert, P. (2005) 'Compassion and cruelty: a biopsychosocial approach', in P. Gilbert (ed.), *Compassion: Conceptualisations, Research and Use in Psychotherapy*. London: Routledge, pp. 9–74.

Given-Wilson, Z., McIlwain, D. and Warburton, W. (2011) 'Meta-cognitive and interpersonal difficulties in overt and covert narcissism', *Personality and Individual Differences*, 50: 1000–5.

Glenn, C. and Klonsky, E. D. (2009) 'Emotion dysregulation as a core feature of borderline personality disorder', *Journal of Personality Disorders*, 23: 20–8.

Gonçalves, M. M., Matos, M. and Santos, A. (2009) 'Narrative therapy and the nature of innovative moments in the construction of change', *Journal of Constructivist Psychology*, 22: 1–23.

Gonçalves, M. M., Mendes, I., Cruz, G., Ribeiro, A.P., Sousa, I., Angus, L. and Greenberg, L. S. (2012) 'Innovative moments and change in client-centered therapy', *Psychotherapy Research*, 22: 389–401.

Gonçalves, M. M., Ribeiro, A. P., Mendes, I., Matos, M. and Santos, A. (2011) 'Tracking novelties in psychotherapy process research: the innovative moments coding system', *Psychotherapy Research*, 21: 497–509.

Goodman, W. K., Price, L. H., Rasmussen, S. A., Mazurem, C., Fleischmann, R. L., Hill, C. L., Heninger, G. R. and Charney, D. S. (1989) 'The Yale–Brown Obsessive-Compulsive Scale. Development, use and reliability', *Archives of General Psychiatry*, 46: 1006–11.

Grandi, S., Sirri, L., Wise, T. N., Tossani, E. and Fava, G. A. (2011) 'Kellner's Emotional Inhibition Scale: a clinimetric approach to alexithymia research', *Psychotherapy and Psychosomatics*, 80: 335–44.

Gratz, K. L. and Roemer, L. (2004) 'Multidimensional assessment of emotion regulation and dysregulation: development, factor structure, and initial validation of the difficulties in emotion regulation scale', *Journal of Psychopathology and Behavioral Assessment*, 26: 41–54.

Gratz, K. L., Rosenthal, M. Z., Tull, M. T., Lejuez, C. W. and Gunderson, J. G. (2006) 'An experimental investigation of emotion dysregulation in borderline personality disorder', *Journal of Abnormal Psychology*, 115: 850–5.

Greenberg, L. S. (2002) *Emotion-Focused Therapy: Coaching Clients to Work Through Feelings*. Washington, DC: American Psychological Association.

Greene, J. O. and Burleson, G. R. (2003) *Handbook of Communication and Social Interaction Skills*. Mahwah, NJ: Lawrence Erlbaum.

Gross, J. J. and John, O. P. (2003) 'Individual differences in two motion regulation processes: implications for affect, relationships, and well-being', *Journal of Personality and Social Psychology*, 85: 348–62.

Grossman, P., Niemann, L., Schmidt, S. and Wallach, H. (2004) 'Mindfulness-based stress reduction and health benefits. A meta-analysis', *Journal of Psychosomatic Research*, 57: 35–43.

Gullestad, F. S., Johansen, M. S., Høglend, P., Karterud, S. and Wilberg, T. (2013) 'Mentalization as a moderator of treatment effects: findings from a randomized clinical trial for personality disorders', *Psychotherapy Research*, 23: 674–89.

Hackmann, A., Bennett-Levy, J. and Holmes, E. A. (2011) *Oxford Guide to Imagery in Cognitive Therapy*. Oxford: Oxford University Press.

Hamm, J. A., Renard, S. B., Fogley, R. L., Leonhardt, B. L., Dimaggio, G., Buck, K. D. and Lysaker, P. H. (2012) 'Metacognition and social cognition in schizophrenia: stability and relationship to concurrent and prospective symptom assessments', *Journal of Clinical Psychology*, 68: 1303–12.

Hayes, S. C. and Strosahl, K. D. (2004) *A Practical Guide to Acceptance and Commitment Therapy*. New York: Springer.

Hayes, S. C., Strosahl, K. D. and Wilson, K. G. (1999) *Acceptance and Commitment Therapy: An Experiental Approach to Behavior Change*. New York: Guilford Press.

Hayes, S. C., Strosahl, K. D. and Wilson, K. G. (2011) *Acceptance and Commitment Therapy, Second Edition: The Process and Practice of Mindful Change*, 2nd edn. New York: Guilford Press.

Herbert, J. D. and Forman, E. M. (2011) *Acceptance and Mindfulness in Cognitive Behavior Therapy: Understanding and Applying New Theories*. Hoboken, NJ: John Wiley & Sons.

Herbert, J. D., Gaudiano, B. A., Rheingold, A. A., Myers, V. H., Dalrymple, K. and Nolan, E. M. (2005) 'Social skills training augments the effectiveness of cognitive behavioral group therapy for social anxiety disorder', *Behavior Therapy*, 36: 125–38.

Hermans, H. J. M. and Dimaggio, G. (eds) (2004) *The Dialogical Self in Psychotherapy*. London: Brunner/Routledge.

Hewitt, P. L. and Flett, G. L. (1991) 'Perfectionism in the self and social contexts: conceptualization, assessment and association with psychopathology', *Journal of Personality and Social Psychology*, 60: 456–70.

Hill, C. E. and Knox, S. (2009) 'Processing the therapeutic relationship', *Psychotherapy Research*, 19: 13–29.

Hollon, S. D. and Beck, A. T. (1979) 'Cognitive therapy of depression', in P. C. Kendall and S. D. Barlow (eds), *Cognitive-Behavioral Intervention: Theory, Research, and Procedures*. New York: Academic Press, pp. 153–203.

Horowitz, L. M., Alden, L. E., Wiggins, J. S. and Pincus, A. L. (2000) *Inventory of Interpersonal Problems (IIP-32/IIP-64)*. London: Psychological Corporation.

Horowitz, M. J. (1987) *States of Mind. Configurational Analysis of Individual Psychology*, 2nd edn. New York: Plenum Press.

Hyler, S. E., Skodol, A. E., Oldham, J. M., Kellman, H. D. and Doidge, N. (1992) 'Validity of the Personality Diagnostic Questionnaire-Revised: a replication in an outpatient sample', *Comprehensive Psychiatry*, 33 (2): 73–7.

Iverson, K. M., Follette, V. M., Pistorello, J. F. and Alan, E. (2012) 'An investigation of experiential avoidance, emotion dysregulation, and distress tolerance in young adult outpatients with borderline personality disorder symptoms', *Personality Disorders: Theory, Research, and Treatment*, 3: 415–22.

John, O. P. and Gross, J. J. (2004) 'Healthy and unhealthy emotion regulation: personality processes, individual differences, and lifespan development', *Journal of Personality*, 72: 1301–34.

Johnson-Laird, P. N., Mancini, F. and Gangemi, A. (2006) 'A hyper-emotion theory of psychological illnesses', *Psychological Review*, 113: 822–41.

Kabat-Zinn, J. (1990) *Full Catastrophe Living: Using the Wisdom of Your Body and Mind to Face Stress, Pain and Illness*. New York: Delacorte.

Kabat-Zinn, J. (1994) *Wherever You Go There You Are: Mindfulness Meditation in Everyday Life*. New York: Hyperion.

Karterud, S. (2012) 'Commentary. Comments on personality disorders with over-regulation of emotions and poor self-reflectivity', *Personality and Mental Health*, 6: 167–9.

Kellner, R. (1986) *Abridged Manual of the Emotional Inhibition Scale*. Albuquerque, NM: University of New Mexico.

Kohut, H. (1971) *The Analysis of the Self*. New York: International Universities Press.

Kramer, U., Berthoud, L., Keller, S. and Caspar, F. (2014) 'Motive-oriented psychotherapeutic relationship facing a patient presenting with narcissistic personality disorder: a case study', *Journal of Contemporary Psychotherapy*, 44: 71–82.

Kramer, U., Rosciano, A., Pavlovic, M., Berthoud, L., Despland, J.-N., de Roten, Y. and Caspar, F. (2011) 'Motive-oriented therapeutic relationship in brief psychodynamic intervention for patients with depression and personality disorders', *Journal of Clinical Psychology*, 76: 1017–27.

Krishnan, K. R. (2005) 'Psychiatric and medical comorbidities of bipolar disorder', *Psychosomatic Medicine*, 67: 1–8.

Kuyken, W., Padesky, C. A. and Dudley, R. (2009) *Collaborative Case Conceptualization. Working Effectively with Clients in Cognitive-Behavioral Therapy*. New York: Guilford Press.

Lafargue, G., Franck, N. and Sirigu, A. (2006) 'Sense of motor effort in patients with schizophrenia', *Cortex*, 42: 711–19.

Lane, R. D. (2000) 'Levels of emotional awareness: neurological, psychological and social perspectives', in R. Bar-On and J. D. A. Parker (eds), *Handbook of Emotional Intelligence*. San Francisco: Jossey-Bass.

Lane, R. D. and Schwartz, G. E. (1987) 'Levels of emotional awareness: a cognitive-developmental theory and its application to psychopathology', *American Journal of Psychiatry*, 144: 133–43.

Lavender, J. M., Wonderlich, S. A., Crosby, R. D., Engel, S. G., Mitchell, J. E., Crow, S. J., Peterson, C. B. and Le Grange, D. (2013) 'Personality-based subtypes of anorexia nervosa: examining validity and utility using baseline clinical variables and ecological momentary assessment', *Behaviour Research and Therapy*, 51: 512–17.

Lee, K., Noda, Y., Nakano, Y., Ogawa, S., Kinoshita, Y., Funayama, T. and Furukawa, T. A. (2006) 'Interoceptive hypersensitivity and interoceptive exposure in patients with panic disorder: specificity and effectiveness', *BMC Psychiatry*, 6: 32.

Leichsenring, F., Salzer, S., Beutel, M. E., Herpertz, S., Hiller, W., Hoyer, J., Huesing, J., Joraschky, P., Nolting, B., Poehlmann, K., Ritter, V., Stangier, U., Strauss, B., Stuhldreher, N., Tefikow, S., Teismann, T., Willutzki, U., Wiltink, J. and Leibing, E. (2013) 'Psychodynamic therapy and cognitive-behavioral therapy in social anxiety disorder: a multicenter randomized controlled trial', *American Journal of Psychiatry*, 170: 759–67.

Leiman, M. and Stiles, W. B. (2001) 'Dialogical sequence analysis and the zone of proximal development as conceptual enhancements to the assimilation model: the case of Jan revisited', *Psychotherapy Research*, 11: 311–30.

Lichtenberg, J. D. (1989) *Psychoanalysis and Motivation*. Hillsdale, NJ: Analytic Press.

Linehan, M. M. (1993) *Cognitive Behavioral Treatment of Borderline Personality Disorder*. New York: Guilford Press.

Linehan, M., Bohus, M. and Lynch, T. R. (2007) 'Dialectical behavior therapy for pervasive emotion dysregulation', in J. Gross (ed.), *Handbook of Emotion*. New York: Guilford Press.

Links, P. S., Mercer, D. and Novick, J. (in press) 'Establishing a treatment framework and therapeutic alliance', in J. W. Livesley, G. Dimaggio and J. F. Clarkin (eds), *Integrated Modular Treatment for Personality Disorders*. New York: Guilford Press.

Liotti, G. (2004) 'Trauma, dissociation and disorganized attachment: three strands of a single braid', *Psychotherapy: Theory, Research, Practice, Training*, 41: 472–86.

Liotti, G. and Gilbert, P. (2011) 'Mentalizing, motivation, and social mentalities: theoretical considerations and implications for psychotherapy', *Psychology and Psychotherapy: Theory, Research and Practice*, 84: 9–25.

Livesley, W. J. (2003) *Practical Management of Personality Disorders*. New York: Guilford Press.

Lobbestael, J., Arntz, A. and Sieswerda, S. (2005) 'Schema modes and childhood abuse in borderline and antisocial personality disorders', *Journal of Behavior Therapy and Experimental Psychiatry*, 36: 240–53.

Lobbestael, J., van Vreeswijk, M. F. and Arntz, A. (2007) 'Shedding light on schema modes: a clarification of the mode concept and its current research status', *Netherlands Journal of Psychology*, 63: 76–85.

Lobbestael, J., van Vreeswijk, M. F. and Arntz, A. (2008) 'An empirical test of schema mode conceptualizations in personality disorders', *Behaviour Research and Therapy*, 46: 854–60.

Luborsky, L. and Crits-Christoph, P. (1990) *Understanding Transference: The Core Conflictual Relationship Theme Method*. New York: Basic Books.

Lysaker, P. H. and Buck, K. D. (2010) 'Metacognitive capacity as a focus of individual psychotherapy in schizophrenia', in G. Dimaggio and P. H. Lysaker (eds), *Metacognition and Severe Adult Mental Disorders. From Research to Treatment*. London: Routledge, pp. 217–32.

Lysaker, P. H., Buck, K. D. and Ringer, J. (2007) 'The recovery of metacognitive capacity in schizophrenia across thirty-two months of individual psychotherapy: a case study', *Psychotherapy Research*, 17: 713–20.

Lysaker, P. H., Buck, K. D., Leonhardt, B., Buck, B., Hamm, J., Hasson-Ohayon, I. and Dimaggio, G. (2014) 'Metacognitively focused psychotherapy for persons with schizophrenia: eight core elements that define practice', in P. H. Lysaker, G. Dimaggio and M. Brüne (eds) *Social Cognition and Metacognition in Schizophrenia: Psychopathology and Treatment Approaches*. Amsterdam: Elsevier Academic Press.

Lysaker, P. H., Erickson, M., Ringer, J., Buck, K. D., Semerari, A., Carcione, A. and Dimaggio, G. (2011) 'Metacognition in schizophrenia: the relationship of mastery to coping, insight, self-esteem, social anxiety and various facets of neurocognition', *British Journal of Clinical Psychology*, 50: 412–24.

Lysaker, P. H., Gumley, A., Brüne, M., Vanheule, S., Buck, K. D. and Dimaggio, G. (2011) 'Deficits in the ability to recognize one's own affects and those of others: associations with neurocognition, symptoms and sexual trauma among persons with schizophrenia', *Consciousness and Cognition*, 20: 1183–92.

Lysaker, P. H., Gumley, A., Leudtke, B., Buck, K. D., Ringer, J. M., Olesek, K., Oscatharp, J., Popolo, R. and Dimaggio, G. (2013) 'Thinking about oneself and thinking about others: evidence of the relative independence of deficits in metacognition and social cognition in schizophrenia', *Acta Psychiatrica Scandinavica*, 127: 239–247.

Lysaker, P. H., Olesek, K., Buck, K., Leonhardt, B., Vohs, J., Dimaggio, G., Popolo, R. and Outcalt, J. (2014) 'Metacognitive mastery moderates the relationship of alexithymia with cluster C personality disorder traits in adults with substance use disorders', *Addictive Behaviors*, 39 (3): 558–61.

Lysaker, P. H., Vohs, J., Ballard, R., Fogley, R., Salvatore, G., Popolo, R. and Dimaggio, G. (2013) 'Metacognition, self-reflection and recovery in schizophrenia', *Future Neurology*, 8: 103–11.

McMain, S. F., Links, P. S., Gnam, W. H., Guimond, T., Cardish, R. J., Korman, L. and Streiner, D. L. (2009) 'A randomized trial of dialectical behavior therapy versus general psychiatric management for borderline personality disorder', *American Journal of Psychiatry*, 166: 1365–74.

McMain, S. F., Links, P. S., Guimond, T., Wnuk, S., Eynan, R., Bergmans, Y. and Warwar, S. (2013) 'An exploratory study of the relationship between changes in emotion and cognitive processes, alliance, and treatment outcome in borderline personality disorder', *Psychotherapy Research*, 23 (6): 658–73.

Maillard, P., Kramer, U. and Dimaggio, G. (2013) *Metacognitive Processes and Biased Thinking Associated with Borderline Personality Disorder: A Pilot Study*. Paper presented at the conference of the Society for the Exploration of Psychotherapy Integration, Barcelona, Spain, July.

Marks, I. (1975) 'Behavioral treatments of phobic and obsessive compulsive disorders: a critical appraisal', in M. Hersen, R. M. Eisler and M. Miller (eds), *Progress in Behavior Modification*, Vol. 1. New York: Academic Press.

Matusiewicz, A. K., Christopher, J. H., Banducci, A. N. and Lejuez, C. W. (2010) 'The effectiveness of cognitive behavioral therapy for personality disorders', *Psychiatric Clinics of North America*, 33 (3): 657–85.

Mayer, J. D., Salovey, P. and Caruso, D. (2001) *The Mayer-Salovey-Caruso Emotional Intelligence Test (MSCEIT)*. Toronto: Multi-Health Systems.

Millon, T. (1999) *Personality-Guided Therapy*. Chichester: Wiley.

Millon, T. and Davis, R. D. (1996) *Disorders of Personality. DSM-IV and Beyond*. Chichester: Wiley.

Millon, T., Millon, C., Davis, R. and Grossman, S. (2009) *MCMI-III Manual*, 4th edn. Minneapolis, MN: Pearson Education.

Mitchell, J. P., Macrae, C. N. and Banaji, M. R. (2006) 'Dissociable medial prefrontal contributions to judgments of similar and dissimilar others', *Neuron*, 50: 655–63.

Mitchell, S. A. (1988) *Relational Concepts in Psychoanalysis*. Cambridge, MA: Harvard University Press.

Modell, A. H. (1984) *Psychoanalysis in a New Context*. New York: International Universities Press.

Monsen, J. T. and Monsen, K. (1999) 'A psychotherapy model integrating Silvan Tomkin's affect-and script-theory within the framework of self psychology', *Progress in Self Psychology*, 15: 287–306.

Murphy, D. L., Moya, P. R., Fox, M. A., Rubenstein, L. M., Wendland, J. R. and Timpano, K. R. (2013) 'Anxiety and affective disorder comorbidity related to serotonin and other neurotransmitter systems: obsessive-compulsive disorder as an example of overlapping clinical and genetic heterogeneity', *Philosophical Transactions of the Royal Society B: Biological Sciences*, 368 (1615): 201–4.

Neimeyer, R. A. (2000) Narrative disruptions in the construction of self', in R. A. Neimeyer and J. D. Raskin (eds), *Constructions of Disorder: Meaning Making Frameworks for Psychotherapy*. Washington, DC: American Psychological Association, pp. 207–41.

Newman, C. F. (2012) *Core Competencies in Cognitive-Behavioral Therapy: Becoming a Highly Effective and Competent Cognitive-Behavioral Therapist*. London: Routledge.

Newman, M. G. (2000) 'Recommendations for a cost-offset model of psychotherapy allocation using generalised anxiety disorder as an example', *Journal of Consulting and Clinical Psychology*, 68: 549–55.

Nicolò, G., Semerari, A., Lysaker, P. H., Dimaggio, G., Conti, L., d'Angerio, S., Procacci, M., Popolo, R. and Carcione, A. (2011) 'Alexithymia in personality disorders. Correlations with symptoms and interpersonal functioning', *Psychiatry Research*, 190: 37–42.

Nicolò, G., Semerari, A., Lysaker, P. H., Dimaggio, G., Conti, L., D'Angerio, S., Procacci, M., Popolo, R. and Carcione, A. (2012) 'Dependent personality disorders unlike avoidant personality disorders are not related to alexithymia after controlling for depression', *Psychiatry Research*, 196: 327–8.

Norcross, J. C. (ed.) (2002) *Psychotherapy Relationships That Work: Therapist Contributions and Responsiveness to Clients*. New York: Oxford University Press.

O'Donohue, W. T. and Cummings, N. A. (2011) *Evidence-Based Adjunctive Treatments*. London: Routledge.

O'Donohue, W. T. and Fisher, J. E. (eds) (2009) *General Principles and Empirically Supported Techniques of Cognitive Behavior Therapy*. Chichester: Wiley.

Ottavi, P., D'Alia, D., Lysaker, P. H., Kent, J., Popolo, R., Salvatore, G. and Dimaggio, G. (2014) 'Metacognition oriented social skills training for schizophrenia. Theory, method and clinical illustration', *Clinical Psychology and Psychotherapy*, 21: 465–73.

Ottavi, P., Passarella, T., Pasinetti, M., Salvatore, G. and Dimaggio, G. (in press) 'Mindfulness for anxious and angry worry about interpersonal events in personality disorders', in W. J. Livesley, G. Dimaggio and J. F. Clarkin (eds), *Integrated Modular Treatment for Personality Disorders*. New York: Guilford Press.

Padesky, C. A. and Mooney, K. A. (2012) 'Strengths-based cognitive-behavioural therapy: a four-step model to build resilience', *Clinical Psychology and Psychotherapy*, 19: 283–90.

Panksepp, J. (1998) *Affective Neuroscience: The Foundations of Human and Animal Emotions*. Oxford: Oxford University Press.

Papageorgiou, C. and Wells, A. (2003) *Depressive Rumination: Nature, Theory, and Treatment*. Chichester: Wiley.

Parker, J. D. A., Taylor, G. J. and Bagby, R. M. (2003) 'The Twenty-Item Toronto Alexithymia Scale-III: reliability and factorial validity in a community population', *Journal of Psychosomatic Research*, 55: 269–75.

Pascual-Leone, A. and Greenberg, L. S. (2007) 'Emotional processing in experiential therapy: why the only way out is through', *Journal of Consulting and Clinical Psychology*, 75: 875–87.

Pellecchia, G., Moroni, F., Carcione, A., Colle, L., Dimaggio, G., Nicolò, G., Pedone, R., Procacci, M. and Semerari, A. (2014) 'Metacognition Assessment Interview: Instrument Description and Factor Structure'. Manuscript submitted for publication.

Persons, J. (2008) *The Case Formulation Approach to Cognitive-Behavior Therapy*. New York: Guilford Press.

Popolo, R., Lysaker, P. H., Salvatore, G., Montano, A., Sirri, L., Buonocore, L., Imbimbo, A. and Dimaggio, G. (in press) 'Emotional inhibition in personality disorders', *Psychotherapy and Psychosomatics*.

Pos, A. E. (2014) 'Emotion focused therapy for avoidant personality disorder: pragmatic considerations for working with experientially avoidant clients', *Journal of Contemporary Psychotherapy*, 44: 127–39.

Rabin, J. S. and Rosenbaum, R. S. (2012) 'Familiarity modulates the functional relationship between theory of mind and autobiographical memory', *Neuroimage*, 62: 520–9.

Rafaeli, E. (2009) 'Cognitive-behavioral therapies for personality disorders', *Israel Journal of Psychiatry and Related Science*, 46: 290–7.

Reeves, T. and Stace, J. M. (2005) 'Improving patient access and choice: assisted bibliotherapy for mild to moderate stress/anxiety in primary care', *Journal of Psychiatry and Mental Health Nursing*, 12: 41–6.

Ribeiro, E., Ribeiro, A. P., Gonçalves, M. M., Horvath, A. O. and Stiles, W. B. (2013) 'How collaboration in therapy becomes therapeutic: the therapeutic collaboration coding system', *Psychology and Psychotherapy: Theory, Research and Practice*, 86: 294–314.

Richardson-Vejlgaard, R., Broudy, C., Brodsky, B., Fertuck, E. and Stanley, B. (2013) 'Predictors of psychotherapy alliance in borderline personality disorder', *Psychotherapy Research*, 23: 539–46.

Ritter, K., Dziobek, I., Preißler, S., Rüter, A., Vater, A., Fydrich, T., Lammers, C.-H., Heekeren, H. R. and Roepke, S. (2011) 'Lack of empathy in patients with narcissistic personality disorder', *Psychiatry Research*, 187: 241–7.

Ritter, V., Leichsenring, F., Strauss, B. M. and Stangier, U. (2013) 'Changes in implicit and explicit self-esteem following cognitive and psychodynamic therapy in social anxiety disorders', *Psychotherapy Research*, 23: 547–58.

Rodebaugh, T. L., Heimberg, R. G., Schultz, L. T. and Blackmore, M. J. (2010) 'The moderated effects of video feedback for social anxiety disorder', *Anxiety Disorder*, 24 (7): 663–71.

Ronningstam, E. (2009) 'Narcissism personality disorder: facing DSM-V', *Psychiatric Annals*, 39: 111–21.

Rosenberg, M. (1965) *Society and the Adolescent Self-Image*. Princeton, NJ: Princeton University Press.

Roth, A. and Fonagy, P. (2005) *What Works for Whom? A Critical Review of Psychotherapy Research*. New York: Guilford Press.

Ryle, A. and Kerr, I. (2002) *Introducing Cognitive Analytic Therapy. Principles and Practice*. Chichester: Wiley.

Safran, J. D. and Muran, J. C. (2000) *Negotiating the Therapeutic Alliance. A Relational Treatment Guide*. New York: Guilford Press.

Salgado-Delgado, R., Tapia Osorio, A., Saderi, N. and Escobar, C. (2011) 'Disruption of circadian rhythms: a crucial factor in the etiology of depression', *Depression Research and Treatment*. Online.

Salvatore, G., Lysaker, P. H., Procacci, M., Carcione, A., Popolo, R. and Dimaggio, G. (2012) 'Vulnerable self, poor understanding of others' minds, threat anticipation and cognitive biases as triggers for delusional experience in schizophrenia: a theoretical model', *Clinical Psychology and Psychotherapy*, 19: 247–59.

Salvatore, G., Nicolò, G. and Dimaggio, G. (2005) 'Impoverished dialogical relationship patterns in paranoid personality disorder', *American Journal of Psychotherapy*, 59: 247–65.

Salvatore, G., Popolo, R. and Dimaggio, G. (in press) 'Promoting integration through reformulation', in J. Livesley, G. Dimaggio and J. F. Clarkin (eds), *Integrated Modular Treatment for Personality Disorders*. New York: Guilford Press.

Sansone, R. A., Levitt, J. L. and Sansone, L. A. (2006) 'The prevalence of personality disorders in those with eating disorders', in R. A. Sansone and J. L. Levitt (eds), *Personality Disorders and Eating Disorders: Exploring the Frontier*. New York: Routledge, pp. 23–390.

Saxe, R., Moran, J. M., Scholz, J., and Gabrieli, J. (2006) 'Overlapping and non-overlapping brain regions for theory of mind and self reflection in individual subjects', *Social Cognitive and Affective Neuroscience*, 1 (3): 229–34.

Schmidt, N. B., Joiner, T. E., Young, J. E. and Telch, M. J. (1995) 'The Schema-Questionnaire: investigation of psychometric properties and the hierarchical structure of a measure of maladaptive schemas', *Cognitive Therapy and Research*, 19: 295–321.

Schultz, J. H. and Luthe, W. (1959) *Autogenic Training: A Psychophysiologic Approach in Psychotherapy*. New York: Grune & Stratton.

Segal, Z., Teasdale, J. and Williams, M. (2002) *Mindfulness-Based Cognitive Therapy for Depression*. New York: Guilford Press.

Seivewright, H., Tyrer, P. and Johnson, T. (2004) 'Persistent social dysfunction in anxious and depressed patients with personality disorder', *Acta Psychiatrica Scandinavica*, 109: 104–9.

Semerari, A. (2010) 'The impact of metacognitive dysfunctions in personality disorders on the therapeutic relationship and intervention technique', in G. Dimaggio and P. H. Lysaker (eds), *Metacognition and Severe Adult Mental Disorders. From Research to Treatment*. London: Routledge, pp. 269–84.

Semerari, A., Carcione, A., Dimaggio, G., Falcone, M., Nicolò, G., Procacci, M., Alleva, G. and Mergenthaler, E. (2003a) 'Assessing problematic states inside patient's narratives. The Grid of Problematic Conditions', *Psychotherapy Research*, 13 (3): 337–53.

Semerari, A., Carcione, A., Dimaggio, G., Falcone, M., Nicolò, G., Procacci, M. and Alleva, G. (2003b) 'How to evaluate metacognitive functioning in psychotherapy? The Metacognition Assessment Scale and its applications', *Clinical Psychology and Psychotherapy*, 10: 238–61.

Semerari, A., Carcione, A., Dimaggio, G., Nicolò, G. and Procacci, M. (2007) 'Understanding minds, different functions and different disorders? The contribution of psychotherapeutic research', *Psychotherapy Research*, 17: 106–19.

Semerari, A., Colle, L., Pellecchia, G., Buccione, I., Carcione, A., Dimaggio, G., Nicolò, G., Procacci, M. and Pedone, R. (2014) 'Metacognition: severity and styles in personality disorders', *Journal of Personality Disorders*. Online.

Semerari, A., Cucchi, M., Dimaggio, G., Cavadini, D., Carcione, A., Battelli, V., Nicolò, G., Pedone, R., Siccardi, T., D'Angerio, S., Ronchi, P., Maffei, C. and Smeraldi, E. (2012) 'The development of the Metacognition Assessment Interview: instrument description, factor structure and reliability in a non-clinical sample', *Psychiatry Research*, 200: 890–5.

Semerari, A., Cucchi, M., Dimaggio, G., Cavadini, D., Carcione, A., Battelli, V., Nicolò, G., Pedone, R., Siccardi, T., D'Angerio, S., Ronchi, P., Maffei, C. and Smeraldi, E. (2013) 'Narcissism, Attachment and Metacognition in a Non-clinical Sample'. Manuscript in preparation.

Semerari, A., Dimaggio, G., Nicolò, G., Pedone, R., Procacci, M. and Carcione, A. (2005) 'Metarepresentative functions in borderline personality disorders', *Journal of Personality Disorders*, 19: 690–710.

Shafran, R. and Rachman, S. (2004) 'Thought-action fusion: a review', *Journal of Behavior Therapy and Experimental Psychiatry*, 35 (2): 87–107.

Shahar, G. and Davidson, L. (2009) 'Participation-engagement: a philosophically based heuristic for prioritizing clinical interventions in the treatment of comorbid, complex, and chronic psychiatric conditions', *Psychiatry*, 72: 154–76.

Shapiro, S. L., Carlson, L. E., Astin, J. A. and Freedman, B. (2006) 'Mechanisms of mindfulness', *Journal of Clinical Psychology*, 62 (3): 373–86.

Sheets, E. S., Duncan, L. E., Bjornsson, A. S., Craighead, L. W. and Craighead, W. E. (2013) 'Personality pathology factors predict recurrent major depressive disorder in emerging adults', *Journal of Clinical Psychology*, 70 (6): 536–45.

Sifneos, P. E. (1973) 'The prevalence of alexithymic characteristics in psychosomatic patients', *Psychotherapy and Psychosomatics*, 26: 270–85.

Solbakken, O. A., Hansen, R. S., Havik, O. E. and Monsen, J. T. (2012) 'Affect integration as a predictor of change: affect consciousness and treatment response in open-ended psychotherapy', *Psychotherapy Research*, 22: 656–72.

Soldz, S., Budman, S., Demby, A. and Merry, J. (1995) 'A short form of the Inventory of Interpersonal Problems Circumplex Scales', *Assessment*, 2: 53–63.

Spielberger, C. D., Gorssuch, R. L., Lushene, P. R., Vagg, P. R. and Jacobs, G. A. (1983) *Manual for the State-Trait Anxiety Inventory (Form Y): Self-Evaluation Questionnaire*. Palo Alto, CA: Consulting Psychologists Press.

Spinhoven, P., Bamelis, L., Molendijk, M., Haringsma, R. and Arntz, A. (2009) 'Reduced specificity of AM in cluster C personality disorders and the role of depression, worry and experiential avoidance', *Journal of Abnormal Psychology*, 118: 520–30.

Spreng, R. N. and Grady, C. (2010) 'Patterns of brain activity supporting autobiographical memory, prospection and theory-of-mind and their relationship to the default mode network', *Journal of Cognitive Neuroscience*, 22: 1112–23.

Spreng, R. N. and Mar, R. A. (2012) 'I remember you: a role for memory in social cognition and the prospection and theory-of-mind and their relationship to the default mode network', *Brain Research*, 1428: 43–50.

Stanley, B., Bundy, E. and Beberman, R. (2001) 'Skills training as an adjunctive treatment for personality disorders', *Journal of Psychiatric Practice*, 7 (5): 324–35.

Stiles, W. B. (2011) 'Coming to terms', *Psychotherapy Research*, 21: 367–84.

Stopa, L., Thorne, P., Waters, A. and Preston, J. (2001) 'Are the short and long forms of the Young Schema-Questionnaire comparable and how well does each version predict psychopathology scores?', *Journal of Cognitive Psychotherapy*, 15: 253–72.

Strauss, J. L., Hayes, A. M., Johnson, S. L., Newman, C. F., Brown, G. K., Barber, J. P., Laurenceau, J. P. and Beck, A. T. (2006) 'Early alliance, alliance ruptures, and symptom change in a nonrandomized trial of cognitive therapy for avoidant and obsessive-compulsive personality disorders', *Journal of Consulting and Clinical Psychology*, 74: 337–45.

Taylor, G. J., Bagby, R. M. and Parker, J. D. A. (1997) 'The 20-Item Toronto Alexithymia Scale IV. Reliability and factorial validity in different languages and cultures', *Journal of Psychosomatic Research*, 55: 277–83.

Taylor, S. (2002) 'Systematic desensitization', in M. Hersen and W. Sledge (eds), *Encyclopedia of Psychotherapy*. Amsterdam: Elsevier Science, pp. 755–9.

Taylor, S. and Gordon, J. G. (2004) *Asmundson Treating Health Anxiety: A Cognitive-Behavioral Approach*. New York: Guilford Press.

Thiel, T., Hertenstein, E., Nissen, C., Herbst, N., Külz, A. K. and Voderholzer, U. (2013) 'The effect of personality disorders on treatment outcomes in patients with obsessive-compulsive disorders', *Journal of Personality Disorders*, 27: 697–715.

Thompson-Brenner, H. and Westen, D. (2005) 'Personality subtypes in eating disorders: validation of a classification in a naturalistic sample', *British Journal of Psychiatry*, 186: 516–24.

Thomspon-Brenner, H., Eddy, K. T., Satir, D. A., Boisseau, C. L. and Westen, D. (2008) 'Personality subtypes in adolescents with eating disorders: validation of a classification approach', *Journal of Child Psychology and Psychiatry*, 49: 170–80.

Tomasello, M., Carpenter, M., Call, J., Behne, T. and Moll, H. (2005) 'Understanding and sharing intentions: the origin of cultural cognition', *Behavioral and Brain Sciences*, 28: 675–91.

Tryon, W. W. (2005) 'Possible mechanisms for why desensitization and exposure therapy work', *Clinical Psychology Review*, 25: 67–95.

Tufekcioglu, S. and Muran, J. C. (in press) 'A relational approach to personality disorder and alliance rupture', in J. W. Livesley, G. Dimaggio and J. F. Clarkin (eds), *Integrated Modular Treatment for Personality Disorders*. New York: Guilford Press.

Unger, T., Hoffmann, S., Köhler, S., Mackert, A., and Fydrich, T. (2013) 'Personality disorders and outcome of inpatient treatment for depression: a 1-year prospective follow-up study', *Journal of Personality Disorders*, 27: 636–51.

van Bilsen, H. and Thomson, B. (2011) *CBT for Personality Disorders*. London: Sage.

Van der Hart, O., Nijenhuis, E. R. S. and Steele, K. (2006) *The Haunted Self: Structural Dissociation and the Treatment of Chronic Traumatization*, Norton Series on Interpersonal Neurobiology. New York: W. W. Norton.

van Dijke, A. (2012) 'Dysfunctional affect regulation in borderline personality disorder and in somatoform disorder', *European Journal of Psychotraumatology*, 3: 10.

Vandereycken, W., Aerts, L. and Dierckx, E. (2013) 'What knowledge do patients have about the physical consequences of their eating disorder?', *Eating and Weight Disorders*, 18: 79–82.

Vanheule, S., Verhaege, P. and Desmet, M. (2011) 'In search of framework for the treatment of alexithymia', *Psychology and Psychotherapy: Theory, Research and Practice*, 84: 84–97.

Vavrichek, S. M. (2012) *The Guide to Compassionate Assertiveness. How to Express Your Needs and Deal with Conflict While Keeping a Kind Heart*. Oakland, CA: New Harbinger Publications.

Vorst, H. C. M. and Bermond, B. (2001) 'Validity and reliability of the Bermond-Vorst Alexithymia Questionnaire', *Personality and Individual Differences*, 30: 413–34.

Vygotsky, L. (1978) *Mind in Society: The Development of Higher Psychological Processes*. Cambridge, MA: Harvard University Press.

Warren, R. (2012) 'Commentary. A cognitive-behavioural perspective on personality disorders with over-regulation of emotions and poor self-reflectivity: the case of a man with avoidant and not-otherwise specified personality disorder, social phobia and dysthymia treated with metacognitive interpersonal therapy', *Personality and Mental Health*, 6: 170–3.

Weiss, J. (1993) *How Psychotherapy Works. Process and Technique*. New York: Guilford Press.

Wells, A. (2005) 'Detached mindfulness in cognitive therapy: a metacognitive analysis and ten techniques', *Journal of Rational-Emotive and Cognitive-Behavior Therapy*, 23 (4): 337–55.

Wells, A. (2008) *Metacognitive Therapy for Anxiety and Depression*. New York: Guilford Press.

Wenzlaff, R. M. and Wegner, D. M. (2000) 'Thought suppression', *Annual Review of Psychology*, 51: 59–91.

Westen, D. and Shedler, J. (1999a) 'Revising and assessing Axis II, part 1: developing a clinically and empirically valid assessment method', *American Journal of Psychiatry*, 156: 258–72.

Westen, D. and Shedler, J. (1999b) 'Revising and assessing Axis II, part 2: toward an empirically based and clinically useful classification of personality disorders', *American Journal of Psychiatry*, 156: 273–85.

Westen, D., Novotny, C. and Thompson-Brenner, H. (2004) 'The empirical status of empirically supported therapies: assumptions, methods, and findings', *Psychological Bulletin*, 130: 631–63.

White, M. and Epston, D. (1990) *Narrative Means to Therapeutic Ends*. New York: Norton.

Whitehead, C., Marchant, J. L., Craik, D. and Frith, C. D. (2009) 'Neural correlates of observing pretend play in which one object is represented as another', *Social Cognitive and Affective Neuroscience*, 4: 369–78.

Wonderlich, S. A., Lilenfeld, L. R., Riso, L. P., Engel, S. and Mitchell, J. E. (2005) 'Personality and anorexia nervosa', *International Journal of Eating Disorders*, 37: S68–71.

Young, J. E. and Brown, G. (2003) *Young Schema Questionnaire*. New York: Cognitive Therapy Center of New York.

Young, J. E., Klosko, J. S. and Weishaar, M. (2003) *Schema Therapy: A Practitioner's Guide*. New York: Guilford Press.

Index